UNDERSTANDING DYSLEXIA

UNDERSTANDING DYSLEXIA

A Practical Approach for Parents and Teachers

Anne Marshall Huston

MADISON BOOKS
Lanham • New York • London

Published by Madison Books
4720 Boston Way
Lanham, Maryland 20706

3 Henrietta Street
London WC2E 8LU England

Distributed by National Book Network

The paper used in this publication meets the minimum
requirements of American National Standard for
Information Sciences—Permanence of Paper for
Printed Library Materials, ANSI Z39.48–1984. ∞™
Manufactured in the United States of America.

Library of Congress Cataloging-in-Publication Data

Huston, Anne Marshall.
Understanding dyslexia : a practical approach
for parents and teachers / Anne Marshall Huston.
p.   cm.
Rev. ed. of: Common sense about dyslexia. ©1987.
Includes bibliographical references.
1. Dyslexia—Popular works.   I. Huston, Anne
Marshall. Common sense about dyslexia.   II. Title.
RC394.W6H87   1992
616.85'53—dc20   90–34364 CIP

ISBN 0–8191–7804–7 (cloth : alk. paper)
ISBN 0–8191–8249–4 (pbk. : alk. paper)

British Cataloging in Publication Information Available

To
JIM
sine qua non

To have striven, to have made an effort,
to have been true to certain ideals—this
alone is worth the struggle.
—Sir William Osler

CONTENTS

PREFACE

This book is intended to help parents, classroom teachers, and others who may be involved with someone who has dyslexia to understand better the nature of this very real disability and the many difficult problems that accompany it. The book is a response in part to many requests from parents, teachers, reading and learning disability specialists, other school personnel involved with students who have special problems, physicians, and, yes, children who have dyslexia. It is the result of over nineteen years of study, research, and experience with dyslexia in public schools, college classrooms, graduate programs, and a reading clinic for the diagnosis and remediation of reading disabilities and dyslexia, which actually is a disability in writing, spelling, speaking, and listening, as well as reading.

Dyslexia is a language communication disability. It includes three general categories. The first, visual dyslexia, is characterized by reversals of letters and numerals; faulty sequencing of letters in words, numbers in series, and events in narrative; disorientation in time and space relationships; and problems in processing, interpreting, and recalling visual images. The second, auditory dyslexia, is characterized by problems of integrating and processing what is heard and recalling those sounds and applying them to the printed symbols representing them. The third category is a combination of the two in varying degrees. Dyslexia is not attributable to any vision or hearing defect; it persists beyond that time when most childhood developmental conditions mature.

The prefix "dys" (Greek) means defective, as in dysfunction, that is, a functional abnormality or impairment, and "lexia" (Greek) refers to the use of words. Words are the means by which we communicate in our language. And dyslexia is certainly a problem with words—in reading, spelling, writing, speaking, and listening. Unfortunately, in the past some have confused dyslexia with the Latin *lexit* (having to do with reading, literally "he has read"). Although, in consequence, some textbooks have inappropriately defined dyslexia as a "general term meaning inability to read" or "a reading disorder," dyslexia is much more than just a reading disability. Dyslexia is a *language communication disability* of which reading is only a part.

Disagreement over the "right" definition creates much dissatisfaction and is sometimes cited to support the contention that dyslexia must not exist if the experts cannot agree on a common definition. Yet pick up a dozen textbooks on how to teach reading and you are likely to find a dozen different definitions of "reading." There are authorities in medicine, psychology, learning disabilities, and reading who acknowledge the existence of dyslexia, while others (mainly in the reading field) deny its existence as a distinct affliction or condition. What is needed at this time is better communication and cooperation which will, of course, result in better understanding. The important thing to keep in mind is that *the focus must always be on the children and their problems*.

There is something of an outcry going on about "labeling" children with the term "dyslexia." Several reading "authorities" prefer the term "severe reading disability"—as if that were not just another label (and at that probably more frightening considering the use of the word "severe"). Special education authorities will place dyslexic children in "learning disabilities" classes—again, just another label. In the past, dyslexia has been called word-blindness, strephosymbolia, primary reading disability, secondary reading disability, constitutional reading disability, specific reading disability, developmental dyslexia, specific dyslexia, maturational dyslexia, and specific language disability. Each became a "label," and another term was then substituted, which then became another label.

In the Library of Congress there are over 170 books about dyslexia, published in sixteen countries. There are 2,394 entries in Evans's *Dyslexia, An Annotated Bibliography*, including journal articles, conference reports, proceedings of symposia, government documents, chapters or parts of books, dissertations, and articles from the popular press. Articles about dyslexia have appeared in *Medical Science, Journal of Genetic Psychology, Annals of Neurology, Developmental Medicine and Child Neurology, Journal of the American Medical Association, Lancet, British Journal of Educational Psychology, Learning Disabilities, Reading Research Quarterly, The Reading Teacher, Journal of School Health, Bulletin of the Orton Society,* and others.

While there have been many books, articles, and studies about dyslexia over the years, programs and methods suggested in many of them are now outdated as a result of our growing knowledge of and experience with dyslexia. Some books recommend a "cookbook" approach to remediation, often with commercial emphasis on buying a particular program—on the assumption that the child needs everything, so give him the whole program.

They do not take into account what he already knows or what he specifically needs. Some authors tend to sit on the fence and try to be all things to all persons, with a "Well, this might work or that might work." Still other books offer comprehensive reviews of the literature on dyslexia which present series after series of studies, one contradicting the other, with very few firm conclusions.

There is a need for professional, comprehensive surveys of the literature on dyslexia, but one must always read the studies with a critical eye. The validity of any research study should be questioned on the basis of its sampling procedures, the use or lack of control groups, the size of the population tested, the accuracy of the diagnosis of "alleged" dyslexia, the length of treatment, information about actual hours of teaching, the training of the teachers, the percentage of children who remain available for post-testing, and so on. A further important consideration ignored in most studies is the subtypes of dyslexia. Lumping all dyslexics together tends to make the subtypes neutralize the data in many ways. A difference in numbers in the subtypes, if grouped together in one study, could result in a skewing of certain results.

Promising research *is* being conducted. Dr. Albert M. Galaburda's investigations of the brains of deceased dyslexics at the Harvard Medical School Department of Neurology, Beth Israel Hospital in Boston, offers hope for new knowledge of dyslexia. Other researchers have uncovered a possibility that a gene localized on chromosome 15 may play an important role in the occurrence of dyslexia. There may be a link between dyslexia and chromosome irregularities. Anti-Ro antibody in mothers may have something to do with dyslexia. These are discussed in Chapter 9, "What Causes Dyslexia?"

We need to keep our feet on the ground when considering dyslexia. We need to use our common sense. We must cut through the controversies in the academic and medical worlds about what particular definition to use, what causes dyslexia, or whether it exists at all. Chapter 1 serves as an introduction to the condition of dyslexia, who can have it, and the incidence of dyslexia. Since dyslexia is a language communication disability, in order to understand dyslexia one must first have an understanding of the nature of our language. This language connection is made in Chapter 2. Chapter 3 presents an overview of the common characteristics of dyslexic students while Chapters 4 and 5 give an explanation of the specific characteristics of visual and auditory dyslexia. With the pressure for early identification of children with dyslexia, Chapter 6 deals with the developmental factors and the dangers of too-early diagnosis in young students. Chapter 7 illustrates these dangers and discusses the progress of five children, with examples of the error of assumption.

A historical perspective is always needed to understand something more clearly, and Chapter 8 discusses early connections and thinking about the evolution of the concept of dyslexia. Chapter 9 deals with the various suggested causes of the dyslexic condition.

The young dyslexic student grows up, often to face many frustrating problems. Chapter 10 examines dyslexia in the middle and high schools, and Chapter 11 follows up with the adult dyslexic in our society.

One hears a steady litany of "famous" persons said to have been dyslexic—always without supporting evidence. Chapter 12 presents some of these notable people and discusses the myths surrounding them.

Chapter 13 covers the factors necessary in alleviating dyslexia success-fully. I receive many calls from parents and teachers throughout the country with questions about reported "cures" for dyslexia. Each time the news media announces another, the calls resume. Chapter 14 deals with these various purported treatments, or "quick fixes," of which parents need to be wary.

Chapter 15 gives suggestions about what parents can do to help their dyslexic child, and Chapter 16 presents ideas for the teachers who must help the dyslexic student in the classroom. The final chapter offers suggestions for future directions in the dyslexia field, from the standpoint of research in general, schools, teacher-training institutions, and the state and federal governments, and includes a special section on medical research.

We are excited about what is happening to our understanding of dyslexia. The more children we can help—both at the clinic and after they return to their schools and classrooms, and through those who read this book—the more worthwhile and contented citizens we will have. And all those years of work and studying and trying this and that to find what works best, and caring for and agonizing with each student who has passed through our doors, will have been worth it all.

Anne Marshall Huston
Lynchburg, Virginia

ACKNOWLEDGMENTS

In addition to the specific acknowledgments given in appropriate chapters in this book, I wish to thank the following for their help and for all that I have learned from them over the years:

—those boys and girls who have come to me seeking help for their various problems,

—and their parents, who have shared their concerns and heartache so candidly,

—and the children's teachers, who worked so hard to help their students but knew additional help was needed, and who were so willing to share information and so appreciative of our work with students,

—my highly dedicated graduate students who spent many conscientious hours planning and preparing not only the work required for our classes but also for those children whose strengths and difficulties had to be uncovered and the latter remediated insofar as was possible. These knowledge-seeking, caring students have been a continuing source of inspiration to me,

—Mrs. Mary Scudder, Mrs. Marjorie Freeman, Mrs. Carol Pollock, Mrs. Linda Harwell, Mrs. Deborah Beckel, Mrs. Helen Bryant, and all the personnel at the Lynchburg College Library, for they were always graciously willing to help find certain books and journals, obtain books and copies of articles through interlibrary loan, and help make my research easier any way they could,

—Dr. Julius Sigler and Dr. James Carico, who took time from their busy schedules to sit down with me and introduce me to the use of the word processor—and the spelling program,

—those at the College Computer Lab, for they, too, were always ready and willing to give me help whenever I needed it. Special thanks go to Wendall Russell, Rick Bourne, Sue Driskill, Kipp Teague, and Gail Troy,

—Dr. Orrie O. Stenroos for his help in obtaining research on twin placentation,

—Mrs. Phyllis Lane and Mrs. Betty Shelton for their skillful typing, care, and concern, and for their wonderful willingness to help with my "Big Emergency,"

—the mother, who cannot be named, who gave me permission to reproduce her letter concerning the problems her son had been having in school,

—the five children described in Chapter 7 and whose names have been changed to assure confidentiality,

—Lynchburg College for providing me with a year's sabbatical leave so that I might complete this book,

—and to my husband, Jim, who was always there to give me help, encouragement, and inspiration through the long hours of researching and organizing information, writing and rewriting, and proofreading.

A.M.H.

PART ONE

GETTING A PERSPECTIVE

We have endeavored . . . to observe a
kind of perspective, that one part may cast
light upon another.
—*Francis Bacon*

CHAPTER 1

INTRODUCTION TO THE DYSLEXIA PROBLEM

Yet all experience is an arch wherethrough
gleams that untraveled world.
—*Tennyson*

My office telephone rang late one October afternoon, and when I answered I heard a woman's voice. She was obviously very agitated. "My daughter has dyslexia! What can I do?"

"Your child has dyslexia?" I asked. "How do you know she has dyslexia?" This is a question that I have learned always to ask.

"Because my sister says so," came back the reply.

"Your *sister*? Who is she? How did she come to this conclusion?" This is another question I have learned to ask.

"She was at the beauty salon and she read an article in one of those parents' magazines that said if a child reverses *b* and *d* or *p* and *q* then the child is probably dyslexic. What are we to do? Can you help us?"

"Now hold on a minute," I answered. "I need more information than that."

I asked her what grade her daughter was in, thinking that if she were in the third or fourth grade (or higher), there *might* be problems of some kind. But the child was in the first grade. I asked her age and was told that she was not yet six years old. I inquired as to the date of her birth and was told that she was born in December. This made her a "young first-grader." (Unfortunately, in our state at that time, children could enter first grade in September if they were to have their sixth birthday before the following January 1, a ruling that disturbed many professional early childhood educators.)

I explained to the mother that it is normal for a child of that age to reverse those letters. I asked if she had had her daughter's vision checked,

3

since certain types of visual defects can cause these difficulties. She had. I explained that the reversal problems would probably disappear by the end of the second grade, or perhaps even earlier. I also asked her to keep in touch with me and to let me know if the difficulty continued beyond that time.

It did not. By the end of the second grade the child was reading and writing without reversals of any kind. When I followed up, the mother recalled how upset and frightened she had been. "How could I have been so foolish?" she asked. "If only I had used some common sense instead of going off on a tangent. I should have known better!"

This child did not have dyslexia, but the story is a good example of how parents and educators can be thrown off the track by "popular" articles written by persons who do not have the training and experience to diagnose dyslexia, or an understanding of child growth and development and how these are related to the reading/spelling/writing processes. Such misinformation is not limited to popular articles. My telephone nearly rang off the hook after a speech by an educational psychologist at our local learning disabilities meeting at which he informed the audience that "any child who, at age five, reverses *b* and *d, p* and *q, saw* and *was, no* and *on, tap* and *pat* is a dyslexic." Unfortunately, the local newspaper picked this up, and the statement appeared in the next morning's paper, frightening many parents unnecessarily. How many five-year-olds are reading those words anyhow? And if they *are*, they are probably not dyslexic.

Scare tactics have no place where children and parents are concerned. Nor where educators are concerned. Diagnosing off the top of the head not only adds fuel to the dyslexia credibility controversy, it contributes to the misdiagnosis of children and the creation of new problems, and to needless anxiety on the part of parents.

When the Child Has Dyslexia

It may be something of a relief when the diagnosis indicates that the child is not a dyslexic, but can be classified as a remedial reader or a corrective reader—neither of which is as serious as dyslexia and therefore can be more easily and quickly alleviated. But at times this is not the case. The evidence is there, and common sense tells us that a spade must be called a spade. When this is done the door is open for remediating the dyslexic difficulties. For the child with dyslexia *can* be helped. Success in alleviating dyslexia is one of the most encouraging developments in education in recent years.

Dyslexia, What Is It?

The word "dyslexia" has been bandied about, been the subject of dissension among friends, left many in a quandary or in disbelief, and so much so that if the word itself could speak it would tell us that it is as bruised as the undiagnosed dyslexic child himself.

Dyslexia is more than just a reading disability. The word refers to a dysfunction or impairment in the use of words. The Greek prefix "dys" means defective, as in dysfunction, that is, a functional abnormality or impairment. The Greek "lexia" refers to the use of words (not just reading) and words are the means of communication in language—in reading, yes, but also in writing, in speaking, and in listening. Words are used in all school subjects, whether it be math, science, social studies, or any other. Students listen for instruction, read textbooks for information, write reports or other papers, copy work from the chalkboard or overhead projector, or solve mathematical problems (thinking as they work, for example, that "six plus four equals ten"—in *words*).

The dyslexic may not only confuse letters in reading and writing such as *m* with *w*, *n* with *u*, *b* with *d*, or *p* with *q*, but may confuse numerals in math and science, such as 2 with 5, or 6 with 9. Problems in sequencing, such as getting letters out of order within words, will cause a dyslexic to switch the order of digits in numbers, such as 245 for 254 or 1856 for 1865. This applies to dates in history as well as numbers in math and science. It is also likely to lead to the transposition of notes when reading music. Sequencing problems contribute confusion in a variety of ways: with the occurrence of events in a basal reader story or, in social studies, with events that have happened in history or with the use of the time line; as well as with the sequential steps in a science experiment, or in math when working long division or word problems; and with following directions, whether written or spoken, in any subject.

Dyslexia is a language communication disability. It includes three general categories. The first, visual dyslexia (sometimes referred to as visuospatial dyslexia), is characterized by inconsistent reversals of letters and numerals; faulty sequencing of letters in words and numbers in series, and disorder of events in life experiences as well as in written narratives, disorientation in time and space relationships; and problems in processing, interpreting, and recalling visual images. The second, auditory dyslexia (at times referred to as auditory-linguistic dyslexia), is characterized by problems of integrating and processing what is heard and recalling those sounds and applying them to the printed symbols representing them. The third category is a combination of visual and auditory dyslexia in varying degrees. Dyslexia is not attributable to any vision or hearing defect; it persists beyond that time when most childhood developmental conditions normally mature.

Dyslexia consists of a syndrome of characteristics that vary in degree according to the severity and kind of dyslexia one has. Just as one can have the symptoms of a mild or a severe chest cold, so, too, with dyslexia. And just as a severe chest cold can go into pneumonia if not treated, so, too, the child with severe dyslexia can become a failure in life, a dropout from our society.

Dyslexia, Who Has It?

There is no general agreement about the total number of dyslexics in our population. Estimates range from 2 percent to 25 percent, depending upon the study or source. The terminology itself can be confusing and misleading. In books and reviews on dyslexia, the subjects of studies are referred to in various ways, such as "learning disabled," "reading retarded," "reading disabled," having "specific learning difficulties," or being "dyslexic." The results of these studies are often compared with one another. And the results of studies on substantially normal populations have been applied indiscriminately to dyslexics—a most questionable procedure. Moreover, since studies of dyslexics have not, in most cases, differentiated among the categories of dyslexia, the results will almost certainly confound the findings. All this brings into question the validity of a great deal of the research on dyslexia.

The accuracy of the diagnoses of dyslexia must also be considered. Were the subjects used in a particular study actually dyslexic? For example, some researchers use as the criterion for determining dyslexia simply as reading two or more grades below grade placement on the basis of standardized reading achievement tests. This is wrong. Literal interpretation of the grade equivalent scores of the standardized tests should be avoided. There are various measurement and interpretive problems with such procedures that can affect any conclusions.[1]

Some children who read below grade level are simply slow learners; they are not necessarily dyslexic. They are intellectually unable to read at a particular grade level. A student may have been ill, had to take time out from school, and thus fallen behind in his reading achievement. Perhaps emotional trauma, such as the death of a parent, interfered with a child's learning progress in school or with his performance during testing. Again, a child may have changed schools and fallen behind because what he had yet to learn had already been covered in his new classroom. There are many reasons why students might be performing two grades below grade level, *other than being dyslexic.* In short, a child may be a "remedial reader" but not a dyslexic. Far too many studies have not made this differentiation.

A study cited in a "current" book compared seven- and eight-year old normal boys with dyslexic boys of the same age and found that the normal group was better able to recognize melody patterns in oral language. In this study a child was labeled dyslexic if he was reading below grade level and had average intelligence.[2] Incredible! *Any* child reading below grade level and of average intelligence being called dyslexic! No wonder there are skeptics. No wonder there is a credibility gap.

There are also children who have been misdiagnosed by poorly trained specialists on the basis of only a few characteristics symptomatic of dyslexia. Diagnoses have been made solely on a student's spelling errors, rather than on the results of a battery of tests with consideration of the child's performance in various areas in order to obtain a comprehensive diagnostic perspective of his overall strengths and weaknesses. An excellent reader may be a poor speller. Indeed, a teacher's method of teaching spelling and reading can affect a child's accuracy and create certain patterns of spelling or reading errors. At times, incorrect diagnoses of dyslexia have occurred during attempts to make a decision of dyslexia in a child who is too young. If these children are used as part of the population in comparative studies, obviously the findings will not be valid. On the other hand, if those children in our schools who do have dyslexia, but are so far undiagnosed, were used in the control groups of studies, the waters would be muddied even more.

The Incidence of Dyslexia

Here are examples of two extreme viewpoints about the incidence of dyslexia in schools. One principal of an elementary school has said that there "are no dyslexic children in my school." Yet nine dyslexic boys attend his school. Since they are not getting the help they need at school, the parents have had to employ a reading specialist, trained in remediating dyslexia, to work with the boys on a private basis after school. Admittedly, dyslexic students can be a real bother to the administrator. They also tend to lower that "all-important" standardized test average on which schools appear to place so much significance. (Yet if the dyslexics were helped, this would contribute to raising the average.)

The principal of another elementary school in the same system told me that she has "a whole school full of dyslexics." Since both schools are "typical" elementary schools with similar populations, it is not likely that one of them, with some hundreds of children, would have no dyslexics and that the other would be "full of dyslexics."

Common sense, experience, and the reasons stated above suggest that a range of from 3 percent to 5 percent is probably a plausible estimate of the incidence of dyslexia. The incidence of *reading retardation* in the schools may be as high as 25 percent, *but not that of dyslexia.*[3]

Dyslexia Around the World

Dyslexia is not limited to any one country or region of the world. In the Library of Congress there are books about dyslexia that have been published in Australia, Austria, Belgium, Canada, Czechoslovakia, Chile, Denmark, France, Germany, Great Britain, Hungary, Holland, the Philippines, and Portugal, as well as the United States. There have been International World Congresses on Dyslexia. Numerous articles have been written in various medical and other professional journals over a period of many years.

The incidence of dyslexia as reported varies a great deal from language to language, with the lowest reported for Japanese and the highest usually for English.[4] There has been much speculation as to the reason for this variance. One assumption is that the answer may lie in the inherent linguistic merits and scripts of the different languages.[5] However, Macdonald Critchley—and others—maintains that this is not credible and suggests the more likely explanation that in Japan the neurologists, educational psychologists, and teachers are not so sensitive to the occurrence of dyslexia. If this were to prove wrong, then Critchley suggests the low incidence of dyslexia in Japan might be due to genetic reasons.[6] At any rate, at the present time, this variance of dyslexia from language to language cannot be explained. What we *do* know is that dyslexia is likely to be found around the world.[7]

Are There Sex Differences?

There are sex differences in the incidence of dyslexia, just as there are in color blindness. The dyslexic child is referred to in most books as "he" for a good reason. While both boys and girls can have dyslexia, boys are far more likely to have it.

As with estimates on the incidence of dyslexia, so, too, is there a lack of consensus on the ratio of dyslexic males to dyslexic females. The estimates vary from study to study: 2–to–1,[8] 3.5–to–1 or 4–to–1,[9] 4–to-1,[10] 5–to–1.[11] In our clinic the ratio of dyslexic males to dyslexic females has been nearly 6–to-1. (However, the method of enrollment acceptance and pairing sex with like sex is likely to have contributed to this higher ratio.)

The difference in the number of male dyslexics as compared to females is well founded and accepted. The *reason* has not yet been established, although there are numerous hypotheses: a greater occurrence of cerebral trauma in males, the hemispheric functioning of the sexes, a mutant at a single locus whose expression is modified by sex, or a polygenic expression that has a lower threshold for males than for females.

What About Intelligence?

Perhaps because of the wording in some of the definitions of dyslexia and learning disabilities in articles and books about dyslexia, the erroneous idea has arisen that dyslexics must be average or above average in intelligence. This misconception may be due partly to well-meaning teachers who are sensitive to the needs of parents to know that their child does not lack intelligence and to the needs of the child, who may fear that he really is "a dummy" because he has so much trouble doing school work and cannot keep up with his classmates. To encourage parents and children, teachers will mention the names of famous people said to have had dyslexia—Einstein, for instance. (Actually, the evidence that Einstein was dyslexic is very weak. More is said about this in Chapter 12, "Some Notable People, Dyslexic or Not?")

Slow learners, average learners, superior learners—any can have dyslexia. The odds are that the child is likely to be of average or above average intelligence simply because about 75 percent of the population falls in those categories (50 percent average, 25 percent above the average range). But the slow learner can also have dyslexia, in which case diagnosis may be more difficult, and remediation will take longer.

Socioeconomic Background

Dyslexia has no favorites in regard to the wealthy or the poor, the cultured or the culturally disadvantaged. Any child from any background can have dyslexia. Money *can* be useful to the dyslexic child from the standpoint of getting private diagnostic help and private tutoring when the schools do not provide adequate services, but the socioeconomic backgrounds of dyslexics are varied.

Birth Order of Dyslexics

Any child in the family can have dyslexia, whether he be the oldest, the youngest, or the in-between child. Research on birth order is sparse. In a study of five hundred dyslexics, 24.6 percent were the oldest in their families, while 36 percent were the youngest.[12] In another study no differences in birth order in the incidence of dyslexia among brothers and sisters were found in 112 families with dyslexics.[13] And in yet another study of 125 children (one hundred boys, twenty-five girls), the birth order of those with alleged dyslexia were as follows:

	Males	Females
First born	31	6
Second born	39	9
Third born	20	5
Fourth born	5	5
Fifth born	3	0
Adopted	2	0

Of those listed above as first born, nine were actually the only child in a family.[14]

In a study of eighty-one dyslexic students, I found thirty to be first born, thirty-one to be second born, thirteen to be third born, six to be fourth born, and one to be fifth born. Of those first born, ten were the only child in the family.

Summary

Dyslexia is a language communication disability, affecting reading, writing, speaking, and listening. It is a dysfunction or impairment in the use of words. Consequently, relations with others and performance in every subject in school can be affected by dyslexia. It can be found around the world, principally among boys. It exists in learners of slow, average, and superior intelligence. The dyslexic child can come from any background, or any income level; and dyslexia may occur in any child in a family regardless of the order in which he is born.

Notes

1. Summarized in Wayne Otto and Richard J. Smith, *Corrective and Remedial Teaching* (Boston: Houghton Mifflin, 1980), p. 196.

2. In the upper grades, the grade equivalent scores do not represent the extent of contrast between raw score medians (for grades immediately above and below) that are indicated by grade equivalents in lower grades. A grade equivalent of one year below a child's grade placement in the second grade would thus signify a larger deviation from the raw score average for the second grade than would a grade equivalent score that is one year below placement in an upper grade. In addition, there is an inclination for grade equivalents to exaggerate minor differences between

scores as a result of the curve fitting operations, and, therefore, large variations within groups tend to be indistinct. A student who is only a little above or below the median for his grade on a particular reading achievement test may seem to be much farther away from this criterion. Another problem with using the grade placement criterion is that some achievement tests use different forms at the different grade levels. Frank R. Vellutino, *Dyslexia: Theory and Research* (Cambridge, Mass.: MIT Press, 1980), p. 26.

3. Hynd and Cohen report that "a variety of studies indicate that it is reasonable to conclude that 10 to 16 percent of the total school population are in need of special education services. . . . Of this number, and on the basis of large-scale investigations of the population of school-age children, it would be conservative to estimate that the percentage of children who could be classified as dyslexic ranges from a minimum of 3 percent to a maximum of 6 percent. . . . Practically speaking, this translates into an expected frequency of approximately 15 to 30 dyslexic children per 500 school children." George W. Hynd and Morris Cohen, *Dyslexia, Neuropsychological Theory, Research, and Clinical Differentiation* (New York: Grune & Stratton, 1983, p. 24.

4. P.G. Aaron, "The Neuropsychology of Developmental Dyslexia," *Reading Disorders, Varieties and Treatments,* R.N. Malatesha and P.G. Aaron, eds. (New York: Academic Press, 1982), p. 53.

5. Notes on inherent linguistic merits and script of languages:

(a) One possible explanation for the lower incidence of reading difficulties among the Japanese, Professor Kiyoshi Makita (Keio University, Tokyo) suggests, lies in the nature of the *kana* script. For one thing, no readable *kana* letters are mirror images of one another such as our *p* and *q* or *b* and *d*. And there is no way to represent the sound of a consonant in isolation in Japanese. Each consonant is phonetically tied to another consonant by an intermediate link of a vowel or vowels, whereas in the Roman alphabet two or more consonants are often joined to become blends or digraphs. While a letter in *kana* script is always read the same way, the letters of our alphabet may be pronounced in various ways, depending on the letters that precede or follow a letter. And while most of our consonant sounds are fairly consistent, our vowels have more than one sound—and often copy one another.

In Japan, the mechanism of reading is entirely different from that used by English-speakers. Our reading is based on 26 letters of the alphabet, and they, singly or in combinations, represent approximately 44 different phonemes (sounds). And in many of our words some letters represent no sound at all; they are silent. The Japanese scripts include two types of *kana* script (*hiragana* and *katakana*), each made up of 48 phonetic letters. There is also the *kanji* script made up of numerous ideographs, mostly borrowed classical Chinese characters which are read differently and are limited to 1,850 characters for daily use.

For his study Makita randomly sampled, by means of a questionnaire, teachers in primary schools in metropolitan Tokyo. Tabulated results indicated that when students with reading problems were divided into poor *kana* readers and poor *kanji* readers, the poor *kana* readers showed a marked drop by third grade, but the numbers of poor *kanji* readers remained relatively large. The Japanese first-grade curriculum requires pupils to read 48 *hiraganas* and 46 of the easier *kanjis*. Second-graders are expected to learn 48 *katakanas* (in addition to the 48 *hiraganas*) and 105 *kanjis*. As students move upward through the grades, *kanjis* of increasing complexity are introduced. By the end of the sixth grade, the students are expected to have learned 977 *kanji* symbols. Requirements continue to grow more complex; consequently, there is a relative increase of reading problems. Makita points out that those having poor intellectual endowment have been able to read *kana* because of its simplicity, but "coping with the complexity of *kanji* was beyond their reach." (p. 612).

Makita's study was limited to one large metropolitan area. He apparently equated dyslexia with reading disability. In the questionnaire the teachers were asked if they had students more backward in reading than the expected level of the last grade, and if they had children with difficulty in reading regardless of normal intelligence. The teacher's opinion was the criterion as to whether a child had a reading disability. No actual testing of intelligence, reading levels, or other behavior was done by the investigator. The validity of the results is thus open to question. Kiyoshi Makita, "The Rarity of Reading Disability in Japanese Children," *American Journal of Orthopsychiatry*, 38 (1968), pp. 599–614.

(b) Harold Stevenson (University of Michigan) questions Makita's position on the orthography issue, on the basis of a study of elementary school children in Taiwan, Japan, and the United States. A reading test was developed, based on an analysis of the vocabulary, grammar, and substance of the reading books used by fifth-grade students in twenty classrooms at ten schools that were selected as being typical of the elementary schools in Taipei, Taiwan; Sendai, Japan; and Minneapolis, Minnesota. (Minneapolis was selected because it has a low percentage of minority and foreign-born families. Taipei and Sendai were then chosen as being the cities in Taiwan and Japan most like Minneapolis in size, cultural, and economic status.) Reading disability was defined as being behind in reading level by at least two years (and neither mentally retarded nor emotionally disturbed). The percentages of these fifth-grade students reading below third-grade level were 8 percent for Taiwan, 2 percent for Japan, and 3 percent for the United States. The severity of reading problems is reflected in the percentages of these students who were reading below *second* grade level: 2 percent for Taiwan, 1 percent for Japan, and 0.5 percent for the United States.

Another definition used for reading disability is that a student have low reading achievement together with average or near-average intelligence. Stevenson calculated the percentages of students who had (1) the lowest 10 percent of reading scores within each city, and (2) those who obtained average scores higher than one standard deviation below the mean for both verbal and performance items in a set of cognitive tasks. The percentages were as follows: 7.5 percent for Taiwan, 5.4 percent for Japan, and 6.3 percent for the United States.

On the basis of his findings, Stevenson concluded that "it is obvious that there is no greater incidence of severe reading problems among children reading English than among those reading Chinese or Japanese. There is no support, therefore, for the belief that because of the orthographic systems of Chinese and Japanese, children reading those languages do not develop disabilities in reading." (p. 300)

In answer to the question of why the existence of such poor reading among elementary school students in Taiwan and Japan has escaped notice, Stevenson suggests:

(1) As a result of little interest, no words to represent the concept of reading disability or severe reading problems were ever devised in either Chinese or Japanese, and therefore it is difficult to even talk about the topic.

(2) There is an absence of objective tests, and there are large numbers of students in classrooms. Standardized reading tests have not been available in Chinese. In Japan only group tests are published. Therefore teachers in both countries rely on their own assessments. With class enrollments of from 35 to 50 students, the determination of accurate reading levels may be hard.

(3) Accurate determination of reading levels is further inhibited in Asian classes because of the extensive use of choral reading, where the variance in individual reading levels is not so obvious.

(4) Eastern philosophy stresses the plasticity of the human being, with the consequence that Chinese and Japanese educators and parents are reluctant to place students into categories. Retardation in reading would likely be attributed to a child's lack of motivation. Harold W. Stevenson, "Orthography and Reading Disabilities," *Journal of Learning Disabilities* 17 (May 1984), pp. 300–301.

(c) Chen-Chin Hsu studied the prevalence of reading disabilities among 240 randomly selected fifth-graders reading the logographic Chinese writing system in Taiwan. His results indicated that reading disabilities and the prevalence rates of reading failure were no lower than among children in the alphabetic writing systems. He concluded that there is no support for the "argument that specific writing systems are easier to learn to read and thus preclude the incidence of reading disabilities" (p.54). Chen-Chin Hsu, "Correlates of Reading Success and Failure in Logographic Writing System," *Thalamus* 6 (Spring 1988), pp. 33–59.

Two other studies replicating Hsu's and carried out in other sections of Taiwan provided similar findings. Guo Yo et al., "A Survey on Prevalence of Reading Disabled Children in Tainan City," Collected Papers, Taiwan Provincial Health Administration, 1984, pp. 253–59, and Y.C. Lee, ed., *Annual Report of the Tung-mun Elementary School* (Taipei City Bureau of Education, 1986), pp. 10–14, as cited in Chen-Chin Hsu's study listed above.

6. Macdonald Critchley, *The Dyslexic Child* (Springfield, Ill.: Charles C. Thomas, 1970), p. 96.

7. In writing about the universality of learning disabilities, Janet W. Lerner reports, "An organization dedicated to fostering international research on learning disabilities is the International Academy for Research in Learning Disabilities (IARLD). Accumulating evidence from this group and other studies shows that learning disabilities exist across nations, in all cultures, and with all languages. The concepts underlying learning disabilities have permeated countries on at least five continents." Janet W. Lerner, "Learning Disabilities and Cultural Diversity," *Educators' FORUM*, (Boston: Houghton Mifflin, Fall 1989), p. 3.

8. John Money, "Dyslexia: A Postconference Review," *Reading Disability, Progress and Research Needs in Dyslexia,* John Money, ed. (Baltimore: Johns Hopkins, 1962), p. 31.

9. T.R. Miles and Elaine Miles, *Help for Dyslexic Children* (London: Methuen, 1983), p. 2.

10. Critchley, op. cit., p. 91.

11. Sandhya Naidoo, *Specific Dyslexia, The Research Report of the ICAA Word Blind Centre for Dyslexia Children* (New York: John Wiley, 1972), p. 25.

12. Edith Klasen, *The Syndrome of Specific Dyslexia* (Baltimore: University Park, 1972), p. 160.

13. Bertil Hallgren, Specific Dyslexia ("Congenital Word–Blindness"); A Clinical and Genetic Study (Copenhagen: Ejnar Munksgaard, 1950); trans. by Erica Odelberg (Stockholm: Esselte aktiebolag, 1950), p. 192.

14. Critchley, op. cit., p. 92.

CHAPTER 2

THE LANGUAGE CONNECTION: READING, WRITING, SPEAKING, LISTENING

> Through experience and through language we learn.
> Experience needs language to give it form. Language
> needs experience to give it content.
> —*Walter Loban*

> Thought is not merely expressed in words;
> it comes into existence through them.
> —*Vygotsky*

Since dyslexia is a language communication disability, we must understand our language and what is involved in reading, writing, speaking, and listening before we can understand dyslexia.

Language is the medium of communication. Human beings communicate their ideas and feelings through language—writing and reading, speaking and listening. Writing and speaking are called *expressive* language processes because information emerges from us in the form of spoken or written words to be heard or read by others. Reading and listening are called *receptive* language processes because that which is read and heard filters into us for processing. We receive information from the author or the speaker. Oral reading is a function of both expressive and receptive language.

We communicate through the words of our language. Words involve a reciprocal relationship—we not only express our thoughts in words, but our ideas come into being through them. Our thoughts are a form of inner speech.

While there are about 2,800 languages spoken in the world today,[1] we are interested here in our own language, English, although many words from other languages have crept into our vocabulary. Our young people often prefer *pizza* or *lasagna* to *broccoli* (Italian). Some like *sauerkraut* (German). They may prefer to *ski* rather than to hear a *saga* (Scandinavian), or to *skate* or sail on a *yacht* (Dutch). Others like to slap on a *sombrero*, sit on the *patio*, and play the *guitar* (Spanish). Young girls may like a touch of *rouge* (French) before going to the *bazaar* (Persian) for a cup of *coffee* (Turkish) on the *Sabbath* (Hebrew).

Our language is flexible, adaptable, and ever changing. In addition to adopting numerous words from other languages, we are continually coining new words and incorporating them into American English. The advent of the computer and other discoveries have created additional words that are now a part of our language. Indeed, other countries are now adopting American words (weekend, car, drugstore, stop).

The words in our language represent ideas or objects; that is, they are symbolic, but of course this is arbitrary and may change with time. Many words have changed in meaning since their inception. For some words, today's definition is not anything at all like the original meaning. For example, in Shakespeare's day *let* meant the same as *stop* does today—that is, it held the opposite meaning. And Shakespeare used the word *owe* as we now would use the word *own*.[2] Young people and adults often enjoy browsing through books dealing with word origins and the remarkable ways in which some of our words have come into the language—Merriam's *Picturesque Word Origins* for young students, or Mencken's *The American Language*, or A.L. Rowse's introduction to his Contemporary Shakespeare Series, "Why a Contemporary Shakespeare?"[3]

Our language tends to be quite orderly, with patterns of expressions that help us to anticipate what is coming next, whether we are listening or reading. Language is thus systematic with common elements that enable us to understand one another. There is a kind of information processing that occurs when we get meaning from an acoustic signal while we are listening to a speaker or from a printed text while we are reading.[4] It is with this information processing that the dyslexic has difficulty.

Certain irregularities in our language make reading and writing particularly difficult for dyslexics. This applies especially to those students who have been limited to a phonics approach to reading or who have had an overemphasis on the phonics word recognition strategy. These words may pose no problem in our everyday speaking and listening. It is when we see them in a book or try to write them that confusion often occurs. Pronounce aloud to yourself the following series of words; listen to what you are saying; and notice the similarity in spelling and the inconsistency in how they sound.

do/go	does/goes/shoes	fat/father
gave/have	hour/four/tour	man/many

alive/give	but/put; but/buy	key/they
on/one	her/here/there	brown/grown
small/shall	ought/bough/cough	home/some
catch/watch	bead/bread/break	ash/wash

Venezky[5] suggests that, in order to be more precise, words such as the above should be referred to as being *predictable* or *unpredictable*, rather than *regular* or *irregular* as is usually done, because of the variance of pronunciation of the phonic elements even though they are written alike. At any rate, since the dyslexic's perception of even predictable words tends to be unstable and insecure, the irregular or unpredictable words present greater and more frustrating obstacles.

Irregular (or unpredictable) words, which are basically "exceptions to the phonics rules," must be incorporated into a child's sight vocabulary so that he can recognize them instantly without having to resort to various strategies to figure them out. Such words give visual dyslexics a great deal of trouble because they must rely on visual recall for these irregularities. The auditory dyslexic can draw more on visual recall, but, he too, has trouble because of all the sound variations, silent letters, and so forth.

In our spoken language we have various words that are understood when heard, but when this language is transferred to print or needs to be written, complications arise. Words that sound alike but have different meanings and spellings (called homophones) such as *meet/meat, blew/blue,* or *pair/pear/pare* confuse the dyslexic. We also have words that are spelled alike but have different meanings and different pronunciations (called homographs) such as *produce* (pro' duce), as in the vegetables in your garden, and *produce* (pro duce'), as in the sentence, "Hens produce eggs." And we have words like *read* which can occur in this manner, "I will read the book that you read last week." (The second *read* sounds like the color *red*.) We have words that are spelled the same and sound alike, but the meanings are different (called homonyms), such as *down* (e.g., down the road, a down mood, a sand dune, soft feathers).

The following poem cleverly but accurately illustrates the inconsistencies in the relationship of spoken language and written language:

Our Queer Language

When the English Tongue we speak
Why is "break" not rhymed with "freak"?
Will you tell me why it's true
We say "sew" and likewise "few"?
And the maker of the verse
Cannot cap his "horse" with "worse"?

"Beard" sounds not the same as "heard"
"Cord" is different from "word"
Cow is "cow" but low is "low"
"Shoe" is never rhymed with "foe"
Think of "hose" and "dose" and "lose"
And think of "goose" and not of "choose"
"Doll" and "roll," "home" and "some"
And since "pay" is rhymed with "say"
Why not "paid" with "said" I pray?
"Mould" is not pronounced like "could"
Where "done" but "gone" and "lone"
Is there any reason known?
And in short it seems to me
Sounds and letters disagree.

—Anon.

A bit confusing, isn't it? But, while our language appears rather complicated, and the connection seems to break down somewhat when we try to match it in print, most people *do* master the interrelationships of our language. The important point is that one must always be thinking, be understanding what is being said and what is being read.

This emphasis on meaning is critical for the dyslexic and is the connecting thread that matches oral language to written language; that is, the sounds of words matched to the symbols that represent them on paper. Thinking, understanding, and making associations form the strongest means that a dyslexic can have to help him progress.

Understanding Reading

Reading is a form of communication by language. The author is trying to convey his thoughts to the reader through the medium of print. There is seldom, if ever, a perfect match of thought between the reader and the author. While the author knows what is in his own mind, the reader cannot "see" into the author's mind. He sees only the printed words on the page. There is no meaning per se in those printed words. Images of what is seen are carried to the mind, and it is here that understanding takes place. It is in the mind that the symbols are recognized, associations made, information processed and interpreted—based on the reader's knowledge and the experience that he brings to whatever he is reading. These may or may not be similar to the author's. This is why different interpretations of books and poems occur among readers. Each reader has his own unique fund of knowledge and experience that influences his interpretation of whatever he is reading. The teacher who expects every student in a class to come up with the same answer to the routine question, "What is the author saying in that poem?" should perhaps substitute the question, "What is *your* interpretation of this poem?"

How Does One Read?

Contrary to what many people assume, our eyes do not flow smoothly across the page as we are reading. Instead, our eyes move in a series of jumps and pauses.[6] These are called saccades and fixations. We only read during the fixations—not when the eyes are moving. When the eyes pause, they take in a portion of visual information (about six or seven items), which is fed into our short-term memory, sometimes called our working memory. This is a sort of holding station where the visual information is processed by the brain. Our working memory is of limited duration. We must give continual attention to this information or we lose it, and while this is going on we cannot attend to anything else. It is as though there is a "shutdown" in our vision while the brain is processing this information.

What happens to the portion of information taken in? If the brain can organize the information and wants to keep it, then the information is transferred into our long-term memory for permanent storage, but recall is not always instantaneous. Sometimes this can be frustrating to us, say, when we want to remember the name of our child's second-grade teacher or the author of a particularly interesting book or the name of a special restaurant.

The dyslexic has serious problems with both short-term memory and long-term memory. Words must be recognized and information organized for the information to be transferred to long-term memory. If what he is trying to read makes no sense, he tries again, and usually his short-term memory becomes overloaded because there is a limit to the amount of visual information that the brain can handle at any one time. Since the maximum is six or seven items, if the dyslexic is trying to "sound out" the individual letters of a word and this results in nonsense, then he has to try again. If unstable letter and word forms change in appearance and if he takes too much time in trying to figure out the word, his short-term memory bogs down. The brain cannot process the nonsensical information fed to it. Furthermore, stress and fear of making a mistake can get in the way of thinking and cause visual-memory overload. This often happens when the dyslexic student is asked to read aloud in front of the whole class.

What the dyslexic already knows and has experienced (sometimes called nonvisual information[7]) plays a part in short-term memory and helps him make sense of what he sees and thus stores in his long-term memory. The effort itself, this trying so desperately to make sense of reading, contributes further to a very slow reading rate. Figure 2.1 illustrates the relationships of the components of the memory system discussed here.

It is common for dyslexics (as well as other retarded readers) to have many regressive eye movements—when the eye goes back to get another look, to try again. Frequent regressions contribute to poor comprehension, lack of fluency, and slow reading.

His problem with short-term memory affects the ability of a dyslexic to copy accurately from the chalkboard, the overhead projector, charts, or books. It affects his ability to keep a visual image or auditory image of a reading or spelling pattern long enough for it to become internalized and transferred into long-term memory. And, remember, it affects any task involving listening as well.

The major problem with long-term memory is in retrieving specific information quickly at a certain time. In many cases, the dyslexic student may not provide an answer to a particular question, written or oral, as quickly as the teacher wishes, and she may turn to another student for the answer, thinking that the dyslexic student does not know it.

Both short-term memory and long-term memory problems can also affect the dyslexic's performance on timed achievement tests.

Understanding Writing

Writing is another form of communication by language. The author is attempting to convey his thoughts to the reader by means of words. Writing is related to both spoken language and reading, but it is not the same. In our country, from ocean to ocean, throughout various geographical regions,

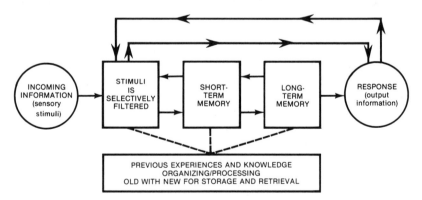

Figure 2.1   The relationships of the components of the memory system.

citizens speak with various dialects. An educated or uneducated Southerner will speak somewhat differently from an educated or uneducated Midwesterner or New Englander. Residents of New York City speak differently from their close neighbors in New Jersey (listen for those dropped "*r*'s" in New York). In fact, within each state there exists a variety of dialects.

In the United States, no one regional dialect is recognized as being *the* national standard. Each geographical region has its own regional standard, but while citizens across our country may speak quite differently, this does not prevent us from reading and understanding the same national newspapers, or magazines, or books on the best-seller lists. We even watch and understand the same national television programs.

What does writing do? It cuts across all the many different dialects, for the conventional form of writing can be read by those who might find another's speech a little difficult to understand. *Writing is a kind of language melting pot for all the variant types of speech.* It is an important form of communication and a significant part of our education; therefore, it should be a major part of the curriculum in our schools.

What is Involved in Writing?

Contrary to what some think, writing is *not* the mirror image of reading. Like reading, writing is actually a complex process, but it is a different ball game from reading. The writer must recall the correct spelling of a word and then encode the word, forming it from the individual letters that make it up. The writer has to recall the exact form of each letter and the sequence in which these letters occur. Does the word begin with a capital letter? Is it a hyphenated word? Must it be underlined? The *t*'s and *x*'s have to be crossed and the *i*'s and *j*'s dotted. Then there must be a space between the individual words and the appropriate punctuation must be chosen—a period, comma, question mark, and so on. Not only do the letters have to be in correct sequence to form a word, but the sequence of the words in a sentence must be considered.

What skills are needed for writing? One must have a good visual image (revisualization) of the spelling of the word, as well as of the formation of the letters that make up the word, and the capacity to recall these from memory. There are no silent letters in spelling! All letters in a word must be written. A sense of sequence is needed for the letters and words to appear in the right order. It is also needed for the orderly development of ideas and the organization of thought in whatever is being written. And the writer must have an understanding of the purposes of punctuation so that the reader will be able to make sense of the material. Recall—retrieving information out of one's long-term memory so as to have something to write about and relating it to other types of information and experiences—is necessary in any writing.

The dyslexic's problems with unstable letter and word formations, his confusions with visual and auditory sequencing, punctuation, and his difficulty in retrieving information from his long-term memory storage in a short time—all contribute to his poor writing abilities.

What about phonics for spelling? Isn't phonics essential in order to spell correctly? Some may think it heresy when I say that students who "spell by ear" are the poorest spellers. Yet, it is true. The following is a letter that shows the types of spelling errors often made by students who have overly depended on phonics and who have been taught to spell by "ear."

> Dear Miz Jonsun,
>   Thay tel me u ar a good teecher. I wont too hav u for my teecher nex yeer. Becauz I hav truble with reeding and riting and speling. Sum uv my teechers tryed too teech me wurds and I had a grate deel of fonix evri day. Wun teecher sed she wuz going too beet fonix n my hed and she wurked hard and I ges she did a thoro job and now I hav truble understanding whut I reed and peepul laf when thay see how I spel wurds. Pleez teech me nex yeer and help me too reed and spel rite.
>
> I luv u,
> Bob

To spell correctly, one must *remember* the spelling of words. Stressing the relationships of the meaning of words will help children to internalize what they know about their language and how words are related. Gradually, developmentally, they will apply this knowledge to their spelling of words and acquire a stock of correctly spelled words. This is how the dyslexic must build up a vocabulary of words to use in his writing. The association of meaning with the word will help him much more than any phonics sounding of letters that at times may vary (to him) in shape as well as sound.

The matter of spelling is treated more fully in Chapter 6, where it is pointed out that children's spelling progresses through a series of stages and that certain types of spelling errors are normal for young children.[8] As they mature, so too, does the development and accuracy of their spelling and writing.

People are often surprised when they hear that the pronunciation of words is a very unreliable guide to spelling. How often do we hear teachers or parents telling children to "sound it out" when students ask for help with spelling a word! Yet one-third of the words in a standard dictionary have more than one accepted pronunciation. A majority of the words in our language have silent letters (as the *k* and *w* in *know* or the *e* in *bake* or the *a* in *beat* or the second *e* in *beet*). One-sixth of the words contain double letters (as in *kitten, bottle,* or *correct*). Many different spellings can be given for most sounds. For example, the vowel *e* can be spelled fourteen ways, only one-fifth of the time with the *e* alone.[9,10] No wonder dyslexics, especially auditory dyslexics, have so much trouble with vowel sounds! Admittedly, teaching the vowel sounds "is undoubtedly the most difficult and confusing part of an entire phonics program."[11] Difficult and confusing for *any* child, not just a dyslexic child! Clearly, phonics cannot ensure correct spelling.

Take the word *work.* If a teacher asked a student to "use your phonics" to spell *work,* the child might write *wurk, werk, wirk, wurc, werc, wirc, wurck, werck, wirck*—none of which correctly spells the word *work,* but all of which are pronounced the same as *work.*

To illustrate the peculiarity of English spelling, George Bernard Shaw constructed the word *ghoti.* This word is pronounced *fish.* Why? The *gh* combination is pronounced like the *gh* sound in *cough* (which is an *f* sound), the vowel *o* is pronounced like the *o* sound in *women* (which is the short *i* sound), and the *ti* combination is pronounced like the *ti* in the word *nation* (which is a *sh* sound). Hence: *ghoti* is pronounced *fish.*[12]

Let's be sensible about teaching spelling. Let's not further disable our dyslexic child by turning him into a "phonics misspelling cripple."

Understanding Speaking

The human vocal apparatus can produce an almost infinite variety of speech sounds for sending words from a speaker to a listener. These have different acoustic patterns caused by the various kinds of articulatory movements used to produce them. Articulation is the process by which the shape of the vocal tract is changed to produce the various sounds.

But speaking is more than just producing speech sounds, more than mere talking. Speaking requires thinking and involves imagination and a sensitivity to the listener. Good speech is produced with ease and confidence and is pleasing to the ear. The tempo, as well as the volume, is suited to the listener.

An individual speaks because he has something to say to someone. He has some information he wishes to share, or an opinion he wants to give. He may have a question to ask, or an answer to a question asked.

In school, it is not the student who does most of the speaking, but the teacher. Actually, teachers need to do less talking and more listening. How else can the students' speaking skills improve? Students need to be encouraged to talk freely with one another in class discussions, in planning a joint project or activity. The object of conversation is to share ideas, and students should have opportunities to present these ideas in logical order, to respond to the ideas of others, and to make suggestions.

Dyslexic students are often quite willing to talk, and, if their self-esteem has not been shattered, will work in groups and make contributions to class discussions. What they have to say is usually based more on their background of knowledge and experiences than on their textbooks, unless they have been given material that they can read with understanding. Sometimes the fund of information that dyslexics have acquired is remarkable in view of their reading problems, since reading is one way to acquire new knowledge.

If, however, you pay close attention to what is being said, you will note that the ideas and events expressed by the visual dyslexic are usually out of sequential order. In school, their verbosity sometimes helps them to get around requirements and slip through the grades. The auditory dyslexic, on the other hand, is not as glib and does not have as great a range of speaking vocabulary as the visual dyslexic. He may not enunciate clearly; his speech frequently may include spoonerisms, twisted syllables, and the like. Both visual and auditory dyslexics often find it hard to recall the right word when needed because of difficulties in retrieving information quickly from long-term memory.

Understanding Listening

Hearing is not the same as listening. We hear with our ears, but we listen with our minds. Listening is more complex than hearing and involves a knowledge of the language, relating what is heard to past knowledge, and making sense out of it. Listening requires giving active and conscious attention to the speaker. It requires thinking, reacting, and associating ideas.

Students in school spend at least 45 percent of their time listening to instruction. Imagine! This much time just listening in the classroom—not really participating in what is going on—just listening. But listening is an active process. Hearing may be inactive, but listening requires involvement on the part of the listener. The good listener *thinks* as he listens and is not distracted. He controls his emotions as he listens to what is said, and he recognizes his responsibility in affording courtesy to the speaker. Because he is thinking as he listens, he is able to react, to respond to what he has heard, or to think of additional information to add to a subject. Good listening is not a passive skill. The listener must pay attention to the words, phrases, and ideas presented by the speaker.

If the material presented by the teacher is interesting or useful to the students, if it means something to them, then they will attend to what is being said. If it is not, they will not. It is as simple as that.

Teachers sometimes, unwittingly, contribute to nonlistening habits when they pitch their instruction at a level higher than the listening level (understanding) of their students, or when they have students who have difficulty reading material aloud stagger through a textbook or story, repeating words and hesitating, so that what they are reading drags on the mind of the listener.

Furthermore, parents and teachers, no matter the difficulties, must listen attentively to youngsters when they have something to say and must serve as listening models for the children.

The visual dyslexic may be a somewhat better listener than the auditory dyslexic, who finds the sounds of language confusing and inhibiting; but the sequencing of thoughts and the retention of ideas is faulty in both. Indeed, because dyslexics tend to be sensitive to the sounds of their environment, many have had to learn to shut them out, to develop a kind of insulation against the distractions of noise. This sensitivity to noise and movement, combined with the difficulties of processing language, makes dyslexics faulty listeners.

The Language Arts

Reading, writing, speaking, and listening are all interrelated. The words of our language are a common bond between them. While reading and listening are the "receptive" components of the language arts, and speaking and writing are the "expressive" components, all require an active participation on the part of the student.

In our everyday life, we tend to speak more than we listen or read, and we read more than we write. On the average, people retain only 50 percent of what they hear (no matter how hard they concentrate), and two months later they generally remember only 25 percent of what they have heard.[13] Elementary school students retain even less. One wonders whether the "lecture method" of instruction in our schools is ever as effective as some believe.

The dyslexic student nearly always has trouble in any lecture type situation. His faulty information-processing system responds better to demonstrations and student-participation exercises and activities than to lectures or textbook reading—in all subjects.

Notes

1. Walter T. Petty and Julie M. Jensen, *Developing Children's Language* (Boston: Allyn & Bacon, 1980), p. 21.

2. A.L. Rowse, "Why a Contemporary Shakespeare?" *King Lear* (Lanham, Md: University Press of America, 1984), p. 6.

3. *Picturesque Word Origins* (Springfield, Mass.: G. & G. Merriam, 1933); H.L. Mencken, *The American Language* (New York: Alfred A. Knopf, 1980); A.L. Rowse, *Introduction in the Contemporary Shakespeare Series* (Lanham, Md: University Press of America, 1984.)

4. Dominic V. Massaro, "Language and Information Processing," *Understanding Language*, Dominic V. Massaro, ed. (New York: Academic Press, 1975), p. 5.

5. Richard L. Venezky, "Regularity in Reading and Spelling," *Basic Studies on Reading*, Harry Levin and Joanna P. Williams, eds. (New York: Basic Books, 1970), p. 42.

6. Edmund Burke Huey, *The Psychology and Pedagogy of Reading* (Cambridge, Mass.: MIT Press, 1908/1968), pp. 15–50.

7. Frank Smith, *Reading Without Nonsense* (New York: Teachers College, Columbia University, 1979), p. 33.

8. There have been a variety of studies concerning the developmental nature of students' spelling progress. You may wish to read further in: J. Richard Gentry, "An Analysis of Developmental Spelling" *GNYS AT WRK, The Reading Teacher* 36 (November 1982), pp. 192–199; "Learning to Spell Developmentally," *The Reading Teacher* 34 (January 1981), pp. 378–381; Edmund H. Henderson and James W. Beers, eds., *Developmental Learning to Spell, and Cognitive Aspects of Learning, A Reflection of Word Knowledge* (Newark, Del.: International Reading Association, 1980).

9. Bradley M. Loomer, *Educator's Guide to Spelling Research and Practice* (Des Moines, Iowa: Iowa State Department of Education; Iowa City, University of Iowa, 1978), p. 18.

10. Ernest A. Horn, "Spelling," *Encyclopedia of Educational Research*, 3rd ed. (New York: Macmillan, 1960), pp. 1338, 1342–1343.

11. Arthur W. Heilman, *Phonics in Proper Perspective*, 5th ed. (Columbus, Ohio: Charles E. Merrill, 1985), p. 65.

12. Lincoln Barnett, "The English Language," *Language Arts in the Elementary School*, Hal D. Funk and DeWayne Triplett, eds. (Philadelphia: Lippincott, 1972), p. 103.

13. Stanford E. Taylor, "Listening," *What Research Says to the Teacher* No. 29 (Washington, D.C.: National Education Association, 1964), p. 4.

PART TWO

THE LANGUAGE DISCONNECTION, DYSLEXIA

> The dyslexic, whether visual or auditory, can look at
> the word and hear the word. The language
> disconnection occurs as the brain sees and listens
> and attempts to make sense of the symbol or sound.
> —*A.M.H.*

CHAPTER 3

OVERVIEW OF THE COMMON CHARACTERISTICS
OF DYSLEXIC STUDENTS

Whatever you cannot understand,
you cannot possess.
—*Goethe*

To be able to call a demon by its name
is halfway to getting rid of him.
—*André Maurois*

This chapter, and the two that follow deal with the characteristics of dyslexia and are offered to help parents, classroom teachers, and principals develop some understanding of the nature of dyslexia and of the numerous problems dyslexics have in coping in the classroom, in the home, and in the world in which they must live from day to day. With deeper understanding and knowledge should come a realization that these children are in special need of supporting, caring adults who are willing "to go the extra mile" to help them overcome their difficulties and to give them the encouragement and acceptance for which they yearn.

This is *not* intended to qualify or enable anyone to diagnose dyslexia. (That will be the subject of a separate book.) Parents should not attempt to diagnose dyslexia. Neither should regular classroom teachers or other school personnel who have not had the appropriate training.

Parents and teachers should, of course, be alert to the characteristics and symptoms of dyslexia, and if dyslexia is suspected (and the child is at least eight years old), steps should be taken to have the child tested for the disability. Use your common sense when observing a child suspected of being dyslexic. Ask yourself if his behavior is really atypical, not that of the "normal" child. Keep a record of your observations and the child's behavior. Keep samples of the child's work: writing, drawings, math, social studies, science, spelling, exercises in reading, and written records of general classroom and playground behavior. Does he need to have directions repeated? Does he make errors when copying from charts or the chalkboard? Has he recently had his vision and hearing checked? Keep all this information in a special folder with his name on it and give it to the person who will be examining the child.

Calling a Spade a Spade

When a student has been diagnosed as being dyslexic—and we do not arrive at this diagnosis without compelling evidence—this must be so stated in order for the child to receive the appropriate treatment. I often think of Mark Twain's answer to the oft-repeated question: "Who *really* wrote Shakespeare's works?" His flippant reply was "They must have been written by some other fellow named Shakespeare." So, too, with diagnosing dyslexia. Mark Twain might, in this respect, have said to the skeptics, "There's no such thing as dyslexia. That ailment is some other condition called dyslexia." And Shakespeare would probably join in with, "What's in a name? That which we call a rose by any other name would smell as sweet."

As for me, I say with Meander (343–292 B.C.), "I call a fig a fig, a spade a spade." When a child has dyslexia, let's say so. If he doesn't, let's not.

The Three Major Categories of Dyslexia

During the past fifteen years, I have found that the dyslexics with whom I work tend to fall into three major categories, or groups, of dyslexia[1]: visual, auditory, and a combination of visual and auditory dyslexia. Visual dyslexia is by far the most common type. Seventy percent of the cases in our Reading Clinic to date have been visual dyslexics, 14 percent have been auditory dyslexics, and 16 percent have been a mixture of both. When a student has a combination of both visual and auditory dyslexia, the visual component is usually, though not always, more pronounced than the auditory.

There are certain characteristic problems that occur with all types of dyslexics. At the same time, there are certain reactions to these problems by the dyslexic, his parents, and his teachers that typically occur, usually as a result of not knowing that the student *is* dyslexic or of not understanding the nature of the condition. The following pages should help pinpoint specific difficulties and illustrate how the dyslexic, his parents, and his teachers have responded in such situations. I hope the result will bring about a modification of attitudes and expectations and a deeper empathy with the dyslexic child.

Slow Work Rate

The dyslexic child usually works very slowly. He is the student who fails to finish his seatwork and often is kept in during recess with firm instructions from his teacher "to finish that work!" Yet day after day this recurs. What the teacher must understand is that the student cannot help this slow rate of work. He is not necessarily a lazy child. He does not need to be "pushed." And he should not be punished by having to stay in the classroom while his classmates go outside to run and jump and play and exercise their muscles, and to socialize with one another. He needs the break even more than the other children because of the pressure on him to perform—which he feels constantly.

Often the dyslexic child must take home the work he does not finish in school with instructions to get it done by the next day. This means the child cannot play outside after school—ride his bicycle, run around, climb trees— or exercise, which he needs to do to grow and to develop normally. Here again, he is being denied opportunities to grow physically, socially, and emotionally, to learn the give-and-take of neighborhood friendship. In a way, this is a form of punishment for parents, too, as one or the other usually has to sit with the child and give him the help that he needs in order for him to complete the work.

So what happens? The dyslexic child feels resentment at what he considers unfair treatment. The parents feel resentment that they must put aside necessary chores, or ignore the crying baby or the other children's questions, or miss a favorite television program, in order to help the dyslexic child with his seatwork. Once in a while, perhaps—but *every* day? The parents resent their child for not "doing what he is supposed to be doing in school." And they resent the teacher for not teaching him so that he does not have to do his work at home. The teacher in turn resents the child for "not doing his work" in spite of all the usually successful tactics she has used. And of course she resents the parents for "spoiling" him. All these feelings of resentment add pressure and tension to an already bad situation.

What to do? First of all, the world will not collapse if teachers reduce the quantity of work. Let the student work ten math examples instead of twenty-five. Let him write half a page instead of two or three, answer five questions instead of ten. Make sure that any work that he is expected to do on his own is on his independent (free-reading) level; that is, that he miss no more than one or two words out of about one hundred words in a narrative passage. And be sure that he understands what he has to do. Work an example out with the child to ensure that he understands what is expected of him. Praise him when he does the work well. And always keep in mind, it is the teacher's job—not the parents'—to "teach" new words, new skills, and other concepts included in the school curriculum.

Even if the work is at the appropriate level for the dyslexic student, even if he has been previously prepared for it, he will still work more slowly than his classmates—not because he is less intelligent than the others but because it takes more time for him to integrate and process the information; that is, to make sense out of what he is seeing and writing.

Timed School Tests

The dyslexic student knows that he works slowly. He cannot get through his work quickly enough nor produce the necessary quantity of work to please the adults in his life. He tries hard, but his best is never good enough. He never seems to be able to catch up with what has to be done. He is constantly feeling the pressure of time and of work. One dyslexic phrased it quite aptly: "I feel as though I am on a treadmill, going around and around and around without ever having a chance to stop and catch my breath."

When the student with dyslexia is faced with a standardized achievement test that has time limits, and the teacher is standing in the front of the room with a stopwatch in her hand, he is likely to panic. Anxiety inhibits his thinking. It increases as the teacher announces, "You have fifteen minutes left. . . . Now you have only ten minutes to finish. Work fast! Five minutes left! Four . . . Three . . . Two . . . ONE! All pencils down!" At that the dyslexic is ready to jump out of his seat and explode.

Following Oral Directions

Following oral directions can be difficult for the dyslexic, and so he asks his teachers and parents to repeat what they have said. This constant need for repetition can get on the nerves of both teachers and parents if they are not aware of the reason that prevents the student from following directions the first time around. It is common for the dyslexic to be told, "If you would just pay attention and listen the first time you would know what to do!" But "just paying attention" is not the major problem.

The visual dyslexic has difficulty remembering a series of directions because of both his sequencing problems and his short-term memory problems. The auditory dyslexic has trouble because of his particular difficulties in processing and understanding what has been said to him. This affects sequential auditory organization. Both types of dyslexics end up with bits and pieces of directions that become jumbled and confused in their minds. And so the directions are not followed as given.

The following directions by a classroom teacher were recorded at the time they were given:

> It's time now to put away your seatwork and get out your math books. Turn to page 81 and look at the word problems on that page. (Turning to a student:) No, Mary, you can't go to the bathroom now. Put your hand down and pay attention. On page 81 . . . (Pointing to another student:) Johnny! Get back in your seat and get out your math book. Now, I want everyone to work the first five problems at your desks, then some of you can come up to the board and show the rest of us how you did your problem.

Directions such as these would confuse any student, but imagine how utterly lost the dyslexic child can become. He knows that he must ask the teacher to restate the directions, and she will probably be cross as a result. Sometimes dyslexics develop the survival technique of pretending to turn to the right page in the book and then peeking at a friend's book to find the correct page. If he gets caught, he may be warned to "keep your eyes on your own work!"—or worse. He may even be accused of trying to cheat— which can have a devastating effect on a child who is valiantly trying to do what he is supposed to be doing.

What about his home life? Here the dyslexic has the same trouble when his parents tell him to finish his supper, and after that to be sure to feed the dog, to empty the trash basket, to hang up his jacket which he left on the living room sofa, and to pass the biscuits, please. When these chores are not done—or only one or two are done—and he neglects to pass the biscuits, he is scolded for not listening or for being lazy.

Neither the teacher nor the parents intend to be unkind to the dyslexic child. Such behavior on their part is usually due to their not knowing that the child is dyslexic, and thus not understanding his inability to behave normally.

Lecture Instruction and Note-Taking

Lecture instruction is the least effective method of teaching for any student. For the dyslexic, the results are dismal. Both visual and auditory dyslexics have trouble with lectures for the same reasons they have difficulty in following directions. Both have processing problems, either because of difficulty in following the sequence and development of ideas presented or because of auditory confusion over what was heard. As a result, note-taking is unsatisfactory—full of incomplete sentences, scraps of ideas, events out of order. The notes provide little or no help in studying for tests and examinations.

Unless the dyslexic condition of the student is discovered and helped before he reaches middle school or high school, where teachers more often use the lecture method, he can become overwhelmed by life at school and his failure to achieve. Unless he gets help from someone quickly, he is likely to withdraw from school—psychologically or physically.

Learning a Foreign Language

Both the visual dyslexic and the auditory dyslexic will have difficulty learning a foreign language or coping with the foreign terms and expressions one finds in prose, especially as the student moves into the upper grades. The visual dyslexic may be able to learn a foreign language by *ear* if he happens to live in a foreign country or is taught strictly by auditory means. It is the written form of the language that presents the stumbling block to learning. By contrast, the auditory dyslexic's processing and synthesis problems with the sounds of the foreign language and understanding the sound-symbol relationships make learning the language highly improbable and an exceptionally frustrating experience for him.

Sensitivity to Sound and Movement in the Environment

As mentioned, dyslexic students tend to be sensitive to what is going on around them and are easily distracted. Noise and movement can divert their attention. This characteristic, of course, varies with the individual student, but clearly the "open classroom" concept *as applied in America* with the ongoing noise and movement in the large rooms without walls is not for the dyslexic student. Neither is a "departmentalized" type of schooling where students move from class to class, period to period, throughout the day. The young dyslexic always feels the pressure of time hanging over him, the need to get his work done before the bell rings; and then he hurries off to the next class only to have the same thing happen all over again. It is unfortunate that so many of our elementary schools have jumped on the departmentalization bandwagon in an ill-advised mimicry of the high schools. It would be far better for the dyslexic student if he did not have to face departmentalization before high school.

The *traditional self-contained classroom*, where children are with one teacher all day, is the best arrangement for the student with dyslexia. In such a classroom, the teacher gets to know the students so well—their strengths and weaknesses, what makes them "tick"—that she is able to plan instruction in flexible blocks of time on a more individualized basis. I am referring to the regular classroom of this type, not the special education classroom for handicapped students. I make the distinction because I suggest that the dyslexic child *can* function in such a situation if the teacher understands the nature of dyslexia and is willing to make certain adaptations in her expectations and instructions, and if the teacher has the help of a reading specialist or other resource person. Here, in a regular self-contained classroom, the dyslexic student feels more secure and less pressured. He does not continually have to adjust to different teacher personalities and other students as he changes classes during the school day while fighting that tyrant, the clock. He is more able to concentrate on applying himself to learning.

Sounds in Isolation Phonics Instruction

Both visual and auditory dyslexics suffer when they are taught the phonic elements *in isolation rather than in a meaningful framework of words and context.* You will recall that in the last chapter *meaning* was considered the critical element in working with the dyslexic student. Dyslexics already have severe problems in organizing and integrating information and making sense of what they try to read. They do not need any more roadblocks thrown up by nonsensical teaching. Words broken down into individual letters "sounded" in isolation are much more difficult to learn than when they appear as a meaningful entity. Why? A letter sounded in isolation has no meaning and sounds like gibberish. The crucial element of meaning is not there.

I do not say that phonics should not be taught, for children must develop a metalinguistic awareness of the sound structure of our language and phonological awareness,[2] an understanding of the segmentation of phonemes in words. I do say that phonics should not be taught in a way that will compound the dyslexic's problems. Most of the basal reader series (books designed especially for the teaching of reading), while emphasizing phonics instruction, do *not* instruct teachers that *r* says *er* or *ruh* or *rur*, or that *l* says *el* or *luh* as teachers have been heard to tell their students). What nonsense! When a teacher tells a child that *b* says *buh*, *a* says *ah*, and *t* says *tuh*, the child comes up with *buhahtuh*—which is absurd. Sometimes, teachers will tell students to "say it fast," thinking that this will help with the blending of the sounds. What actually happens is that child says *buh-ah-tuh, buh-ah-tuh, buhahtuh*, resulting in a three-syllable nonsense word for the one-syllable word *bat*. (No wonder such children have trouble with syllabication!) The child might end up with the words *batter* or *butter* or *barter* for the word *bat*, which will make hash out of what he is reading. Such instruction can be disastrous for the dyslexic child.

As the late Doris J. Johnson, formerly with the Department of Communication Disorders at Northwestern University, and Helmer J. Myklebust, well-known scholar in language, psychology, and neurology, and also at Northwestern University, have pointed out, when a vowel sound is added to the consonant (or blend or digraph), as illustrated above, "it is nearly impossible for children to blend sounds into words."[3] They relate this experience with a child: "An eight year old tried to sound out the word *pat* and said, 'puh-a-tuh—puh-a-tuh?' What does that mean?"[4] Nothing. It is meaningless, and a typical reaction to this kind of instruction. Yet how often does one hear from teachers (and parents, probably quoting the teacher) that "Johnny knows all his sounds. His problem is, he just can't *blend* them." Or, this statement: "Johnny knows all his sounds. His problem is not with phonics. It's his *comprehension.* He just doesn't seem to understand what he reads."

The dyslexic child has enough trouble with comprehension without adding the sounds-in-isolation barrier. Such instruction also results in slow, labored reading—another problem the dyslexic already has—and excessive lip movements.

How do children learn? They tend to "chunk" meaningful units. By chunking, I mean grouping items. For example, it is far easier for a child to "chunk" meaningful words than isolated letters. And since they can "chunk" up to six or seven items at a time, more words can be read in this manner. Is it not better to take in six or seven words than six or seven individual letters that may or may not make up one word, and which are likely to cause a short-term memory overload?

Any program that advocates teaching the sounds of letters in isolation should be avoided at all costs for the dyslexic student, whether his affliction is visual or auditory. A child *can* learn to read in this way, but (1) his progress will be ever so much slower, (2) his comprehension will be poor, (3) his reading will be slow, (4) his fluency in reading will be poor, and (5) he will likely develop the habit of lip movements.

Proponents of teaching the phonic elements in isolation often quote Dr. Jeanne Chall of Harvard University, and author of *The Great Debate*, as recommending this type of phonics instruction. Her book made a great impact upon educators, journalists, and some politicians, and influenced the recommendations of *Becoming a Nation of Readers: The Report of the Commission on Reading.* However, assumptions were made that are not warranted. Jeanne Chall herself points out that "teaching only phonics—and in isolation—was not a recommendation of *The Great Debate* in 1967 or in 1983."[5]

The notes for this chapter provide some comments by eminent educators concerning the teaching of sounds in isolation.[6]

The critical ingredient in any instruction of the dyslexic child must be to emphasize meaning. Dyslexic students are already handicapped in school. Let's not be guilty of making phonics cripples of them, too.

Reluctance to Read Aloud

After so many problems in reading and so many mistakes made when reading aloud in front of the class, the dyslexic has naturally developed a fear of performing in front of his classmates and his teacher. He knows that he will make mistakes, say the wrong words, and read in a halting and repetitious manner. He knows that when he reads aloud, his classmates do not enjoy listening because of his faltering manner and use of incorrect words, which make it hard for them to follow the thread of thought. These fears come to the fore and create feelings of anxiety so that he even misses words that he *does* know. Panic takes over. If you observe closely you can notice his flushed face, rapid breathing, clenched hands, stooped posture.

Unfortunately for the dyslexic, there are still some teachers who use the "round-robin" technique to teach reading—each student takes a turn reading aloud from a book—although this is not the recommended procedure suggested in the basal reader teacher's manual. Nor is this taught to prospective young teachers by up-to-date professors in the teacher-training colleges, because of the problems it can cause even normal students. It is the least effective way to teach reading. It also demands the least preparation, the least imagination, and the least effort on the part of the teacher.

Some upper elementary, middle, and high school teachers use the round-robin technique when "teaching" science, social studies, or other subjects. Down one row and up the next, the students take turns reading aloud from their textbooks. (This is "teaching?") The excuse often given for this procedure at the upper levels of school is that "the textbook is too hard for some of the students and this is how to make those students know what's in the book." Sometimes, the teachers ask for "volunteers," and so the same capable students end up reading in class day after day. (And what is this telling the other students?)

But we know the problems the dyslexic already has with listening and retaining information. When the pressure and anxiety of being called on to read the textbook aloud, in front of others, is added, no wonder the dyslexic tries to find some way out—leaving the room or creating a diversion or just plain refusing and thus invoking the wrath of the teacher.

Reluctance to Write

The dyslexic student has had trouble with his spelling and his handwriting since the beginning of his school years. So many papers have been returned to him covered with red ink and corrections that he has developed a way to cope with the increasing demands of writing—he writes as little as he can, and when he does he uses the words he thinks he can spell. For example, when asked to write about his favorite animal he may want to write *dinosaur* or *elephant* or *squirrel*, but instead he will write *cat* because he knows he can spell that word. (He may avoid *dog* because of the unstable *d* and *g*, but if he does he is likely to capitalize the *d*.) His favorite movie may have been *The Abyss*, but when asked to write about this topic, he may write *Batman* instead because of the simpler spelling. Results of some tests and inventories, where the dyslexic student must fill in blanks to answer questions or finish incomplete sentences, are invalid for this reason. The substance of what he has written appears immature, of course, and his sentences are usually choppy or of the run-on kind.

Figure 3.1 shows a story written by a student in our summer clinic. How old do you think Keith was when he wrote this story? In what grade would you place him? Would you say his intelligence is at a low, average, or above average level?

Keith's story is included here as an example of how a low stock of spelling words can affect a student's writing. His writing appears fairly neat, with only ten strike-overs and two misspelled words (*stell* for *still* and *like* for *likes*). At its highest, the readability level of this paragraph would be beginning third grade. Most of the words used are one-syllable words; it is the length of the sentences that makes the readability level as high as it is. Is this the writing of an eight-year-old child in the third grade?

Hardly. It is the writing of a high school auditory dyslexic who had learned to circumvent those red corrections on papers by using words that

Figure 3.1   An example of Keith's writing.

he was fairly certain he could spell correctly—but which in no way indicated the capability of Keith. When he wrote this story, Keith was almost eighteen years old and in the eleventh grade—with an IQ of one hundred twenty-five.

The dyslexic has learned that another way to cope with the demands of writing is to copy from books rather than give the information in his own words. He may make some mistakes in his copying, but the errors will be far fewer than if he had written on his own. He finds a survival technique in plagiarism that helps to make his life run more smoothly. It is another way to help him get from day to day.

In a way, these self-protective coping devices have made the dyslexic student act dishonestly in setting down what he truly thinks and truly feels. Yet he is basically as honest as any other child, and, this, in turn, increases his feelings of guilt and lowers his self-esteem.

Attention Deficit Disorder (ADD)

Is attention deficit disorder (ADD), initially referred to as hyperactivity,[7] a common characteristic of dyslexia, as often claimed in articles and books on the disability? Are all dyslexics overactive, full of energy, constantly in motion, excessively talkative, into everything?

The answer is no. This may be symptomatic of certain brain damage and can even be symptomatic of an emotional disturbance, or of certain physical diseases. Such characteristics may be the result of frustration, boredom in class, or even a particular learning style. Dyslexics, however, are not necessarily hyperactive; some are and some are not.

In a study of five hundred dyslexic children, ages six to eighteen, only 26.8 percent were found to be hyperactive, 22 percent of them boys and 4.8 percent girls. And 13.8 percent of the boys and 4.6 percent of the girls were found to be *hypoactive;* that is, lethargic, lacking energy.[8]

One Category: A Combination of Visual and Auditory Dyslexia

Some children have a combination of visual and auditory dyslexia. My experience has been that usually the visual dyslexia is more pronounced than the auditory dyslexia, though the reverse may be the case at times.

I have found 16 percent of the dyslexic cases diagnosed at the clinic to be a combination of both types. It would seem that having one kind of dyslexia is enough of a burden without being saddled with both kinds, but it does occur. In such a case, depending upon the severity, the prognosis is less encouraging. But, these children *can also be helped*. It is harder to alleviate the difficulties and it takes longer. The residual remnants of difficulties tend to be stronger, and it is to be expected that some difficulties may be lasting to a certain degree.

"Sam" came to the College Reading Clinic when he was eight years old (with a mental age two years higher). He had repeated the first grade and was now scheduled to repeat the third grade. His instructional reading level—that used by the teacher for the formal teaching of reading with his basal reader—was first grade. His independent or "free-reading" level was preprimer, which is the first step above reading readiness. His dyslexia had not been diagnosed prior to his coming to the clinic. He had a combination of both kinds of dyslexia.

The following is a copy of Sam's story, which he wrote after the Fourth of July holiday. It took Sam twelve minutes to write the story. When he had finished, he was asked to read what he had written. See Figure 3.2. This is what he read:

> It was the Fourth of July and somebody shot out a little rocket. It hit the castle.

When "Jack" came to us for help with his reading and writing problems he was nine years old, with the mental age of a fifteen-year-old. His instructional reading level was at the primer level. Like Sam, his dyslexia had not been diagnosed prior to his coming to the reading clinic. He, too, had a combination of visual and auditory dyslexia.

Jack was asked to write about something that he especially enjoyed, and he wrote the following story about his Honda. After he finished writing it, his teacher asked him to read what he had written and she taped what he said. Later, she wrote what he had said below his story (see Figure 3.3).

Children such as Sam and Jack definitely require remediation on a one-to-one basis, as frequently as can be arranged (and afforded), in order to make the most progress. Progress will be slow, but with hard work on the

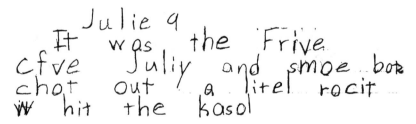

Figure 3.2   A story written by Sam, C.A. 8-6, M.A. 10-6.

Figure 3.3   A story written by Jack, C.A. 9-1, M.A. 15-0.

part of the specialist and the student, with the cooperation of the parents and teachers, such students *can* accomplish a great deal.

The following two chapters will deal specifically with the particular characteristics of visual dyslexia and auditory dyslexia as different categories of the disability.

A Word About Dysgraphia

Dysgraphia is sometimes spoken of as being another type of dyslexia. It is a disorder of visual-motor integration—the hands and eyes working together smoothly. The handwriting of a child with dysgraphia can be difficult to read and at its worst is said to resemble "chicken tracks."

Yet the "symptoms" of dysgraphic handwriting apply also to the handwriting of the visual and auditory dyslexic. Their writing may be hard to read because of their problems with visual memory in copying, in spelling, in writing, in retrieving visual images, or in trying to match auditory images of sounds with the printed letters. The dyslexic's handwriting is slow and laborious. His writing is usually filled with corrections, strike-overs, and erasures. Their papers are usually messy in appearance.

Other than being a result of visual and auditory dyslexia, poor handwriting can also be the result of finger agnosia, which is a kind of short-circuit in the neural pathways from the brain to the fingers (or vice versa). A child with finger agnosia produces poor letter formation, insecure writing with letters of varying size and spacing, strike-overs, and frequent erasures. The writing rate is slow, and writing is a laborious task. A child with finger agnosia might show no other symptoms except poor handwriting and certain types of misspellings and reversals in words.

Students thought to have dysgraphia have been referred to me (with no mention of dyslexia or finger agnosia). Yet the symptoms of dysgraphia exhibited by these students were caused by dyslexia or finger agnosia—or both, for a dyslexic can also have finger agnosia.

I question the existence of dysgraphia as a separate entity and suggest that it is either a manifestation of an existing dyslexic condition or of finger agnosia. Of course, certain types of injury to the writing hand could affect a child's handwriting, but this would be because of the injury rather than dysgraphia.

Notes

1. Notes on categories of dyslexia:

(a) Ingram, in his discussion on the nature of dyslexia, speaks of three kinds of dyslexia: some predominantly "visuospatial" in type, some predominantly "audiophonic," and others a combination. Thomas T.S. Ingram, "The Nature of Dyslexia," *Early Experience and Visual Information Processing in Perceptual and Reading Disorders* (Washington, D.C.: National Academy of Sciences, 1970), pp. 412, 431, 437.

(b) Ingram, Mason, and Blackburn, in a retrospective study, suggest three categories: visuospatial, audiophonic, and one with "correlating" difficulties. From their description, it would appear that the third category corresponds with my third type of a combination of visual and auditory dyslexia. Thomas T.S. Ingram, A.W. Mason, J. Blackburn, "A Retrospective Study of Children With Reading Disability," *Developmental Medicine and Child Neurology* 12 (1970), p. 273.

(c) Johnson and Myklebust describe two major types of dyslexia: visual and auditory. They do not mention a combination of visual and auditory as a third type, although they state that "dyslexia is rarely found in isolation. Other disabilities are manifested as a part of the total syndrome." They also describe the writing disorder called dysgraphia and the math disorder called dyscalcula. Doris J. Johnson and Helmer R. Myklebust, *Learning Disabilities, Educational Principles and Practices* (New York: Grune and Stratton, 1967), pp. 150, 152–271.

(d) Later, in 1978, Myklebust speaks of visual dyslexia, auditory dyslexia, and an inner-language dyslexia. He refers to inner-language dyslexia as *word-calling* and says that usually there are deficiencies in both auditory and visual verbal processing (combination type). He says that the letters and words are perceived and the child can say them (because he can "read"), but the level of meaning is bypassed. Helmer R. Myklebust, "Toward a Science of Dyslexiology," *Progress in Learning Disabilities* IV, Helmer R. Myklebust, ed. (New York: Grune and Stratton, 1978), pp. 15–16.

(e) Jordan describes the three kinds of dyslexia as being visual, auditory, and dysgraphia. No mention is made of a separate combination subtype, although note was made that "few children are handicapped by only one form of dyslexia." Dale R. Jordan, *Dyslexia in the Classroom*, 2nd ed. (Columbus, Ohio: Charles E. Merrill, 1977), pp. 1–9.

(f) Aaron and Bakes have found three groups in their work with college students who have "specific reading disabilities." These are called the Acoustic Short-Term Memory Deficient Group, the Visual Short-Term Memory Group, and the Lexical Access Deficient Group. P.G. Aaron and Catherine Bakes, "Empirical and Heuristic Bases for Diagnosis and Remediation of Specific Reading Disabilities," *Topics in Learning and Learning Disabilities: Issues in Reading Diagnosis* 2 (Gaithersburg, Md: Aspen, 1983), p. 37.

(g) Boder also reports on three subtypes: visual, auditory, and mixed. Those with visual channel problems she calls *dyseidetic* (Gestalt-blind), those with auditory channel problems she called *dysphonetic*, and the mixed group is called *dysphonetic-dyseidetic* (or *alexia*). In contrast to my findings, more of her dyslexics fell in the auditory group, with less in the visual group. However, her study has been criticized for questionable diagnostic assessment procedures involving a word recognition task and its determination of gestalt or phonetic approach through timed versus untimed responses, the spelling test of known and unknown *reading* vocabulary words for visual and auditory classification, and the possibility of interpreting such errors in other ways. For example, *rough* is an irregular word. Why would a child be expected to sound this out? The word *doubt* has a silent *b*. Visual recall is what is needed with these irregular words. Other interpretations of behaviors can also be questioned. Samples of errors analyzed were small. Any of these could affect the placement of a dyslexic into a particular group. And no diagnosis of dyslexia should be made on the basis of a spelling test alone. Many excellent readers are poor spellers, and her selection procedures could include nondyslexic as well as dyslexic children. A word of caution: there have been several studies using Boder's system. The validity of such studies and conclusions should be weighed carefully. Elena Boder, "Developmental Dyslexia: A Diagnostic Approach Based on Three Atypical Reading Patterns," *Developmental Medicine and Child Neurology* 15 (1973), pp. 663–87. Elena Boder, "Developmental Dyslexia: A Diagnostic Screening Procedure Based on Three Characteristic Patterns of Reading and Spelling," *Learning Disorders* Vol. 4, B. Bateman, ed. (Seattle, Wash.: Special Child Publications, 1971), pp. 297–342. Elena Boder, "Developmental Dyslexia: Prevailing Diagnostic Concepts and a New Diagnostic Approach," *Progress in Learning Disabilities* Vol. 2, Helmer Myklebust, ed. (New York: Grune and Stratton, 1971), pp. 293–321. Elena Boder, "Developmental Dyslexia: A New Diagnostic Approach Based on the Identification of Three Subtypes," *Journal of School Health* 40 (1970), pp. 289–90.

(h) Bryant and Impey of the University of Oxford describe two types of dyslexia: surface and phonological. They describe the surface dyslexic as one who is able to use phonological rules without much difficulty, but who seems to have little idea as to the visual appearance of words. While regular nonsense words can be pronounced fairly well, irregular words present difficulty and tend to be pronounced phonetically. Words containing silent letters are confused. The phonological dyslexic has problems with letter-sound correspondences, difficulty converting letters into sounds, and leans on the visual appearance of words. Peter Bryant and Lawrence Impey, "The Similarities Between Normal Readers and Developmental and Acquired Dyslexics," *Cognition* 24 (1986), pp. 122–23.

(i) Omenn and Weber in the Division of Medical Genetics, University of Washington, undertook a series of studies of dyslexic children of normal intelligence and their families in a search for phenotypic and genetic evidence of heterogeneity. They identified pedigrees for eleven families classified as visual-predominant, seven as auditory-predominant, and three as mixed subtypes of dyslexia. Gilbert S. Omenn and Bruce A. Weber, "Dyslexia: Search for Phenotypic and Genetic Heterogeneity," *American Journal of Medical Genetics* 1 (1978), p. 335.

(j) Pirozzolo has been able to identify two neurological subtypes of dyslexia, based on a comprehensive neuropsychological test battery. One is visuospatial, having symptoms of higher-order visual disturbances characterized by a higher Verbal IQ relative to Performance IQ and Raven IQ, and with reading and writing errors that involve faulty encoding of visual information, finger agnosia, left-right disorientation, and spatial dysgraphia. The other is auditory-linguistic, with symptoms of a language disorder characterized by a lower Verbal IQ relative to Performance IQ and Raven IQ, and with reading and writing errors that involve faulty grapheme-to-phoneme translation, articulation disorders, difficulty remembering names of persons and objects, and developmentally delayed language. Francis J. Pirozzolo, *The Neuropsychology of Developmental Reading Disorders* (New York: Praeger Press, 1979), pp. 69–70 and 86–87, and "Language and Brain: Neuropsychological Aspects of Developmental Reading Disability," *School Psychology Review* 10 (1981), pp. 352–53.

2. Keith E. Stanovich, "Matthew Effects in Reading: Some Consequences of Individual Differences in the Acquisition of Literacy," *Reading Research Quarterly* 21 (1986), p. 362.

3. Johnson and Myklebust, op. cit., pp. 157–58.

4. Ibid., p. 158.

5. Jeanne S. Chall, "Learning to Read: The Great Debate 20 Years Later—" *Phi Delta Kappan*, 70 (1989), p. 525.

6. Notes on phonics instruction, sounds in isolation:

(a) "In teaching each phonic element, deal only with words as units, not with sounds isolated from words" George D. Spache and Evelyn B. Spache, *Reading in the*

Elementary School, 5th ed. (Boston: Allyn and Bacon, 1986), p. 484; also George D. Spache, *Diagnosing and Correcting Reading Disabilities*, (Boston: Allyn and Bacon, 1986), p. 250.

(b) "In general, consonant phonemes should not be pronounced in isolation because they become distorted unless used with a vowel. For example, the sound represented by <b> pronounced alone is apt to become *buh*. The sound represented by <d> tends to be *duh*. Thus, if the word *bed* were blended letter by letter, the resulting *buh-e-duh* would be a distorted blending of the phonemes." Nancy B. Tanner, "Phonics," *Teaching Reading*, J. Estill Alexander, ed., 3rd ed. (Glenview, Ill.: Scott, Foresman/Little, Brown, 1988), p. 78.

(c) "We strongly believe that phonics should be taught not in isolation, but through context whenever possible. This makes sense if you consider the idea that the sound or sounds a letter makes are partially determined by the other letters in a word." Robert J. Marzano, Patricia J. Hagerty, Sheila W. Valencia, and Philip P. DiStefano, *Reading Diagnosis and Instruction, Theory Into Practice* (Englewood Cliffs, N.J.: Prentice-Hall, 1987), p. 137.

(d) "The logic of phonics instruction is that letters can be coded as sounds, or sounds as letters. Then these can be blended to produce reading or writing. But that doesn't produce meaningful language—it only produces strings of sounds or letters. . . . Readers are seeking meaning, not sounds or words. They may use their developing phonics generalizations to help when the going gets tough. If they are lucky enough not to have been taught phonics in isolation, with each letter equally important, then they will not be diverted from developing the strategies necessary to select just enough graphic information to get to the sense they are seeking." Ken Goodman, *What's Whole In Whole Language?* (Portsmouth, N.H.: Heinemann, 1986), pp. 37–38.

(e) "Teachers should not present initial consonants in isolation from words. . . . Teachers may state a number of words beginning with the initial consonant. They may ask the children to listen to the words: *ball, book,* and *bee*. They should write the words on the board. They should ask how *ball, book,* and *bee* are similar. They all have the same beginning letter *b*. They all start with the same sound." Dorothy Rubin, *Diagnosis and Correction in Reading Instruction* (New York: Holt, Rinehart & Winston, 1982), p. 192.

(f) "When teaching initial consonants, do not stress sounds; instead, emphasize each sound within the context of the word." Diane Lapp and James Flood, *Teaching Reading to Every Child* (New York: Macmillan, 1978), p. 225.

(g) "Originally, the sounds of individual letters were taught but mainly in the last decade linguists have pointed out that letter-sounds are never produced singly but in the context of words, and that usually the positioning of the letter determines its particular sound. If individual letters are sounded there is a tendency for *uh* to be added, so that one gets the distorted pronunciation *huh, ruh,* and *guh*. When the sounds of individual letters are 'blended' or synthesized, one gets the word *bat* sounding more like *barter,* which can be very confusing to some children." Elizabeth J. Goodacre, "Methods of Teaching Reading," *The Reading Curriculum,* Amelia Melnik and John Merritt, eds. (Morristown, N.J.: General Learning Press, 1972), p. 118.

(h) "While materials account for many of the errors found in phonics instruction, teachers sometimes contribute errors quite on their own. Certainly, this is so of teachers who have been heard saying to children that the sound of *r* is *er;* that the sound of *l* is *ul;* that the sound of *fr* is *fur;* and so on." Delores Durkin, "Phonics: Instruction That Needs to be Improved," *The Reading Teacher* 28 (November 1974), pp. 152–56.

(i) "It is true that one cannot separately pronounce letter sounds, which taken together constitute the pronunciation of English words, and children are not asked to do so. They are taught that a particular letter represents the same speech sound in many different words, and they are invited to think or sub-vocalize this sound when the letter occurs in a word they are attempting to solve." Arthur W. Heilman, *Phonics in Proper Perspective*, 5th ed. (Columbus, Ohio: Charles E. Merrill, 1985), p. 10. Also, "Neither consonants nor vowels should be sounded in isolation (*cat = kuh-ah-tuh*)." Arthur W. Heilman, Timothy R. Blair, and William H. Rupley, *Principles and Practices of Teaching Reading* (Columbus, Ohio: Charles E. Merrill, 1986), p. 141.

(j) "Word-attack skills must be taught as a first-aid to meaning. Words must be introduced in a communication context so that, as the reader moves along, meaning clues to recognition may also be a first-order, functional source of help. Phonics must be taught in a pronunciation unit or in context, but not in isolation." Russell Stauffer, "Dictated Experienced Stories," *The Reading Curriculum,* Amelia Melnik and John Merritt, eds. op. cit., p. 155 (also University of London Press).

(k) "In my judgment children who believe they can read unfamiliar words just by 'blending' or 'sounding' them out are likely to develop into disabled readers, the type of secondary students who are condemned for being 'functionally illiterate' because they do exactly what they have been taught and try to read by putting together the sounds of letters. Besides, I think it would be difficult to exaggerate the complexity and unreliability of phonics. To take just one very simple example, how are the letters *ho* pronounced? Not in a trick situation, as in the middle of a word like shop, but when *ho* are the first two letters of a word? Here are eleven common words in each of which the initial *ho* has a different pronunciation: *hot, hope, hook, hoot, house, hoist, horse, horizon, honey, hour, honest.* Can anyone really believe that a child could learn to identify any of these words by sounding out the letters?

"Incidentally, the preceding illustration underlines an important requirement of phonics that is never explicitly taught at school—that phonics requires reading from right-to-left. The eleven different pronunciations of *ho* that I have just given all depend on the letters that come next." Frank Smith, *Reading Without Nonsense* (New York: Teachers College, Columbia University, 1985), p. 53.

7. Edward A. Kirby and Lliam K. Grimley, *Understanding and Treating Attention Deficit Disorder* (New York: Pergamon, 1986), p. 3.

8. Edith Klasen, *The Syndrome of Specific Dyslexia* (Baltimore: University Park Press, 1972), pp. 67, 71, 193–94.

CHAPTER 4

VISUAL DYSLEXIA

True wisdom consists not only in seeing what is
before your eyes, but in foreseeing what is to come.
—Terence

In the little world in which children have their
existence, whosoever brings them up,
there is nothing so finely perceived and so
finely felt, as injustice.
—Charles Dickens

A child is not a visual dyslexic because of any loss of vision. We *look* with our eyes, but *it is our brain that sees and makes sense of that which is seen.* A visual dyslexic has difficulty with processing and interpreting the images received by looking. Light rays from whatever it is we are looking at pass through the cornea of our eye, and on through the pupil, the lens, the vitreous humor (the soft, jelly-like material that maintains the shape of our eyeball), until they reach the retina, the inner layer of the eyeball occupying about four-fifths of the inner circumference of the eye and situated toward the rear of the eyeball. Figure 4.1, a diagram of the eye, will help in understanding the location of the various parts.

When light strikes the sensitive cells of the retina, it stimulates nerve cells. Messages then flow along the optic nerve to the *visual cortex,* which is the "seeing" part of our brain.[1,2] The brain must now do something with these images; it must make sense of them by classifying, organizing, relating and making associations, and integrating them with knowledge that has been

47

PARTS OF THE EYE

The human eye is a complex organ. The part we normally see is only about one sixth of the· complete eye, *below.*

SCLERA   CHOROID   RETINA
CILIARY MUSCLE
IRIS
PUPIL
CORNEA
LENS
IRIS
CILIARY MUSCLE
VITREOUS HUMOR
OPTIC NERVE
BLIND SPOT

FOVEA CENTRALIS—AREA OF SHARPEST VISION

Figure 4.1   The parts of the eye. (Used with permission from "Eye," by John McWilliams, *World Book Encyclopedia,* Vol. 6, Chicago: Field Enterprises Educational Corporation, c 1968)

stored previously in the brain. This is a process of interpretation, and it is with this process that the visual dyslexic has trouble.

Parents and teachers need to know that several types of vision defects can create symptoms similar to those of dyslexia. For example, *nearsightedness* (myopia) results in blurred distant vision. A student with this defect can have trouble copying correctly from the chalkboard or the overhead projector—as does the visual dyslexic. Students who are *farsighted* (hyperopia) will find close seatwork and reading in books fatiguing and will likely try to get out of these tasks whenever possible—as does the visual dyslexic.

With *astigmatism,* vision tends to be blurred and distorted. Such a vision problem will cause a child to tire easily and to avoid close work or prolonged copying. Letters and words that are similar in form are often confused. Reversals may occur. The student with astigmatism will experience difficulty in any sustained reading task. Headaches are common. Most of this behavior is also typical of the visual dyslexic.

Muscular imbalance (strabismus) can cause a blurring of letters and words, and even double vision in severe cases. The same word (or letter) may appear differently at different times. Lines of print may be jumped over. A word in one line may be transferred to a line above or below (insertion errors). Again, these too are symptoms of visual dyslexia.

Lack of fusion and *aniseikonia* (the lenses of the two eyes are not in focus) can cause readers to mix letters in words (transpositions), to make reversals, to lose their place, and to read very slowly. Sounds like dyslexia, doesn't it?

One can understand that certain eye defects can affect the accurate assessment of a child's problems and can affect a student's performance not only in his reading class but in other subjects as well. Any student who is having trouble with reading and writing should have a complete vision examination by an eye doctor.

This is not a chapter on diagnosis. I shall not attempt to discuss in detail other problems that can cause symptoms similar to those of the visual dyslexic. This is simply a plea for common sense, for not jumping to conclusions when certain types of errors occur in reading and writing. For example, very often I have heard parents and teachers make an automatic and often unwarranted assumption in such statements as "Johnny reversed his letters (or words) and he must have dyslexia." Pause and consider the following possible reasons for reversal problems, other than dyslexia:

1. Could the child possibly have an eye defect?

2. Has he had sufficient left-to-right orientation? We read and write in a left-to-right direction, but this does not come naturally to children. Primary teachers should spend a good amount of time in this area.

3. Is the child a left-hander? Left-handed children need much more training in left-to-right orientation than right-handed children. It is common for young left-handers to reverse letters and to begin writing from the right side of the page (mirror writing).

4. Are the words or letters reversed quite similar in appearance? The child may need more visual discrimination work. The words *was* and *saw* or *no* and *on* have the same shape. Perhaps the child needs to learn to direct his attention to the distinguishing features of such words and letters—to consider what makes them different from one another.

5. How old is the child? Visual immaturity can cause reversal errors of

letters and words, as well as visual discrimination types of mistakes. (This is discussed more fully in Chapter 6 concerning early identification of dyslexia.)

6. Is it likely that self-consciousness, anxiety, worry, stress, or fatigue is causing the child to make reading and writing errors similar to the dyslexic patterns?

7. Is the child expected to read in a book that is too difficult for him?

Sequencing Difficulties

The inability to understand the sequence of things and events is a major problem of the visual dyslexic. He has difficulty with the sequencing of letters in words, with learning a series, such as the order of the letters in the alphabet from A to Z, the days of the week, the months and seasons of the year, sets of numbers in series, the progression of time on the clock, and the score by innings on a baseball scoreboard.

The months of the year (Figure 4.2) were written by Roger, a visual dyslexic, age nine years and ten months. Roger was to repeat the fourth grade in the fall.

Roger was asked to write the months of the year "in order, beginning with the first month of the year." As you can see he began with October and wrote November and December, skipped to March, skipped to June, July, August, then jumped back to January, then to August (spelled another way this time), and September. He omitted February, April, and May.

The visual dyslexic may at first appear to be fluent in retelling a story, but listen carefully and you will note that he has trouble relating the events of a story in the order in which they occurred, or predicting outcomes, or making inferences about what has been read. The main idea of a story may escape him altogether.

Indeed, the visual dyslexic usually has difficulty relating the incidents in his own life in correct order. For example, he may tell you that his dog died last month (when it was a year ago), and that he went to the circus a year ago (when it was only a month ago). He has problems with chronology in history and with the order of steps in a science laboratory experiment or the logical steps in proof of a theorem in geometry.

This flaw in sequencing is why the visual dyslexic has trouble following oral directions. It is also the reason he has trouble following any written directions involving several steps. Baking a cake or making a souffle requires a sequence of actions that can frustrate the visual dyslexic. If given a kit for constructing model airplanes or toy automobiles, he will probably begin assembling the pieces right away rather than first reading the written directions. The adult dyslexic, when faced with assembling his new lawn

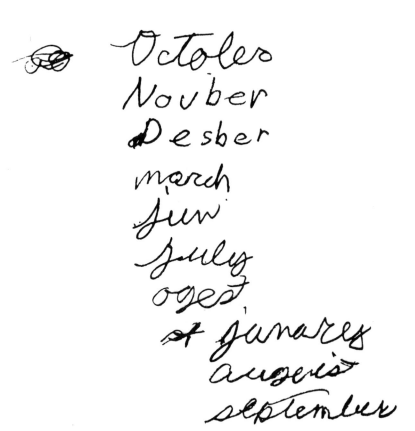

Figure 4.2 Months of the year written by Roger, a visual dyslexic.

mower or a new bicycle for his child, will proceed immediately by trial and error—and common sense—with the unused directions often blowing away unheeded.

A young visual dyslexic may like to play catch with his dad in the backyard, enjoying the companionship and attention of his father, but games such as baseball can be confusing because of the sequence of plays and calls and the need to grasp visually what is going on in the game, let alone keeping track of the score by innings. Sports of this type usually have a low priority in the visual dyslexic's life, although he may "mouth statistics" with the guys, which helps him to be part of the group. He is likely to prefer sports such as fishing or hunting or swimming.

Working jigsaw picture puzzles can be frustrating. There is a sequence of development in joining the various pieces of a puzzle. Visual imagery is important in such a task, and visual dyslexics have difficulty relating the parts to the whole. Visual analysis and synthesis are hard for them.[3]

In school, taking multiple-choice tests and examinations can throw the visual dyslexic into a panic because of the requirements for sequence, recall, and visual memory.

Because of his poor visual memory, he has trouble copying from any of the materials used by teachers in instruction. For, when copying, the visual dyslexic makes mistakes in spelling, omits certain punctuation or capital letters, and may even skip a line of writing, even though the model is there in front of him. Teachers often find this hard to understand, and they display their impatience—"there it is, right in front of your eyes!"

Figure 4.3 is a story copied from a chart by Mark, a nine-year-old visual dyslexic. He took ten minutes to copy these lines and still did not complete the entire story.

This is the original from which he was to copy:

Bob and Dan saw Sam Watts walking on the dock. The three men stopped.
  "See the big ship?" asked Sam.
  "Sure did!" Bob and Dan said. "Must be a mile long."
  Bob and Dan saw Sam was in a hurry. "Got to run," Sam said. "See you!"
  "Sure," said Bob and Dan. "See you, Sam."

Observe Mark's intermixing of cursive and manuscript writing as well as of capital and lower-case letters. Note the various errors:

Figure 4.3 A story copied by Mark, a visual dyslexic, from a chart.

In the first sentence, he
—reversed the final letter *b* of *Bob*, so that it appears to be a *d*,
—added an additional *n* in *and*,
—substituted a *d* for the *n* in *Dan*, so that the word appears as *Dad*,
—originally reversed the beginning *s* of *saw* but corrected it by writing over the reversed letter,
—omitted the word *Sam* altogether (or did he omit *saw* and write *Sam* as *saw*, reversing the *m*?),
—wrote *Watts* as *watts*, with the *w* in lower case,
—omitted the word *walking*,
—wrote *dock* as *Dock*, with the *d* capitalized,
—had no space for the period, so he placed it at the beginning of the next line.

In the second sentence, he
—did not begin the sentence with a capital *T*, but used the lower-case *t* instead,
—reversed the *s* and the two *p*'s in *stopped*.

In the third sentence, he
—continued on the same line as the second sentence instead of beginning another paragraph,
—began and ended the sentence with *zam* for *Sam*, with the *s* reversed and not capitalized,
—wrote *big* as *Big*, with the *b* capitalized,
—omitted ending quotation marks,
—reversed the *s* in *asked*,
—omitted the final *d* in *asked*,
—placed the period at the level of the top of the *m* which it followed.

In the fourth sentence, he
—reversed the *S* in *Sure*,
—ran his exclamation and quotation marks together,
—wrote *Bob* as *Bod*, with the final *b* reversed,
—wrote *Dan* as *Ban*, substituting *B* for *D*.

In the fifth sentence, he
—omitted *Bob and Dan saw Sam was*,
—wrote *a hurry* as *aherie*, the two words joined as one, with the *er* substituted for *ur* and *ie* substituted for *y*,
—omitted the period.

In the sixth sentence, he
—omitted beginning quotation marks,
—added an *o* to *to* (too)
—misplaced *Sam* at the end of the sentence, with the *s* reversed and not capitalized,
—omitted the period,
—omitted beginning quotation marks,
—substituted a comma for the exclamation mark,
—wrote the closing quotation marks in the opposite direction.

Mark did not copy the last sentence.

Such errors are typical of a visual dyslexic's far point copying. He also has trouble copying the questions from the end of a chapter of a book. The frequent instruction, "Copy the questions at the end of the chapter and then answer them for homework," becomes a laborious task for the visual dyslexic student. He will also find difficulty in drawing what he sees at the end of a microscope in science class or copying a map in social studies class.

Drawings of the Visual Dyslexic

The visual dyslexic has difficulty describing accurately his bedroom or house or classroom, and when asked to draw them, items of furniture, windows, and doors often are omitted or misplaced and out of proportion. Indeed, his drawings as a whole tend to be poor and lacking in details. Whether the picture is of a room, flower, tree, or human being, it appears to be the work of an immature child.

Figure 4.4 shows a visual dyslexic's self-portrait. This child was nine years old at the time. Note the omission of such details as the nose, mouth, ears, eyebrows, hair, and items of clothing. Also note the lack of proportion of the figure as a whole—head, hands, trunk, legs, and feet.

Figure 4.5 is an example of a self-portrait of an older boy, age fourteen. More details are included in the face, but the ears are missing. And while he has drawn his belt, other details of his clothes are missing so that the drawing appears to be that of a belted nude on a skateboard! Note the insecurity of the drawing—the erased lines, the strike-overs.

Figure 4.6 is a drawing of the room where a visual dyslexic and his teacher worked. The boy was ten years old. He had been working in this room each weekday morning for four weeks. The teacher took him to another room in the building and asked him to draw a picture of the room where they worked. He was asked to try to make it look just like the room.

Figure 4.4   A self-portrait drawn by a visual dyslexic, age nine.

Figure 4.5   A self-portrait drawn by a visual dyslexic, age fourteen.

You can see that many details are missing. He did include the round table and the two chairs, marking his particular plaçe. Another chair and a triangular table are included, but bookcases, other tables lining the walls, and pieces of furniture are omitted. The window is drawn out from the wall and is greatly out of proportion. Another window is missing. An arrow indicates where he erased part of the line to make a door. Notice the insecurity of the lines, the strike-overs, the incorrect strokes.

The visual dyslexic, of course, has trouble with his visual memory—with revisualizing (picturing in his mind) how something or some place looks. Hence the lack of details, the incorrect proportions, the omission of objects, the insecure lines—all of which result in immature and unrealistic drawings.

Irregular (Unpredictable) Words

Irregular words, sometimes called unpredictable words, give the visual dyslexic student a great deal of trouble because these words must be *visually recalled* since they are exceptions to the phonics rules or have letters that are not pronounced (silent letters). Thus, phonics provides little or no help

Figure 4.6   A sketch of the remedial classroom drawn by a visual dyslexic, age ten.

with these words. Examples of such words in our English language are *once, one, does, ought, bough, cough, though, rough, break, are, night, gnaw, know, love, their, eyes, to, mother, father* (not *fat her*)—and hundreds more. The student must store a visual image of these words, both for reading and for spelling. Then he must revisualize how these words appear and apply this to what he is reading or spelling.

Words with the diminished vowel stress (called the "schwa")—where any vowel can take the sound—such as the *o* in *button* (but'ən), the second *e* and the *a* in *elephant* (el'əfənt, or the *i* and second *e* in *president* (prez'ədənt) present huge barriers to a dyslexic in reading and spelling certain words correctly.

Visual Discrimination Errors/Reversals

Letters and words similar in form are likely to be confused or reversed at times. A child may confuse *b* with *d* or *was* with *saw*, but not all the time. Some authors of books and articles on dyslexia have erroneously referred to a dyslexic's problem as "reading backwards" or "writing backwards." If this were the case, all the letters and words would be reversed and reading could be learned simply by learning the reversed letters. What does occur is an inconstancy, an instability of form. It is common for the visual dyslexic to capitalize certain letters in writing so as to circumvent this inconstancy of form. You will recall that Mark wrote the word *big* as Big and *dock* as *Dock*. Dyslexics may write *baby* as BaBy or bad as *Bad*. Usually it is not the last letter that is capitalized.

Confusion of words such as *got/get, house/horse, want/went, tam/tan, how/now,* is typical of the visual dyslexic. Confusing words such as *bad/dad, big/dig, god/dog, pan/nap, saw/was* and *no/on* is also common for the visual dyslexic. Did you note the reversed letters and words in this second group?

I have found that the following letters give the visual dyslexic the most trouble. The letters within each set tend to be confused with one another:

b-d-p-q-h	t-f-j, j-i	M-W, m-w
r-h-u-n	h-p-y	N-Z, n-z
v-w-y-u	e-o-c	S-Z, s-z
r-c-s	a-e	o-u

Look closely at the above letters. Note the similar features. Turn *N* on its side and you have a *Z*. You can understand how inconstancy of form will create such confusions at times.

Letters are not alone in being confused by the visual dyslexic. Numbers, too, can give him trouble. You may find that the visual dyslexic will also confuse:

2–5   6–9   3–E   7–f

Spelling

Just as in reading, irregular words give problems in spelling. The speller not only must remember which letters make up the word and what these letters look like, but also the sequencing of the letters in the word. He must revisualize exactly what a particular word looks like and its specific components. The visual dyslexic will make errors in spelling of the same letters (listed above) as those that confuse him in visual discrimination.

Figure 4.7 was written by Bobby, age nine and a half, and of above average intelligence. Note that reversal of the numeral 5 occurs three times.

The visual dyslexic will write letters out of order in words (called transposition errors). For example, he may write *left* for *felt, paly* for *play, who* for *how, pna* for *pan,* or *clam* for *calm.* Silent letters within words are

Figure 4.7 A list of spelling words written by Bobby, a visual dyslexic, age nine and a half.

often omitted and sometimes transposed. The visual dyslexic just cannot revisualize these words correctly in a consistent manner.

As I have already stated, these characteristics of the visual dyslexic are not being illustrated for diagnostic purposes, but only as a matter of information to help in better understanding his problems. I should note here, however, that if a nondyslexic child has been taught phonics by sounds in isolation, he may make certain errors typical of the dyslexic. Therefore, the method of instruction should be investigated before arriving at any final conclusions. (See Appendix A for examples of such errors, which have thrown some diagnosticians off the track.)

Handwriting

Letter formation by the visual dyslexic is usually poor because of the inconstancy of his letter forms and his revisualization deficiencies. When he writes, his letters tend to be irregular in size, with frequent rotations, reversals, strike-overs as he tries to form the letters, and lots of erasures. There will be an intermixing of capital and lower-case letters and of cursive and manuscript styles of writing. Mark's writing in Figure 4.3 illustrates the inconstancy of writing typical of the visual dyslexic.

It is easy to understand that learning shorthand symbols or coding symbols would be very difficult for a visual dyslexic to master. He has enough trouble with his own alphabet!

Arithmetic

The visual dyslexic will have trouble in arithmetic for the same reasons that he has trouble with reading, spelling, and handwriting. Language is as necessary in math as it is in all subjects. In arithmetic words are often used to represent certain concepts. But number symbols and operations on numbers are more specific than those used for reading and writing. The visual dyslexic has problems with arithmetical language development, just as he has problems in the language arts.

Even if he could read all the words in the arithmetic directions and word problems, his sequencing difficulties would still affect his thought processes. He cannot organize the information given in the problem. Facts related to simple addition and subtraction may be remembered, but the more complex ones tend to be forgotten. He may carry or borrow (regroup) the wrong digit. Multiplication tables can drive him up the wall. Processes may be reversed while computing. Numerals may be reversed—a *2* may be changed to a *5* or a *6* to a *9*—which can result in major errors in calculation.

Referring to tables and bar graphs or copying geometric figures is likely to result in errors. His poor visual discrimination and unstable memory will cause the symbols for addition and multiplication ("+" and "x") or the subtraction and equal signs ("-" and "=") to be confused at times—just as with the letters *b* and *d* or *u* and *n*.

The vocabulary used in arithmetic, such as *quotient, subtrahend, associative,* and *product* are difficult for the visual dyslexic to understand and learn.

The concept of time is also hard to master. Learning to read time presents problems because of the sequencing of the numerals around the clock face and the visual dyslexic's reversal difficulties. He may read 6:00 as 9:00. Even if a child has a digital watch and he reads the numeral correctly, the digits may be transposed.

Social Studies, Science, and Other Subjects

Visual dyslexics have trouble reading maps and globes. The keys (legends) to maps are hard to use. They have difficulty reading any kind of floor plan. Estimating distance is difficult. They become confused with dates and times of events in history. They can get lost trying to create a time line as part of a history assignment. They even have trouble remembering the date of their own birthday, of other special family events, and of holidays commemorating famous people.

Some visual dyslexics may have an ear for music and be able to play an instrument, but reading the notes (or the words to the music) is another matter, depending upon the severity of the condition. Just as with music, the visual dyslexic may be able to learn a foreign language by ear if exposed to the language auditorily, but reading and writing the language will be difficult or nearly impossible.

Standardized Achievement Tests

Parents are often concerned about the scores of their child on the various standardized tests required by the schools. These require reading, of course, and any child with a reading problem is likely to score poorly even though he may know the necessary materials asked. He may simply be unable to read all the words in the questions and so he cannot give the correct answer.

Teachers have wondered about the variance in reading achievement subtest scores. The visual dyslexic tends to score higher on the vocabulary subtest (usually consisting of finding synonyms or meanings for words) and lower on the comprehension subtest, where he reads narrative passages and then answers certain questions. This is because of his sequencing difficulties and the confused order of the material in his mind. His memory weaknesses inhibit his looking back at the passage to try to find the answer. He has a hard time even keeping the question in his mind. He will probably give up and begin checking the answers in a random manner.

He is also likely to score higher on an oral reading test than on a silent reading test. On the Wechsler Intelligence Scale, Revised (WISC-R), his Verbal IQ score is apt to be relatively higher than his Performance IQ score.[4]

Oral Reinforcement When Working

The visual dyslexic will softly repeat words to himself as he works. He is drawing on his auditory modality to help him make sense of what he is reading. Even when he is asked to write the alphabet in sequence, he is likely to sing "The Alphabet Song" quietly to himself over and over—using it as a mnemonic device to help him recall the letters until he is finished. He may do the same when spelling words. (He is *not* trying to cheat or give away answers. He is trying to draw on a device to help him do what he has been asked to do.)

While it is customary for first grade children to use oral reinforcement (softly reading the words aloud to themselves) as they read, usually by second or third grade children have moved into silent reading successfully, no longer using obvious lip movements (unless they have had round-robin instruction on a regular basis). This development is desirable, for one can read silently much faster than aloud. Comprehension tends to be better, too.

But for the visual dyslexic we must make an exception. He needs to whisper the words softly to help him make sense of his reading and to serve as a self-corrective aid. This is his crutch. He needs it. Let him keep it.

Auditory Discrimination

The visual dyslexic usually has good auditory discrimination and can distinguish between similarities and differences in words when he hears them. His problem is with distinguishing between similar words when he *looks* at them.

Consonant Blends and Digraphs

When reading, the visual dyslexic is likely to transpose blends and digraphs, such as *three* for *there*, *gril* for *girl*, *calm* for *clam*, and *how* for *who*. But, as has been stated, one must be cautious here, for children who have been taught the phonic elements in isolation may have the same pattern of errors in both reading and spelling as dyslexics. (For example, if they have been taught that the blend *gr* says *gir* the child may read or write the word *grill* as *girl*.)

Configuration Word Recognition Strategy

Configuration refers to the shape of something. The shape of a word (or a letter) can be a clue to recognition, particularly if it is distinctive. Children tend to recognize the word *grandmother* rather easily because of its unusually long shape which begins with a letter dropping below the line. The word *elephant* is another word with a rather unusual shape and one that children learn easily. Figure 4.8 illustrates the concept of configuration.

The configuration word recognition strategy is of the visual type. The reader must "picture" the shape of the word in his mind—and do so very quickly for the strategy to be effective. The visual dyslexic tends to have

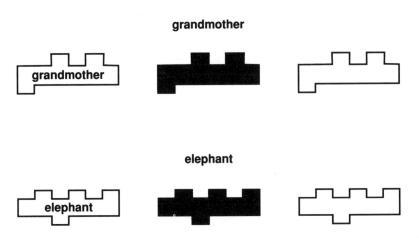

Figure 4.8   Shapes of words help in recognition of the words (configuration word recognition strategy).

trouble making use of this clue to identify words because of his problems with revisualization. This technique will be of more help to the auditory dyslexic.

Miscellaneous Problems of Orientation

In addition to problems with letter and word reversals, the visual dyslexic has a disorientation of time and space. He may draw heavily on his common sense, but this still may not be enough in many situations.

The visual dyslexic child may be the one who remains on the playground after the others have returned to class. This is the child who gets lost in hide-and-seek games or peeks before the time is up. This is the student who, when sent with a message to the office, gets lost on the way. This is the child at home who does not know when to come in for dinner or the child who, when his mother sends him to the neighborhood store with a list, arrives home two hours later without any satisfactory explanation. Where schedules are concerned, he seems to dawdle. If he attends a school where he must change rooms from class to class, he is often late (and may offer no reason, because he is too embarrassed to admit he lost his way).

Teachers and parents find it hard to accept any of the visual dyslexic's explanations as to why he is late. What they must constantly remember is that the visual dyslexic *cannot help it.* He is not being deliberately disobedient. He is not a truant. He may not seem to care—but he does, very much. He knows these things are happening; he does not understand why; he would much rather that they not happen.

The same problems create difficulties in traveling—reading maps and getting around town, or across the country. The visual dyslexic can get lost—anywhere, anytime.

Summary

The visual dyslexic's major problems are with sequencing, revisualization compounded by the instability of letter and word forms, and other orientation difficulties. These can affect every school subject, many sports, his family relations, and the various community activities in which he may participate. They can affect any traveling he may do, which includes finding his way around his hometown and his community.

Notes

1. Stanley W. Jacob, Clarice Ashworth Francone, and Walter J. Lossow, *Structure and Function in Man* (Philadelphia: W.B. Saunders, 1978), pp. 312–14.

2. John R. McWilliams, "Eye," *The World Book Encyclopedia* (Chicago: Field Enterprises Educational Corporation, 1968), pp. 358–59; Morton F. Goldberg, "Eye," *The World Book Encyclopedia* (Chicago: World Book, 1985), pp. 358–67.

3. Doris J. Johnson and Helmer R. Myklebust, *Learning Disabilities, Educational Principles and Practice* (New York: Grune and Stratton, 1967), pp. 153, 156.

4. F.J. Pirozzolo, "Language and Brain: Neuropsychological Aspects of Developmental Reading Disability," *School Psychology Review* 10 (1981), pp. 350–55.

CHAPTER 5

AUDITORY DYSLEXIA

To children the whole isn't a collection of parts, it's a
complete unit. So, paradoxical as it may sound,
to go from the whole to the part is to proceed
from the simple to the complex.
—*Kenneth Goodman*

When you know a thing, to hold that you know it;
and when you do not know a thing, to allow
that you do not know it: this is knowledge.
—*Confucius*

A child is not an auditory dyslexic because of any loss of hearing. The
auditory dyslexic often has keen hearing. We *hear* with our ears, but *it is our
brain that listens and makes sense of what is heard.* An auditory dyslexic has
trouble processing and interpreting the oral information that he hears.

How do we hear? There are three main parts of the human ear—the
outer ear, the middle ear, and the inner ear. We actually hear sound deep
inside the inner ear. Figure 5.1 illustrates the three major parts of the ear.

Sound waves (vibrations) can travel directly through the bones of our
skull. The bones send the sound waves on to our inner ear. The outer part
of our ear also collects sound waves in the fleshy, curved, cuplike part
attached to the side of our head (the auricle). These vibrations are directed
into the hole or passageway (external auditory canal) and are guided to the
middle ear through the eardrum—or a second eardrum if the first was
ruptured at one time—on across three bones into the inner ear, which has
numerous intricate chambers and passageways. As the sound waves move
along they cause the fibers (24,000 of them) that lie within the cochlea to
move, and these fibers cause a vibration in specialized sense cells that make

WORLD BOOK illustration by Colin Bidgood

The Human Ear extends deep into the skull. Its main parts are
(1) the outer ear, (2) the middle ear, and (3) the inner ear.

Figure 5.1   The three major parts of the ear. (Used with permission from "Ear," by
David D. Caldarelli and Ruth S. Campanella, *The World Book Encyclopedia*, Vol. 6,
Chicago: World Book, © 1985)

up the organ of Corti. The vibration of these sense cells (called hair cells) stimulates nerves that are attached to them. Messages flow through an auditory nerve to the center of hearing in the brain (temporal lobe), where the sounds are classified, processed, and interpreted.[1,2] Figure 5.2 illustrates how sounds travel to the inner ear.

Parents and teachers need to be aware that abnormalities of the ear (or ears) can cause symptoms that are similar to some of those of an auditory dyslexic. Any child who is having academic problems in school should have his hearing tested with an audiometer by a trained examiner to determine if hearing defects may account for his difficulties.

Some school systems have a policy of regular screening for hearing problems. The person administering the test should be well trained and skilled. Usually there is a speech and hearing clinic within driving distance, where experienced examiners are available. Most cities have medical doctors who specialize in eyes, ears, nose, and throat who could give such hearing examinations.

What is so difficult about the ear is that a child can have normal hearing one week, then have an infection or injury, and suffer a hearing loss. Thus, parents and teachers need to be alert continually to the danger.

Disease or injury may cause partial or total deafness. Sound vibrations may be blocked by wax or foreign bodies that can lodge in either the external or the middle ear, or by adhesions of the bones in the middle ear. A ringing in the ear (tinnitus) can affect hearing and may be caused by wax in the ear, holes in the eardrum, fluid in the middle ear (including water from swimming), and sometimes by taking drugs. Aspirin and streptomycin are two common drugs that can cause ringing in the ears.

Perforation of the eardrum can cause hearing loss, the extent of the loss

How Sounds Travel to the Inner Ear

Sound waves enter the ear through the external auditory canal. They strike the eardrum, causing it to vibrate. The vibrations flow across the malleus, incus, and stapes. The footplate of the stapes vibrates within the oval window, creating waves in the fluid that fills the ducts of the cochlea.

WORLD BOOK Illustration by Colin Ridgood

Figure 5.2   How sounds travel to the inner ear. (Used with permission from "Ear," by David D. Caldarelli and Ruth S. Campanella, *The World Book Encyclopedia*, Vol. 6, Chicago: World Book, © 1985)

depending upon the size and location of the hole. But even with almost complete loss of the eardrum, a person can hear slightly because of the sound waves that pass through the bones of the skull, bypassing the eardrum, to the inner ear.[3]

Children who have allergies, with stuffy noses and blocked Eustachian tubes, can have temporary hearing loss of varying degrees.

Hearing loss can affect the auditory discrimination of students; that is, the ability to distinguish the minute differences in letters and words—as is the case with the auditory dyslexic. A child may not hear directions or instructions clearly, may not listen attentively because he hears only portions of what is said and thus his interest wanders. Obviously, abnormalities in hearing can affect the validity of the diagnosis of a child and the assessment of his performance in school.

If you have a child who is having problems with phonics, with structural analysis, taking notes, following oral directions, and paying attention to what is being said, consider the following before you refer him to a specialist for possible auditory dyslexia:

1. Has he had a head injury or ear infection?
2. Could he possibly have a hearing loss?
3. Does he have frequent head colds?
4. Does he appear to have allergies?
5. Have you considered the possibility of a wax build-up in his ears?
6. Has he frequently been absent from school, and thus missed specific instruction in auditory activities such as phonics and syllabication?
7. Is the seatwork assigned him for these auditory activities at a level that he can read easily? That is, when new skills are taught, is there follow-up material that will not itself provide a block to the application of the new elements taught?
8. Is the child taking any kind of drug, such as aspirin, streptomycin, or others?

In the chapter on visual dyslexia, I spoke of the difficulty of *revisualizing*, or remembering and "picturing" words, objects, and places formerly seen. The auditory dyslexic has difficulty in *reauditorizing*, remembering and "hearing" the sounds and sound patterns formerly heard and then applying them to his reading and spelling. When he looks at a word, he may be unable to say it even though he knows what the word means. For this reason, he will read silently better than orally. He can associate the word with meaning but cannot change the visual symbol of the word to the auditory symbol.[4]

Let us hope that the auditory dyslexic does not have a classroom teacher who uses the round-robin technique to teach reading or other subjects, nor that his teacher assigns oral reading for homework—stories to be read aloud each evening at home. He needs to read silently at these times. Oral reading should be limited to diagnostic and remedial purposes.

Auditory Integration and the Dyslexic

The auditory dyslexic has trouble with certain intrasensory auditory functions, such as distinguishing between the sound units of language and synthesizing them into words, or taking a word and dividing it into parts like syllables. As a result, he cannot learn if taught by a synthetic (sounds in isolation) approach to teaching the phonic elements. He has trouble perceiving the relationship of the sounds of language with those represented by print; that is, matching the sound of the word with the printed word—or matching the phoneme (sound of a letter) with the grapheme (the letter as we write it).

Phonics and spelling rules are almost meaningless to him, as are the diacritical markings used in dictionaries to designate the pronunciation of words.

Auditory Discrimination

The many disorders in auditory discrimination make it difficult for the auditory dyslexic to make sense out of what he is hearing and trying to read. One of the major limitations caused by auditory dyslexia is the difficulty in distinguishing minimal differences in letters and words that are similar in sound. For example, he may confuse the sound of *m* with that of *n* (as in *man* and *Nan*), the sound of *v* with that of *f* or *th* (as in *vine, fine,* and *thine*). The letters *b, d, t, p,* and *g* may sound alike to him. He may say that the words *back, pack,* and *tack* are the same. He may not perceive that the words *boy* and *big* begin with the same sound, or that *got* and *not* end with the same sound.

The Vowels and Vowel Digraphs

Variations of the vowel sounds really throw the auditory dyslexic into a quandary. He is bewildered when trying to discriminate between the short and long vowel sounds, such as those heard in *fat* and *fate* or *bet* and *beat*. He confuses some short vowel sounds with others, such as those heard in *got* and *get,* or *pin* and *pan* and *pen*. He especially has trouble with vowel sounds when heard in isolated form, but when words containing certain vowel sounds are given in a sentence he can draw on context clues to help him make sense of what he is reading and predict the correct word.

The "schwa" vowel sound like the *o* in *button*, which any vowel may represent in certain words, is nearly impossible for him to distinguish. (Actually, teachers should not even attempt to teach this perplexing concept to the auditory dyslexic.) To make matters worse and even more confusing for this student, the vowels in our language copy other vowel sounds, such as the short *u* sound in *mother* (written with an *o*, not a *u*), or the short *o* sound in *watch* (written with an *a* not an *o*), or the *ai* in *said,* which has the short *e* sound (but is not spelled that way).

The auditory dyslexic may spell the word *meet* in either of several ways—*met* or *meat* or *mete*. And then, too, he may spell *meat* as *meet, met,* or *mete*. His spelling can be truly appalling.

Phonics must be kept in proper perspective for the dyslexic student. Trying to "pound" phonic elements into his head will not make him proficient at spelling or reading. On the contrary, it will only add to the confusing bits and pieces of sounds already floating around in his head.

The Consonant Blends and Digraphs

Since the auditory dyslexic already has trouble distinguishing between certain consonant sounds, it follows that he will have difficulty with consonant blends. He tends to write the blends with the letters in a transposed order, such as *calm* for *clam* or *paly* for *play* (as does the visual dyslexic, but his reasons are different). As stated before, one must find out how the auditory dyslexic has been taught his phonic elements, since having learned them in isolation will contribute to these errors.

Sometimes the auditory dyslexic will omit one of the letters of a blend, for example, mat for mast. He has special trouble with the *l* and *r* blends (such as in *block, clock, float, glad,* and *bread, crack, drive,* and *frog*).

As for the consonant digraphs (two letter combinations having one sound, such as the *ch* in *chop* or the *th* in *that* or the *wh* in *what*), the auditory dyslexic will come up with just about anything. He often acquires certain mnemonic (memory) devices to help him figure out words. For example, if you listen to him as he reads, you may hear him softly talking to himself as he tries to remember the words. When confronted with *what* he may say, "This word, *what,* is *at* with a *wh* in front of it," (which it really isn't, of course), or, "*Then* is *hen* with a *t* in front." This is one reason his reading is so very slow and labored and, naturally, this affects his understanding of what he is reading.

Rhyming

Because of his difficulty in distinguishing between words that are similar or different in sound, the auditory dyslexic will not be able to rhyme with any facility, whether he is asked to say words that rhyme or to write words that rhyme with a given word. He does not seem to be able to hear a part of a word and then go through the mental process of relating and associating and supplying words with the same ending. Even high school auditory dyslexics have trouble with rhyming elements.

For example, when asked to say some words that rhyme with *man*, the auditory dyslexic may respond with *mat* or *men*. He may throw in some nonsense words such as *zan, lan,* or *gan*. When asked to write rhyming words, he may just run through the alphabet writing words that rhyme with the key word but which are also gibberish: *ball, call, dall, eall, fall, gall, hall, jall,* and so on. Of course, what he is actually doing is copying the phonogram *all* and then just placing a letter in front of it. The rhyming concept has escaped him. In written rhyming exercises, look for the auditory dyslexic to do this especially if there is an alphabet writing chart in plain sight!

Syllabication

Since the auditory dyslexic has difficulty with auditory analysis and synthesis, he cannot distinguish the different syllables in words. He has problems with dividing words into syllables and with building a word from syllables. Naturally, this disorder affects both reading and spelling. Since he has trouble with syllabication, he has a tendency to omit syllables in both reading and writing, to reverse syllables, and at times to add syllables.

Scrambled Words, Phrases, and Sentences

The auditory dyslexic has trouble accurately retrieving words from his auditory memory. This, together with his difficulty in blending, sometimes results in a garbled pronunciation of certain words. Spoonerisms, such as saying "tons of soil" for "sons of toil," are not uncommon. Tongue twisters are very difficult for him to say, even slowly. He really does seem to trip over his own tongue.

While it is common for young children to pronounce *animal* as *aminal* or *spaghetti* as *pasghetti* or *aluminum* as *alunimum* or *enemy* as *emeny*, the older child should be able to articulate these words correctly. But the auditory dyslexic will continue to have trouble with them. The letters and syllables of words seem to scramble into different combinations. Too often, at school and at home, people will laugh at and mimic the auditory dyslexic when he comes up with these misarticulations. This may be fun for the others; it is no fun at all for the dyslexic. Unaware of what he has just said, he cannot understand what sets them off. He feels uneasy, self-conscious, and at times defensive.

Parents, brothers and sisters, and teachers need to be sensitive to such mistakes and reactions. They must understand that what is funny to them is embarrassing and humiliating to him. As a defense, the auditory dyslexic may resort to silence—saying as little as possible in front of others—a tragedy, indeed.

It is possible for the auditory dyslexic to learn to laugh along with the others—but only when he feels happy and secure in his environment.

A further point: many of the auditory dyslexics in our clinic have had a history of some early speech disorders that required speech therapy.

Spelling

The spelling errors of the auditory dyslexic result from his difficulty in matching sounds with written words and in retaining the auditory memory of the words. His troubles with vowel sounds, consonant blends, and digraphs have been mentioned. Incorrect vowels will be written, consonant blends broken, letters and syllables added or omitted, and the spelling rules (such as i before e except after c) are meaningless. Words that are similar in sound confuse him. He is just as likely as not to spell *cat* as *kat* or *city* as *sitee*. He cannot reauditorize the rules or the sounds. He tends to spell "phoneti-cally"—*bot* for *boat*, *mene* for *many*, or *gos* for *goes*.

He has a great deal of difficulty in acquiring a stock of correct spelling words. His spelling can be more bizarre than that of the visual dyslexic.

"Sarah" came to our reading clinic for help with her reading and spelling problems the summer before she was to enter the sixth grade. She was eleven years old. Testing indicated that she had the mental ability to be able to read at the seventh-grade level. However, her instructional reading level was second grade, and her independent or "free reading" level was preprimer. Her instructional spelling level was first grade.

Sarah was very frustrated by her inability to read the assignments in her textbooks and to do the work expected of her in school. She was frank about dreading the arrival of September when she would have to return to school. When asked to write the days of the week in order, Sarah wrote what is shown in Figure 5.3.

Observe that Sarah wrote the days of the week in correct sequence, even in a left to right, top to bottom order. This was not her problem. Note also

Figure 5.3   The days of the week written by Sarah, an auditory dyslexic, C.A. 11-0, grade 6.

that only Monday was spelled correctly and that she did know how to spell *day* correctly in each word. Her spelling errors consisted of omitting the vowel combination *ue* in Tuesday and substituting the vowel *o*, omitting the *d* and *es* in Wednesday, omitting the *h* as part of the digraph *th* and the *ur* in Thursday, substituting the vowel *e*, omitting the *r* in the *fr* blend in Friday, substituting the vowel *e*, omitting the *ur* in Saturday, and substituting the vowel *o* for the vowel *u* in Sunday. These errors are typical of the auditory dyslexic's writing.

Handwriting

The auditory dyslexic writes slowly, but his letter formation is usually better than the visual dyslexic's. He frequently marks over and erases what he has written, but this is because of his uncertainty in spelling rather than a visual inconstancy of letter formation.

Other Subjects in School

As a result of his serious reading and writing disabilities, the auditory dyslexic has difficulties in the other subjects. He has difficulty reading textbooks with understanding. He has trouble attending to lectures and taking notes.

He generally does not enjoy musical recitals and concerts, and has difficulty with the rhythm of music and dancing. He will avoid music classes and band if at all possible. But, to be accepted as "one of the gang," he will often pretend to be "up on the latest," attend rock concerts, and put on a great act.

The dyslexic (whether auditory or visual) often withdraws and isolates himself. Or he may take the opposite course and become the "bully" or ring leader of a gang to try to prove his worth to himself and others.

Auditory dyslexics often are good in vocational shop, woodworking, and athletics.

Trying to learn a foreign language can drive an auditory dyslexic to distraction. His auditory processing problems with sound and synthesis make this very difficult for him. Any foreign language requirement should be waived for the auditory dyslexic. He has enough problems with his own language. Learning shorthand or a code, such as the Morse code, presents the same problems of discrimination, association, and processing. The Morse code also requires a sense of rhythm and the use of sound units of dots and dashes.

Standardized Reading Achievement Tests

The auditory dyslexic generally scores higher on the comprehension subtest than on the vocabulary subtest. The words in isolation on the vocabulary test, if unknown, must be figured out by phonics analysis or mental substitution (a form of phonics), or by breaking the word into syllables—all tasks difficult for him—or even configuration (but then several words may have the same shape). The auditory dyslexic is at a loss and is likely to zip through the test, guessing at the answers, marking them at random.

On the comprehension test containing narrative passages, he knows the meaning of some of the words, and he can draw on the context of the story or exercise to figure out others. His visual memory, usually strong, can also help him to locate answers. He will work very slowly, trying to make sense of what he is reading, but as the paragraphs become harder he will probably give up and begin guessing—especially with the pressure of time bearing down on him.

His silent reading score will likely be higher than his oral reading score. On the Wechsler Intelligence Scale, Revised (WISC-R), his Performance IQ score is apt to be higher than his Verbal IQ score.[5]

Summary

The auditory dyslexic's major problems are with his ability to integrate and process the sounds of language and to associate them with the written symbols in reading and writing. He has difficulty with reauditorizing what he has heard, and this affects any situation in which listening is involved as well as any in which his own speaking is involved. Every subject in school can be affected by his auditory dyslexia. His dyslexia colors his whole life—home, community, school—and affects his relations with his teachers, classmates, family, and others with whom he comes into contact.

Notes

1. Stanley W. Jacob, Clarice Ashworth Francone, and Walter J. Lossow, *Structure and Function in Man* (Philadelphia: W.B. Saunders, 1978), pp. 319–25.

2. David D. Caldarelli and Ruth S. Campanella, *The World Book Encyclopedia*, Vol. 6 (Chicago: World Book, 1985), pp. 5–8d.

3. Jacob, Francone, and Lossow, op. cit., pp. 325–26.

4. Doris J. Johnson and Helmer R. Myklebust, *Learning Disabilities, Educational Principles and Practices* (New York: Grune and Stratton, 1967), p. 175.

5. F.J. Pirozzolo, "Language and Brain: Neuropsychological Aspects of Developmental Reading Disability," *School Psychology Review* 10 (1981), pp. 350–55.

PART THREE

KEEPING OUR FEET ON THE GROUND

To know just what has to be done, then to do it,
comprises the whole philosophy of practical life.
—Sir William Osler

CHAPTER 6

COMMON SENSE AND "EARLY IDENTIFICATION" OF DYSLEXIA

Nothing astonishes men so much as
common sense and plain dealing.
—*Ralph Waldo Emerson*

The push is on for "early identification" of dyslexia; the rallying cry is, "The sooner we can catch these children the sooner we can begin the remediation of the dyslexia. So let's test as soon as we can to see if we have any dyslexics."

Sounds good, doesn't it? But attempts at identifying dyslexia too early are fraught with problems. The possibility of error carries with it a real danger of premature efforts at remediation, which may aggravate a disability or even create one where none existed before. As yet, no test instruments have been devised to identify positively, with validity, those children in nursery school, kindergarten, or first and second grade who have dyslexia and those who do not.

Just as it is difficult to distinguish between the young cygnets of the trumpeter swan and those of the whistling swan until the cygnets have matured to a certain degree, so too is it difficult with our young children to determine who may or may not have dyslexia.

At our clinic, a part of the criteria for acceptance is that a child must be at least eight years old or in the third grade. There are reasons for intervention at this age, rather than earlier, that go far beyond any limitations of space, materials, or personnel. These have to do with the child himself—that is, his biological development (maturation), which is gradual and progressive. This is true for all children, although all do not develop at a uniform rate. Children are individuals and they grow as individuals. Each child's maturation and progress in learning are intricately, inevitably intermingled. Some children mature early; others need more time. In diagnosis, we refer to what is called the "magical age of eight" for good reasons.

Vision Development

The type is large in primary reading books and gradually decreases with each grade. The reason for this is that most young children are naturally farsighted (hyperopic), but as the child grows, develops, and matures, the eyeball lengthens, and the farsightedness gradually decreases.[1,2] The typical child is about eight years old when his eyes become sufficiently mature to cope with the demands of a school's numerous near-point vision tasks.

When children are farsighted and are asked to do a great deal of close work, the letters and words tend to blur, and they become tired, get headaches, and, of course, lose interest in the work at hand. They may become restless, get into mischief, and create problems in the classroom. The teacher is likely to view them as being "hyperactive" and "unable to attend to the task" in the workbook, skill sheets, reading book, or textbook.

Among the various refractive conditions that cause reading disabilities, farsightedness is the most frequently listed. Farsightedness causes both excessive accommodation and convergence.[3] Since many learning disability cases do not have good near-point acuity, most being farsighted,[4] the question may be: might some of these children have been diagnosed as learning disabled (LD) at an early age, before their vision had matured?

There are some educational implications to be considered with regard to children's visual immaturity. Too much close work, too much busy work, too many purple dittoed worksheets, too many workbook pages for young pupils may well be a major factor in contributing to vision problems. Too much close work is being required in too many classrooms, including remedial reading and learning disability classes, where young students are frequently deluged by page after page of skill sheets from commercial "cookbook" programs of remediation. It is easy for teachers to use such printed materials to excess.

Early identification? Caution and common sense are needed. As Emerald Dechant has pointed out, "Unfortunately, too many teachers fail to recognize the relationship between visual immaturity and failure in reading in the first grade."[5]

Visual Discrimination Development

Visual discrimination is not to be confused with visual acuity—overall vision, the ability to see clearly as determined by vision tests. Visual discrimination is the ability to differentiate between similarities and differences in letters and words, such as between *b* and *d* or *pan* and *pen*. While certain defects in visual acuity may cause some errors in visual discrimination (vision screening should always be a part of diagnostic testing), a child may have excellent vision but poor visual discrimination. Here, too, there are developmental factors to keep in mind when making a diagnosis.

Some authors of articles and books on dyslexia stress the need to assess dyslexia at the earliest possible moment, and have stated that one of the early identification symptoms to look for is if a child confuses *p* and *b* and *d*, or *no* and *on*, or *horse* and *house*, and the like. As any primary teacher knows, such errors are common among kindergartners, first-graders, and even second-graders. As the students get older and more mature, these types of errors should disappear.[6] It is when such behavior *persists* that we become concerned. Although maturation cannot be hurried, a child's visual discrimination can be sharpened by experience and practice.[7] But care must be taken that this does not involve an excessive amount of near-point work.

Auditory Discrimination Development

Auditory discrimination should not be confused with auditory acuity—overall hearing, the ability to hear sounds of varying pitch and at differing degrees of loudness as measured by a hearing test, such as with an audiometer. Auditory discrimination is the ability to differentiate between similarities and differences in speech sounds (phonemes) and combinations of sounds, as in "*b*ig" and "*d*ig," or "*p*ay," "*l*ay," "*pl*ay," or "*p*en," "*p*an," "*p*in," or "*m*ad" and "*m*ade." Say the following letters aloud and listen to the similarity in sound even though each is different:

$$b, c, d, e, g, p, t, v, z$$

Some linguists have maintained that if a child can pronounce most words accurately, then he must have adequate auditory discrimination. This would appear to be true; however, the ability to abstract a sound from a spoken word and then compare it with a sound in another word is a cognitive proficiency that many five- and six-year-olds have not yet developed.[8] Those familiar with Piaget's theory of cognitive development will know that this task requires a child to attend to different features and their relationship to the whole word. This is called "decentration."

As with vision, certain kinds of auditory acuity defects (such as a hearing loss of fifteen decibels or high-frequency hearing losses) may cause auditory discrimination errors. A child may have excellent overall hearing but poor auditory discrimination. Maturational factors affect the development of a child's auditory discrimination.

Again, as with visual discrimination, certain authors of articles and books on dyslexia who stress early diagnosis state that problems in auditory discrimination are symptomatic of dyslexia. Yet young children show differing degrees of ability in auditory discrimination; furthermore, auditory discrimination rarely is fully developed before the age of eight.[9,10,11] Experienced primary teachers know that it is when most children's auditory discrimination errors persist for no apparent reason that we should become concerned.

Auditory Sequential Memory

Auditory memory difficulties are a part of the syndrome of dyslexia. Again, one should be cautious in applying any such diagnosis to young children. Auditory memory has to do with a child's ability to remember accurately what he has heard, whether it is words in isolation or in sentences, or digits in a certain sequence. Auditory memory affects the child's ability to follow oral directions or, indeed, to perform *any* listening task.

The act of reading requires the reader to make the association of a visual sequence of letter symbols (the written word) with an auditory sequence of speech sounds (the spoken word). When a child applies phonics and structural analysis knowledge to the written word, he must reauditorize the sounds, note similarities, make associations, and keep them in order in his mind (memory) as he figures out the word. The longer the word, the greater the load placed on auditory memory as the word is synthesized.

Writing and spelling require remembering the sequential order of letters that make up a word. The child may transpose letters within words, such as *aminal* for *animal* or *paly* for *play*. Substitutions, omissions, or distortions of words and numbers may occur when the child is asked to repeat what he has heard. The young child may pronounce *spaghetti* as *pasghetti* or *enemy* as *emeny*. Any kind of dictation or note-taking exercise is difficult for a child with auditory memory problems, as is recalling lengthy series of numbers.

The ability to recall sequences is developmental in nature. The child gradually becomes able to recall longer and longer series of words, sentences, and numbers. Usually there is little change in scores on various tests of auditory sequential memory between the ages of seven and eight. The most significant changes occur between the ages of six and seven[12]—that is, generally students in the first and second grades.

Visual Memory

Visual memory refers to the ability to remember letters, words, objects, and events seen. A strong visual memory is essential for learning and remembering those words in our language to which the phonics rules do not apply (irregular words), such as *head, break, once, does, through, though,* or *rough.* A child will never read fluently until he has acquired a stock of sight words—words that the reader must recognize instantly without having to interrupt his reading to figure them out. Visual memory is necessary for acquiring a necessary stock of words. It is also needed to learn handwriting and to remember how each letter is shaped. Intelligence is considered to be a related factor, although it is possible for a very bright child to have poor visual memory.

The maturity of a child's development in vision and visual discrimination plays an important role in visual memory and must be taken into account before a diagnosis of dyslexia can be made with confidence.

Spelling

A strong visual memory is far more important than phonics for accurate spelling. Spelling is basically a matter of convention and etymology. It is the meaning of the words that often provides clues to their spelling. For words that contain silent letters, such as *heat* or *light,* and irregular words, the child must draw upon his visual memory. He must "see" (revisualize) the *gh* in *light* because those letters are not heard. He must remember that these letters are in the word so as not to spell the word as *lite.* He must keep a *visual image* that *one* is not spelled *wun,* the way it sounds.

Spelling errors are often analyzed and used in the diagnosis of dyslexia. This practice with very young students is highly questionable in view of the various stages of spelling that children go through. As children are growing and gaining experiences, they seem to construct tentative rules based on their knowledge of the language, and then they apply the rules to their spelling. Primary teachers know well how *yor* eventually becomes *yours,* how *tod* becomes *tode* and then *toad,* and *lafwts* becomes *elefant* and finally *elephant.* A child's visual memory and the development of an understanding of spelling principles play a part in this evolution of accuracy in spelling. Recent studies have established that there is a sequence of spelling stages through which children go, and their knowledge about written words is acquired in a systematic, developmental, and gradual manner.[13,14]

Dyslexics cannot be placed neatly and cleanly within the developmental spelling stages. It is as though their spelling progress had been arrested at points along the way, with ups and downs in a rather erratic pattern of progress. Both visual and auditory dyslexics can have bizarre misspellings, although auditory dyslexics tend to have more.

Too early attempts at identification of dyslexia on the basis of errors in spelling may result in misdiagnosis, with serious implications for the child. There are *normal* types of errors that children make as they progress through the developmental spelling stages, each child in his individual manner. All do not make exactly the same errors.

These types of spelling errors must not be misconstrued as dyslexia symptoms in the young child. Later, if such errors persist, appropriate steps for referral should be taken.

Visual-Motor (Eye-Hand) Coordination

Visual-motor coordination refers to the ability of a child's eyes and hands to work together in such tasks as writing, copying, cutting with scissors, pasting, coloring, tying shoelaces, buttoning coats, stringing beads, using hammers, and throwing, catching, or batting a ball. These tasks may be required when testing a child for hand preference. Writing a story and copying from a chart are two tasks required in the dyslexia diagnostic battery of tests.

Gross motor skills are developed before the finer motor skills. The latter are required for the tasks mentioned above. For this reason, children are usually first introduced to the manuscript ("printing") style of writing. The straight lines, circles, and spacing forms are much simpler for the young child than the more complex movements required for cursive writing. Most authorities believe that until about the third grade—or about the age of eight—many children do not acquire the intricate muscular development and maturity needed to learn cursive writing.[15,16,17]

Various experiments indicate that cursive writing can be learned in the third grade, after two years of manuscript writing, more easily than in the first or second grades, and the quality of writing in the upper grades is equal to or superior to the writing of children who begin cursive in the first grade.[18]

Children tend to write more if they are permitted to continue using manuscript in the primary grades. They use a greater variety of words and more running words. Indeed, one study[19] of third-grade students indicated that each half-year delay in teaching cursive writing increases the mastery of the written language.

—2,623 different words were used by those who had changed to cursive writing in the second grade,

—3,798 different words were used by those who had changed in the first half of the third grade,

—4,636 different words were used by those who had changed in the second half of the third grade, and

—7,681 different words were used by those who had continued using manuscript writing throughout the third grade.

The Bender Visual-Motor Gestalt Test used by some in "detecting" dyslexia requires the child to copy certain designs containing curved and straight lines, dots, little circles, and open and closed figures, with the forms becoming increasingly more complex. Of interest here is that the Bender test score *tends to improve during the primary grades*[20]—that is, as the child matures and as he develops his fine motor control. Any difficulty may not be due at all to the child's inaccurate perception of the figures. Actually, the reliability of the Bender test with young school children is poor, and test-retest scores vary considerably, especially during the first two school years.[21]

Visual-motor coordination seems to reach maturity somewhere between age six and age eight.[22] Since the finer muscle development of most little boys lags behind that of most little girls, the majority of boys will take longer to acquire the maturity needed for such coordination.

Lateral Awareness/Directional Confusion

Lateral awareness refers to a child's ability to discriminate right from left, and difficulty with this is often regarded as being one of the symptoms of dyslexia. But young children are often confused when a teacher gives directions involving the use of the words *right* and *left*. When they do not follow these directions they are considered disobedient. A child may be told to get the book on the right side of the bookcase, and then when he stands there in confusion he may be scolded for not doing what he has been told to do. Such experiences occur at home as well as at school. Children may have trouble in physical education classes for the same reason.

By the age of seven, a child may have developed an awareness of the right and left parts of his *own* body (left eye, right foot), which is sometimes referred to as "personal space awareness." Most children are able to do this by age eight, but some are not until age nine, and mental age has an influence upon the performance level. However, the lateral awareness for such tasks, as in the example above—where the teacher gave directions regarding the bookcase, called "extra-personal space awareness"—is not established until children are between the ages of nine and twelve years.[23,24] Note that a range of ages is given, not one certain age where this occurs for *all* children.

Problems in personal space awareness and extra-personal space awareness are usually considered symptomatic of dyslexia, and tests for such difficulties are included in the dyslexia diagnostic battery. But parents and teachers (and diagnosticians) must keep in mind that there are developmental aspects involved in acquiring this lateral awareness. The maturity of the child must be taken into account before any final decision can be made as to whether a child is dyslexic.

Language Acquisition

Young students are still learning to speak distinctly and to produce sounds correctly. There is a relationship between hearing and auditory discrimination and speech development. Of course a hearing loss can affect the development of speech in a child. So, too, while a child may have a keen sense of *hearing,* problems with being able to discriminate auditorily between the various sounds can contribute to difficulties in speech. But beyond this, many normal children in the beginning years of school cannot articulate certain sounds well. Young children make frequent common substitution errors which follow a pattern. It is not unusual for young students age six to age eight to substitute the following sounds:[25]

/f/   for /v/, and sometimes /v/ for /f/
/f/   *for the* /th/ sound heard in *thin*
/s/   for /z/
/k/   for /t/
/n/   for /m/
/th/ as heard in *thin* for the /th/ as heard in *that* and also for /s/

Young students seem to have particular problems in pronouncing /r/, /l/, and /s/, and these sounds (phonemes) make up the major articulation therapy loads of public school speech therapists.[26,27] It follows that primary grade children have special trouble with the *r, l,* and *s* blends, such as *tr, dr, cr . . . bl, cl, fl . . . sc, sk, sl . . .* and so on.[28]

Young students have more difficulty producing certain sounds in the middle of words and at the end of words than they do at the beginning. Growth and maturation, however, eliminate many articulation errors in the first few grades.

The pattern of speech development has implications for any phonics assessment, since auditory discrimination is linked to speech development.

Some teachers try to teach certain phonic elements to children who cannot even pronounce those elements accurately, much less discriminate between those sounds.

Authors of articles and books on dyslexia often mention that confusing the sounds mentioned above, as well as making errors in the middle and end of words, is symptomatic of dyslexia. It would be very easy to come up with a misdiagnosis of dyslexia if one tested children at too young a developmental age.

There are certain developmental shifts in children's acquisition of language. These shifts concern not only the speech sounds and changes of sounds, but also the patterns of words in sentences and the meanings of words and how these meanings can change. These are referred to as the phonological, syntactical, and semantic shifts in a child's language development.

The periods between the ages of five and eight and then again between the ages of twelve and fourteen are marked by instability in linguistic development. These are then followed by growth and stable linguistic performance. During these two periods there are large increases in the child's new grammatical constructions and high error rates in some kinds of these constructions.[29,30]

These age ranges concur with Piaget's cognitive development transition points, when the child moves from preoperational thought to concrete operations (age five to eight) and from concrete operations to formal operations (age eleven or twelve and up).[31] The concrete stage is the first stage of operational intelligence, and it is here that the child begins to classify and group ideas and to understand numbers and things in series, but he needs real (concrete) objects in order to learn and to apply these concepts. Formal operations involve considering various alternatives in a situation, making propositions, understanding proportions in mathematics, and solving problems on the basis of logic.

Language development and cognitive development are intimately interwoven with developmental patterns that must be taken into account when one is planning instruction or diagnosing dyslexia.

Finger Agnosia/Finger Localization

Finger agnosia refers to the relative, or absolute, inability to indicate which fingers, or how many, have been touched by an examiner. Children who have finger agnosia tend to have poor handwriting with inconsistent letter formation and size. In both spelling and reading they will transpose letters within words, such as *clam* for *calm*. They erase frequently and tend to have many strike-overs of letters. Their handwriting rate is slow, so that such children often cannot finish their work in the time allotted. Students with this problem are likely to do poorly on drawing tests, such as the Bender-Gestalt Test or the Slosson Drawing Coordination Test, thus confounding the findings.

Finger localization shows a progressive development beginning at about the age of four; by age eight or nine most tasks can be performed by the average child. The localization of stimulated single fingers on a tactual basis alone shows rapid development through years seven to nine. By the age of nine, performance is about 93 percent correct as compared with 67 percent by age six. Performance in the localization of single fingers on a tactual-visual basis is 98 percent by age eight, as compared with 88 percent by age six. Mental age has a strong influence on performance.[32]

A child can have finger agnosia and not be dyslexic. Yet all too frequently children with finger agnosia are misdiagnosed as being dyslexic because their writing and spelling errors are similar to those of the dyslexic. This test is sometimes administered to children at too early an age for any valid conclusions to be drawn from the results.

Myelination Within the Brain

Nerve cells in our brains contain a nucleus and a long fiber, or projection, of varying length (along which the nerve impulse travels) called the *axon,* and a diverse but extensive number of branching fibers of varying length called dendrites that reach outward toward other nerve cells. There is a fatty substance that covers the axon, called the *myelin sheath* (Figure 6.1). A nerve impulse is carried along the length of the axon, where it ends on various numbers of dendrites or cell bodies of other nerve cells.

What is important to our discussion on early identification of dyslexia is that the myelination process of a nerve axon is not completed until late childhood.[33,34] This type of maturation in the brain is said to have implications in teaching abstract concepts and certainly could affect the validity of early identification of dyslexia in very young students.

Some Other Matters to Consider in the Identification of Dyslexia

There are other matters that need to be taken into account, and to which common sense should be applied, when attempting any early identification of problems in young students. A child just simply may not care for the

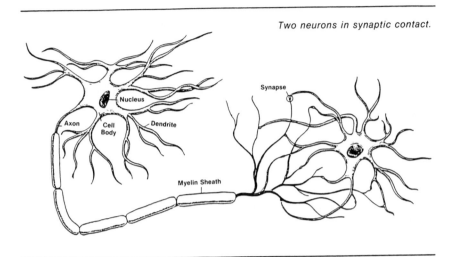

Two neurons in synaptic contact.

Figure 6.1   Myelin sheath encasing the axon. (From *The Brain*, by Richard M. Restak, New York: Bantam, © 1984, p. 27)

whole idea of school and would far prefer to stay home. He may have a "personality conflict" with his teacher and have no desire to please her, particularly with progress in schoolwork. It is possible, too, that he may have hostile feelings toward his parents, who pressure him to read—and so he won't. It is conceivable that a child just may not understand at the time what reading and writing are all about, and thus may not be at all interested in learning, in which case more time is needed for barriers to be overcome and for the business of learning to get under way.

Reading Readiness Tests

What about reading readiness tests? Don't they examine some of the very factors that have been discussed in this chapter?

Of course they do. They can be used to *help* a teacher decide if a particular child is ready to be moved into formal reading instruction. A reading readiness test, along with a checklist of behavior and achievement in various areas based on observations, and probably some type of mental maturity test, can make a useful contribution to the teacher's experienced judgment.

But the results of a reading readiness test should never be used alone to make a decision for formal reading instruction or in an attempt at early identification of dyslexia. They are by no means infallible. The range of positive correlation with school achievement is from .40 to .70 for most major reading readiness tests. This may be fairly substantial for a whole group, but it is of little value in predicting the achievement of an individual student. Clearly, the prediction for success (or lack of success) in reading does not hold for a large percentage of the children taking the test. In any case, readiness for reading cannot be equated with the actual reading process. Reading readiness serves as a foundation for and a bridge *into* reading.

Reading readiness tests may reveal certain areas of weakness as well as strengths to help the teacher in planning certain activities, but a child is not just a collection of various skills. (Nor is reading.) The *whole* child is involved in learning. Reading readiness tests and other types of developmental tests do *not* specify which students are dyslexic and which are not.

Summary

Early attempts at identification of dyslexia—prior to the age of eight—are ill-advised. Many of the symptoms of dyslexia are related to the normal developmental growth of the child, mentally and physically, so the possibility of misdiagnosis is great. Unfortunately, such misdiagnoses are being made. Misdiagnoses not only harm children but also create a great credibility gap when such findings are examined by experts in child growth and development, who are aware of the relationship of maturation to reading, writing, and spelling. This, no doubt, has contributed to the present confusion about dyslexia.

As far as possible, the developmental factors contributing to dyslexia-like symptoms must be ruled out first. For example, at the present time there is no valid way to determine whether the reversal of *b* and *d* in a six- or seven-year-old is due to the level of development of visual discrimination and spatial perception or to dyslexia.

It *is* possible, of course, to determine if a vision defect is contributing to certain problems. It should be possible to discover if a child has been taught the phonic elements in isolation, thus viewing the *d, i,* and *g* in the word *dig* as three separate elements, rather than viewing the word as an entity, and tending to reverse either the *d* or *g*.

The instruction of a child must be considered in any diagnosis as a possible cause of certain types of errors similar to those caused by dyslexia. The school curriculum must be considered from the standpoint of whether a child has had the opportunity to learn certain information. For example, the days of the week and the months of the year are usually part of the dyslexia test battery. One must ask: Is a child unable to say these in sequence because he is dyslexic, or simply because he has not yet had an opportunity to *learn* them in school? Common sense must be applied in any such situation.

When the dyslexic pattern of errors persists and the child gets older and moves through the grades, then our concern is with a correct diagnosis followed as soon as possible by a program of remediation designed to alleviate the various difficulties which result from this very real disability.

Notes

1. Emerald Dechant, *Diagnosis and Remediation of Reading Disabilities* (Englewood Cliffs, N.J.: Prentice-Hall, 1981), p. 164.

2. Albert J. Harris and Edward R. Sipay, *How to Increase Reading Ability,* 7th ed. revised (New York: Longman, 1980), p. 28.

3. Eldon E. Ekwall, *Diagnosis and Remediation of the Disabled Reader* (Boston: Allyn and Bacon, 1976), p. 198.

4. George Kaluger and Clifford J. Kolson, *Reading and Learning Disabilities* (Columbus, Ohio: Charles E. Merrill, 1978), p. 128.

5. Dechant, op. cit., p. 164.

6. (a) Moyer and Newcomer note that "For many years, the tendency of many children to reverse letters or words when they write or read has received a great amount of attention in education. Although this behavior is recognized as normal in 5 or 6 year old children and is expected to disappear without special attention during the first or second grade, it causes concern when it persists beyond that time." Sandra B. Moyer and Phyllis L. Newcomer, "Reversals in Reading: Diagnosis and Remediation," *Exceptional Children* 43 (April 1977), p. 424.

(b) Gibson studied the development of visual discrimination of letter-like forms for 167 children aged four through eight, in kindergarten through third grade. Findings indicate that there is the greatest developmental change between ages four and eight years in the tendency to confuse rotations and reversals, with line-to-curve errors showing the next greatest drop (p. 901). Errors in rotations and reversals were high at age four, but for the eight-year-olds these had declined to zero. Errors for changes of lines to curves were relatively high for the four-year-olds, but dropped for the eight-year-olds. At age four, all differences were significant; at ages five, six, and seven, all but one of the six differences were significant (p. 900). As a validity check, the experiment was repeated with real letters and the same letter-like forms. While fewer errors were made for the letters (the children were also two months older by now), the same developmental results occurred, and the correlations between transformations were significant in every case. "Overall errors decreased with age . . ." (p. 905). Eleanor J. Gibson, James J. Gibson, Anne D. Pick, and Harry Osser, "A Developmental Study of the Discrimination of Letter-Like Forms," *Journal of Comparative and Physiological Psychology* 55 (1962), pp. 897–906.

(c) George and Evelyn Spache note that "Reversals are seldom present among individuals who read above primary levels. Their frequency drops markedly as the reader matures, demonstrating that they are not due to handedness, mixed eye-hand dominance, or lack of cerebral dominance, as some writers suggest. If reversals were due to anatomical relationships, they would not disappear while handedness, eyedness, and the like persisted. In fact, most research studies show no consistent relationship between reversals and these physical factors. The error is characteristic of the beginning reader and it spontaneously disappears as skills improve." George D. Spache and Evelyn B. Spache, *Reading in the Elementary School*, 5th ed. (Boston: Allyn and Bacon, 1986), p. 449.

(d) Kennedy studied reversals of letters and words in kindergarten, first- and second-grade students in three Pasadena city schools (California) and found a steady decrease in reversal errors as the students got older. She concluded that reversal errors of all the types studied are normal for students in the earliest grades, and that it is equally normal for such reversal errors practically to disappear as the child progresses through the first several grades. Helen Kennedy, "Reversals, Reversals, Reversals!" *Journal of Experimental Education* 23 (December 1954), pp. 165, 169.

7. Arthur W. Heilman, Timothy R. Blair, and William H. Rupley, *Principles and Practices of Teaching Reading,* 5th ed. (Columbus, Ohio: Charles E. Merrill, 1981), p. 104.

8. Harris and Sipay, op. cit., p. 26.

9. Dainis Turaids, Joseph M. Wepman, and Anne Morency, "A Perceptual Test Battery: Development and Standardization," *Elementary School Journal* 72 (1972), p. 352.

10. Anne Morency, "Auditory Modality, Research and Practice," *Perception and Reading*, Helen K. Smith, ed., (Newark, Del.: International Reading Association, 1968), Vol. 12, Part 4, p. 18.

11. Dechant, op. cit., p. 250.

12. Ibid., p. 252.

13. James W. Beers, "Developmental Strategies of Spelling Competence in Primary School Children," *Developmental and Cognitive Aspects of Learning to Spell: A Reflection of Word Knowledge*, Edmund H. Henderson and James W. Beers, eds. (Newark, Del.: International Reading Association, 1980), pp. 36–45.

14. J. Richard Gentry, "An Analysis of Developmental Spelling in GNYS AT WRK," *The Reading Teacher* 36 (November 1982), pp. 192–200; "Learn to Spell Developmentally," *The Reading Teacher* 34 (January 1981), pp. 378–381.

15. Paul C. Burns and Betty L. Broman, *The Language Arts in Childhood Education* (Chicago: Rand McNally College, 1979), pp. 330, 338.

16. Gertrude A. Boyd, *Teaching Communication Skills in the Elementary School* (New York: Van Nostrand Reinhold, 1970), p. 44.

17. Virgil E. Herrick, "Children's Experiences in Writing," *Children and the Language Arts*, Virgil E. Herrick and Leland B. Jacobs, eds. (Englewood Cliffs, N.J.: Prentice-Hall, 1955), pp. 271–72.

18. Boyd, op. cit., p. 44.

19. Louis Ada Wilson, "A Study of Some Influencing Factors Upon and the Nature

of Young Children's Written Language," *Journal of Experimental Education* 31 (1963), p. 374.

20. Albert J. Harris and Edward R. Sipay, *How to Teach Reading* (New York: Longman, 1979), p. 42. Also: Edwards, Alley, and Snider in an investigation found no evidence that a diagnosis of minimal brain dysfunction based on a pediatric neurological evaluation and/or visual-motor impairment as measured by the Bender-Gestalt is a useful predictor of academic achievement. The investigators deem that a multidisciplinary approach is necessary in the diagnosis of learning problems. R. Phillips Edwards, Gordon R. Alley, and William Snider, "Academic Achievement and Minimal Brain Dysfunction," *Journal of Learning Disabilities* 4 (March 1971), pp. 17, 20.

21. Elizabeth M. Koppitz, *The Bender Gestalt Test for Young Children* (New York: Grune and Stratton, 1971), pp. 38–39. Also: Spache states, "If the Bender gave some diagnostic information for the teacher . . . there might be some justification for its use in readiness testing. But in view of its unreliability and lack of constructive interpretation I could not recommend it." George D. Spache, *Diagnosing and Correcting Reading Disabilities*, 2nd ed. (Boston: Allyn and Bacon, 1981), p. 38.

22. Dechant, op. cit., p. 256.

23. Arthur L. Benton, "Right-Left Discrimination," *Pediatric Clinics of North America* 15 (1968), p. 753; *Right-Left Discrimination and Finger Localization, Development and Pathology* (New York: Harper and Brothers, 1959), pp. 27, 36.

24. Spache, op. cit., p. 44.

25. Katherine Snow, "A Comparative Study of Sound Substitutions Used by 'Normal' First Grade Children," *Speech Monographs* 31 (1964), pp. 138, 141.

26. Mildred C. Templin, "The Study of Articulation and Language Development During the Early School Years," *The Genesis of Language, A Psycholinguistic Approach*, Frank Smith and George A. Miller, eds. (Cambridge, Mass.: MIT Press, 1966), pp. 176–77.

27. Alvin M. Liberman, "General Discussion: Temple Presentation," *The Genesis of Language, A Psycholinguistic Approach*, Frank Smith and George A. Miller, eds. (Cambridge, Mass.: MIT Press, 1966), p. 183.

28. Boyd, op. cit., p. 110.

29. David S. Palermo and Dennis L. Molfese, "Language Acquisition From Age Five Onward," *Psychological Bulletin* 78 (December 1972), p. 422. Also: The left side of the angular gyrus (inferior parietal lobule in the brain) is critical for receptive language and is the last cortical area to reach full cellular development, often not until late childhood. Paul Satz and Sara S. Sparrow, "Specific Developmental Dyslexia: A Theoretical Formulation," *Specific Reading Disability, Advances in Theory and Method*, Dirk J. Bakker and Paul Satz, eds. (The Netherlands: Rotterdam University Press, 1970), p. 25.

30. Paula Menyuk, "Middle and Late Childhood," *Language and Maturation* (Cambridge, Mass.: MIT Press, 1977), pp. 89–122.

31. Jean Piaget, "The Stages of the Intellectual Development of the Child," *Readings in Child Development and Personality*, Paul Henry Mussen, John J. Conger, and Jerome Kagan, eds. (New York: Harper and Row, 1965, 1970), pp. 196–97.

32. Benton (1959), op. cit., pp. 67–69, 145.

33. Drake D. Duane, "A Neurologic Overview of Specific Language Disability for the Non-Neurologist," *Bulletin of the Orton Society* 25 (1974), p. 15.

34. William H. Calvin and George A. Ojemann, *Inside the Brain* (New York: New American Library, 1980), p. 193.

CHAPTER 7

FIVE CHILDREN: DYSLEXIC OR NOT?

There are no unteachable children. There are only
schools and teachers and parents who fail to teach them.
—*Mortimer J. Adler*

No bubble is so iridescent or floats longer than that
blown by the successful teacher.
—*Sir William Osler*

In order to illustrate the hazard of attempting to diagnose serious
problems in young students, I have summarized the reading achievements of
five children as they progressed through kindergarten and the early elementary grades. All of these children were of average or above average intelligence. Their profiles indicate their individual patterns and will help in
understanding why a too-early "diagnosis" of dyslexia can be perilous.

Mary

Mary's growth in reading was steady throughout her early school years.
Her progress record is typical of many children. She was a stable, self-
confident child, somewhat large for her age. With her birthday in February,
she was not a "young" kindergarten child when she began school. In fact,
she was almost a year older than some of the children in her class. She was
popular with her classmates and teacher and often was chosen as a leader in
group activities. She enjoyed story and reading time, and when she was in
kindergarten and first grade she would pick up picture books and sit quietly
looking at them. As she acquired independent reading skills, she began

reading books on her own whenever she could. Fortunately, she was in a school where the principal's priority was for "the teachers to have the tools to do the job," and so each classroom had a variety of books at different levels for the students to use during their free-reading time, for which time was set aside each day in addition to the time a child might have after finishing the assigned work.

As Mary moved up through the grades, her teachers reported that her enjoyment of reading served as a motivation for her to finish her seatwork quickly, so that she would have additional time for reading.

Mary liked to write stories. She quickly mastered manuscript writing and began writing short stories of her own, which she would illustrate. Her writing was well formed and was soon reduced in size, and she began writing on one line instead of two. She probably could have learned cursive easily in the second grade, but she was in a school system where cursive writing was introduced in the third grade. At that time her teacher, who individualized handwriting instruction, decided that Mary could begin instruction right away. Mary then learned cursive writing very quickly, and her writing was excellent.

From the beginning her spelling showed good progress. Her visual

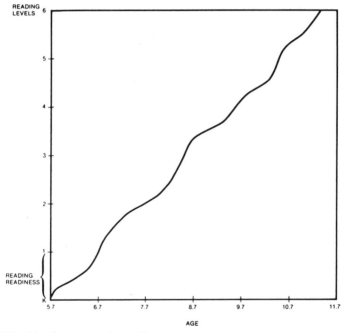

Figure 7.1   Mary's progress in reading.

memory was strong, and she retained the irregular spellings of words with little difficulty.

When administered the reading readiness test at the beginning of first grade, Mary's scores in all areas were high. The prediction then, based on testing and observations, was that she would perform successfully in reading. This she did, as indicated by her reading achievement progress profile (see Figure 7.1).

Tommy

Tommy was a little live wire, full of energy, curious, not the least bit interested in sitting at his desk and doing his seatwork. Fortunately for Tommy, his kindergarten teacher believed that this was a time for children to continue to grow and develop in all areas, not just in academic skills. Periods of inactivity and sitting quietly were interspersed with periods of action and movement, singing and dancing, acting out stories, finger painting, working with clay, pretending to be animals or butterflies or trains or whatever.

Readiness groups were set up after the Christmas holidays, and by the end of the year a couple of the children were beginning to read. A reading readiness test was given at the end of kindergarten, and Tommy's scores were somewhat low. In the fall, after several weeks of school, Tommy's first grade teacher gave the reading readiness test again to use as a diagnostic instrument to give her some direction as to his areas of weakness and strength. His scores were just about the same as in kindergarten.

He had some reversal problems, confusing b with d, and p with q. The possibility of dyslexia did not enter the teacher's mind. Again Tommy was fortunate, for his teacher understood that he was somewhat immature for his age. (He was born in June.) She gave him work that he could do at his level of achievement.

The teacher set up groups within her class according to the different children's needs. At first all were in various readiness groups, but six children were soon moved into a formalized reading group and began their practical charts and preprimers. The teacher used experience charts with all groups and for many different activities. Tommy was happy in first grade. It did not bother him that he was only at the primer level by the end of the school year. It did bother his parents, who thought that Tommy would do better with a teacher who "used more structure" than those Tommy had had in kindergarten and first grade. They asked the principal to place Tommy in Mrs. X's class the following year because she had the reputation of being a strict disciplinarian.

Tommy's second-grade year was disastrous. His teacher arranged the chairs in rows rather than in nests of tables because "this kept children out of mischief and their hands to themselves." She had only three reading groups, and Tommy was in the lowest. While she worked with one group, the other children had workbook pages and dittoed seatwork sheets "to keep them busy and quiet," and when this was done there was always work to copy off the chalkboard.

Tommy never got to the chalkboard work; he rarely finished his seat-work, and every day he had to take the incomplete work home with him to finish after school. He resented having to stay in afternoons when he wanted to climb the big tree in his yard and work on the tree house with his buddy. He resented losing the "privilege" of swimming with a "bunch of the guys" at a nearby indoor pool each Saturday because he always had all that unfinished schoolwork to do. His parents told him that when he began doing his work at school as he was supposed to, he could do these other things. And his mother reported that she resented having to sit with him every afternoon when he got home from school to see that the work got done, as well as after dinner when she had to bathe the baby, get her to bed, and get the supper dishes washed.

What happened to Tommy? He became balky and moody, both at school and at home. He was not a happy child. His scores took a nose dive. He was still confusing b with d and would often write the capital B for the lower case, as in BaBy. The teacher suggested to his parents that this was a symptom of dyslexia, which Tommy probably had, and she went on to say that there was nothing much that could be done for children like that. She recommended that Tommy repeat the second grade.

The parents, in turn, talked with the principal and explained Tommy's problems in class. The principal did not say much other than that perhaps Miss Jones should be his third grade teacher. Since the parents were not very happy about the possibility of Tommy repeating the second grade, they agreed to this arrangement.

Third grade was a completely different story. Miss Jones was a bubbly, enthusiastic, creative teacher. It was obvious that she enjoyed being with children and teaching. After a few weeks of various activities—games for reviewing vocabulary words and skills, easy reading books for some children and picture books for others, lots of experience chart stories (and always a positive attitude with Tommy and the other children) and keeping them busy in ways other than with workbooks and dittoed skill sheets—Miss Jones administered several tests so as to set up various groups in her classroom according to the individual needs of the children.

She called Tommy's parents in for a conference and tactfully suggested that they "back off a bit" and lessen the pressure on Tommy. She shared the information she had obtained from her testing and explained what she intended to do to help Tommy. The parents returned home, encouraged about Tommy's school situation, still worried somewhat but optimistic about his third-grade year with Miss Jones.

Within a very short time, Tommy's attitude and performance showed a dramatic change. His progress soared steadily, and it continued to rise. By the end of the third grade he was reading at the third-grade, first-semester level—a big jump from the preprimer level to which he had sunk in the second grade. As shown by Figure 7.2 illustrating Tommy's progress, by the end of the fourth grade Tommy was just moving into the fifth-grade level.

Suppose Tommy had been diagnosed as being dyslexic on the basis of his low kindergarten scores or first-grade scores as part of some early identification program. Was his slow start due to developmental factors, or to dyslexia? Was his drop in achievement in the second grade due to dyslexia as his teacher suggested, or to his school experience, his relationship with his teacher, her teaching style, and the quality of instruction?

Of course Tommy was not dyslexic, or he could never have made such rapid progress in the third grade and thereafter. It is probable that had his second-grade classroom been different, things would have fallen into place sooner and his achievements would have been even higher in the later grades.

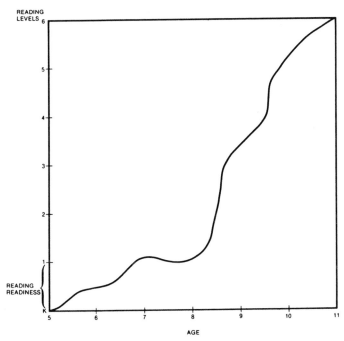

Figure 7.2 Tommy's progress in reading.

Sue

Sue was a September birthday child. Her progress was a bit slow until third grade, when she began performing on grade level. Then her progress speeded up, and by the time she was ten years old and in the fifth grade she was reading over a year above grade level.

Her profile shows plateaus amidst her rising progress in reading. Such plateaus are typical in children's learning. In Sue's case, she got off to a slow start, achieving mediocre to low scores on the reading readiness test; but, given time to mature, with nurturing and understanding, encouragement and quality instruction, she took off and progressed steadily. Her progress is shown in Figure 7.3.

Had Sue been mistakenly identified as a dyslexic or a child with learning disabilities on the basis of her slow start and test scores, her story might well have been different. Luckily for Sue, she was in a school where the principal and teachers understood the developmental factors that may temporarily affect early progress in school. They were ready to give her special help if she did not begin to improve, but no intervention became necessary.

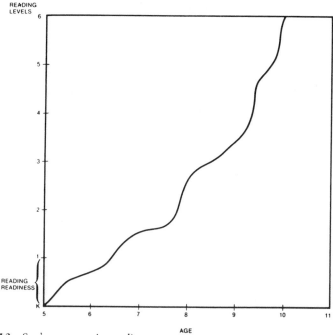

Figure 7.3 Sue's progress in reading.

Larry

Larry was born in November, and thus was a young child in kindergarten. Some of his classmates were almost a year older. He was small for his age and the youngest child in his family. It was especially difficult for his mother to let go of him, her last little chick, and Larry sensed her reluctance. The first few weeks of kindergarten were rough for all: child, teacher, parent. Eventually, the transition was made, and the tears ended.

Larry's scores were low on the various developmental tests and on the reading readiness test administered at the conclusion of kindergarten. They were still low when the test was administered again a few weeks after first grade began. The predictions were that he would be likely to continue to have problems and that his progress would be slow. Larry's parents were greatly concerned and had frequent conferences with his teachers and the principal. They kept insisting that more special testing be done, and toward the end of the first grade this was arranged. The school evaluation team consisted of his classroom teacher, a school psychologist, a learning disabilities teacher, a Chapter I reading teacher, and a special education supervisor. It was agreed that Larry showed many of the symptoms associated with dyslexia. And this was the diagnosis.

The next year Larry began going to a special learning class for one hour three times a week. He was not happy doing this, and told his parents that "there are a bunch of dummies in there and I'm *not* a dummy!" He also told his parents that all they did was work on phonics skill sheets in workbooks. He was happy, however, with his second-grade teacher, who planned special work for him at his level, encouraged him to act out stories he had heard or read, and gave him much positive encouragement. Toward the end of the second grade she was sure that he was beginning to make progress at a faster rate. She suggested to his parents that they contact a reading specialist acquaintance of hers and make arrangements to have him tutored over the summer on a regular basis. She also cautioned them to avoid pressuring him and to let him enjoy the summer activities attractive to a boy his age.

Larry hit it off right away with the reading specialist, who was quite creative, had a variety of concrete and interesting materials to use, and provided challenging and exciting reading, spelling, and writing experiences for each session.

Larry's chart shows the startling change in his rate of achievement. At the beginning of third grade, at the recommendation of the tutor and the parents, Larry was not put in any special classes. The parents did request the reading specialist to continue to work with him one afternoon a week on a private basis. This she did for about six months. By fourth grade, Larry was reading comfortably at grade level, as can be seen by his progress in Figure 7.4.

Larry had been diagnosed as dyslexic because of his poor performance in early testing. Had he been tested at age eight, no such diagnosis would have been made.

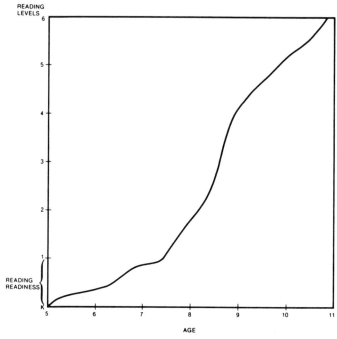

Figure 7.4   Larry's progress in reading.

Bruce

Bruce's chart is similar to Larry's in kindergarten and the early grades, except that Bruce repeated the second grade. Unlike Larry, Bruce did not begin to show rapid progress, but continued in his poor achievement.

Bruce came to the clinic when he was ten years old, reading on a first-grade level. An analysis of the total test findings and observations revealed that Bruce did have dyslexia.

An examination of Bruce's school records indicated that at first Bruce was considered just immature. As time went on his parents were told that he could do the work if he weren't so lazy, but that he also needed more time to grow up. He was retained in second grade because of his low reading achievement, but he was also having serious problems in arithmetic. All this was very upsetting to Bruce, who knew that he was having trouble and was not doing the same level of work as most of his classmates but could not understand why he could not move to the next grade with his friends. (Later, in the clinic, he told me that he used to go home after school and crawl under his bed and cry, holding an old blanket against his face to muffle any sound.)

His progress in second grade the second time around was no better. (See Figure 7.5.) It was as though he sat in class each day and nothing happened, according to the end-of-the-year achievement test scores. The school did not want to retain him again at the lower level, and he was promoted to the third grade, where his teacher took a special interest in him. She sensed something was really wrong. She "didn't know what, but there was something there I couldn't put my finger on." She knew that Bruce was intellectually capable of learning because she had the results of a special school psychological test. Bruce made a little progress during his year with her, but very little.

In January, his teacher called his parents and asked that they come in for a conference. At that time she recommended that they contact me for possible diagnostic testing. Bruce attended school some forty miles away, and for various reasons no testing could be done until the following summer, when his parents enrolled him in our summer clinic.

Bruce's mother and father were deeply concerned about him. They had continued in their support of Bruce and had done some of the things many parents do in such cases. They had gone along with the school for a while, then blamed the first-grade teacher (she "didn't push phonics" hard enough), proceeded to have his vision and hearing checked by medical doctors, and visited a psychologist for mental tests and to discover why his attitude was so bad and why he would not work at school.

Bruce began wetting his bed, and his parents decided on their own that the pressure of everything was just too much for him. They stopped the visits to the psychologist, whose office was about fifty miles from their home and caused a major logistical problem because both parents were working. There was no change either for the better or the worse, except in the summer Bruce stopped wetting his bed.

Being kept back in school had upset Bruce so much that he refused to play anymore with two of his neighborhood friends, who had been in his class but had moved on to third grade when Bruce stayed back. Up to this time, in spite of his problems in school, Bruce had always been popular with the children in both his class and his neighborhood, and he had been something of a leader, sometimes into mischief. He was a good swimmer

Figure 7.5   Bruce's progress in reading.

and had been on the swimming team at the neighborhood swimming pool. Now he began to shun activities and to become something of a loner.

Bruce was feeling that sense of failure, frustration, and loss of self-esteem so common to children with his difficulty and experiences. We would have liked to have begun work with him a year earlier, before such feelings had taken a toll, yet after the required time for the maturational pattern to unfold. For Bruce, intervention came at a good enough time to help him with his problem, and before he had developed the hard, protective facade frequently acquired by dyslexics as a coping device, which often fools others into thinking the young student means it when he says he doesn't really care—about learning, about school, about anything.

This is nonsense, of course, for children like Bruce *do care* —very much.

CHAPTER 8

THE HISTORICAL DEVELOPMENT OF THE CONCEPT OF DYSLEXIA

Progress, therefore, is not an
accident, but a necessity.
—*Herbert Spencer*

The concept of dyslexia has its roots in two other types of disorders. One is alexia, which refers to a condition in persons who were previously literate but who have lost their ability to read as a result of an acquired disease of or injury to the central nervous system. Alexia (note the prefix "a" which means "without") is thus different from dyslexia, which refers to the disability that *prevents* the child from normally acquiring the developmental reading skills. Alexics *could* read at one time. The other type of disorder is aphasia, which is the loss of speech.

Some Early Connections

The early findings that showed that the ability to read might be impaired by brain damage have led to many current investigations of the neurological abnormalities in children with severe reading, writing, and spelling difficulties. In 1834, Professor Lordat of Montpellier, France, who had recovered from a speech disorder in 1825, described his previous inability to make sense of the printed word.[1] He could hear and understand words, but had lost his ability to read. He wrote:

The alphabet alone was left me, but the function of the letters for the formation of words was a study yet to be made. When I wished to glance over the book which I was reading before my malady overcame me, I found it impossible to read the title. I shall not speak to you of my despair, you can imagine it. I had to spell out slowly most of the words, and I can tell you by the way how much I realized the absurdity of the spelling of our language. After several weeks of profound sadness and resignation, I discovered whilst looking from a distance at the back of one of the volumes in my library, that I was reading accurately the title *Hippocratis Opera*. This discovery caused me to shed tears of joy.[2]

Lordat's story had a happy ending, for his loss of the ability to read was temporary. The point here is that this problem occurred in connection with a speech disorder. As time went on, other physicians described instances of patients who had aphasia and became unable to read.

In 1872, Sir William H. Broadbent,[3] physician to and joint lecturer on medicine at St. Mary's Hospital, London, described a case to the Medical and Chirurgical Society where a man suffered an acute cerebral attack after which he was unable to read printed or written words, except his own name. The patient, Charles D., wrote correctly from dictation and wrote letters with a little prompting, but could not read what he had written. He conversed intelligently, using an extensive vocabulary, but occasionally forgot names, streets, persons, and objects. He was unable to name his arms or legs or the colors of things. The man died soon afterwards from another vascular attack. An autopsy revealed one new and two old lesions ("clots") in his brain. Broadbent believed that one of the older lesions caused the reading difficulty because of its specific location in the man's brain, the left angular (and supramarginal) gyrus. Figure 8.1 shows the location of the angular gyrus in the brain, as well as the location of other areas specifically involved in the language process.

In this case the patient could speak and pronounce words correctly and could write from dictation, but he could not recall certain names nor could he read.

In 1877, a German physician, Adolph Kussmaul, coined the term "word-blindness." He noted that while the ability to read could be lost, vision, the power of speech, and the intellect might remain.[4]

Kussmaul (and Broadbent) were among the first to point out that word-blindness could be dealt with clinically as an isolated condition, and that it represented the pathological condition of a special faculty.[5]

In 1877, Dr. Rudolf Berlin of Germany coined the term dyslexia (dys-lexie) as an alternative to word-blindness. Berlin had collected six case histories over a period of twenty-three years. In each case, the patient's manner of reading was the same. Each could read the first three to five words, but no more. Their speech remained fully intact.[6]

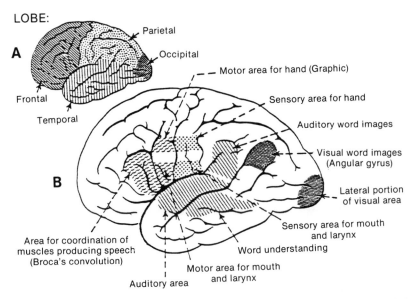

Figure 8.1 (A) Lobes of the surface of the left hemisphere of the brain, and (B) the hemispheric sites involved in the language processes. (Used with permission from "A Neurologic Overview of Specific Language Disability for the Non-Neurologist," by Drake D. Duane in *Bulletin of the Orton Society* 24, p. 13, 1974)

Dyslexia—Congenital?

The suggestion that dyslexia might be a congenital (constitutional) problem probably began with the reports of Doctors James Hinshelwood, W. Pringle Morgan, and James Kerr.

Dr. Hinshelwood[7] was an ophthalmologist in Glasgow, Scotland. He was surgeon to the Glasgow Eye Infirmary and assistant to the professor of clinical medicine at the University of Glasgow. Over a number of years, various persons had come to him because of their sudden loss of the ability to read, and they thought that the problem might be the result of a vision defect, which proved not to be the case. The patients had lost their reading ability after "fits" or strokes or periods of extreme mental worry.

From 1895 on, Dr. Hinshelwood wrote a series of papers for *The Lancet* about these alexics. He noted that (1) some could recognize the individual letters of the alphabet but not words, (2) some could read a few words and then no more (similar to Dr. Berlin's patients), (3) some could recognize neither letters nor words but could recognize Arabic numerals, and (4) some could read words but not letters. Among these, some patients tended to lose their way in familiar surroundings.

Then, in 1900, within two months of one another, two boys, ages ten and eleven, were brought to Dr. Hinshelwood because the medical attendants where they were examined suspected that their difficulty in learning to read might be due to some cerebral problem. These boys were intelligent but were having an extremely hard time in school. Hinshelwood observed that their symptoms and problems with reading were similar to those that appeared in adults who had suffered brain injuries and lost their ability to read. He also noted that there were often several cases of such reading problems in one family. Hinshelwood noted further that these two cases were excellent examples of different degrees of "congenital word-blindness" in which there were congenital deficiencies in visual memory for words and letters. He also reported on two other congenital word-blindness cases that he had read about in an article by Dr. W. Pringle Morgan, whom Hinshelwood credited with reporting the first case of congenital word-blindness.

Dr. Morgan was a general practitioner who lived in the small town of Seaford in Sussex, in the southern part of England. He had become acquainted with a fourteen-year-old boy, Percy F., who was the oldest son of an intelligent family. In 1896, Morgan wrote a report for the *British Medical Journal* in which he described some of Percy's problems. Morgan had read Dr. Hinshelwood's article on word-blindness and visual memory, published in *The Lancet* in 1895, concerning adults with alexia. Morgan could find no reference anywhere to the possibility that the condition was congenital, and yet Percy F. had had trouble learning to read from his earliest schooling. Morgan stated that Percy's condition followed "upon no injury or illness" and was "evidently congenital, and due most probably to defective development of that region of the brain, disease of which in adults produces practically the same symptoms—that is, the left angular gyrus."[8] (See Figure 8.1.) Morgan wrote:

> His great difficulty has been—and is now—his inability to learn to read. This inability is so markable, and so pronounced, that I have no doubt it is due to some congenital defect. . . .
>
> The following is the result of an examination I made a short time since. He knows all his letters and can write them and read them. In writing from dictation he comes to grief over any but the simplest words. For instance, I dictated the following sentence: "Now, you watch me while I spin it." He wrote: "Now you word me wale I spin it"; and again, "Carefully winding the string round the peg" was written: "Calfuly winder the sturng rond the Pag."
>
> In writing his own name he made a mistake, putting "Precy" for "Percy," and he did not notice the mistake until his attention was called to it more than once. . . .
>
> I then asked him to read me a sentence out of an easy child's book

without spelling the words. The result was curious. He did not read a single word correctly, with the exception of "and," "the," "of," "that," etc.; the other words seemed to be quite unknown to him, and he could not even make an attempt to pronounce them. . . .

He seems to have no power of preserving and storing up the visual impression produced by words—hence the words, though seen, have no significance for him. His visual memory for words is defective or absent; which is equivalent to saying that he is what Kassmaul has termed "word blind." . . .

I may add that the boy is bright and of average intelligence in conversation . . . his eyesight is good. The schoolmaster who has taught him for some years says that he would be the smartest lad in the school if the instruction were entirely oral.[9]

A short time later, in 1897, Dr. James Kerr, a school medical officer of Bradford, in the Midlands of England, wrote a school hygiene essay in which he called attention to mentally intelligent children with problems similar to Percy F.'s who were extreme cases needing consideration by the school and teachers.[10]

Dr. Hinshelwood continued to collect data on such cases, which were now referred to as "congenital word-blindness," and he published another book on the subject in 1917. Others began reporting similar observations over the following years, with the result that "word-blindness" in those early days was suspected as due to either cerebral damage or a congenital defect in children with normal or undamaged brains.

In the United States, a neuropsychiatrist, Dr. Samuel T. Orton, had been observing some children with reading and writing problems who reversed letters and seemed to find it easier to write from right to left. He coined a new term, "strephosymbolia" (from the Greek), which literally means the turning or twisting of symbols. Dr. Orton believed that these difficulties were due to an abnormality of brain function, a confusion in the memory images of symbols. Like Hinshelwood, Orton considered that the problem was congenital. Orton, however, suggested that strephosymbolia was caused by the genetically determined failure of one brain hemisphere to assume the dominant role in mediating language and speech functions.[11] But this theory has never gained general acceptance because the patterns of reading, writing, and spelling mistakes of dyslexic children cannot be adequately explained in terms of such confused mirror images, and also because of the difficulty in testing the neurological propositions.[12,13,14,15]

It is interesting to note that Dr. Orton worked in the pathology department at the Boston City Hospital during his early career. This is the same institution where Dr. Albert Galaburda and Dr. Thomas Kemper studied the brain of their first childhood dyslexic.[16] (Dr. Orton's theory of strephosymbolia and results of dyslexic brain studies by Doctors Galaburda and Kemper, and others, are explained in more detail in the next chapter.)

Actually, as time has passed we have discovered that Dr. Orton was right about some things—and not right about others. He noted the high degree of similar problems in the families of his patients and the likelihood of a genetic factor, the preponderance of males having the condition, the frequency of delayed speech in some children, and the possible location of the difficulty in the brain. He was not right about the brain being symmetrical (the human brain is structurally asymmetrical) or about the disorder being present on both sides of the brain.[17]

Nevertheless, Dr. Orton is considered an American pioneer in dyslexia, and an organization dedicated to helping children with dyslexia and other learning disabilities has been named after him. His work and that of his disciples aroused interest in children who had severe problems in learning to read, with the result that papers about such children began appearing in the United States as well as in Europe.

Over the years, we have learned more about the localization of reading ability. While it was once believed to be in the region of the angular gyrus in the left hemisphere, we now know there is more to be considered. In man, the location of the angular gyrus is at the juncture of the parietal, temporal, and the occipital lobe association zones—all of which we now know are important in reading.[18]

Help on the Way

Help for the dyslexic child was on its way, although it would be some time before it would become effective. The deluge of papers, studies, and reports—some clear, some ambiguous; some objective, some biased; some valid, some not; some in agreement, some contradictory; some professional, some amateurish—contributed to the growing knowledge, yet also succeeded in muddying the waters of research and providing ammunition for the skeptics.

Notes

1. Macdonald Critchley, *The Dyslexic Child* (Springfield, Ill.: Charles C. Thomas, 1970), p. 1.
2. Ibid.
3. Sir William Henry Broadbent, "On the Cerebral Mechanism of Speech and

Thought," *Medico-Chirurgical Transactions,* The Royal Medical and Chirurgical Society of London 37 (London: Longman, Green, Reader, and Dyer, 1872), pp. 162–65.

4. Sandhya Naidoo, *Specific Dyslexia, The Research Report of the ICAA Word Blind Center for Dyslexic Children* (New York: John Wiley, 1972), p. 2. As time passed, more and more autopsies were performed and lesions, softenings, or hemorrhages in the occipito-parietal region of the left cerebral hemisphere were found in some of these persons. The occipital lobe and the parietal lobe are in the cortical areas behind the central fissure. (The latter is the slight furrow that runs downward from the top over the outer portion of the hemispheres, and with the longitudinal sulcus, a deep ditch running front to back, and the Sylvian fissure along the outer side of each hemisphere at about the level of the angle of the jaw—divides the cerebral hemispheres into artificially separate territories.)

5. James Hinshelwood, *Congenital Word-Blindness* (London: H.K. Lewis, 1917), p. 1.

6. Rudolph F. Wagner, "Rudolf Berlin: Originator of the Term Dyslexia," *Bulletin of the Orton Society* 23 (1973), pp. 60–61.

7. James Hinshelwood, "Word-blindness and Visual Memory," *The Lancet* (Dec. 21, 1895), pp. 1564–70; "A Case of Dyslexia: A Peculiar Form of Word-Blindness," *The Lancet* (Nov. 21, 1896), pp. 1451–54; "A Case of 'Word' without 'Letter' Blindness," *The Lancet* (Feb. 12, 1898), pp. 422–25; "'Letter' Without 'Word' Blindness," *The Lancet* (Jan. 14, 1899), pp. 85–86; "Congenital Word-Blindness," *The Lancet* (May 26, 1900), pp. 1506–8; *Congenital Word-Blindness* (London: H.K. Lewis, 1917), p. 77.

8. W. Pringle Morgan, "A Case of Congenital Word Blindness," *British Medical Journal* (Nov. 7, 1896), p. 1378.

9. Ibid.

10. James Kerr, "School Hygiene, in its Mental, Moral, and Physical Aspects," *Journal of the Royal Statistical Society* 60, (1897), p. 668.

11. Samuel T. Orton, "'Word-blindness' in School Children," *Archives of Neurology and Psychiatry* 14, No. 5 (November 1925), p. 610; *Reading, Writing, and Speech Problems in Children* (New York: W.W. Norton, 1937), pp. 68–118.

12. Donald G. Doehring, *Patterns of Impairment in Specific Reading Disability, A Neuropsychological Investigation* (Bloomington: Indiana University Press, 1968), p. 8.

13. M.D. Vernon, *Backwardness in Reading, A Study of its Nature and Origin* (Cambridge: Cambridge University, 1958), pp. 82–110.

14. Calvin Tomkins, "The Last Skill Acquired," *The New Yorker* 39 (Sept. 14, 1963), p. 146.

15. Naidoo, op. cit., p. 8.

16. Norman Geschwind, "Why Orton Was Right," *Annals of Dyslexia* 32 (1982), pp. 23–24.

17. Ibid., pp. 15–17, 19, 24–26.

18. George W. Hynd and Cynthia R. Hynd, "Dyslexia: Neuroanatomical/neurolinguistic Perspectives," *Reading Research Quarterly* 19 (Summer 1984), p. 488.

CHAPTER 9

WHAT CAUSES DYSLEXIA?

Somebody said that it couldn't be done,
But he with a chuckle replied,
That "maybe it couldn't,"
but he would be one
Who wouldn't say so till he'd tried.
—*Edgar Guest*

What causes dyslexia? Have the neurosurgeons, general medical practitioners, psychiatrists, geneticists, developmental experts, education specialists, or school psychologists finally found any answers over all these years? The answer is: maybe partially. Knowledge is accumulating, but until diagnoses become more consistently accurate, criteria of research more clearly established, reports of findings more carefully drawn, and until explorations of the functioning of the brain are more complete, and objectivity replaces concern for pet theories, no final answers can be expected.

The search must continue. In spite of all the barriers erected by those whose major interests lie elsewhere, in spite of all the criticisms of ill-informed skeptics, in spite of all the frustrations of working with contradictory reports and incomplete information, the search must continue for the sake of those who do have dyslexia. We can, in fact, diagnose dyslexia accurately, but accurate diagnosis does not necessarily imply any definitive answer as to the cause.

Common sense and high standards of professionalism must prevail in all cases. Undoubtedly, a major factor in extravagant claims concerning a "cure" for dyslexia is due to a misdiagnosis in the first place. For example, one person (a psychiatrist) claims to have cured "thousands" of dyslexics over the last ten years. He has attracted a good deal of attention in the media with the assertion that he has THE cause of dyslexia, and the cure is drugs and vitamins. However, upon reading his books, one finds that some of his "dyslexics" were excellent readers and spellers. (One excellent speller was a *proofreader!*) True, his child patients were having problems in school and at home, such as poor attitudes, dislike of schoolwork or school, inconsistency in work performance, headaches, stomach-aches, moodiness, emotional problems, hyperactivity, and so forth. He even made the statement that *all* of his "phobic patients were found to have dyslexia."

As of the present time, just what have we investigated? Why does dyslexia occur in a small percentage of the population? What is the progress to date?

Is Dyslexia Inherited?

Research on the question of whether genetics may be a factor in dyslexia has followed three principal directions. One is a behavioral approach that studies families of dyslexics and analyses of data on sets of twins. The study of twins particularly provides more accurate reflections of both the environmental and genetic contributions to the condition.

The second approach is cytogenetic. This deals with the phenomena of heredity and variation in relation to the formation of cells. Using elaborate cytogenetic techniques, the researcher studies chromosomes under a microscope to determine possible variations that may account for the disorder.

The third approach concerns the mapping of genes that cause disorders on specific chromosomes. Chromosomes carry the genes (hereditary determiners) like beads on a string (sometimes referred to as a "linear map"). Specific genes have fixed locations (called "loci"), and distances (linkage) between two loci can be estimated from the frequency of recombination between specific genes in the offspring. The more often two characteristics are associated with one another across several generations, the closer the two fixed locations are to each other. By finding one locus, one may approximate the location of a linked gene. By studying families in which there are multiple cases of dyslexia, the search for a gene that may be a cause of dyslexia can be narrowed.[1]

The progress of some investigations about the inheritance of dyslexia will be summarized according to the particular method of study used.

The Behavioral Approach

The first studies about possible genetic connections with dyslexia were mainly investigations on the concordance (both twins having dyslexia) of

identical (single-ovum/monozygotic) twins and the concordance of nonidentical (dizygotic) twins, or family history and pedigree analysis.

Studies of twins have been sparse, especially those dealing with dyslexia
(as opposed to "reading disability"), but the concordance has been 100
percent for identical twins and about 33 percent for nonidentical twins. The
conclusion that genetic factors must play a role in the occurrence of at least
some dyslexia is inescapable. Information on Hermann's[2] studies of forty-five
sets of twins and Zerbin-Rubin's[3] summary of ten studies of fifty-three sets of
twins is given in Appendix B.

What about the families of dyslexics? Is there a tendency in other
members of the family to have similar disabilities? A pedigree chart can
illustrate the affected and unaffected brothers, sisters, parents, and other
relatives of dyslexics and the distribution of dyslexia (if any) in families. One
should be aware of certain problems in making such a pedigree analysis with
regard to the occurrence of dyslexia in several successive generations. In the
case of the grandparents of the dyslexic child, it may be difficult to make a
diagnosis of dyslexia because the researcher may not be able to get the
satisfactory historical data. Even if one or more of the grandparents did have
dyslexia, the condition may have been relatively mild and could have been
unobserved for various reasons at that time. It is also possible that a dyslexic
adult may deny that he has dyslexia for one reason or another.

Figure 9.1 is an example of a pedigree chart of three generations. The
following symbols and abbreviations are used:

> Squares designate males.
> Circles designate females.
> Solid black indicates dyslexia.
> One slash indicates a person who was too young for diagnosis or who died
> before reaching the "age of manifestation."
> Crossed lines indicate data were lacking for an accurate diagnosis of
> dyslexia.

As can be seen by the chart, the grandfather was dyslexic; the grandmother was not. They had seven children of whom two sons and one
daughter were dyslexic. A son and daughter were definitely not dyslexic, but
the conditions of another son and daughter could not be determined because
of insufficient data. One dyslexic son married a nonaffected woman, and they
had two children, a dyslexic son and a daughter who was not dyslexic.
Another dyslexic son married a nonaffected woman and they had four
children, two of whom were dyslexic, one daughter who was not, and one
son who was too young for a diagnosis of dyslexia to be made. Dyslexia is
known to have occurred in three generations in this case.

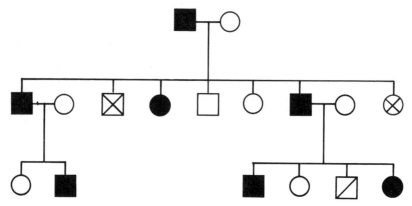

Figure 9.1   Pedigree chart of dyslexia for three generations.

Figure 9.2 is a pedigree chart prepared by Hallgren.[4] The dyslexic child was sent to him by his colleagues, and he was able to trace dyslexia for four generations. He reported that the majority of the members of this family were very talented, and their intellectual capacity was high. Nonetheless, dyslexia caused definite difficulties at school and later in life for family members who did have the condition. The numbers 1, 2, 3, and 4 on the chart show the four generations of dyslexics. Members with A? have suspected specific arithmetical disability. The letter N by the youngest dyslexic indicates that he is a "problem child."

Since the family was "selected," Hallgren did not include it in his genetic-statistical analysis of dyslexia in 112 families. Here he found that in ninety families, one parent had dyslexia. In three families, both parents had dyslexia. In nineteen families, neither parent was dyslexic. Direct inheritance in three generations was found in twenty families. In four of these families, two or more affected members belonging to the same generation had dyslexia.[5]

These two pedigree charts merely indicate the condition of dyslexia as it occurred in families. There was no differentiation as to the type of dyslexia. This "lumping" of all dyslexics into a single entity or category has not been useful in identifying a uniform pattern of transmission.

Later studies of families by Omenn and Weber[6] indicated differences in the dyslexic condition. They found that visual-predominant dyslexia tended to cluster in families of dyslexics with that type of dyslexia, while auditory-predominant dyslexia tended to cluster in families of dyslexics having that subtype.

The following three illustrations are pedigree charts of families that reflect this clustering. The following symbols and abbreviations are used:

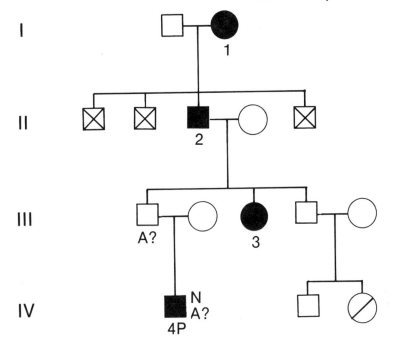

FAMILY B.

Figure 9.2 Hallgren's pedigree chart showing four generations of dyslexics. (Used with permission from *Specific Dyslexia ("Congenital Word-Blindness"); A Clinical and Genetic Study*, by Bertil Hallgren, Copenhagen: Ejnar Munksgaard, © 1950; translation from the Swedish by Erica Odelberg, Stockholm: Esselte aktiebolag, 1950, p. 272)

Squares designate males.
Circles designate females.
Black indicates dyslexia.
Black to the left indicates visual dyslexia.
Black to the right indicates auditory dyslexia.
Solid black indicates mixed dyslexia.
Stripes indicate difficulties, but insufficient information to type with confidence.
Numbers beneath the symbols are the ages.
Small black arrows point to the dyslexic being studied.

Figure 9.3 portrays the pedigrees of eleven families of visual dyslexics studied by Omenn and Weber. In family V5, note the numerous cousins with dyslexia (all in specific learning disability classes in the Seattle schools).

Figure 9.3   Pedigree chart of eleven families of visual dyslexics. (From "Dyslexia: Search for Phenotypic and Genetic Heterogeneity," by Gilbert S. Omenn and Bruce A. Weber, in *American Journal of Medical Genetics* 1, p. 339, 1978; with permission of Wiley-Liss, a division of John Wiley and Sons, Inc.)

Figure 9.4 shows the pedigrees of seven families in which the subjects had auditory-predominant dyslexia. Figure 9.5 illustrates pedigrees of three families in which the subjects had the combination, or mixed, type of dyslexia.

Other family history studies have revealed the following information:

Study 1: 40 percent of the parents had reading problems, while less than 10 percent of the parents of nondyslexic children had reading problems.[7]

Figure 9.4 Pedigree chart of seven families of auditory-predominant dyslexics. (From "Dyslexia: Search for Phenotypic and Genetic Heterogeneity," by Gilbert S. Omenn and Bruce A. Weber, in *American Journal of Medical Genetics* 1, p. 337, 1978; with permission of Wiley-Liss, a division of John Wiley and Sons, Inc.)

Study 2: 39.7 percent of the dyslexics had one or more close relatives with related learning problems.[8]

Study 3: 36.7 percent of the families of dyslexics had problems, compared with 22.5 percent for those of a control group.[9]

Study 4: In sixteen families with a child having "specific reading disability," in which both parents were tested and classified, three dyslexics had both parents affected, ten had only one parent affected. Three children had neither parent affected.[10]

Study 5: Twenty-nine dyslexic children formed a "hereditary" subgroup with a familial incidence of dyslexia. Of these, twenty parents were dyslexic and were treated as probands (subjects), forming a sample of forty-nine dyslexic cases for analysis. Six dyslexics had both parents affected, sixteen had dyslexic fathers, and five had dyslexic mothers.[11]

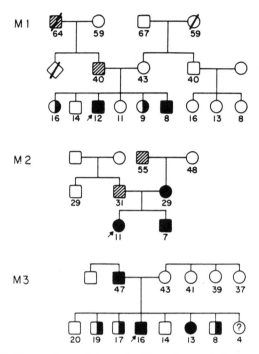

Figure 9.5 Pedigree chart of three families of mixed dyslexics. (From "Dyslexia: Search for Phenotypic and Genetic Heterogeneity," by Gilbert S. Omenn and Bruce A. Weber, in *American Journal of Medical Genetics* 1, p. 340, 1978; with permission of Wiley-Liss, a division of John Wiley and Sons, Inc.)

Possible Cytogenetic Connections

Learning problems may be connected with certain sex chromosome disorders,[12] especially a particular kind of karyotype, a group of chromosome sets having one or more characteristics in common. Normally, human beings have forty-six chromosomes. These are divided into twenty-three pairs, two of which are sex chromosomes. The chromosomal makeup of a normal male is 46,XY. For a normal female it is 46,XX. The most frequent sex chromosome abnormalities occur when a male has an extra X chromosome (47,XXY karyotype) or an extra Y chromosome (47,XYY karyotype), or when a female has an extra X (47,XXX karyotype) or is missing all or part of an X (called X monosomy). Reading problems in individuals having sex chromosome abnormalities are often reported from around the world. Many have difficulties with language and spatial ability. It is possible that such disorders in the chromosomal makeup may affect a child's growth, including his endocrinological and neurological development.

We are still a long way from understanding the full implications of these chromosome irregularities. Could this be one of the causes of dyslexia? Much more study will be necessary before any firm conclusions are drawn concerning a relationship between dyslexia and disorders in chromosomal constitution.

Potential Linkage Connections

If two genes are inherited together they are often said to be "linked." Both genes must be located close together on the same chromosome. Four researchers, Shelley D. Smith and William J. Kimberling of the Boys Town Institute for Communication Disorders in Omaha, Nebraska, Bruce F. Pennington of the University of Colorado, and Herbert A. Lubs of the University of Miami, pioneered the first study[13] of linkage analysis in sixteen families with a history of dyslexia. Their findings suggest a linkage between a major gene influencing dyslexia and chromosome 15p heteromorphisms (deviations from the norm).

This study needs to be replicated, and further studies of this type are required. If future investigations confirm these findings we will have taken a giant step forward in our search toward understanding the causes of dyslexia. Genetic differences may be only one cause, and we still have the perplexing problem to answer as to why there are so many more male than female dyslexics—but this difference in itself suggests a genetic factor in dyslexia.

Is dyslexia inherited? Findings such as these would indicate that certainly in some cases dyslexia is genetically determined, that it does seem to "run" in some families. But while there appears to be a genetic aspect to dyslexia, the linkage has not yet been definitely established. Various hypotheses have been made, studies are continuing, but nothing has been conclusively proved.

Maturational Lag

Is maturational lag the cause of dyslexia? A maturational lag is the slow or delayed development of those brain areas that bring about the acquisition of certain developmental skills which are basically age-linked. In Chapter 6, concerning the early identification of dyslexia, I explained the developmental factors that can affect achievement in certain school tasks. These maturational factors were spelled out in terms of the typical child's development, and it was pointed out that some children develop earlier, some later, but within a certain range of age, usually by age eight, most children have acquired the required maturity. A maturational lag implies cerebral immaturity.

It is true that some children get off to a slow start in school, and as time passes, some of these "late bloomers" begin to sail along and catch up. The question is: Are these children really dyslexic, or is their individual developmental pattern only somewhat deviant from that of the "typical" child? Some children just need more time to get moving; others take off right away and progress faster. The child who learns to read later may become a better reader than one who begins earlier.

Children do not progress in a lock-step fashion, all together and at the same time. They are *individuals* and progress in an individual manner, although the *overall pattern* may be similar. Their individual perceptual boundaries change with age because of the structural and functional alterations in their general growth processes, and the consequent decentration of perception.[14] Levels and rates of maturation may vary a great deal among *normal* children.

Much of the discussion on maturational lag as a cause of dyslexia rests on pure speculation. The research has been done mainly with kindergarten, first-grade, and second-grade children, with a few at other levels. What were the findings of such studies? Some children were more advanced in certain perceptual skills (such as visual discrimination and auditory discrimination) and knowledge; others less so. Surely this was not unexpected. Any kindergarten or primary grade teacher knows that some children start off slowly, test poorly, and then, after a few weeks or months, things seem to "jell" and they move up. In other words, poor readers may develop into good readers. Of course, some young children perform poorly and continue to do so. Unfortunately, in many of the studies no mention of intelligence is made—a factor that can certainly affect a child's academic progress, and a variable that should be taken into account in any such study.

It is possible that there may be some kind of maturation lag for a number of children as a result of cerebral immaturity, but this could happen to children who are *not* dyslexic as well as to those who are.[15] This may be a partial explanation for those "late bloomers." And *if* maturation lag were the cause of dyslexia, then it would follow that there would be three different kinds of "lag"— one that causes visual dyslexia, another that causes auditory dyslexia, and still another that causes a mixture of visual and auditory dyslexia.

If this really were the basic cause, would not dyslexics naturally "grow out" of the condition in time?

The notion that maturational lag causes dyslexia remains just that at the present time—a notion based on speculation only. It is highly improbable that any *tangible* evidence will emerge anytime soon.

Cerebral Dominance (Lateral Dominance)

The brain is divided into two hemispheres, the left hemisphere controlling the right side of the body and the right controlling the left side of the body. (See Figure 9.6.)

Frontal pole

Frontal lobe

Great longitudinal
fissure

Precentral gyrus

Central sulcus

Postcentral gyrus

Parietal lobe

Occipital lobe

Occipital pole

Figure 9.6   Superior view of the two hemispheres of the brain. (Used with permission from *Structure and Function in Man*, by Stanley W. Jacob, Clarice Ashworth Francone, and Walter J. Lossow, Philadelphia: W. S. Saunders, © 1982, p. 242)

Consistency in the use of one side of the body to dominate motor functions (right-eyed, right-handed, right-footed, or vice versa) is usually considered as evidence of neural integrity in the central nervous system. But many people do not have this clear-cut dominance. Some are left-eyed, right-handed, and right-footed (or right-eyed, left-handed, and right-footed, or any other variety of combinations). This is called mixed or crossed dominance.

Some dyslexics have crossed dominance; some do not. Some superior readers and spellers have crossed dominance; some do not. About 90 percent of the population is right-handed, with 10 percent left-handed, but approximately 60 percent of the left-handers process speech in the left hemisphere just as right-handed persons do. The other 40 percent of the left-handers appear to use both sides.[16]

There is a fine, but important, distinction between the terms *ambidexterity* and *ambivalency* in the use of the hands. An ambidextrous person is able to use both hands equally well for some tasks, and may do this even though one hand is considered the dominant or preferred hand. But ambivalency (in the technical sense used here) implies a conflicting use in the hands, using either one about half the time, with no dominant (preferred) hand, and is sometimes referred to as unestablished dominance. Some researchers have found a correlation between ambivalency in the use of hands and reading, writing, and spelling problems (not necessarily dyslexia).

Dr. Samuel Orton suggested in 1925 that strephosymbolia (dyslexia) was caused by confusion between the two hemispheres of the brain. He believed that memory images in the right hemisphere are the exact mirrored counterpart of those in the left hemisphere. For example, if the word *not* were stored in the left hemisphere, it would be stored as *ton* in the right hemisphere. If *saw* were stored in the left hemisphere, its mirrored counterpart in the right hemisphere would be *was*. He believed this was the reason for the twisted symbols and reversals of dyslexics.[17]

Figure 9.7 illustrates Orton's theory of mirrored images in the two hemispheres. Note that the letters *ABC* in the left hemisphere are shown in reversed form in the right hemisphere.

By 1937, Orton was suggesting that the confusion of the two brain hemispheres was caused by mixed or crossed dominance. Although Orton's views are no longer accepted, the notion that mixed or crossed dominance is the cause of reading difficulty or dyslexia still persists among some educators. Occasionally, one hears in the classroom the comment, "Oh, he has reading problems. He has mixed dominance, you know."

Research has never established that mixed or crossed dominance causes dyslexia or any other type of reading disability.

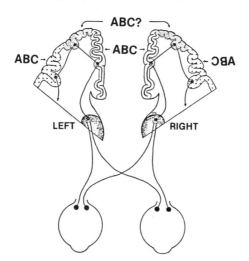

Figure 9.7   Orton's theory of memory images in the left hemisphere having mirrored counterpart images in the right hemisphere. (Used with permission from " 'Word-blindness' in School Children," by Samuel T. Orton, *Archives of Neurology and Psychiatry*, November 1925, 14, p. 609; © 1925, American Medical Association)

Neurological Dysfunction

In the preceding chapter on the historical development of the concept of dyslexia, the term *alexia* was explained as a condition in which persons who were previously literate had lost their ability to read as a result of acquired disease of or injury to the central nervous system. The term in general use today is *acquired dyslexia*. Research is both scarce and rather mixed on acquired dyslexia. Reference to control groups in the literature is rather sparse, even though control groups are essential to establish whether certain errors in reading and spelling are due to an improper reading and spelling development (stages, etc.) or to dyslexia.

Another term the reader will encounter is *developmental dyslexia*, which implies no brain damage. Yet various doctors have suggested that the dyslexic's difficulties may be neurological in origin. Parents can become greatly upset by such terms as "minimal brain dysfunction" and the like. Unfortunately, some educators have become confused, and they view dyslexia as a medical condition. As a result, in some schools improper screening procedures are used to identify children with learning problems. For example, in preschool screening, some school personnel make indefensible assumptions about motor development and certain types of neurological difficulty affecting reading, writing, and spelling achievement in school. As a consequence, some schools have set up "motor development programs" where children walk beams, jump through old tires, throw balls and bean bags, draw big circles, and go through other similar activities with the idea that this will make the children better readers and spellers.[18] The connection has not been made. All this will probably do nothing but improve the children's balance, throwing, and drawing, and give them a little fun and exercise.

It has been suggested that dyslexia could be caused by certain diseases or high fever affecting the child's brain, but there is no solid proof of this. Certain prenatal difficulties or birth complications such as anoxia (lack of sufficient oxygen) may cause dyslexia but research so far has not established this linkage.

There is a possibility that the presence of anti-Ro antibody in mothers may have something to do with a child's having dyslexia. This antibody assaults the Ro antigen, a substance that exists in the brains (and hearts) of developing fetuses, causing irritation and inflammation. In one study[19] of forty-five mothers of dyslexic children, nine percent tested positive for this antibody. This was a frequency over twenty times greater than that found in the two control groups combined. It may be that, as in congenital heart disease, anti-Ro plays a part in congenital cerebral pathology. Certainly this possibility warrants further examination.

Dyslexia and Neurodevelopmental Pathology

Progress in technological techniques that can be used to study the functioning of the brain and to assess impaired forms and structures has been extraordinary in the last ten years. However, certain problems arise in applying these procedures to dyslexic children. The brain is not completely developed until early adulthood. Thus it is difficult to determine what normal cortical-functional organization is in a young person, much less in one who is undergoing added delay or deficiency in the neuroanatomical system.[20] Moreover, one would hesitate to use certain invasive approaches, such as the sodium amytal technique that requires the use of barbiturates, or the regional cerebral blood flow procedure that uses radioactive substances,[21] even though these are used with adults (and, questionably by some researchers, with teenagers.)

Some of the technological procedures used with dyslexics are briefly explained below. Findings have been inconsistent.

Computed Tomography (CT Scan)

Computed tomography has an "acceptable" degree of radiation hazard and is used for visualization of the brain. Basically it is an X-ray of the brain. Computer-generated images show density values of compartments of brain matter.

Findings from research studies based on this technique are inconclusive. Indeed, interpretations of the scans may vary according to who is making the interpretation. In one study[22] two radiologists who knew nothing about the subjects' physical or academic histories ("blind" to clinical findings) read twenty-five scans. The first radiologist read fifteen scans as normal, nine as slightly abnormal, and one as borderline atrophic (a halt in growth). The other read thirteen scans as normal, twelve as slightly abnormal, and none as atrophic. Five CT scans were read as "slightly abnormal" by *both* radiologists (only a 20 percent agreement).

There is another limitation in the use of CT scans. Since these are based on the density of the compartment of the brain tissue scanned, if irregularities at the cellular level occur sufficiently enough to interfere with function, but not enough to change significantly the overall density of the tissue, then CT scans may not reveal any irregularities.[23]

The Electroencephalogram (EEG)

The validity of the electroencephalogram (EEG) to indicate different modes of brain pathology has been established for years, but the use of the

EEG with children is laden with complications. Significant evolutions in EEG patterns are related to conceptual age, and significant variability appears among children of the same age. EEG patterns may be affected by intervening illnesses or by metabolic disturbances.[24] And as mentioned before, defining what is "normal" in children is always open to question.

The usefulness of the EEG with dyslexics has been the subject of a great deal of dispute, and the controversy continues. Some dyslexics have "abnormal" EEG findings; some do not. Some superior readers and spellers have "abnormal" EEG findings; some do not.

How does the EEG work? Pieces of metal, which act as conductors (electrodes), are placed on different parts of a person's scalp. These electrodes pick up brain waves transmitted from the part of the brain nearest to the electrode. These waves are passed into a machine, where they are amplified and then traced onto moving graph paper. The neurologist examines these patterns to determine if the brain is functioning normally. For example, the presence of slow waves in the occipital region, or positive spike patterns, or epileptiform discharges are characteristic of abnormal EEGs.

There have been numerous studies made, but no EEG pattern has been established as a correlate of dyslexia; that is, there is no proved relation between the two. For example, in a study of eighty-two dyslexic children, where detailed information was obtained from families, maternity hospitals, nurseries, nursery schools, regular schools, attending doctors, and hospitals, it was found that on neurological investigation, the most severe degree of dyslexia could exist without any evidence of brain damage.[25]

In fact, C. Keith Conners reviewed a number of studies and concluded that they could just as easily be "interpreted as showing the *absence* of EEG abnormalities among dyslexics," and that the better-controlled studies especially lead to this interpretation.[26] (A list of the various problems that Conners encountered with studies is included in the notes for this chapter.)

The notion that some general, unspecific neurological abnormality causes dyslexia has not been proved.

Beyond the EEG with the BEAM and SPM

Brain electrical activity mapping (BEAM) is a way of adding to the amount of information obtained on a standard EEG. When the neurologist reads the EEG, he analyzes the brain waves recorded on the graph paper. The BEAM does not create new data, but converts the squiggly lines of the EEG into a color-coded map. The results can be compared to what happens when a column of numbers is converted into color graphics. The information already there becomes more apparent.[27]

After the electrical activity, either in response to a stimulus or in a resting condition, is recorded, the data are transformed statistically to what is called Significance Probability Mapping (SPM). This defines the areas in which a particular EEG pattern deviates from the normal pattern. These SPMs are used mainly in the delineation of abnormal areas of the brain during the clinical evaluation of BEAM images. Dr. Frank Duffy of Boston Children's Hospital and his colleagues have studied the use of the BEAM and SPM as a way to map the brain waves of dyslexics as they react to words, sounds, and sights. They concluded that the computer program can separate dyslexics from nondyslexics with 80 to 90 percent accuracy.[28] However, Dr. Drake D. Duane of the Department of Neurology, Mayo Clinic, points out that a number of constraints operate against using the BEAM as a diagnostic procedure to determine the existence of dyslexia. He notes that "each point generated on the video screen is an arbitrarily selected point in time which, in reality, represents group rather than individual comparisons. Furthermore, the data base upon which the computer comparison is made is predicated on the average performance of three dyslexics compared with the average performance of three controls. At no point is there a comparison of any individual dyslexic with any individual control."[29]

Dr. Martha Denckla of the National Institute of Neurological and Communicative Disorders also stresses that SPMs are of questionable value. "The existence of a difference does not indicate which group is more or less normal, i.e., it does not localize or even imply processing deficit, much less a 'lesion' in the usual neurodiagnostic sense."[30]

Due to the use of such small numbers of subjects in the various studies, lack of consistency in the diagnostic procedures used including no consideration of the subtypes of dyslexia, lack of congruity with regard to the ages of the subjects, and poor descriptions of the cognitive activation techniques employed, no conclusions can be drawn at this time about either the diagnosis of dyslexia or the *cause* of dyslexia.

If the validity of using the EEG to diagnose dyslexia is disputable, then, since the BEAM and SPM interpretations are based on the EEG, should not the validity of these results be equally suspect?

Specialization Within the Brain

As already mentioned, the brain is divided into two hemispheres. At one time there were two conflicting views. The traditional view held that the two hemispheres of the brain were simply mirror images of each other (Orton's view, for example), with no reason to designate particular functions to one hemisphere rather than to the other. The other view was that the hemispheres were specialized, and that some things were done better by one hemisphere or the other. The latter view has come to be accepted. The left hemisphere is concerned mainly with language, verbal reasoning, and certain motor skills, while the right hemisphere is more adept at certain kinds of spatial functions, such as understanding and working with maps, visualizing and remembering faces, and other performances that do not depend on verbal descriptions.

We now know, however, that the functions of each hemisphere, though specialized, are not necessarily exclusive. A number of exceptions have recently led neuroscientists to re-evaluate their thinking about specialization within the brain. Further experiments have indicated that the brain does not just break down, as has previously been suggested, into neat little categories—each hemisphere with its own functions altogether exclusive of the other hemisphere.

With the discovery of the PET Scanner (Positron Emission Tomography), which currently is being used to "map" the brain, new knowledge is being uncovered about the functions of the hemispheres. Hemispheric specialization has been found to occur along *different* lines in *different* people.[31]

Music awareness has been considered a right hemisphere function. In a "landmark experiment" at the University of California at Los Angeles, research scientists have compared PET scans of persons listening to music after having been given certain directions. The scientists discovered that the brain responds differently depending upon the cognitive strategies that the listener uses! An example task: two musical chords were sounded and the person was asked if the chords were the same ones or different. If the person just listened and answered reflexively (perhaps by pushing one button if the chords were alike or another if they were different), the right hemisphere of the brain was likely to carry out the task, thus responding according to perceptions. But if the person responded by mentally arranging the chords along the piano keys, drawing on visual memory and imagery, then the task shifted to the more symbolic mode of the left hemisphere.[32] What is important here is the cognitive strategy used by the listener and the fact that *either* hemisphere could be used.

Other research has expanded our understanding of the functions of the brain hemispheres. Rather than saying that the left hemisphere is specialized for language, the more accurate phrasing would probably be that the left hemisphere is specialized for symbolic representation; whereas the right hemisphere deals more with representations that reflect reality more directly—that is, those chunks of experience that do not use language. To make it clearer and to avoid oversimplifications, one might say that the brain is divided into the *symbolic-conceptual hemisphere* (left) and the *nonsymbolic directly perceived hemisphere* (right).

But it is not exactly true that the right hemisphere is wholly lacking in language ability, for it can decode words such as "dog" or "house," after some practice, although it may have trouble with symbolic words such as "liberty" or "honesty." It seems, in any case, as if the right hemisphere can get meaning more easily from concrete objects and events.[33]

It appears also that we need *both* hemispheres for language, although the left is considered the more important of the two for this function. Why? An injury in "Broca's area" (in the *left* hemisphere; see Figure 9.8) can cause a person to be unable to say a simple straightforward sentence, such as, "Is this what you really wanted?"

Recent research at the Texas Health Center in Dallas and also at Harvard University has shown that disorders in the *right* hemisphere can cause a person to lose the capacity to distinguish the *important nuances* of everyday speech, such as subtle shades of meaning and emotional tones of sarcasm, disbelief, or irony. It is as though the right hemisphere furnishes us with the emotional aspects of our speech—the color, the liveliness, the spirit. For example, an injury to our right hemisphere could make it impossible to intone some subtle irony, such as saying the above sentence in this way, "Is THAT what you really wanted?" Our words would ring flat. Figure 9.9 illustrates the multifaceted brain in a picturesque way.

There is no doubt that both sides of our brain are needed. In fact, along

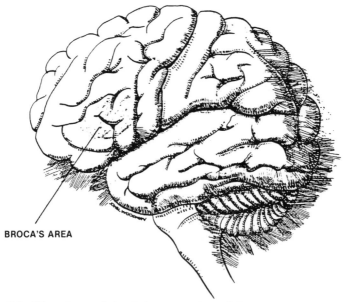

BROCA'S AREA

Figure 9.8 "Broca's area" is vital to speech and language ability. (Used with permission from *The Brain* by Richard M. Restak, New York: Bantam, © 1984, p. 238)

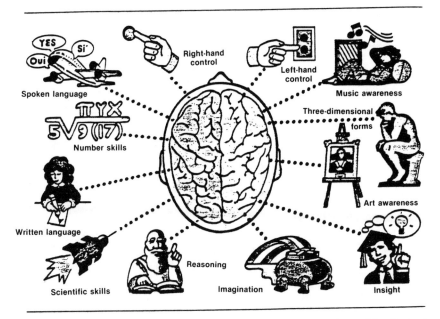

Figure 9.9 The multifaceted brain. (Used with permission from *The Brain* by Richard M. Restak, New York: Bantam, © 1984, p. 260)

with Restak, one can say with "equal validity that we are not just the right and left sides of our brain but simply we are our brain."[34]

What does specialization within the brain have to do with dyslexia? While neurological dysfunction has not been proved to be a cause of dyslexia, most of the dyslexia research to date appears to have viewed the two hemispheres as having separate functions. But surely the recent discoveries concerning the crossover and interrelationship of the two hemispheres suggest that further thinking along this line is needed. Some researchers[35] even speak in terms of "R-type dyslexics" (excessive development of right-hemispheric reading strategies) and "L-type dyslexics" (excessive development of left-hemispheric reading strategies).

Should not this "either-or" mentality be altered to consider the interrelationship of both hemispheres? What about the different hemispheres used in responses by different persons? Do these new findings not have implications for the remediation of dyslexia?

Obviously, we need to know more about the workings of the brains of dyslexics. We need to get *inside* their brains to determine what answers may lie there. The opportunity to examine a brain occurs frequently, but the chance to examine the brain of a diagnosed dyslexic is very rare.

Cytoarchitectonic Studies of Dyslexics' Brains

The first published post-mortem study[36] concerning dyslexia appeared in the *Journal of Learning Disabilities* in 1968. It was conducted by Dr. William E. Drake, Jr., who at that time was associated with the Veterans Administration Hospital in San Francisco. A child had been referred to him from the Child Center in Kentfield, California. Drake described "Billy" as a likable twelve-year-old boy who had serious difficulty in reading and in retaining what he read, some trouble with arithmetic, slow production of poor quality writing and spelling, and slowness in learning to tell time. While he was not disruptive in the classroom, at home he had unexpected temper outbursts (sometimes hitting or throwing things), and at times he seemed to enjoy aggravating members of his family. His mood changed frequently and abruptly; he often burst into tears for no apparent reason. Billy had dizzy spells with blackouts. Often his attention would lapse into empty stares into space. His younger brother also had a serious reading problem.

One afternoon Billy had an unsettling temper outburst. A little while later he complained of a dull headache in the back of his head and became lethargic. Later he went to bed, and during the night he suffered a massive cerebellar hemorrhage and died.

In his post-mortem examination of Billy's brain, Drake found an abnormal convolutional pattern (folds or ridges on the surface of the brain) bilaterally in the parietal lobes (see Figures 8.1 and 9.6), a thinned corpus callosum, and neurons (see Figure 6.1) out of place deep in the white matter. These problems are caused by disturbed cellular migration during gestation. They are not the consequence of brain damage. These abnormalities are consistent with what was suggested by Broadbent in 1872 and Morgan in 1896 (see Chapter 8); that is, they were identified with areas of the cortex important in visual and auditory association, visual imagery, and cross-modal integration—all significant in reading, spelling, and writing.[37] (Dr. Drake speculated that the headaches and blackouts that Billy experienced were caused by either atypical migraines or minor epileptic seizures.)

Eleven years were to pass before another such study was conducted. In the meantime, in 1970, Roger E. Saunders (then president of the Orton Dyslexia Society) recommended that the feasibility of establishing a brain bank for neuroanatomical research be investigated. By 1977, the Society agreed to begin a program of basic research in the anatomical analysis of dyslexic and nondyslexic brains. (The brains of nondyslexics are needed as controls and for comparison purposes in the post-mortem studies.) Prospective brain donors needed to be interviewed and tested so that a uniform standard of classification could be developed and maintained.[38]

The Society sent a questionnaire, requesting information on any current research relating brain structure and function to dyslexia, to over three hundred medical institutions in the United States. Most of the replies referred to research being done at the Harvard Medical School Department of Neurology at Beth Israel Hospital in Boston. Indeed, this was the only institution doing this type of research.[39]

And so we come to the next post-mortem examination of a dyslexic's brain. In 1979, a twenty-year-old male "dyslexic" died of multiple internal injuries resulting from an accidental fall from a great height. His brain had not been directly injured in this fatal accident. Dr. Albert M. Galaburda and Dr. Thomas L. Kemper[40] from the Departments of Neurology, Harvard Medical School and Boston University School of Medicine, and the Neurological Units, Beth Israel Hospital and Boston City Hospital, obtained permission to examine the young man's brain.

His difficulties with reading and spelling caused him to repeat the first grade and the diagnosis of dyslexia was made at that time, during which a routine neurological evaluation indicated no abnormal findings.

He was the youngest of four children, three boys and one girl. His father and both of his brothers were slow readers, but not his mother or his sister. He, and several other family members, were left-handed. He received special tutoring but continued to have trouble with the language arts. Table 9.1 shows his reading achievement test scores at various ages.

Note how very little progress was made in *six* years, with scarcely any between the ages of fifteen and nineteen. One wonders what kind of help he received, whether he was a visual or auditory dyslexic, or if the diagnostician knew the difference. Note that the diagnosis of dyslexia was made at an early age. Obviously his special tutoring did not help very much. When he was sixteen years old he developed nocturnal seizures, but these were easily controlled with phenytoin. No other member of his family had seizures. At

Table 9.1   Results of Reading Achievement Tests*

Test	Age at Testing			
	13	14	15	19
Stanford Achievement Test				
Paragraph meaning	2.4	3.9	3.5	3.5
Word meaning	3.0	2.0	3.5	4.0
Spelling	3.0	3.5	3.5	3.5
Gray Oral Paragraphs	1.6	2.9	3.5	4.0
Gates-MacGinitie Reading Tests	–	3.7	3.5	4.0

*Results are given in grade levels. At 6 years of age the patient's IQ (Stanford-Binet) was 105; at 13 years it was (WISC): full scale 88; verbal 95; nonverbal 83. From "Cytoarchitectonic Abnormalities in Developmental Dyslexia: A Case Study," by Albert M. Galaburda and Thomas L. Kemper, *Annals of Neurology*, 6 August 1979, p. 95. Used with permission.)

age sixteen he had repeated neurological examinations, but no abnormalities were noted. Except for one sleep study indicating borderline slowing over the right hemisphere, routine electroencephalograms were normal. An isotope brain scan was also normal.

His arithmetic performance was thought to be better than his reading and spelling, but he scored at the fourth-grade level on an arithmetic assessment when he was eighteen years old. At this time it was noted that he had some mild problems with left-right orientation and finger recognition.

Dr. Galaburda and Dr. Kemper examined the young man's brain and found no gross abnormalities and no abnormalities in myelination, size of ventricles, or thickness of the corpus callosum. The abnormalities that were found were all confined to the left cerebral hemisphere. Here, within the language areas, the doctors found a disordered cortex (the layer of gray matter covering most of the surface of the brain) with frequently fused layers, scrambled and whirled, and with numerous abnormally large cells scattered "throughout the thickness of the cortical ribbon, often extending into the subcortical white matter for a short distance." This abnormal neuronal architecture was found mainly in the areas of the brain that are concerned with the auditory region and language.[41]

In addition to the above, Galaburda and Kemper found that the planum temporale (temples) on both sides were symmetrical. (Usually the left is larger.) But the doctors pointed out that this finding did not necessarily represent an abnormality, since such symmetry in the extent of the planum can occur in as many as 24 percent of normal persons.

Though the left cerebral hemisphere was consistently wider than the right hemisphere, the implications were not clear to the researchers. As the doctors pointed out:

> It is not possible to tell from a single case whether or not the anatomical findings have any causative relationship to the clinical findings—much less whether the malformation is responsible for the seizure disorder, the learning disability, both, or neither.[42]

Following the publication of this brain study by Galaburda and Kemper, the Orton Dyslexia Society selected Harvard as the institution to carry on research of dyslexics' brains. The William Underwood Company contributed $100,000 to provide equipment for a new laboratory. In 1981, an advisory board to the research division was selected. The Charles A. Dana Laboratories of the Beth Israel Hospital and Harvard University were dedicated in 1982. At this dedication, the Powder River Corporation, a company founded by a dyslexic, announced a contribution of $50,000 for operating expenses.[43]

The technique of cytoarchitectonics (cell architecture) is highly specialized. It requires sectioning the brain into 3,000 to 4,000 sections. Certain sections are stained and examined for differences in cells. The process is exceptionally time consuming for it requires hundred of hours from the beginning to the final step. As a consequence, only three to five brain examinations can be completed in a year.[44]

The next two brains to be studied in the Charles A. Dana Laboratories were those of a diagnosed dyslexic female and a German male dyslexic (the first in the study from outside the United States).[45] Of the ten brains that have been studied so far, seven were from males and three were from females. All indicated symmetry of the temporal plane.[47] (This symmetry occurs in about 21 percent to 25 percent of the general population.)

All of the male brains revealed asymmetric (left hemisphere more than right) cortical nerve cell anomalies. The latter are residue of defects of fetal neuronal cell migration and consist of clumps of immature nerve cells close to the brain's surface. Nerve cells were irregularly arranged instead of being layered. There were small enfoldings inside the brain where none should have been. Changes of these types occur between the eighteenth and twenty-fourth weeks of pregnancy. Two of the three female brains and one male brain revealed multiple placques (scarring within which a myelin coating has developed). This abnormality can occur as early as the seventh month of pregnancy or as late as two years after birth.[47]

Researchers theorize that these abnormalities may result from some intricate injury to the brain of the fetus from a virus, a diminutive stroke, variation in testosterone some time during the last five months preceding birth or the first month after birth, or even stress on the part of the pregnant mother.

Some specialists have speculated that there may be a connection between autoimmune disorders and the disturbances in neuronal migration described above. Some of the cases whose brains were studied did suffer from autoimmune disorders, such as allergies and asthma.[48]

Again, caution and common sense must be emphasized in any attempt to interpret the findings of the studies discussed in this section. Were those persons whose brains were examined truly dyslexic? Hynd and Semrud-Clikeman, in a critical review of these studies, point out that

the diagnosis of dyslexia in these studies is based primarily on history, which is often poorly documented, and the measures of reading attainment in these studies are inconsistent, the tests given at different assessment intervals, and the results of achievement tests are reported in grade equivalents and not standard scores, which would have facilitated appropriate comparisons with IQ measures. Also, the distribution of neurodevelopmental abnormalities in these few cases is more left frontal-temporal rather than left temporal-posterior, as the historical formulations would predict. . . . Further, the autopsy results are somewhat inconsistent with the dysfunctional cortical regions suggested by Duffy et al. (1980). Although the results of these various studies offer grist for interesting speculation, one must keep in mind that the data are based on very small numbers, and conclusions drawn from these data must be viewed as tenuous.[49]

Cerebellar-Vestibular (C-V) Dysfunction

The theory that cerebellar-vestibular dysfunction is a cause of dyslexia is being treated separately and placed at the end of this chapter for a reason. I have mixed feelings about even presenting this notion, which has received quite a bit of media attention, but which has been repudiated by neurologists, psychiatrists, educators, and organizations dealing with dyslexia. However, in true education one must be aware of the thinking of others, must consider the issues and the facts, and must draw conclusions based upon knowledge and experience.

Harold N. Levinson, a psychiatrist, has written two books.[50] The first book is rather technical, somewhat lengthy, and requires persistence to get through. The second presents his information in a manner more readable for the general public.

First, some background information is needed to understand Levinson's theory about the cause of dyslexia. The cerebral cortex controls numerous muscles with the aid of the cerebellum, which has been called our biological computer. There are different kinds of activities that are performed by the cerebellum, but the following example will relate to Levinson's theory. Try holding your index finger in a vertical position approximately six inches in front of your face. Then begin moving your hand from side to side as quickly as you can. What happened? Your finger became just a blur. Now try it from the opposite approach. Hold your hand (and finger) very steadily while moving your head from side to side as fast as you can. Now what happened? There was much less blurring. The reason for this is that the *vestibul occular reflex* (VOR) largely prevented the blurring. The VOR extends from the *vestibular center* in the inner ear and served to keep your eyes on the fixed target of your finger as you moved your head from side to side.

Levinson holds that the root of dyslexia lies in this area; that is, in an inner ear dysfunction that can be treated with varying dosages and combinations of medication. Levinson reports that some of his "dyslexics" have been excellent readers and spellers in school, and he has "found" that all of his phobic patients have dyslexia. He devised an instrument called a 3–D Optical Scanner to measure eye-tracking defects, and this he uses as a diagnostic screening tool to detect "dyslexia." He asserts that 95 percent accuracy is obtained with this instrument.

Some criticisms of Levinson's studies and work are as follows:

1. Dyslexia is a complex disability. Dyslexics have problems in reading, writing, spelling, listening, and speaking. They do *not* excel in schoolwork, as did some of Levinson's "dyslexics." So the first question must be whether his patients were truly dyslexic, or just persons with emotional problems, various phobias, psychosomatic disorders, hyperactivity, or other behavioral difficulties. One parent in Levinson's book was told that her daughter's "work, when she did it, was all above average."[51] Dyslexics *cannot* do their work at the expected grade levels—much less perform well above average.

2. No "double-blind" studies were done. A "double-blind" study is one in which some of the participants (the "control group") take placebos (such as sugar pills), while others are given the real medication under study. These studies are called double-blind because neither the participants nor the examiners know which is the phony pill and which is the real pill, though of course the directors of the research do.

3. Neurologists have criticized Levinson's neurological examinations, which identified cerebellar dysfunction, and have disputed that these can identify vestibular dysfunction.

4. The children who participated in the "Queens Study" blurring-speed experiment were kindergarten students. The question of visual and other developmental immaturity and their possible effect upon such young children must be raised, with the consequence of invalid results as far as the diagnosis of dyslexia is concerned.

5. The children who participated in the "Staten Island Study" were students in nursery school, kindergarten, and first and second grades. The same question regarding visual and other developmental immaturity must be asked.

6. Levinson later admitted that the results of the blurring-speed studies were confounded by "unwittingly" comparing premedication with postmedication subjects.

Additional and more technical criticisms of Levinson's theory and diagnostic procedures are listed in note 52 in the references following this chapter.

Full Circle

We do not yet know all the causes of dyslexia, but we do know that it exists. Brain injury and certain illnesses can cause acquired dyslexia. Heredity plays a role in some cases of dyslexia, but how this occurs in some families is not known at the present time. In other words, the specific linkage has not been established. And, more boys than girls have dyslexia.

We are not going to make much progress in discovering the cause(s) of dyslexia until our diagnoses become more accurate, and experiments and other research tighten up. In a sense, progress in dyslexia knowledge may have been impeded by the "research, publish, or perish" dicta at our large universities. Too much hasty, sloppy, questionable research has been turned out. Longitudinal studies take *time*; any well-designed and well-researched study takes time and conscientious, intelligent, objective evaluation of the findings.

Somehow, this message must be gotten across if we are ever going to reach the end of the road. So far, the dyslexia route has been circular, tortuous, and frustrating.

Notes

1. Sadie N. Decker and Bruce G. Bender, "Converging Evidence for Multiple Genetic Forms of Reading Disability," *Brain and Language* 33 (1988), p. 206.

2. Knud Hermann, *Reading Disability, A Medical Study of Word-Blindness and Related Handicaps* (Springfield, Ill.: Charles C. Thomas, 1959), pp. 86–87.

3. Edith Zerbin-Rubin, "Congenital Word Blindness," *Bulletin of the Orton Society* 17 (1967), p. 50.

4. Bertil Hallgren, *Specific Dyslexia ("Congenital Word-Blindness"): A Clinical and Genetic Study* (Copenhagen: Ejnar Munksgaard, 1950); trans. by Erica Odelberg (Stockholm: Esselte aktiebolag, 1950), p. 272.

5. Ibid., pp. 194–95.

6. Gilbert S. Omenn and Bruce A. Weber, "Dyslexia: Search for Phenotypic and Genetic Heterogeneity," *American Journal of Medical Genetics* 1 (1978), pp. 333–42.

7. Donald G. Doehring, *Patterns of Impairment in Specific Reading Disability, A Neuropsychological Investigation* (Bloomington: Indiana University Press, 1968), p. 83.

8. Edith Klasen, *The Syndrome of Specific Dyslexia* (Baltimore: University Park Press, 1972), p. 78.

9. Sandhya Naidoo, *Specific Dyslexia* (New York: John Wiley, 1972), pp. 96–97, III.

10. Joan M. Finucci, John T. Guthrie, Anne L. Childs, Helen Abbey, and Barton Childs, "The Genetics of Specific Reading Disability," *Annals of Human Genetics* 40 (London, 1976), p. 17.

11. M. Zahalkova, V. Vrzal, and E. Kloboukova, "Genetical Investigations in Dyslexia," *Journal of Medical Genetics* 9 (1972), pp. 49–50.

12. Additional notes on sex chromosome abnormalities:

(a) Decker and Bender also report that "anomalies of the sex chromosomes often result in mild developmental delays, learning problems, and minor physical anomalies." Sadie N. Decker and Bruce G. Bender, "Converging Evidence for Multiple Genetic Forms of Reading Disability," *Brain and Language* 33 (1988), p. 204.

(b) Bender et al. report that chromosome abnormalities occur in one out of two hundred births, of which about one-half are sex chromosome abnormalities (p. 176). In a review of various studies of children having sex chromosome abnormalities, conclusions indicated that most such children "have learning disorders and, rarely, mental retardation. . . . Some specific LD patterns are present in the karyotype groups: 47,XXY boys often develop dyslexia associated with their language disorders, and 45,X and partial X monosomy girls frequently have impaired spatial ability. Girls with SCA [sex chromosome abnormalities] are more generally impaired than boys" (p. 197). Bruce G. Bender, Mary H. Puck, James A. Salbenblatt, and Arthur Robinson, "Cognitive Development of Children with Sex Chromosome Abnormalities," *Genetics and Learning Disabilities, Shelley D. Smith, ed.* (San Diego, Cal.: College-Hill Press, 1986.)

13. Smith et al. note that the probability of linkage is expressed as a lod score; that is, the lod of odds of the likelihood of linkage. A lod score of 3.421 was obtained for the linkage in this study (p.174). They go on to explain that "a maximum lod score greater than 3 has generally been considered sufficient to establish linkage, whereas a lod score less than −2 refutes linkage" (p. 170). S.D. Smith, B.F. Pennington, William J. Kimberling, and H.A. Lubs, "A Genetic Analysis of Specific Reading Disability," *Genetic Aspects of Speech and Language Disorders*, Christy L. Ludlow and Judith A. Cooper, eds. (New York: Academic Press, 1983), pp. 172, 174–77. Also, Shelley D. Smith, William J. Kimberling, Bruce F. Pennington, and Herbert A. Lubs, "Specific Reading Disability: Identification of an Inherited Form Through Linkage Analysis," *Science* 219 (March 18, 1983), pp. 1345–47.

14. David Elkind, John Horn, and Gerrie Schneider, "Modified Word Recognition, Reading Achievement, and Perceptual Decentration," *Journal of Genetic Psychology* 107 (December 1965), p. 248.

15. Notes on the developmental lag hypothesis:

(a) Stanovich et al. contend that the developmental lag model is in fact more helpful in understanding the variations of normal achievement in nondyslexic children. In a study of third- and fifth-grade students, Stanovich found that the skilled third-grade readers and the less skilled fifth-grade readers were nearly matched on overall reading level. The reading-related cognitive performance profiles of the two groups of readers were very much alike. They had comparable levels of vocabulary development, phonological skill, pseudoword decoding proficiency, picture-symbol naming fluency, and word naming both alone and in context. The researchers concluded that this pattern of performance correspondences implies a developmental lag model of the reading skill deficiencies exhibited by the less skilled fifth-grade students. Keith E. Stanovich, Ruth G. Nathan, and Marilyn Vala-Rossi, "Developmental Changes in the Cognitive Correlates of Reading Ability and the Developmental Lag Hypothesis," *Reading Research Quarterly* 21 (Summer 1986), pp. 267–83. (Note: A follow-up study on the achievement of the fifth-grade students a couple of years later might have contributed additional information as to whether these children did indeed mature and "catch up," thus indicating that some type of developmental lag had formerly existed.)

(b) In another study of third-, fifth-, and seventh-grade students who were tested and placed in skilled and less skilled subgroups for each grade level, Stanovich et al. found comparable results in the performance profiles of older less-skilled students when matched with younger skilled students. The researchers state that these findings confirm the hypothesis of the earlier study mentioned above: that the performance of students who read poorly (but have not been classified as LD or dyslexic) show the cognitive pattern of a developmental lag model. Keith E. Stanovich, Ruth G. Nathan, and Judith E. Zolman, "The Developmental Lag Hypothesis in Reading: Longitudinal and Matched Reading-Level Comparisons," *Child Development* 59 (1988), pp. 71–86. (Note: Again, valuable information might have been obtained if these students, supposedly falling in the "developmental lag category," were followed up at a later date to monitor progress in their achievement.)

(c) Scarborough states that if specific reading disabilities result from a developmental lag, then disabled readers should catch up to their peers at maturity. In a study of adults who had childhood reading disorders and those who did not, Scarborough found that most of those who had reading problems at an earlier age continued to have difficulty into adulthood, and that the developmental lag theory could not account for such problems. Hollis S. Scarborough, "Continuity Between Childhood Dyslexia and Adult Reading," *British Journal of Psychology* 75 (1984), pp. 329–48.

16. Richard M. Restak, *The Brain* (New York: Bantam, 1984), p. 173.

17. Samuel T. Orton, "'Word-blindness' in School Children," *Archives of Neurology and Psychiatry* 14, No. 5 (November 1925), pp. 607–9.

18. C. Keith Conners, "Critical Review of Electroencephalographic and Neurophysiological Studies in Dyslexia," *Dyslexia, an Appraisal of Current Knowledge*, Arthur L. Benton and David Pearl, eds. (New York: Oxford University Press, 1978), p. 260.

19. Wilhemina Behan, P.O. Behan, and Norman Geschwind, "Anti-Ro Antibody in Mothers of Dyslexic Children," *Developmental Medicine and Child Neurology* 27 (1985), p. 538–40.

20. John E. Obrzut, "Dyslexia and Neurodevelopmental Pathology: Is the Neurodiagnostic Technology Ahead of the Psycho-educational Technology," *Journal of Learning Disabilities* 22 (April 1989), p. 218.

21. Ibid., p. 217.

22. Martha B. Denckla, Marjorie LeMay, and Catherine A. Chapman, "Few CT Scan Abnormalities Found Even in Neurologically Impaired Learning Disabled Children," *Journal of Learning Disabilities* 18 (March 1985), pp. 133–34.

23. George W. Hynd and Margaret Semrud-Clikeman, "Dyslexia and Neurodevelopmental Pathology: Relationships to Cognition, Intelligence, and Reading Skill Acquisition," *Journal of Learning Disabilities* 22 (April 1989), p. 206.

24. Ibid.

25. T.T.S. Ingram, A.W. Mason, and J. Blackburn, "A Retrospective Study of 82 Children With Reading Disability," *Developmental Medicine and Child Neurology* 12 (1970), p. 280.

26. Conners' (1978) critique of EEG studies, op. cit., pp. 259–60:

(a) Most studies employ nonblind readings of unknown reliability.

(b) Studies vary in the definition of the dyslexic group.

(c) Studies frequently do not rule out associated conditions such as behavior or neurological abnormalities.

(d) Matching of experimental and control samples is usually poor, and where it is good there is no EEG-reading association.

(e) More recent and well-controlled studies show significantly less abnormality than is reported for earlier studies.

(f) The range of degree-of-abnormality reported is too large to inspire confidence in the reliability of the findings.

(g) No consistent findings have appeared with respect to either the locus or type of abnormality associated with dyslexia.

(h) In the cases where follow-up evaluations of EEG-studied dyslexics were performed, the EEG contributed nothing to prediction of outcome.

(i) There are several instances where the greater degree of abnormality of the EEG is associated with the milder conditions of the reading disorder.

(j) There are several instances where the greater degree of abnormality among the dyslexics is less than that found in other studies among controls.

27. Restak, op. cit., pp. 351–52.

28. Frank H. Duffy, Martha B. Denckla, Peter H. Bartels, Giulio Sandini, and Louise S. Kiessling, "Dyslexia: Automated Diagnosis by Computerized Classification of Brain Electrical Activity," *Annals of Neurology* 7 (1980), pp. 421–28.

29. Drake D. Duane, "Neurodiagnostic Tools in Dyslexic Syndromes in Children: Pitfalls and Proposed Comparative Study of Computed Tomography, Nuclear Magnetic Resonance, and Brain Electrical Activity Mapping," *Dyslexia: Its Neuropsychology and Treatment*, George Th. Pavlidis and Dennis F. Fisher, eds. (New York: John Wiley, 1986), pp. 72–73.

30. Martha B. Denckla, "Issues of Overlap and Heterogeneity in Dyslexia," *Biobehavioral Measures of Dyslexia*, David B. Gray and James F. Kavanagh, eds. (Parkton, Md.: York Press, 1985), pp. 44–45.

31. Restak, op. cit, p.248.

32. Ibid., p. 250.

33. Ibid., p. 250–51.

34. Ibid., pp. 250, 252, 257–60.

35. Bryon P. Rourke, Dirk J. Bakker, John L. Fisk, and John D. Strang, *Child Neuropsychology, An Introduction to Theory, Research and Clinical Practice* (New York: Guilford Press, 1983), pp. 104–105.

36. William E. Drake, Jr., "Clinical and Pathological Findings in a Child With a Developmental Learning Disability," *Journal of Learning Disabilities* 1, No. 9 (September 1968), pp. 486–502.

37. George W. Hynd and Margaret Semrud-Clikeman, "Dyslexia and Neurodevelopmental Pathology: Relationships to Cognition, Intelligence, and Reading Skill Acquisition," *Journal of Learning Disabilities* 22, No. 4 (April 1989), pp. 204–16.

38. Elinor L. Hartwig, ed., "History of the Research Division," *Medical Research Update: Perspectives on Dyslexia* (Baltimore: The Orton Dyslexia Society, 1984), p. 2.

39. Ibid.

40. Albert M. Galaburda and Thomas L. Kemper, "Cytoarchitectonic Abnormalities in Developmental Dyslexia: A Case Study," *Annals of Neurology* 6 (August 1979), p. 94–100.

41. Ibid., p. 96.

42. Ibid., p. 99.

43. Hartwig, op. cit., p. 2.

44. Ibid., p. 3.

45. Drake D. Duane, "Commentary on Dyslexia and Neurodevelopmental Pathology," *Journal of Learning Disabilities* 22, No. 4 (April 1989), p. 219; also see Albert M. Galaburda, Gordon F. Sherman, Glenn D. Rosen, Francisco Aboitiz, and Norman Geschwind, "Developmental Dyslexia: Four Consecutive Patients with Cortical Anomalies," *Annals of Neurology* 18 (1985), pp. 228–29; Albert M. Galaburda, Gordon F. Sherman, and Norman Geschwind, "Developmental Dyslexia: Third Consecutive Case with Cortical Anomalies," *Abstracts of Society for Neuroscience* 9 (1983), p. 940; Albert M. Galaburda and Thomas L. Kemper, "Cytoarchitectonic Abnormalities in Developmental Dyslexia: A Case Study," *Annals of Neurology* 6 (August 1979), p. 95.

46. Duane, op. cit., p. 219; Galaburda says that "subtle and more obvious distortions of cortical architecture have been demonstrated in the left hemisphere of the dyslexic brain, and this type of distortion probably dates back to the period of neuronal migration occurring somewhere between the 16th and 24th week of gestation." Albert Galaburda, "Developmental Dyslexia: Current Anatomical Research," *Annals of Dyslexia* 33 (1983), p. 51.

47. Duane, op. cit., p. 219.

48. Hynd and Semrud-Clikeman, op. cit., p. 208.

49. Ibid.

50. Harold N. Levinson, *A Solution to the Riddle Dyslexia* (New York: Springer-Verlag, 1980); *Smart But Feeling Dumb* (New York: Warner Books, 1984).

51. Levinson (1984), op. cit., p. 58.

52. Additional notes on Levinson's C-V Theory:

In a review of Levinson's book, *A Solution to the Riddle Dyslexia*, Dr. Richard Masland and Dr. Celia Usprich find "inadequate scientific evidence to justify the author's treatment or to support his theory." (p. 256) They write:

(a) His interpretation that soft neurological signs are attributable to c-v function is based on his own view of the cerebellum, a view which rests on an expanded notion of what cerebellar function might be. This includes giving the cerebellum a major role in cognition. No evidence of such a role is provided. Levinson tends "to leap from *if* to *it is true*" and writes as though his view is a fact.

(b) In the blind ENG study 75 dyslexics were referred to hospitals for electronystagmography. Levinson says that of the 70 children who completed the ENG testing, 90 percent revealed some abnormality of c-v function. About 50 pages later Levinson says that of these 70 dyslexics "20 percent were reported to have spontaneous and/or positional forms of a subclinical or ENG-detectable nystagmus" (p. 138). He goes on to state that "one can assume either that the remaining 80 percent of the ENG-tested c-v dyslexics have no subclinical nystagmus or that all c-v dyslexics have a subclinical nystagmus but that present day ENG methodology can detect this nystagmus only 20 percent of the time" (p. 138). Levinson assumed the existence of a subclinical nystagmus in all c-v dyslexics. "As a result of these ENG-detectable subclinical nystagmus in dyslexia was raised from 20 percent to over 65 percent—lending significant support to the thesis that all c-v dyslexics have a subclinical nystagmus" (p. 138). When, where, and by whom the 20 percent was raised to 65 percent is not stated. No data is given as to the proportion of nondyslexic normal children who show such ENG abnormalities using his modified procedures; hence, conclusions remain unconvincing.

(c) In the Staten Island study dyslexics were found to have slower blurring speeds than the normal controls in the study. There are a variety of experimental questions concerning this study. Independent investigators who did a blind study could not confirm Levinson's results. He then conducted two additional studies because he was convinced that blurring speed deficits are present in dyslexics and are diagnostic of the dyslexia condition. The reviewers state that, "the author was emotionally biased against unnecessary blind studies and biased in favor of historical responses and content" (p. 260). For more information read Richard Masland and Celia Usprich's review of Levinson's book in *Bulletin of the Orton Society* 31 (1981), pp. 256–61.

PART FOUR

DYSLEXIA IN ADOLESCENCE AND MATURITY

'Tis education forms the common mind:
Just as the twig is bent the tree's inclined.
—*Alexander Pope*

CHAPTER 10

DYSLEXIA IN THE MIDDLE SCHOOL AND HIGH SCHOOL

> True, children are educable in varying degrees, but
> the variation in degree must be of the same kind and
> quality of education. If "the best education for the
> best is the best education for all," the failure
> to carry out that principle is the failure on the
> part of society—a failure of parents, of
> teachers, of administrators—not a failure on the
> part of the children.
> —*Mortimer J. Adler*

If the dyslexia is not detected in the elementary school, remediation for the dyslexic student tends to take longer and may be more difficult to achieve because of his age. There are several reasons for this. The student's self-esteem has been damaged over years of being unable to keep up with his fellow students in school or to satisfy the performance expectations of his teachers and his parents. Feelings of frustration and anxiety have built up inside him as a result of continuing failure and low grades. His motivation and drive to take on certain tasks is deadened. "What's the use?" he thinks. Since his difficulties have not been overcome or even ameliorated, he continues to reinforce his incorrect responses to the point where they become internalized and automatic.

The older dyslexic often develops the pretense of not caring about the quality of his schoolwork or his grades. He may try to act superior, belittling or putting down those to whom he may feel inferior. He is thin-skinned, with a prickly personality, and is subject to irritability and verbal (and sometimes physical) explosions. He may burst out with a nasty retort and withdraw to

149

his desk at school or to his room at home. By now he may have been diagnosed as "emotionally disturbed," and the underlying dyslexia may have become eclipsed by its own creation.

Often the middle school or high school dyslexic becomes a loner. By evading social interchange he naively believes that he can prevent the other students from finding out that he cannot read the textbooks, cannot perform as he thinks they do. Each year in school the gap increases between his chronological age and his academic achievement—unless he gets the help he needs—and his social withdrawal is likely to become more pronounced.

The lecture method of instruction is common in middle and high school classes. And of course the dyslexic student has difficulty listening to a lecture, following the sequence of what the teacher is saying, and remembering what he has heard. He has trouble recording the notes of the lecture because of his problems with immediate recall, sequencing, spelling, and writing. His lecture notes are likely to be scanty, disorganized, in bits and pieces, and almost impossible to study for a review. The faster the teacher talks (or reads), the more confused the dyslexic's notes become.

Some middle and high school teachers fill the chalkboards with notes prior to class and expect the students to spend a large part of the period copying the notes for future study. Often diagrams or charts must also be copied. All of this is very difficult for the visual dyslexic, as is copying notes or diagrams from the overhead projector, which teachers in the upper grades frequently use, for the student has to look up repeatedly to see the material, then look down at his paper to reproduce it. His visual memory and integration problems interfere with the smooth transference of letters, words, and punctuation. He must work slowly. Often he does not complete the copying, usually to the dismay of his teacher. A teacher may also find it hard to understand the errors in copying, since "it is all right there in front of you!" or the messiness, which is a tendency of both visual and auditory dyslexics.

School essays, book reports, science or social studies reports, and other such projects present special problems to the older dyslexic. But by this age, he has developed certain "survival techniques" (sometimes called "avoidance techniques") as a result of receiving papers covered with red ink corrections—sometimes with sarcastic remarks about his numerous errors and sloppiness in spelling and handwriting—and the inevitable low grades. (He writes as little as possible, using only those words that he thinks he knows how to spell, or he plagiarizes, although he makes some errors in copying.)

Scores on tests and examinations may be low because of his reading and writing problems in class. They may also be low, not because he does not know the answers, but because he is unable to read the significant words in the questions or because his short-term memory and sequencing problems distort his perception of what is being asked. Few and fortunate are the dyslexic students who are placed with an understanding teacher (who has a caring, courageous, and supportive principal), who is allowed to read and clarify test questions for them, or who will take the time to tape the questions of a test. When this is done the dyslexic student benefits by looking at the words of the directions as he hears them being spoken.

The dyslexic student needs additional time to write his answers because of his mental processing problems and his slow handwriting rate. If he can speak the answers to the questions softly into a tape recorder for the teacher to check later, the result will be a more realistic assessment of the student's progress.

The dyslexic student is, obviously, likely to have trouble with foreign languages in high school. The elimination of foreign language requirements by many colleges and universities may have distressed educators, foreign service personnel, and others, but it has been a great help to the dyslexic who seeks higher education. For the auditory dyslexic, a foreign language may present an impossible task. For the visual dyslexic, writing the language is the hurdle that must be overcome, not speaking it. Some visual dyslexics have learned to speak a foreign language by ear; that is, by living in a foreign country or by participating in a conversation class that requires no writing.

The older visual dyslexic student finds the requirements of geometry trying, such as the need to reproduce various geometric designs, compare figures, take measurements, and write logical proofs. Depending upon the severity and type of dyslexia, band, chorus, and music appreciation classes may be difficult because of the need to read musical notations, to keep in step during precision drills, and simply to keep in time. Visual dyslexic students have trouble with algebra mainly because of transposition and sequencing problems.

Secondary school teachers should take a page from the elementary teacher's book of methods. Rather than predominantly using the lecture method in the classroom, the "unit" method of teaching would be most successful with the dyslexic student. This technique can be used for *any* subject. Here the students are not sitting passively at their desks taking or copying notes but are *actively* involved in the instruction through various shared activities, planning, demonstrating, and so on. Books containing the basic concepts but written at lower reading levels are used. Rather than having a single textbook at one level for all students in a class (regardless of the level of their reading), there are a variety of books on the curriculum topics, and at differing reading levels.

Some teacher-training institutions require their graduates to have a knowledge of unit teaching, but too often they leave this knowledge at the college, either because they are employed by a school system that mandates a single textbook in a class or does not provide the funds for a variety of books at differing levels, or because the teachers give in to the simpler and less time-consuming use of one textbook and let it dictate what is to be taught and how it is to be taught. It is unfortunate when the teacher becomes the tool and the textbook the master, because it is the student who suffers.

By law, students are required to remain in school until a certain age. As a result of "social promotion" (because of age) students are moved to the next grade, sometimes after repeating a year or more in elementary school. But all children in a particular grade, say the tenth grade, are not reading at the tenth-grade level. In a typical tenth-grade class, the range of reading levels is likely to cover a span of seven grades or more. Yet it is common practice for schools to adopt a single textbook for each subject at each grade level. All students are expected to read the same textbook both in and out of class, whether or not the reading level makes for ease of reading and understanding. No wonder so many middle and high school teachers feel frustrated when they haven't the least idea what to do with the students who cannot read the required textbook.

According to the latest *NASDTEC Manual* (Manual on Certification and Preparation of Educational Personnel in the United States), a course, such as the teaching of reading or applying reading to a high school subject, is neither specified nor required of any secondary teacher seeking certification in twelve of our fifty states. Four states include reading only as one of a group of courses that *may* be taken, which means that some other course may be elected in its place. Three states require a reading course for English teachers only. One state requires this of only English and social studies teachers. One requires the course for all teachers except those in art, home economics, industrial arts, music, or physical education. Another merely states that whether a reading course is taken depends on "the endorsement obtained and renewal period."[1] Only twenty-eight states require courses in the teaching of reading or reading in the content areas for all secondary school certification. Here is another reason our dyslexic students have been falling by the wayside. In addition to note-taking problems during lectures, they have problems with the textbooks and the required reading in their classes.

During the upper-level school years, nearly 90 percent of a student's studies will depend upon his reading achievement.[2] As a result, the dyslexic public high school student often ends up in vocational shop classes. Early diagnosis of the problem with the necessary treatment to alleviate the disability would help many capable and highly motivated dyslexics move toward higher education.

What About College for the Dyslexic?

Of course it is possible for a dyslexic to attend college, although his preferred college may not be the best for him. The degree of his success in college will depend to a considerable extent upon the severity of his dyslexic condition. It will also depend upon his intelligence, interest, motivation, drive, self-discipline, persistence, health, and energy level.

Special tutoring will probably be necessary, and this will add to the cost of college. Often this can be provided by another college student who has done especially well in a particular course in which the dyslexic needs help. A typewriter for term papers and special reports is essential. Better yet, hire a typist for this job (more cost to the dyslexic student). Help in proofreading anything handwritten is essential, but both the help and the reason for it should be made known to the professor.

Learning to use a word processor could be helpful for the dyslexic student in writing papers, particularly if it included a spelling correction program, although these do not catch all the misspellings. Proofreading would still be necessary. For example, if one were to write "he went into the house" as "he went in to the house," the spelling program would not pick up the word *into* because *in* and *to* are correctly spelled. Also not picked up as a misspelling is the incorrect use of homophones (words that sound alike but have different spellings and meanings, such as their/there, meat/meet, blue/blew, buy/by, and too/to/two). Errors of this type are common to the dyslexic.

Little research has been done with longitudinal and follow-up studies of dyslexics—testing students in elementary school and then following up and retesting them as adults to determine their academic progress, educational attainments, and occupational status. We also need ongoing (not retroactive) information about the kinds of remedial help being given; the frequency of remedial instruction and whether it is on a one-to-one or group basis (and size of group); whether the students remain in regular classrooms and receive special remedial help or spend all day in special classes; and the yearly progress of each student. Ongoing, progressive records of such information are highly preferable to retroactive information with its many gaps.

The information obtained from the few follow-up studies that have been done is contradictory. It leaves doubts about what really can be expected of the dyslexic. Of course, the severity of the condition, the time of the diagnosis, the quality and amount of remedial help, the intelligence of the dyslexic, and various personality factors combine to affect the progress of a dyslexic student and his future life (see Chapter 13). One must also take into account the accuracy of the diagnoses when considering the progress of students who have fallen behind for one reason or another.

Forty young men who had been diagnosed as being dyslexic at the Hawthorn Center, a mental health facility in Michigan for children and adolescents, were retested to determine their academic progress over approximately ten years after they were first diagnosed.[3] They continued to have serious difficulty, and many of the types of errors noted earlier persisted.

The highest reading level score of these men was 8.4 (eighth grade, fourth month). The highest spelling level score was 6.6 (sixth grade, sixth month). These reading and spelling levels are not likely to gain one admission to college, much less allow one to succeed in college after getting there.

Several aspects of this study should be noted. The Wechsler Intelligence Scale for Children (WISC) was administered at the time of diagnosis. The Verbal IQs varied from 66 to 103, with Full Scale IQs varying from 80 to 112. No follow-up Wechsler Adult Intelligence Scale (WAIS) was given. The researcher does not indicate the number of students at each level of intelligence, and if the range of IQs was skewed to the left—more scores falling at the lower end of the scale—one cannot expect the same amount and rate of progress for those of lower intelligence as for those of higher intelligence. Some of the symptoms of low intelligence are similar to those of dyslexia (such as poor sequencing, some reversals, problems with abstract concepts, immature drawings, and poor auditory discrimination). Were some of the participants in this study simply slow learners, or slow-learning dyslexics?

The quantity and quality of remedial help is not known. Remedial help was defined as assistance by specially trained persons in a group of ten or fewer outside the classroom two or three times a week. But the *total* amount of remediation given each dyslexic *varied tremendously*, ranging from only one to five semesters for nine students to sixteen to twenty-four semesters for six students. (The researcher "concluded" that there was no relationship between the amount of reading assistance and the adult reading levels!)

In contrast to the above study, published in 1978, is a prior follow-up study published in 1968, of twenty dyslexic boys[4] (eight "moderately" dyslexic and twelve "severely" dyslexic). Most of the boys were found to have progressed steadily through secondary school. Three severe and two moderate dyslexics repeated grades, but all graduated from high school. All but two went on to graduate from college. Four completed a year of graduate study, one earned a law degree, one a graduate degree in divinity, and three were doctoral candidates. Five had their doctoral degrees.

What happened to these dyslexic boys? Why had they not fallen by the wayside? There may be several reasons. Their dyslexia was diagnosed at a fairly early age and special help was given. The researcher, Rawson, states that one of this particular school's most valuable contributions was "to the self-concepts of the boys, a persistent faith in their intelligence and capacity to achieve, transmitted to the boys directly and indirectly."[5] The home environment must have had a great deal of influence. The families were "professionally oriented, highly educated, intelligent, 'intellectual,' upper-middle-class, financially solvent but not wealthy, educationally nonconventional, and individualistic."[6] The range of IQs was from average to superior—no slow learners.

One must add that this is a rather old study, and the boys were diagnosed as being "dyslexic" while still in elementary school. Much less was known about diagnosing dyslexia at that time, and it is possible that some of these boys were not dyslexic at all. No mention was made about the types of dyslexia.

The students in the above study began receiving help to alleviate their difficulties at a fairly early age. But the middle school or high school dyslexic who was not diagnosed at an earlier age can take heart from former Vice President Nelson A. Rockefeller who, a dyslexic himself, had an interesting story to tell about his travels through the Land of Dyslexia Frustration and about his decision in the ninth grade to tackle his problem. He wrote the following article in connection with a television special called "The Puzzle Children." Older students will be able to identify with some of his experiences:

Don't Accept Anyone's Verdict That You Are Lazy, Stupid or Retarded

By

Vice President Nelson A. Rockefeller

Those watching the Public Broadcasting Service program "The Puzzle Children" will include a very interested vice president of the United States.

For I was one of the "puzzle children" myself—a dyslexic, or "reverse reader"—and I still have a hard time reading today.

But after coping with this problem for more than 60 years, I have a message of encouragement for children with learning disabilities—and their parents.

Based on my own experience, my message to dyslexic children is this:

• Don't accept anyone's verdict that you are lazy, stupid or retarded. You may very well be smarter than most other children your age. . . .

• You can learn to cope with your problem and turn your so-called disability into a positive advantage.

Dyslexia forced me to develop powers of concentration that have been invaluable throughout my career in business, philanthropy and public life.

And I've done an enormous amount of reading and public speaking, especially in political campaigns for governor of New York and president of the United States.

No one had ever heard of dyslexia when I discovered as a boy, along about the third grade, that reading was such a difficult chore that I was in the bottom one-third of my class.

None of the educational, medical and psychological help available today for dyslexics was available in those days.

We had no special teachers or tutors, no special classes or courses, no special methods of teaching—because nobody understood our problem.

Along with an estimated three million other children, I just struggled to understand words that seemed to garble before my eyes, numbers that came out backwards, sentences that were hard to grasp.

And so I accepted the verdict . . . that I wasn't as bright as most of the rest of my class at the Lincoln School in New York City. Fortunately for me, the school (though it never taught me to spell!) was an experimental, progressive institution with the flexibility to let you develop your own interests and follow them.

More to the point, I had a wise and understanding counselor in Dr. Otis W. Caldwell, the headmaster.

"Don't worry," he said, "just because you're in the lower third of the class. You've got the intelligence. If you just work harder and concentrate more, you can make it."

So I learned, through self-discipline, to concentrate, which in my opinion is essential for a dyslexic.

While I could speak better French than the teacher, because I'd learned it as a child, I couldn't conjugate the verbs. I did flunk Spanish—but now can speak it fluently because I learned it by ear, later, at the Berlitz School.

My best subject was mathematics; I understood concepts well beyond my grade level. But it took only one reversed number in a column of figures to cause havoc.

When I came close to flunking out in the ninth grade—because I didn't work very hard that year—I decided that I had better follow Dr. Caldwell's advice if I wanted to go to college.

I even told my high-school girl friend that we would have to stop dating so I could spend the time studying in order to get into Dartmouth.

And I made it by the skin of my teeth.

I made it simply by working harder and longer than the rest—eventually learning to concentrate sufficiently to compensate for my dyslexia in reading.

I adopted a regimen of getting up at 5 A.M. to study, and studying without fail. And thanks to my concentration and the very competitive nature I was born with, I found my academic performance gradually improving. . . .

I owe a great debt to my professors and to President Erneste M. Hopkins. I had met Dr. Hopkins earlier and was so impressed that I had made Dartmouth my goal. Most of all, however, I think I owe my academic improvement to my roommate, Johnny French.

Johnny and I were the exact opposites. He was reticent, and had the highest IQ in the class. To me, he was that maddening type who got straight A's with only occasional reference to books or classes. He was absolutely disgusted by my study habits—anybody who got up at 5 in the morning to hit the books was, well, peculiar.

Inevitably, Johnny made Phi Beta Kappa in our junior year, but my competitive instincts kept me going. We were both elected to senior fellowships and I made Phi Beta Kappa in my senior year. . . .

Looking back over the years, I remember vividly the pain and mortification I felt as a boy of 8, when I was assigned to read a short passage of Scripture at a community vesper service during summer vacation in Maine—and did a thoroughly miserable job of it.

I know what a dyslexic child goes through—the frustration of not being able to do what other children do easily, the humiliation of being thought not too bright when such is not the case at all.

My personal discoveries as to what is required to cope with dyslexia could be summarized in these admonitions to the individual dyslexic:

Accept the fact that you have a problem—don't just try to hide it.

Refuse to feel sorry for yourself.

Realize that you don't have an excuse—you have a challenge.

Face the challenge.

Work harder and learn mental discipline—the capacity for total concentration—and

Never quit.

If it helps a dyslexic child to know I went through the same thing . . .

But can conduct press conferences today in three languages . . .

And can read a speech on television . . .

(Though I may have to rehearse it six times . . .

(With my script in large type . . .

(And my sentences broken into segments like these . . .

And long words broken into syllables) . . .

And I have learned to read and communicate well enough to be elected Governor of New York four times . . .

And to win Congressional confirmation as Vice President of the United States . . .

Then I hope the telling of my story as a dyslexic could be an inspiration to the "puzzle children"—for that's what I really care about.[7]

Rockefeller had "true grit" and self-discipline, plus high intelligence and a goal very important to him. He did not have auditory dyslexia and was able to do much learning by ear, as evidenced by his learning to speak Spanish at the Berlitz School and to speak French as a child. *Writing* the language was another story because of his visual dyslexia, which also contributed to his problems in math and reading.

In Rockefeller's school days, very little, if anything, was known about dyslexia by most of those in education. Today, there is no excuse for anyone connected with the education of children to be ignorant of this disability. School priorities may need to be reorganized so that dyslexics will be detected and receive the help they need. This means that trained reading specialists must be available at the elementary, middle, and high school levels to detect dyslexics and to work with them. New lights or an enlarged stadium or new band uniforms may need to take a lower priority, if necessary, to enable the business of educating all the children in our schools to proceed in our democratic society.

College Tests: Services for Dyslexic Students

Since 1939, the College Board has made available special editions of its tests for handicapped students. This includes students with dyslexia. Special editions of the Scholastic Aptitude Test (SAT) and the Test of Standard Written English (TSWE) may be administered during an extended time period for dyslexic students. They may also work with cassettes and may use a typewriter or an abacus, but not a calculator.[8]

The American College Testing (ACT) Assessment also provides special accommodations for dyslexic students. However, the SAT makes a notation if any test is taken under the above nonstandard conditions, whereas the ACT makes no reference to any special testing arrangements unless extended time is used.

The dyslexic student, his parents, and the school counselor should decide what special arrangements are needed. They may wish to consider the possibility of taking the test both ways. For some students, taking the test with and without special accommodations, may be worth the additional cost and investment of time.

The need for a special test must be documented by an individual educational plan that states the nature and effect of the handicap as well as the modified testing arrangements required. In the absence of such documentation, statements signed by qualified personnel must be provided describing the handicap and the need for a special testing arrangement. The high school counselor should order the tests, answer sheets, and practice materials.

If additional information is needed on the Admissions Testing Program of the College Board, contact:

ATP: Services for Handicapped Students
Box 2891
Princeton, New Jersey 08541
Telephone: (609) 734-3867

If there are questions concerning the American College Testing Assessment, contact:

The ACT Assessment—"Special Testing Guide" Test Administration
P.O. Box 168
Iowa City, Iowa 52243
Telephone: (609) 337-1332

Which College to Choose?

Finding the right college for the dyslexic student is not easy and must be done with care and caution. Before a decision is made, one must determine what programs are offered, what type of help is available for the student, the philosophy of the college as a whole with regard to dyslexic students, and whether the environment is right for the dyslexic. As much information as possible must be obtained from the college, and this should be discussed with the dyslexic's parents and the school counselor.

A visit to the college is very important. Prepare in advance a list of questions you will need answered, and do not hesitate to ask these. Make no commitment until you have given careful thought to the information you have obtained. Compare what you have learned about the different colleges you have considered and visited.

Listed below are two books that contain information about colleges with programs for dyslexic students. These should provide preliminary help in considering a particular college:

Mangrum, C.T., and Strichart, S.S., *Peterson's Guide to Colleges with Programs for Learning Disabled Students* (Princeton: Peterson's Guide, 1985).

Straughn, C.T., and Colby, M., *Lovejoy's College Guide for the Learning Disabled* (New York: Monarch Press, 1985).

The high school guidance counselor will probably have other books of this type to examine.

Notes

1. *The NASDTEC Manual* (Manual on Certification and Preparation of Educational Personnel in the United States), National Association of State Directors of Teacher Education and Certification, Robert A. Roth and Richard Mastain, eds. (1984), pp. G–6 through G–8.

2. Herman K. Goldberg, Gilbert B. Schiffman, and Michael Bender, *Dyslexia, Interdisciplinary Approaches to Reading Disabilities* (New York: Grune and Stratton, 1983), p. 6.

3. John G. Frauenheim, "Academic Achievement Characteristics of Adult Males

Who Were Diagnosed as Dyslexic in Childhood," *Journal of Learning Disabilities* 2 (October 1978), pp. 21–28.

4. Margaret B. Rawson, *Developmental Language Disability: Adult Accomplishments of Dyslexic Boys* (Baltimore: Johns Hopkins Press, 1968), pp. 74, 76.

5. Ibid., p. 110.

6. Ibid., p. 109.

7. Nelson Rockefeller, "Don't Accept Anyone's Verdict That You Are Lazy, Stupid or Retarded," *TV Guide* (October 16, 1978), pp. 12–14. Reprinted with permission from TV Guide® Magazine. Copyright © 1976 by Triangle Publications, Inc., Radnor, Pennsylvania.

8. "Information for Students with Special Needs," Admissions Testing Program, College Entrance Examination Board, Princeton, New Jersey (1984), pp. 1–4.

CHAPTER 11

THE ADULT DYSLEXIC IN OUR SOCIETY

> There are golden ages yet to be made and times of
> trouble to be survived. The book is a shield, a tool
> and a power-pack. It is an instrument for intellectual
> and emotional navigation. It is men's own sovereign
> remedy against the ills and confusions of a changing
> universe. The more competent readers a society
> has, the greater will be its capacity for doing good
> itself. Wakeful happiness should be the best
> condition of men.
> —*Frank G. Jennings*

There is no way of determining the number of adult dyslexics in our
society. Many are part of that larger number of functionally illiterate adults
who are unable to perform productively as citizens, family members, con-
sumers, or workers. The National Commission on Literacy has reported that
30 million adult Americans cannot read a want ad or a newspaper. One in
five high school seniors cannot perform basic reading tasks upon graduation.[1]

Conflicting, confusing, and somewhat alarming statistical figures of
literacy and illiteracy are constantly being thrown at us these days by
politicians and the media. Part of the problem lies in defining these terms.
Webster's Dictionary defines the word *illiterate* as someone who does not
know how to read or write; however, some people today are defining it as
functioning below the eighth-grade level. Certainly the latter definition would
result in a higher estimate of illiterate citizens in our society than Webster's
or that used by the United States Census Bureau, which defines as illiterate a
person who is at least fourteen years old but who has not finished the fifth
grade.

In the past, most newspaper articles and wire service dispatches were thought to be written at about a fourth- or fifth-grade readability level. Recent research indicates, however, that the readability of these materials actually ranges from the eleventh-grade level to that of a college freshman.[2]

A sixth-grade reading level is needed to understand a driver's license manual. An eighth-grade reading level is necessary to follow the directions for cooking a TV dinner and to read the federal income tax form. A tenth-grade reading level is needed to understand the directions on an aspirin bottle, and a twelfth-grade reading level to read and understand an insurance policy.[3]

In answer to a class action suit brought by Legal Services for the Elderly against Medicare in the federal court in New York, a letter sent by Medicare to claimants was found to have a readability level that ranged from the twelfth to the sixteenth grade (college senior). The court found that 48 percent of the residents of New York age sixty-five and older have an eighth-grade education or less.[4]

When the adult dyslexic enrolls his children in school and is asked their dates of birth he may not be able to recall them. This is likely to shock the school recorder. Often I have heard the remark, "Would you believe that man doesn't even know when his children were born? Doesn't he *care* about his family?" She would be even more surprised to know that the same person may not remember the date of his marriage, when he had that car accident, or in what order he was supposed to stop by the classroom, the secretary's office, and the principal's office. And none of these has a thing to do with caring for his family.

The adult dyslexic has trouble using the telephone directory, dictionaries, encyclopedias, and other indices, and filing papers because of his problems with alphabetical order and spelling. For this he needs a competent secretary.

The adult visual dyslexic should keep a small pocket notebook in which he can make notes or keep lists to use as a check on what things he needs to do and when he is supposed to do them. For some, a digital watch may be easier to read than the ordinary type that has two (sometimes three) hands and twelve numbers, because of sequencing difficulties. Care must be taken, though, when reading the numbers that these are not transposed and thus read out of order—12:15 read as 12:51—and of course reversals can still occur—9:26 becomes 6:29 or 9:56 becomes 6:59. Some modern watches have only dots or lines to indicate where the numerals should be. These, too, may present problems for the visual dyslexic because he must draw on memory and visual imagery to place the appropriate numerals and count the minutes (in sequence). A wristwatch with an alarm will help remind the dyslexic of appointments and time schedules. Here again, care must be taken when setting the alarm that the correct numerals are used. Double-checking the setting should be habitual.

A dyslexic artillery observer might confuse the numbers in his map coordinates and call down fire on his own forces!

Reading road maps or traveling by train, bus, or the subways can be troublesome. The dyslexic may need to record the stops before his destination in his notebook and refer to them as he travels. He may wish to ask the conductor or bus driver to announce his stop. He should *never* be hesitant to ask someone for help if in doubt.

The visual dyslexic must use a calculator with caution and much double-checking, because visual memory, transposition and other reversal errors, and sequencing problems may result in tabulating inaccurate information. Still, it will probably be more accurate than trying to figure without a calculator. Referring to and copying from sets of mathematical tables can result in serious mistakes for the same reasons.

Obviously, reversals and sequencing errors with numerals can lead to mistakes in the preparation of income tax returns. I would advise the dyslexic to have someone check his figures.

When participating in parades, the adult dyslexic may confuse right with left and have difficulty keeping in step. Piloting an airplane could be very dangerous. One example of this was a case where certain air force pilots seemed to be involved in a larger number of accidents or incidents. A psychologist, Gerhardt, was asked to investigate the matter. He discovered that many of the pilots often confused right and left directions (and also were poor readers and spellers),[5] which resulted in disastrous consequences when they had to make quick decisions concerning a right or left action.

Learning a special code, such as the Morse Code, is a difficult task for both the visual and auditory dyslexic. Accurate sequencing of coded symbols is necessary, and dots and dashes must be in correct order.

When writing an incident report, policemen must relate the occurrence of events in accurate order. Indeed, included in the multiple-choice examination given to applicants by the New York City Police Department are tests requiring the applicants to place disconnected sentences in "logical order."[6]

Reading the subtitles used with foreign movies is frustrating to the dyslexic because the lines are usually exposed for too short a time for him to be able to process the information.

Can Adult Dyslexics Be Helped?

Motivation, drive, a strong need to learn, and a willingness to work hard and long will speed the adult's remediation. He usually feels that time is passing him by, giving a sense of urgency to his attitude.

A young man in his early thirties, "S," called and asked for help. He was a salesman—energetic, likable, convincing, and doing well at his job. Why did he need help? He had been offered a promotion with the firm for which he worked, but he knew he would be unable to read and write the necessary reports. Up to that time his wife had been writing out all his orders for him from notes he made on a pad.

But his wife could hardly follow him into the office and be his helpmate there as she had been at home. He wanted to accept the offer very much because it would mean less traveling, which he did not enjoy. He said that he was under constant strain to get where he was going—not just to the particular town or city, but even to the business office on which he was supposed to call. This was especially difficult if the place were strange to him.

The young man came in for the necessary series of diagnostic tests. Findings indicated a moderate degree of visual dyslexia. A conference was set up with "S" and his wife to discuss several possibilities of action. I was impressed with his wife's genuine desire to help her husband in any way she could. She said that helping him kept her busy and made her feel important in his life. She obviously admired her husband for what he was trying to do. Their relationship was one of warmth and mutual trust. Each had a sense of humor and could laugh at some of their experiences in life.

I was relieved to hear that in the new job "S" would have the services of a secretary, although he had to share her with another employee. The secretary had been trained to use a dictating machine, and he was able to requisition one for his office. Having a secretary meant that he would have help with making telephone calls, typing, filing information folders and letters—and retrieving them from the files when needed. He could dictate letters, reports, and memoranda. If he needed to bring home any papers or reports, his wife would help him.

We also set up a practical "crash" program of remediation, working first on urgent needs. "S" was a young man of high intelligence, healthy, energetic, disciplined, and certainly highly motivated. With these attributes working for him he could see some progress within a reasonably short time. This encouraged him to work even harder.

I am no longer working with "S," who was transferred to another city, but I do hear from him occasionally, and he and his wife are coping with the situation well. There remains a residual of difficulty—and there probably always will be—but this young man's success can serve as an inspiration for others who find themselves in similar situations.

The Center for Social Organization of Schools and certain members of the Department of Pediatrics at The Johns Hopkins University have done a study of adult dyslexics that gives encouraging results.[7] It was a large-scale, long-term follow-up of several hundred men who had attended the Gow School in South Wales, New York, and had graduated in the years 1940 through 1977.

Gow is a college preparatory school with grades seven through twelve. Students come from all over the United States to attend this boarding school for dyslexic boys. Most of the boys in the study had repeated a school grade before entering Gow. More than two-thirds attended Gow for at least two years, with several returning to their regular high schools at home. Average IQ of those in the study was 118 as measured by the Stanford-Binet Scale, which was administered to the students while at Gow. Only 3.3 percent had an IQ score of 100 or below.[8]

About half of the Gow alumni have only a high school diploma. Of those with a college education, only a few have advanced degrees.[9] Over 80 percent of the Gow men have white collar jobs. Sixty percent of these are professionals or managers—but of the professionals, only a few are lawyers or physicians. Most are technicians or school teachers. Some of those in managerial or sales work are vice presidents, presidents, or chief executive officers. Many are owners of small businesses such as retail stores, and construction, and real estate companies.[10]

Attending Gow is not inexpensive. These men came from homes of sufficient means to allow them to attend this boarding school.

Can dyslexics be successful as adults? The answer is yes. But this yes must be qualified with the statement that there is no doubt that high intelligence and advantaged social backgrounds can weigh the scales in their favor, both as to the degree of success and opportunity. Nevertheless, determination, discipline, and a willingness to work hard—true grit—are almost as important. The adult dyslexic can be helped and can succeed if he is willing to put in the time and effort. Again, the severity of the dyslexia, previous experiences in coping with the difficulty, the amount and quality of any remediation that may have been received—all will affect the level of accomplishment of the dyslexic adult.

Which Career to Choose?

It is just plain common sense to consider a vocation in which dyslexics can succeed. True, dyslexics may *possibly* become lawyers or even physicians, but these vocations pose special problems with the reading, writing, spelling, speaking, and listening involved in both the academic preparation and the career itself. Not only the severity of the dyslexia, but the level of intelligence and the personality of the individual must be taken into account.

The dyslexic might give thought to sales work or certain technician jobs or managerial positions (if secretaries are available). I have some serious reservations about recommending the teaching profession to dyslexics. Teachers have a responsibility to serve as models for their students whenever speaking or reading to them and also in writing, whether on their papers, on the chalkboard, or in notes sent home to their parents. They must also listen and respond carefully to students. Their instruction must be presented in an organized manner with clarity and preciseness of thought. Ambiguity and disorganized lessons will not result in successful learning on the part of the students.

If a teacher should spell a word incorrectly on the chalkboard or on a student's paper, the child may be confused and learn the incorrect spelling of the word, especially if he is to copy the word on paper. Reversals of numerals in arithmetic will, of course, add to the general confusion.

Students in kindergarten and the primary grades must develop a left-to-right/top-to-bottom directional orientation, since this is how we read and write in our society. In physical education or in band-marching practice, miscalled directions concerning left or right could result in real chaos.

Students must learn the sequencing of ideas, events, and numbers, and apply this to all subjects. But how can they if their teacher is unable to do it accurately?

In a study[11] of families involving 105 individuals with a history of dyslexia (primarily to determine genetic analysis of the disability) the researchers reported a concentration of jobs in the building trade. They noted, however, that the dyslexics included both a physician and a lawyer, and one female English teacher.

But here again, one must consider the severity of the dyslexia, the level of intelligence, and the personality of the individual.

The Adult Dyslexic and His Family

We cannot leave this section on the adult dyslexic without some specific comments about how this condition may affect the family. What about the emotional development of the children? Are there adjustments that must be made by the wife (or husband)? By the children?

These questions cannot be answered in a few words or with a flat yes or no. Each case is different. The answers depend on many things: how serious the dyslexic condition is, whether it was diagnosed early, the extent of effective remediation, the emotional stability of the dyslexic and that of the spouse, the self-esteem of the family as a whole, how they perceive the dyslexia problem, and the mutual caring and respect and love that exists among the family members.

Earlier in this chapter I mentioned the willingness of the wife of "S" to help her husband with his job, and his endeavors to seek help and work at improving his condition. What will happen when the children begin arriving and the young wife has less time for her husband's work? Will he understand? Will he feel threatened and insecure? Will feelings of resentment build up in her because of the many demands upon her time? Will the children, as they enter school and learn to read and write, note their father's difficulties? Will they think less of him? Be embarrassed by his problem? Will the father try to hide his problems from them?

(In the case of this particular young family, I do believe that the couple will cope well with the increased responsibility of children and the support needed by all.)

Little research has been done on the dyslexic's family as a whole to determine what happens in such families and how the members respond to each other as a result of having a dyslexic in the family. Psychologists Lenkowsky and Saposnek[12] have done a case history on a dyslexic male whose family almost fell apart. Mr. White was a thirty-five-year-old dyslexic, a high school graduate who earned $16,000 a year as a respected trouble-shooter machinist for a major automotive company. His innate intelligence helped him get through school, where it seems he managed to talk his way out of situations that required reading. His teachers continued to pass him to the next higher grade, until he graduated from high school.

He developed a plan to set up a campground on municipal property, but since he was unable to draw or read blueprints accurately, he had to explain the project to the city officials while actually on the grounds. He would walk to the various spots and point to where different structures should go and where the plumbing pipes should lie.

At work in the machine shop, he had to devise a mnemonic (memory) ritual to locate objects on the job since he could not read the inventory lists.

No one knew of his inability to read other than his immediate family, his reading tutor, and a few psychotherapists whom he had seen. This secrecy required the complicity of the other members of his family, especially his wife, who had to take care of budget decisions, bank transactions, paying the bills, ordering meals in restaurants, and other tasks that require reading and writing.

As time passed, Mr. White saw himself increasingly in a role dependent on and subordinate to his wife. He felt inadequate, unmasculine, and helpless. When frustrated, he frequently gave in to fits of rage during which he would break the furniture or become physically violent to his family, much to his wife's resentment. She also resented his insistent demands for praise for whatever he did. She began to treat him less like a husband and more like a child.

As so often happens when husbands and wives are at odds with one another, Mrs. White drew closer to their two daughters. The husband became more like a peer to the children, and he began to think of his wife as a strict, stern parent. He felt guilt-ridden and incompetent. The relationship deteriorated to the point where almost all their time together was spent fighting. The older daughter, Susan, age fifteen, aware of the precarious balance of her parents' marriage, began to delve into drugs, made some token suicide attempts, and became promiscuous. She perceived that her actions united her parents in an attempt to help her.

Eventually Susan ended up in a state hospital, committed by her parents and diagnosed as having "sociopathic trait disturbance with mild schizophrenic tendencies." While Susan was away, the younger daughter started to assume Susan's mediator role with the parents. When Susan's stay in the hospital was prolonged, Mr. White lost control and threw his younger daughter and wife out of the house, threatened suicide with a gun to his head, and set flares around the house. He was hospitalized and diagnosed as a "paranoid schizophrenic with sociopathic tendencies." Upon his release, he lived alone for a while but then returned home.

When Susan was in turn finally released from the hospital, the family was referred for outpatient family therapy. The father was encouraged to seek help in learning to read, and family relationships were improved during the sessions, as each began to understand what had happened to the family unit—and the reasons why.

This case history is rather extreme and probably atypical of most cases of dyslexia. For here the father, while a dyslexic, did not have the emotional stability essential for successful family relationships. In this case too, the father tried to hide his problem rather than bring it out in the open and get help, as did "S." In addition to having dyslexia, Mr. White was paranoid schizophrenic! No wonder his family had difficulties. Even had Mr. White not had dyslexia, I doubt that life would have been "normal" for the White family.

How can anyone unable to read manage to graduate from high school? I cannot answer this question, yet I know that it does happen. How can a student go through twelve years of school and not have dyslexia diagnosed? This, too, I cannot answer. Again, I know it does happen.

Mr. White's dyslexia had not been diagnosed in school, and thus he received no remedial help to alleviate the condition. However, neither had Nelson Rockefeller, who, in spite of his frustrations in school, retained a stable personality and faced up to his problems squarely while still in school, resolving to tackle the situation rather than designing ways to avoid certain requirements.

True grit can pay off for the dyslexic. Emotional stability is a must if he is to achieve lasting, caring relationships with others and attain a rewarding place in society.

Notes

1. *Written Word, An AAAA Project to Promote Communication in the Field of Functional Illiteracy* (Lincoln, Nebr.: AAAA Contact Center, May 1979).

2. John Micklos, "Reading Levels of Newspapers," *Reading '84* 1 (Newark, Del.: International Reading Association, February 1984), p. 3.

3. "Ahead: A Nation of Illiterates?" *U.S. News and World Report* (May 17, 1982), pp. 53–55.

4. "Poor Writing Can Have Legal Consequences," *Reading Today* 2 (Newark, Del.: International Reading Association, December 1984–January 1985), p. 7.

5. Michael Thomson, *Developmental Dyslexia* (Baltimore: Edward Arnold, 1984), p. 221.

6. "Readings . . . Finding New York's Finest," *Harper's* (February 1986), pp. 16–18. Apparently, the significance of testing for sequencing ability was lost upon those who quoted those items in this selection.

7. Linda S. Gottfredson, Joan M. Finucci, and Barton Childs, "The Adult Occupational Success of Dyslexic Boys: A Large Scale, Long-Term Follow Up," Report No. 334 (Baltimore: Center for Social Organization of Schools, The Johns Hopkins University, March 1983), p. 8.

8. Ibid., p. 9.

9. Ibid., p. 57.

10. Ibid., p. 56.

11. Shelley D. Smith, Bruce F. Pennington, William J. Kimberling, and Herbert A. Lubs, "A Genetic Analysis of Specific Reading Disability," *Genetic Aspects of Speech and Language Disorders*, Christy L. Ludlow and Judith A. Cooper, eds. (New York: Academic Press, 1983), p. 175.

12. Linda Klein Lenkowsky and Donald T. Saposnek, "Family Consequences of Parental Dyslexia," *Journal of Learning Disabilities* 11 (January 1978), pp. 60–64.

CHAPTER 12

SOME NOTABLE PEOPLE: DYSLEXIC OR NOT?

A man should never be ashamed to own he has been
in the wrong, which is but saying, in other words,
that he is wiser today than he was yesterday.
—*Alexander Pope*

Behold the turtle: he makes progress
only when he sticks his neck out.
—*James B. Conant*

Nelson Rockefeller, former vice president of the United States, was a notable person who was able to overcome the handicap of dyslexia. His article, reproduced in Chapter 10, reflects the heartache of a boy who was having trouble in school but did not understand why. It also reflects the courage of a young student who decided that he was going to do something about his problem, the success he achieved, and how he continually had to cope with the problem.

Frequently, in books and articles on dyslexia, writers report a number of notable adults reputed to have had dyslexia. Repetition of these names has become almost a litany. These names are usually just listed in a series in books, with rarely any explanation or evidence given as to why the person is considered to have been dyslexic. The few times any evidence is given it is scanty—often irrelevant or questionable. The problem here seems to be one of follow-the-leader and self-perpetuation. A writer mentions that it is possible that so-and-so *may* have had dyslexia. Another writer picks up the name and goes on to state that such-and-such *did* have dyslexia. And so it goes.

Yet, in our desire to reassure and to give hope to the dyslexic himself and to the parents of dyslexic children, we must ever be on guard as professionals to avoid perpetuating mistruths, and we must couch our language in such a way that new myths are not created. The statement that "so-and-so had problems in school, "too" is far more appropriate than a flat statement that "so-and-so had dyslexia just like you."

The scant evidence that has been presented has been usually based on an after-the-fact (or "after-life") diagnosis of the person's handwriting and his reputed problems at school. But much more information than this is needed for an accurate diagnosis of dyslexia. In Chapter 9 concerning the possible causes of dyslexia, I mentioned the difficulty of adequately tracing dyslexia back three generations because of the problems in obtaining the necessary information to make a proper diagnosis of dyslexia. The same is true with these notable persons who lived a number of years ago and are reputed by some to have had dyslexia. Misspelled words, poor handwriting, and school problems do not necessarily add up to dyslexia! Yet a number of writers have made diagnoses on this basis.

Often there are more simple explanations for the difficulties these personages are said to have had. Pseudodyslexic symptoms may be caused by certain types of vision or hearing defects, inadequate or incorrect instruction in school, emotional problems, stress, anxiety, finger agnosia, or merely haste in writing in order to get thoughts down quickly on paper. Caution and careful investigation must be used—as well as plain common sense—in making any diagnosis, much less one based on historical assumptions.

Dr. Macdonald Critchley, a neurologist, and author of several books and many articles on dyslexia, has studied more than 1,300 cases of dyslexia and characterizes the person who has been diagnosed as dyslexic at a young age, who has made progress while at school, and who has later embarked upon a career as follows:

> I suspect that he does not read for the sheer pleasure or fun of it like non-dyslexic individuals. He is not bookish; he doesn't browse in libraries like his contemporaries in age and intellectual attainment. . . . [He] always continues to be a slow reader, so that it will take him an inordinate length of time to wade through a volume or a technical communication which would be skimmed through quite rapidly by a non-dyslexic. He is slow, furthermore, in getting the gist of a document or business statement, or quickly identifying the nub of an argument or a legal brief. Maybe too, he is a somewhat inaccurate reader, and this may betray itself in his conversation. For example, he may consistently mispronounce certain words which are familiar enough to him from his reading, but which he does not associate with their spoken equivalents. The result is that in his conversation . . . [he] may make rather odd malapropisms when he comes to articulate words which are unusual or relatively infrequent in usage.
>
> He is a most reluctant writer. In the same way he will be a slow writer and, I need scarcely say, an inaccurate speller. . . . [There is] comparative

brevity of [his] writings. Within a given unit of time, say thirty minutes [he] commits to paper far less materials than a non-dyslexic [and there is] a reduction of different words utilized. . . . The dyslexic's writing is more monotonous. He does not employ particularly long sentences nor for that matter particularly short sentences. The average sentence length is inter-mediate and does not vary from sentence to sentence.

An important factor in writing is word-choice and word-usage. [He] rarely uses words of three or more syllables . . . will utilize an undue proportion of first person pronouns—I, me, we—which recur in his writings to an inordinate extent. Normal subjects are less personalized in their script and resort to far more abstract attitudes in the narrative. [The dyslexic] avoids utilizing abstract conceptions and is much more happy when he expresses on paper notions which are absolutely clear-cut, concrete, and identified with personal experience. [He is] very sparing of punctuation marks, and may limit himself solely to full stops. [One] would scarcely expect to find in [his] essays any foreign terms or expressions such as one might well come across in the prose of someone of comparable educational status and socio-cultural background.[1]

The above characteristics of dyslexics out of school and involved in careers are mentioned specifically in this chapter so that you can consider them as you read about the lives of certain persons described below. They are notable persons reputed to have been dyslexic. Among those most frequently cited are:

- Hans Christian Andersen (Denmark's author of fairy tales)
- King Charles XI of Sweden (Karl XI)
- Winston Churchill (British prime minister during World War II)
- Thomas Edison (American inventor)
- Albert Einstein (renowned theoretical scientist, best known for his theory of relativity)
- Leonardo Da Vinci (Italian Renaissance artist)
- Woodrow Wilson (twenty-eighth president of the United States)

These persons are no longer with us, of course, and they lived in times and places in which dyslexia was either unknown or little known. The diagnosis and remediation of dyslexia was certainly not part of a school's services. Any attempted diagnosis of dyslexia now, when these personages are no longer living, would have to rest purely upon speculation—risky business, surely, for those who consider themselves professionals.

Let us briefly examine the lives of these men.

Hans Christian Andersen (1805–1875)

No one would deny that Hans Christian Andersen was the very talented, imaginative writer of many enchanting fairy tales. Less known is the fact that Andersen also wrote plays, novels, and travel books.

In respect to dyslexia, various points should be noted: effective stories must have an organized sequence of events; details in a tale, play, novel, or travel book are important; and visual imagery is essential for imaginative writing.

One source reported that Hans Christian Andersen only relatively recently has been discovered to have been a dyslexic, and this came about as the result of some "expert analysis" of his handwritten manuscripts.[2] Arriving at a diagnosis of dyslexia on the basis of handwriting alone is highly questionable. Spelling and handwriting errors may not be due to dyslexia at all but to a lot of reasons, such as transposition and other reversal errors caused by finger agnosia, haste in getting racing ideas down on paper, stress, or just plain carelessness about spelling or handwriting. I do not read the Danish language, but an examination of a reproduced sample of Andersen's handwriting did not show the numerous overwriting, erasures, and crossovers so common to dyslexia. If they exist in other samples, they could still be caused by any of the reasons given above.

His misspelled words could easily be due to Andersen's inadequate education. One has to have the opportunity to learn to spell words. While Andersen did attend a school for poor children in his hometown for a few years, he quit at age eleven after his father, a sickly indigent shoemaker, died. Left alone, and entirely to his own devices, he built a toy theater and sat at home making clothes for his puppets—and, "avid reader" that he was, he read all the plays he could borrow, including those of Ludvig Holberg, the father of Danish drama, and Shakespeare.[3,4]

When Andersen was fourteen years old he went to Copenhagen because he "was ambitious to become an opera singer,"[5] and he was befriended by the musicians Christoph Weyse and Siboni (and later by the poet Frederik Hoegh Guldberg). When Andersen's voice failed to achieve his operatic ambitions, he was admitted as a dancing pupil at the Royal Theater.[6]

When he was seventeen years old he published his first book, *The Ghost at Palnatoke's Grave* (1822). He then was sent by his patron, King Frederick VI, to the grammar school at Slagelse. The king insisted that he remain there until he (the king) considered that Andersen was "educated." Andersen said that those five years were the darkest and bitterest of his life.[7]

But the assumption must not be made that his academic problems were due to dyslexia. It might well have been that his education at the Odense school for poor children had not prepared him for the performance expectations of the grammar school. The difference, moreover, in social back-ground between the other students and Andersen may have embarrassed the sensitive young man. After having been on his own for six years, he may simply have found the rules and regulations of the school too restrictive.

At any rate, it is not likely that someone who possessed the vivid visual imagery and imagination of Andersen, the mastery of sequence, the ability to organize thoughts and set them down in stories, plays, and novels, and who willingly traveled on long journeys throughout Europe in order to write travel books the way Andersen did, would be a visual dyslexic. Nor is someone with operatic aspirations or who has been accepted in the Royal Theater dancing school likely to be an auditory dyslexic. Certainly a young dyslexic boy would not be considered an "avid reader," motivated to read on his own and to understand and enjoy plays by Ludvig Holberg and Shakespeare at age eleven. Andersen, moreover, enjoyed the acquaintance of Franz Liszt (the composer), Heinrich Heine (the poet), and Charles Dickens and Victor Hugo (the novelists), for they had interests in common.

Hans Christian Andersen surely was *not* a dyslexic.

King Charles XI (Karl XI) of Sweden (1655–1697)

King Charles XI may have had dyslexia. He apparently was a disappoint-ing scholar, mainly because of his difficulty in learning to read. His progress in reading was extremely slow. As an adult he relied on personal interviews rather than on written reports—but many busy executives do this to save time. The difference lay here: if handed a paper, King Charles might hold it upside down and pretend to read it.[8] Could these problems be due to dyslexia? Could they be due instead to some kind of vision defect? This far removed in time we cannot know. We may never know.

His spelling is said to have been highly unconventional. He omitted letters in words, transposed letters (often starting with letters from the middle of the word), and reversed both letters and whole words. In an examination of his journals and other writings, Macdonald Critchley[9] discov-ered a number of interesting spelling mistakes, such as *ta* for *att* (transposi-tion error plus omitted letter), *faton* for *aftou* (transposition error plus vertical reversal of *u* with *n*), *kraken* for *klockan* (blend and vowel confu-sions, plus silent letter omission), and *recyteran* for *rekryter* (letter substitu-tion, blend error, letter omission, addition of letters at the end of the word). Such spelling mistakes continued up to the time of King Charles's death.

But were these spelling mistakes due to reasons other than dyslexia, such as a vision defect? We cannot be sure at this late date. He certainly did have serious ongoing problems with reading and with writing, and it is possible that he had a combination of both visual and auditory dyslexia. All in all, "perhaps" is the word we should use if we wish to name King Charles XI as an example of a renowned dyslexic.

Winston Churchill (1874–1965)

Sir Winston Churchill was, among other things, an outstanding, spellbinding speaker, a noted historian and biographer, and a war reporter. He was a man of boundless energy with a vigorous mind. His command of the English language has been called "matchless," and he won the Nobel Prize for Literature in 1953.

Why is Churchill said to have had dyslexia? Probably because of his trouble with schoolwork, his refusal to learn Latin, and the fact that he spoke with a stutter as a child. (He also had a lisp.) As a boy his high spirits tended to get on everyone's nerves, and his stubborn nature did not help the situation. His personality and strong will affected his schoolwork and antagonized his teachers. He worked hard for those masters he admired and respected, but not for those for whom he had no regard.

His speech problem must have been highly exasperating and frustrating to a boy with such a quick mind. On another front, his mother and father had many duties and responsibilities and could spare little time for their son. Trouble with schoolwork is one way to gain attention from parents. While we do not know that this was the case with Churchill, it is a possibility to be considered. The answer is more likely to lie in his competitiveness, his indifference to the authority of others, and his robust constitution. Only rarely did he play with other children, although he did enjoy football. His tastes, manners, recreation, and thinking reflected the adult world of politics in which he lived.[10]

Churchill's formal schooling began at Ascot, a fashionable and expensive institution. He ended up in the "caning room" frequently for "the headmaster was a sadist of a sort not uncommon in schools of that period, a man with whom flogging reached religious fervor. He felt that he was scourging out devils, and he sang at his work."[11] Such experiences were not likely to serve as a motivating educational force for a young boy of Churchill's nature. And it was at Ascot that he refused to learn Latin. He viewed "the subject as a piece of calculated persecution on the part of the authorities."[12] Not learning Latin has been given as a reason to consider Churchill a dyslexic. But later, when he began writing speeches, he sat down and memorized a complete dictionary of Latin quotations![13] At Ascot, he also began writing a newspaper of his own, *The Critic*—not the type of task a dyslexic is likely to attempt.

While at Ascot, Churchill read *King Solomon's Mines* by H. Rider

Haggard. The young Churchill persuaded a relative of his to arrange a meeting with the author. Haggard came over and Winston quizzed him about various obscure passages in the book. "Now what do you mean by this business?" the child asked at one point, pointing to the passage in question. Haggard became very rattled and after reading the passage over, he admitted that he really did not have "the slightest idea."[14] This incident is not illustrative of typical dyslexic behavior and accomplishment.

When Churchill was twelve years old he entered a leading English secondary school, Harrow School, where it is said he acquired his love of the English language. With regard to dyslexia, I should mention Churchill's performance in qualifying in first place for Moriarty's Army Class. (Moriarty was the master who headed the Army Class and a man whom Churchill especially admired.) While many boys of high scholastic standing failed this examination, Churchill learned 1,200 lines of Macaulay's "Lays of Ancient Rome" and recited them without a single error—again, not something a dyslexic is likely to be able to do.

For the army test Churchill knew that the contestants would be required to draw a map. The evening before he placed a collection of maps in his hat and then withdrew one, which turned out to be of New Zealand. He set about learning it, and Lady Luck was with the young Churchill, for he was asked to draw a map of New Zealand. His memory was in "well-oiled shaped; he filled it in with such specificity, including streams of a dozen yards' breadth and whistle stops on the narrow-gauge railroads, that Moriarty never quite got over it."[15] Again, such detail and accuracy are not common to the visual dyslexic.

True, when it came time for Churchill to take the entrance examinations for the Royal Military College at Sandhurst (the English equivalent of West Point), he failed the examinations twice before passing them. This has been cited as part of the "proof" that Churchill had dyslexia. But never mentioned is the fact that he ended up *graduating eighth in a class of 150 students!* At Sandhurst he was particularly adept in tactics that involved fire and movement on the battlefield—finding ways of getting around the enemy. This, of course, required an adroitness in reading maps, a sense of organization, movement, and direction in space, immediate recall, and the ability to shift one's thinking with quickness and clarity. Also, in the classrooms at Sandhurst, Churchill was "competent and quiet, in astonishing contrast to his classroom manner at Harrow."[16]

While stationed in Bangalore in southern India, Churchill read many of the books that he had neglected to read earlier. Among his favorites were the works of Edward Gibbon and Thomas B. Macaulay—certainly not the type of books that a dyslexic would select for pleasure reading, or would be able to read at all.

A dyslexic has difficulty processing information quickly and setting his thoughts down on paper in an organized fashion. Winston Churchill was most adept at doing this and had no problems with details and sequence in his writings. He was a productive writer.

He also, quite obviously, had an excellent sense of direction. When Churchill was riding on an armored train during the Boer War in South Africa, the Boers ambushed the train and Churchill was captured. He escaped by scaling the prison wall and then crossed three hundred miles of enemy territory (in a country strange to him) by traveling on freight trains—a remarkable feat even for a nondyslexic.

One has only to listen to a record or tape of Sir Winston Churchill's speeches to be impressed with the fluency of his speech, his command of the language, and the orderliness, depth, speed, and clarity of his thought. He was famous as a master of repartee in parliamentary debates—his sharp mind and well-integrated speech flashed a quick retort at the propitious moment. He won the Nobel Prize for "his mastery of historical and biographical presentation and for this brilliant oratory."[17]

Sir Winston Churchill was neither a visual nor an auditory dyslexic.

Thomas Alva Edison (1847–1931)

Thomas A. Edison had a phenomenal mind, endless curiosity, an abundance of energy, tremendous initiative and drive, and enormous "stick-to-it-ive-ness." What he accomplished in his lifetime is incredible. He was certainly one of the great technical geniuses in history. His inventions include an electric vote-recording machine, a typewriter that later became the Remington, the quadruple telegraph repeaters for simultaneous dispatch of several messages over a single wire, the phonograph, the incandescent electric lamp, the electric dynamo, the mimeograph machine, the motion-picture camera, the transmitter, and others too numerous to list.

The evidence given as proof of Edison's dyslexia was that he was considered a dunce at school, that he could not learn the alphabet or arithmetic tables by heart, and that his spelling and grammar remained poor throughout his life.[18,19] Yet the truth of the matter is that because of his need to know the "why" of things, and his tenacity in asking questions, he remained in public school for *only three months*. It seems that Edison irritated his schoolmaster by asking too many questions. When Edison overheard his teacher refer to him as "addled," he told his mother, a former school teacher herself. She immediately confronted the schoolmaster and told him that her son had more sense in his little finger than the schoolmaster had in his entire body (which Edison probably did have), and she withdrew Thomas from school and set about teaching him at home.

Edison's mother believed that learning did not have to be drudgery but could and should be fun. Edison was enchanted with this approach and progressed so rapidly that his mother could no longer instruct him. He was not a "dunce" at all, nor "addled." Indeed, Edison read a chemistry book (by Richard G. Parker) with such understanding that he questioned certain statements made by the author and set about proving them incorrect. Hardly something a dyslexic boy would do.

When he was sixteen, Edison became a telegrapher—another task difficult for a dyslexic because of the coding and sound patterns, sequencing, and need for memory and immediate recall. He was supposed to check in with the Toronto office every hour by telegraph signal. This was a nuisance, so the ingenious Edison constructed a means of sending the hourly signal by attaching a gadget to a clock. Edison lost several jobs because of his fondness for reading and his boredom with routine, uncreative work. He read intensely throughout his life. When on the path of inventing something, his procedure would be to seclude himself for days reading everything he could get his hands on concerning the topic, not only from his vast library next to his laboratory, but from whatever his literary agent could obtain. Only then, after a thorough review of the subject, would he begin his laboratory work. By doing this he avoided the failures of others as well as the fruitless repetition of old experiments.[20]

Thomas Alva Edison a dyslexic? Hardly. A nine-year-old dyslexic is not likely to read a chemistry book at all, much less with such understanding. Nor would he have a fondness for reading in general as did Edison. Learning and using the Morse code would be next to impossible. Scientific experiments require very careful, methodical steps and organized thinking, and an ability to focus on a task for long periods of time. Dyslexics are not likely to immerse themselves in a variety of books on a particular topic for days and days at a time. The evidence does *not* support the notion that Edison was a dyslexic.

Albert Einstein (1879–1955)

Einstein is probably the most often cited "dyslexic" in books and articles on dyslexia. But, as Macdonald and Eileen Critchley point out in their book, *Dyslexia Defined*, "The evidence for Einstein being a true case . . . is slight."[21] They do not elaborate upon this statement.

What is the evidence for Einstein's being dyslexic? The following proof is offered by several writers. Einstein did not talk until he was three years old nor read until he was nine.[22,23] There was evidence of frustration in Einstein's early education, such as when at age five, during a session with his special tutor for lessons and music, it seems that he became so upset that he threw a chair at his teacher who left and was never to return. He was a fair-to-middling student in the early school years (but by the age of twelve he was a brilliant mathematician and physicist). He had no gift for languages. He failed his language requirement at the public school in Munich and left at age fifteen without a diploma. He also failed the language requirements for admission to technical school and enrolled in a small canton school where there was a minimum of verbal communication and a maximum use of diagrams, maps, charts, as well as demonstration.[24]

What is the meaning of this "evidence"? It is not unusual for some highly intelligent children to delay their speaking, but when they do speak they tend to speak in complete sentences, rather than speaking one or two words in isolation. Age five, furthermore, is early to begin formal lessons. We know nothing about the teacher's relationship with Einstein or the teaching techniques used or the performance expectations for the child. The temper tantrum could well have been the result of a young five-year-old on whom too many expectations were placed. Intellectually gifted children can be mediocre students for many reasons, especially if they are creative and are expected to conform, and if they are bored in class. As far as the language requirements are concerned, Einstein's interests quite obviously lay in other directions. As an adult, he could speak and write in English in addition to his native German.

Visual dyslexia? One of the sources reported that Einstein was unusually adept at working puzzles, including geometric puzzles, before the age of ten! And he read, marked, and annotated a geometry book at age twelve.[25] Using diagrams, charts, and maps requires visual memory. His unique ability to grasp concepts of space, mass, motion, time, and gravitation at any level is nigh miraculous—indeed, he changed the way we think about things. Einstein wrote about these concepts with clarity, precision, and orderliness. The development of his different theories required exact steps in sequence and clearness of thought.

Auditory dyslexia? Einstein was very fond of classical music and enjoyed playing the violin, neither of which is probable with auditory dyslexia. He also spoke and wrote in English, a difficult language to learn.

The verdict? It is exceedingly doubtful that Einstein was a dyslexic, either visual or auditory, and he should not be cited as such. The publication of children's books, such as *Einstein and Me* (about a dyslexic boy who attends Einstein School, and in which Einstein is referred to as a dyslexic), should be discouraged.

Leonardo da Vinci (1452–1519)

Leonardo da Vinci is often reported as having been a dyslexic, yet he was a painter, sculptor, musician, architect, experimental scientist, military engineer, art critic, and fiction writer! His figures, portraits, and designs were true to life, exceptionally realistic; these required a strong visual memory, an eye for detail, a sense of direction, a sureness of touch. Architectural drawings are like maps and charts and require a high level of accuracy in planning and execution, and a strong perception of direction, size, and space.

Leonardo was a lute player and had a beautiful voice. He studied the physics of music and understood the fundamentals of acoustics and the physics of the echo.[26]

He had a country schoolboy's education. "He grumbled at not having Latin and Greek," writes Richie Calder in his biography of Leonardo, "but he set out to teach himself, just as he taught himself, quite effectively, advanced forms of mathematics to the level where he would vaunt 'Let no man who is not a mathematician read the elements of my work'—echoing Plato who inscribed over the entrance to his Academy 'Let no one ignorant of geometry enter here.'" Leonardo had a natural curiosity and a thirst for knowledge of all things which were not discouraged by his early schooldays.[27]

"Apart from his uncommon 'common sense,'" Calder goes on—"the brain, the recipient sense common to all physical senses, his faculties, certainly those of sight and hearing, were exceptionally acute. . . . His color register [discrimination] was similarly exceptional not just in seeing the obvious colour differences in painting, but in the subtlety of hues which he expressed in his theory of colours. . . . His [hearing] sensitivity suggests a range and a precision which was not really available scientifically until we had the microphone and high-fidelity recordings, and the cathode ray oscillograph to make sound visible. . . . He was lucky to be apprenticed to Verrocchio at a time when perspective had become a preoccupation of artists. This at its simplest was the geometry of drawing. . . . Leonardo could encompass, as well as create, the knowledge of his times. He was exceptional in his perceptions and his breadth of awareness. No single man today could embrace all the knowledge of all the disciplines which he embodied. . . . He relied upon his senses, but was always insistent that the senses were the servants of 'the common sense,' the brain."[28]

Leonardo had such a keen intellect that he acquired information with little effort. He studied geometry, physics, astronomy, anatomy, and physiology *on his own*. He was a renowned inventor. Among his numerous inventions were the free-moving ball bearing, the needle-sharpening machine, the chimney cowl to divert smoke, the diving suit, the military tank, the sliding ladder, the machine gun, the oil lamp, and the swing bridge. He was a successful engineer, and "perhaps the deepest thinker and most profound investigator into all the known branches of science of his age."[29]

Leonardo da Vinci wrote *Treatise on Painting*, intended as a guide for his own pupils and as a reflection on his own work as well as that of other artists. He kept voluminous notes, and there are today almost seven thousand pages remaining, containing comments, notes, sketches, and his philosophy of life.

He was ambidextrous, able to use both hands equally well in writing. *He read and wrote competently in the conventional forms.* On his sketches he wrote special notes for himself *in Latin* with his left hand, in a right to left direction from the margin. He created his own style of shorthand—grammalogues, combining words and phrases and using symbols.[30,31,32]

Some historians claim that he wrote in this manner deliberately so as to disguise his thoughts and protect his inventions. But, unfortunately, someone saw these unique notes on Leonardo's sketches and rushed to the conclusion that he was dyslexic because of his "mirror-writing," without investigating the situation further. And thus, was birth given to the myth that Leonardo da Vinci was a dyslexic.

Understanding of true "mirror-writing" is limited, and any explanation of this phenomenon is highly speculative.[33,34] But one can be certain that de Vinci did not suffer from the spatial, orientation, and directional confusions that usually cause mirror-writing. Leonardo was simply a genius, a gifted artist who created his own special form of shorthand for his own particular purposes. As already mentioned, he could write quite proficiently in the conventional manner. It is ludicrous to use Leonardo da Vinci as an example of a famous dyslexic.

George S. Patton, Jr. (1885–1945)

Now the general's name is being thrown into the collective basket of notable dyslexics. One source reports that Patton could not read well, although he had a fantastic "verbal memory," and that he had to have someone write down his examination answers for him.[35] Another writes that "he got through West Point by memorizing whole lectures and texts and parroting them verbatim."[36]

What are the facts in the case of Patton? In the early years, Patton did not have to go to school. His father did not believe in formal education for his children, although he was a cultured man of wide knowledge gained by study and reading. He believed that young brains were unduly burdened with the strict stereotyped curricula of schools, especially the three R's—reading, 'riting, and 'rithmetic. He preferred to impart whatever education he thought they needed by reading the classics to them on long evenings in front of their huge fireplace. By the time he was seven years old, George Patton could recite long passages from the *Iliad* in Pope's translation and knew much of the Bible by heart.[37] Ask yourself, is this something that a seven-year-old dyslexic would be able to do?

When Patton was twelve years old his father decided to begin his formal education. Patton could neither read nor write—not because he was a dyslexic but because he had never been taught! He could recite long passages (with the correct sequencing), but he could not put them down on paper. Yet "Georgie quickly managed to learn to read and became an accomplished writer—as shown by the many brilliant articles which he contributed to the old *Cavalry Journal*; by the facile style of his diary; the lucid notes in his *War As I Knew It*; his letters to his wife—and especially by his crisp and highly professional instructions and orders to his troops."[38]

True, Patton never did learn to spell well, and he was weak in arithmetic. But why just assume that this was due to dyslexia? He missed all those early years of schooling when a stock of spelling words and the basic math facts are acquired. We do not know whether Dr. Stephen Cotter Clark's Classical School for Boys gave individual attention to these deficiencies.

Patton went on to graduate from Pasadena High School, spent a year at the Virginia Military Institute, and passed the entrance examinations for West Point. (I have found no mention of the West Point examination answers being written by someone else. At any rate, it is doubtful that this would have been allowed.) He did flunk his math test in his plebe year at West Point. The reason for this may be because he had been trained by his father to memorize "everything verbatim," and he found the problems in Smith's *Algebra* very difficult.[39] But he read avidly whatever books he could find dealing with military history.[40] He read in depth and retained the information to the minutest detail. His recall, even years later, was remarkable regarding time, detail, sequence, movement, direction, location, space, number, and action. Map reading, topographical features of the terrain, flexibility and change in direction gave him no problems.

Patton's difficulties were likely due to his lack of formal education in those early years, rather than to dyslexia. I would not include him in any list of dyslexics.

Woodrow Wilson (1856–1924)

Another name recently added to the "dyslexia file" is that of Woodrow Wilson, twenty-eighth president of the United States. He was a professor of history, president of Princeton University, a political leader, and a popular and distinguished lecturer and writer. He had a great deal of energy, a magnetic personality, and a fantastic mind.

He graduated from Princeton University thirty-eighth in a class of 106. While there, he practiced public speaking, was a leader in debating, and read widely on public affairs; and he was managing editor of the college newspaper. He then entered law school at the University of Virginia, where he was active in the debating societies. He was an outstanding student at UVA but ill health forced him to leave the following winter.

After a brief interlude as a practicing lawyer, Wilson wanted to be a college teacher and did graduate work at Johns Hopkins, where he received his Ph.D. degree in 1886.

Wilson was a family man, an avid reader, and spent many evenings with his three daughters telling stories and reading aloud from Dickens, Wordsworth, and Scott. He wrote a number of books including *The State, Congressional Government* (his doctoral dissertation), *Division and Reunion, Constitutional Government, A History of the American People* (five volumes), *George Washington*, and *The New Freedom* (his campaign speeches).

Some of the "evidence" given for citing Wilson as being dyslexic is based on his handwriting.[41] Wilson felt the frustration and stress of being unable to write his thoughts down fast enough to keep up with his quick, active mind—so he taught himself shorthand. Learning these symbols would be difficult for a true dyslexic under any circumstances, and it is unlikely a dyslexic would teach them to himself. Anyone who has learned shorthand knows that some of these symbols tend to creep into ordinary handwriting when one has to write something in a hurry.

Wilson turned to the typewriter no doubt for the same reason many other writers do—to keep up with a fast-moving, creative mind so that the flow of thoughts will continue with no interruption in fluency.

Wilson, at age seventeen, had attended a year at Davidson. He had been poorly prepared for college. He had been conditioned in Cicero and in ancient geography by his father, but he entered his Greek and mathematics classes on probation, and he was required to make up a heavy amount of back work. His report card for the first term was a follows:[42,43]

Composition and English	96
Logic and Rhetoric	95
Declamation [oratory]	92
Latin	90
Greek	87
Mathematics	74
Deportment	100

For the second term report, his grades were:[44]

English	97
Composition	95
Latin	94
Declamation	92
Greek	88
Mathematics	88
Deportment	100

As shown here, Wilson's highest grades were in composition and English, the lowest in mathematics and Greek. But these grades in these subjects, including Latin and Greek, could not be called typical of courses taken by and grades won by any young seventeen-year-old dyslexic. (Interestingly, some writers have used difficulties in foreign language as symptomatic of dyslexia, yet Wilson did quite well in both Latin and Greek, and also mastered German and French—but the critics seem to have overlooked this fact.)

Several sources reported that Wilson was dyslexic because "he did not learn his letters until nine" or learn to read until he was eleven.[45,46,47] But the truth of the matter is that Wilson did not even start school until he was nine years old because the Civil War had closed so many of them.[48] One of Wilson's biographers mentions that "he did not even learn his letters until he was nine years old; and could not read readily until he was eleven," but the biographer went on to add, "What need was there when a boy could spend eight hours in delightful listening while others read aloud? [His father and sisters read aloud to him frequently.] He loved always the spoken word, the roll of language."[49] The process of reading is complex, and two years would be a normal time period for a bright child to begin reading "readily" from the time of first learning his alphabet letters. It is worth speculating that Wilson, an eminent man of letters, may actually have had an advantage in not being forced to learn to read at too early an age!

While Wilson's father taught him a great deal at home, his grandfather, who was a frequent visitor and a devotee of the ancient classics, also contributed substantially to Wilson's training. The young Wilson made short trips with his father, after which the boy would be encouraged to relate what he had seen. His father stressed that an exact expression of ideas was essential for clear understanding. This the young boy was able to do competently.

One of Wilson's main interests when he was a youngster was a club that he organized himself. The members played baseball, challenging the neighborhood teams. While Wilson was not the best player, he was president of the club and he wrote a constitution for it before he was ten years old. Rules of strict parliamentary procedure governed all debates of the club members![50] These are not likely activities for a ten-year-old dyslexic.

One of Wilson's classmates at Davidson spoke of him as a "fine, graceful young man, brilliant in his studies and as an athlete. As a short stop on the college team he was a handy player." At Princeton he sang in the Glee Club, was president of the Athletic Committee and president of the Baseball Association. He made "deep friendships that were never broken."[51] Another biographer stated that "as in his student days, he formed strong friendships. . . . Every Sunday afternoon for years an intimate little group met . . . for tea and hours of animated talk."[52] Yet Woodrow Wilson has been described as being "a loner," and this given as evidence of his dyslexia![53]

You will recall, as quoted at the beginning of this chapter, that adult dyslexics are "slow . . . identifying the nub of an argument or legal brief." Wilson was admitted to the bar in 1885.[54]

An examination of Wilson's speeches and writings and a study of his life reveal a clarity and fluency of thought, skillful manipulation of details and organization of facts, excellent recall, and a zest for reading and the acquisition of knowledge.

> All his life he had been a reader: no casual reader, but one of the eager and passionate kind who is not content until he tears out the very heart of a book. This was true not only of so-called serious books, but of romances and poetry as well. When the boy read Cooper's novels, he wished afterward to act them out; if he read sea stories, he made pictures of the ships described; and he was not content with Scott's romances until he had found someone—his father was his best resource—with whom he could discuss the characters and incidents. Many of the volumes of his reading remained in his library at his death. They are indicative of his passion to know completely and accurately what the author had to say. Here, for example, are such books as *The Federalist*, Green's *Short History of the English People*—and Macaulay and Bagehot—with the pages underscored and marginally noted to the last degree, and often written synopses appended to the chapter.[55]

In a commendable effort to dispel one myth about Woodrow Wilson, i.e., Freudian interpretations for a number of things, two researchers (an educational psychologist and a historian)[56] have fallen into the trap of perpetuating another myth—that Wilson had dyslexia. They even threaten to publish a whole volume on historic persons who allegedly, on highly questionable grounds, had dyslexia.[57]

Woodrow Wilson a dyslexic? Balderdash! The facts do not support this notion, and this myth should not continue to be fostered.

Others Reputed to Have Been Dyslexic

There are other notable persons less frequently cited as having been dyslexic. Some of these are Harvey Cushing (the pioneer in brain surgery[58] and a prolific writer, who won the Pulitzer Prize in biography for his book, *The Life of Sir William Osler*); Paul Ehrlich (the German bacteriologist and discoverer of the drug to destroy the specific organism of syphilis); David Lloyd George (British prime minister during World War I); William James (American philosopher and psychologist who wrote philosophy in a wonderfully readable style); Abbott Lawrence Lowell (former president of Harvard University); Michelangelo (the Italian Renaissance artist); and Auguste Rodin (the French sculptor).

As in the cases of the persons discussed earlier, an examination of these men's lives and their works and a search for plausible explanations for certain academic problems raise serious doubts about labeling any as dyslexic. It is highly improbable that they were, and they should not be cited as such in view of the insufficient evidence proffered.

The Credibility Gap

If we are ever to achieve a cooperative, interdisciplinary approach to the dyslexia problem, we who work with dyslexics must earn the respect of those in the various disciplines. Perhaps the credibility gap that now exists is partly due to a few well-meaning persons who have been eager to bring about acceptance of the dyslexia concept and have been too eager to reassure dyslexics and parents by citing as dyslexics persons of substantial accomplishments. Of course we want dyslexics and their parents to feel good about themselves and to hope for a brighter future, but hope must have a firmer basis in reality than quoting myths.

In some cases, this mythologizing has produced ludicrous results. I know of instances where parents will insist that a child is dyslexic, though there are other causes for the problems, because for them the term dyslexia has become some kind of status symbol—look at all the famous intellects who have had it, they crow. For some who cannot accept the real reasons for their children's problems, dyslexia is a comforting explanation.

Those of us in the professional fields must keep our feet on the ground, always using a common-sense, professional approach in these matters. Diagnosis should never be made on the basis of a few symptoms and insufficient information. We need to search for all possible reasons behind a problem and consider the facts objectively. For example, if a sample of mirror-writing is uncovered, one does not immediately jump to the conclusion that a person is dyslexic. Teachers and others who need to explain things are sometimes placed in situations where they must write backward on a glass, allowing a viewer on the opposite side to read the information. Technicians and noncommissioned officers in the military services write backward on glass charts. Merchants write backward on display windows. Television weathermen sometimes write backward on the glass weather chart. Left-handed children in the early grades seem to have a natural tendency to begin writing from right to left.

I can remember as a child exchanging secret letters with friends which were written backward, and later we would hold these up to a mirror so we could more easily read what was written. (Would someone finding one of these letters tucked away in the attic conclude that we were dyslexic?)

Of course, one must always consider the possibility that a printer at one time or another may have simply reversed the negatives of an illustration or made typographical errors. Some Shakespearean "purists" still get very upset if certain words are changed in his works—some of which are the result, not of Shakespeare's writing, but of a printer's error.

Most people will occasionally transpose letters when dialing a telephone number, especially when in a hurry. What typist has not transposed letters when typing—again, especially when in a hurry or under stress? Who has not transposed letters in simple words when writing letters? These errors tend to occur also when the people do not have their mind on what they are doing. Just plain carelessness is probably the number-one culprit of errors in spelling. Diagnosing dyslexia on the evidence of a person's writing alone is altogether unreliable.

But what if there are many such errors? Again, caution is advised. Look to the schooling of the person. Did he have the *opportunity* to learn? What about his personality? Was he the type of person who would place a priority on correct spelling—or were other things more important, such as getting his ideas down quickly any way he could?

What about his reading? Did he read early and widely? What types of books did he read? Was he an excellent reader but a careless speller? Could he set his ideas down in written form in an organized, sequential manner? Was he a fluent speaker, expressing himself with clarity, conciseness, and orderliness? Did he enjoy music? Play a musical instrument? Sing in the choir? Was he a good dancer?

In sum, it should be remembered that (1) in any diagnosis of dyslexia the whole person must be considered—his background, his opportunity to learn, what he has accomplished in various areas, and his personality, (2) a diagnosis cannot be made on any single factor, and (3) any retroactive diagnosis, as in these cases, is highly precarious.

Obviously none of the notable persons cited in this chapter had access to any program for diagnosing and remediating dyslexia. If the purpose of perpetuating the myth of their dyslexia is to reassure dyslexic children and their parents, the essence of the message is actually: "You do not need to do anything. You do not need to see a reading specialist or a learning disability teacher for regular remediation of your dyslexia condition. It will go away with time. In fact, you are likely to be a far greater achiever than the so-called normal persons."

Nonsense!

Notes

1. Macdonald Critchley, "Some Problems of the Ex-Dyslexic," *Bulletin of the Orton Society* 23 (1973), pp. 9–13. Used with permission.

2. Bevé Hornsby, *Overcoming Dyslexia* (New York: Arco, 1984), p. 12.

3. "Andersen, Hans Christian," *The Encyclopedia Americana* Vol. 1 (1946), p. 658.

4. Edmund Gosse, "Andersen, Hans Christian," *The Encyclopedia Britannica*, 11th ed., Vol. 1 (1911), p. 958.

5. "Andersen, Hans Christian," *The Encyclopedia Americana* Vol. 1 (1946), p. 658.

6. Gosse, op. cit., p. 958.

7. Ibid.

8. Macdonald Critchley, *The Dyslexic Child* (Springfield, Ill.: Charles C. Thomas, 1970), p. 114.

9. Ibid., pp. 114–15.

10. Robert Lewis Taylor, *Winston Churchill, An Informal Study of Greatness* (Garden City, N.Y.: Doubleday, 1952), p. 47.

11. Ibid., pp. 53, 55.

12. Ibid., p. 54.

13. Ibid.

14. Ibid., pp. 58–59.

15. Ibid., pp. 70–71.

16. Ibid., p. 91.

17. Carol L. Thompson, "Churchill, Sir Winston Leonard Spencer," *The World Book Encyclopedia* Vol. 3 (1969), p. 425.

18. Hornsby, op. cit., p. 12.

19. Lloyd J. Thompson, "Language Disabilities in Men of Eminence," *Journal of Learning Disabilities* Vol. 4 (January 1971), pp. 39–44.

20. "Edison, Thomas Alva," *The Encyclopedia Americana* Vol. 9 (1946), p. 588.

21. Macdonald Critchley and Eileen Critchley, *Dyslexia Defined* (Springfield, Ill.: Charles C. Thomas, 1978), p. 133.

22. Hornsby, op. cit., p. 10.

23. Thompson, op. cit., p. 116.

24. Richard L. Masland, "The Advantages of Being Dyslexic," *Bulletin of the Orton Society* 26 (1976), pp. 15–17.

25. Ibid., p. 17.

26. Richie Calder, *Leonardo and the Age of the Eye* (New York: Simon and Schuster, 1970), p. 87.

27. Ibid., p. 260.

28. Ibid., pp. 260–61, 273–74.

29. "Vinci, Leonardo da," *The Encyclopedia Americana* Vol. 28 (1946), p. 100.

30. Raymond S. Stites, "Da Vinci, Leonardo," *The World Book Encyclopedia* Vol. 5 (1969), p. 41.

31. Sidney Colvin, "Leonardo da Vinci," *Encyclopedia Britannica* 11th ed., Vol. 16 (1911), p. 453.

32. Calder, op. cit., p. 36.

33. Frank R. Vellutino, *Dyslexia: Theory and Research* (Cambridge, Mass.: MIT Press, 1979), p. 137.

34. Note on mirror-writing: Mirror-writing does not make one a dyslexic. I have observed that when young children first learn to write they will sometimes begin to write from the right margin to the left. The problem can be simply solved by marking the left side of the paper, or by placing a watch or ring on the left hand, and calling the child's attention to this. Usually it can be solved by simply telling a left-handed child to begin starting at the edge of the page on the same side as the hand he uses for writing. The right-handed child is told to start on the side across from his "writing hand." I have noticed that lefties tend to be more persistent in this behavior. For older students who have not had the difficulty firmly corrected and have had insufficient left-to-right orientation practice, I have found this procedure plus tracing techniques (a line of writing) has worked quite successfully. Indeed, as far back as 1943, Grace Fernald reports on correcting an eleven-year-old's mirror-writing in a period of only five days in these simple methods. Grace Fernald, *Remedial Techniques in Basic School Subjects* (New York: McGraw-Hill, 1943), pp. 90–91.

35. Hornsby, op. cit., p. 12.

36. Thompson, op. cit., p. 116.

37. Ladislas Farago, *Patton: Ordeal and Triumph* (New York: Dell, 1963), pp. 55–56.

38. Ibid., p. 56.

39. Ibid, pp. 56, 57–58.

40. Ibid., p. 45.

41. Mary Wade Atteberry, "Dyslexia, Do Its Victims Have Unusual Ability?" *The Indianapolis Star* Section F (Nov. 4, 1984), pp. 1–2.

42. Ray Stannard Baker, *Woodrow Wilson, Life and Letters; Youth 1856–1890* (New York: Doubleday, 1927), pp. 74–75.

43. Ruth Cranston, *The Story of Woodrow Wilson* (New York: Simon and Schuster, 1945), pp. 15–16.

44. Baker, op. cit., p. 74.

45. Hornsby, op. cit., p. 12.

46. Thompson, op. cit., p. 116.

47. Elizabeth Fleming, *Believe the Heart* (San Francisco, Calif.: Strawberry Hill, 1984), p. 39.

48. Arthur S. Link, "Wilson, Woodrow," *The World Book Encyclopedia* Vol. 20 (1969), p. 269.

49. Baker, op. cit., p. 36.

50. Cranston, op. cit., pp. 8–9; Baker, op. cit., p. 45.

51. Josephus Daniels, *The Life of Woodrow Wilson* (Chicago: John C. Winston, 1924), p. 43, 48, 58.

52. Cranston, op. cit., p. 53.

53. Atteberry, op. cit., p. 2.

54. Arthur S. Link, *Wilson, The Road to the White House* (Princeton, N.J.: Princeton University, 1947), p. 8.

55. Baker, op. cit., p. 86.

56. P.G. Aaron and Robert G. Clouse at Indiana State University.

57. Atteberry, op. cit., p. 2.

58. Cushing was a noted brain surgeon at Johns Hopkins, Harvard, and Yale. How would you feel about having a dyslexic with problems in sequence and left/right, up/down, in/out concepts and directions operate on you or your loved ones? Obviously, Cushing did not have that kind of difficulty.

PART FIVE

WHAT CAN WE DO ABOUT IT?

Nothing in education is so astonishing as the amount
of ignorance it accumulates in the form of inert facts.
—*Henry Adams*

CHAPTER 13

ALLEVIATING DYSLEXIA

> Nothing can be taught unless it has the potential of
> making sense to the learner, and learning itself is
> nothing but the endeavor to make sense. The effort
> to teach or to inform, therefore, can be nothing but
> an endeavor to make sense, to be comprehensible.
>
> *Frank Smith*

If a child has visual dyslexia, it can generally be more readily alleviated and in less time than auditory dyslexia. This statement, however, should not be taken to imply that visual dyslexia always can be very quickly remediated, or that auditory dyslexia is beyond help. The length of time for the alleviation of any type of dyslexia depends upon several factors:

- The severity of the dyslexia
- The intelligence of the dyslexic student
- The willingness of the student to work
- The age of the dyslexic
- The expertise of the person alleviating the dyslexia
- The materials available in the classroom and clinic
- The cooperation and understanding of the parents
- The cooperation and understanding of the classroom teacher
- The duration and frequency of periods and length of remediation

- Whether the remediation is on a one-to-one basis or in a small group situation

The Severity of the Problem

I have found that the dyslexic condition can range from severe to moderate to mild. Just as when a child has a physical illness such as pneumonia, the more severely ill a child is, the longer the recovery. The milder the case of pneumonia, the more quickly the child snaps back. The same is true of dyslexia.

The Intelligence of the Dyslexic Student

Intelligence is a major factor in learning and progressing in school. The more intelligent student tends to pick up new concepts and vocabulary more quickly and to learn at a faster rate. Retention of material learned is better. The slow learning child needs much more repetition and review. There is less retention; hence the need for additional repetition and review, which takes more time. These differences have added significance for the dyslexic.

The Willingness of the Student to Work

The willingness of the dyslexic to work is no doubt just as important as intelligence, for no matter how intelligent a student may be, if he is not motivated and does not want to work and to learn, he won't. In remediation, as in all education, the sixty-four dollar question for teachers becomes, "How can I motivate this child, and get him interested in learning?"

A dyslexic who has been having problems in school—given work that he cannot do and then reprimanded by the teacher for not doing it—who has received low grades for which he has been chastised by his parents, who has become aware that he cannot do the same work as his classmates, and who has been kept in at recess and sometimes after school to complete work that is frustrating to him—this child is not likely to continue to have that curiosity and zest for learning that are natural to any child and that he brings with him when he enters school.

What happens? He will be afraid to try, to take a chance on making a mistake, for he is fearful of failure, fearful of ridicule, fearful of seeing red marks all over his papers with the customary low grade written at the top or comments by the teacher such as "You can do better if you only try," or "Pay attention in class. You should have learned this material."

But these students *can* be motivated. They *can* become excited about learning and progressing. In the clinic, we find that in the first week of attendance, the children are inclined to be somewhat on the defensive, sometimes putting on the facade of not caring about anything. But as time goes on, and they find themselves in a secure environment of trust and faith that they can learn, find out that they are not really "dumb," see that they are learning each day, get work and materials of particular interest to them, receive frequent encouragement and praise—then they become willing to take another chance, to try to learn even though they might make mistakes . . . and then to try again.

Learning takes initiative and drive, but these do not automatically occur in a classroom or in a child who has had repeated failures. The child must be nourished. Those around him must trust in his ability to learn. They must be able to "turn him on" so that he will be willing to try, willing to work hard. Successful teaching results in a bond between the teacher and the student. Each becomes inspired by and an inspiration to the other. Both become learners in this process.

The Age of the Dyslexic

The longer a child is ill, the more worn down he becomes and consequently the longer his recovery. The older the dyslexic child (beyond the age of eight or nine), the longer he has endured failure and frustration, the lower his self-esteem—how he sees himself and how he perceives that others in his world view him. He has had to learn all kinds of coping and survival techniques to make it in school and at home. Negative behaviors, reinforced over and over, have become habitual.

The older the dyslexic is, the farther behind he has fallen in his school work. He may have had to repeat one or more grades, and he is embarrassed and humiliated when his friends leave him behind and move on to higher grades. He may truly believe that he is stupid. He may have arrived at the point of desperation: "What's the use of trying?" Such negative concepts have to be eliminated, of course, before remediation can be effective.

The following statement is especially appropriate in dealing with a dyslexic student:

> Every time we succeed at something which is important to us, we make a deposit in our emotional bank account. Each time we are diminished by something someone does or says, we make a withdrawal. Some people, some children, are always in the red, always overdrawn.[1]

I have found that the older a dyslexic student is, the more overdrawn is his emotional bank account.

The Expertise of the Person Alleviating the Dyslexia

The knowledge, training, understanding, and experience of the person working with the dyslexic student will affect the progress of the remediation. What good does it do to diagnose dyslexia, pinpoint specifically the deficiencies of the dyslexic, and then send him to someone for remediation who does not know what to do about alleviating the various problems?

Ignorance on the part of this person can in fact compound the problem and even create new problems where none existed before. In some college and university programs, graduate students are required to take diagnostic courses, but not a remediation course for disabilities. Other schools of education offer a one-semester course combining both diagnosis and remediation, with the result that diagnosis usually gets the major emphasis. In any case, in the latter situation the students tend to get too much information too fast—not enough time to absorb and retain the necessary knowledge to be proficient in both diagnosis and remediation.

A competent person who knows exactly what to do to alleviate dyslexia, and how to do it, can accomplish a great deal in a reasonable length of time. Do these troubled young dyslexics deserve any less than the best? They have already paid the price.

Materials Available in the Classroom and Clinic

All too often administrators, rather than teachers, decide what materials to order and then tell the teachers to do the job without giving them the appropriate tools to do it effectively. This can be frustrating to even the most capable and conscientious teachers. How can a mechanic possibly make repairs to the engine of a car without the proper tools for the job? How can a surgeon possibly operate without the necessary medical instruments to perform the operation? There are tools that teachers need in order to teach interesting and creative lessons that will result in successful learning on the part of the students.

I am not talking about tables full of basal reader workbooks, multiple phonics workbooks, stacks of purple dittoed skill sheets, or various commercial "cookbook" programs. This type of material too often becomes a crutch for lazy or ill-prepared teachers. Too frequently such materials end up determining the remediation program. I am referring to quantities of books at various levels of difficulty and on different topics that would be of interest to the individual students. I am referring to materials that would not insult or humiliate the more mature student. The older dyslexic student who may be reading at the preprimer, primer, or first-grade level is embarrassed to have to read something like, "The duck says quack, quack, quack. Come here, duck. Come here, duck. Can you say quack, quack, quack?" There are books available that do not have the appearance of "baby books"; they have smaller type, the lines of print are closer together, and they have illustrations of older children rather than first-graders. (Listed in Appendix C are the names and addresses of publishers of "high-interest, low vocabulary" books designed for use with older students not reading at grade level.)

Teachers will need plenty of chart paper for experience charts and practical charts for teaching new words, and sentence strips and pocket charts for teaching new vocabulary and developing sequencing. They also need construction paper, paste, scissors, magic markers, crayons, string, blocks, puzzles, sand and glue for preparing kinesthetic tracing materials, wooden letters in both capitals and lower case, dolls and clothing, boxes and cans from the grocery store, and boxes and cards for the students' word banks.

For older students, materials should include driver's license manuals, hunting and fishing pamphlets, magazines about such sports as tennis, swimming, skating, surfing, hockey, baseball, football, basketball, and soccer, and books and magazines about airplanes, racing cars, motorbikes, and bicycles. There should be cookbooks; Cub Scout, Brownie, Boy Scout, and Girl Scout books; clothing and fashion magazines; telephone books; travel guidebooks; maps of the city, county, state, the United States and the world; copies of *TV Guide*, and other popular magazines—even a few comic books.

Magazines and books such as these can be used for the application of all kinds of learning. One does not need a phonics workbook to teach phonics; any of the above will do. New words, sequencing skills, dividing words into syllables—and many other items and skills—can be taught by using common materials.

Spending day after day filling in the blanks on workbook pages or dittoed sheets, keeping quiet, and sitting still will not contribute much to the rapid remediation of dyslexia. These students need to be active and involved. They need concrete materials that they can see and feel and manipulate and use for associating and relating new skills and knowledge. They need materials that are interesting to them. Finding pictures of items that begin with a certain consonant or vowel sound in a Sears and Roebuck or Best catalog, or circling words that begin with a newly learned consonant blend in their own story or experience chart—all are far more interesting than using workbooks and dittoed sheets. Of course, such materials need to be used occasionally, but only to fit certain needs of individual children at certain times. Our dyslexic students have already been "workbooked" and "dittoed" to death. They need new and different materials with which to work.

The subhead of this section included the words, *classroom* and *clinic*. This means the regular classroom in which the dyslexic student sits with all the students of his class as well as the special room where the dyslexic receives specific remediation on a regular basis by a specially trained person. *Both* teachers should use materials such as those referred to above. The regular classroom teacher will soon find that not only the dyslexic student but the other students in the class as well will become more motivated, will better retain what they learn, and will be able to transfer skills more successfully.

The Cooperation and Understanding of the Parents

I have found that, on the whole, parents are genuinely concerned about their dyslexic child and have been greatly worried about the problems that he has been having in school. They have brought their child to the clinic and are willing to pay the necessary tuition, which can be a real sacrifice to some. The parents are willing to be inconvenienced and to make all kinds of necessary arrangements to get their child to the clinic on time each day and to pick him up, as well as to make additional trips if more testing and special remediation are required.

A parent rarely goes about the neighborhood bragging that his child has dyslexia, using the condition as a sort of "status symbol." Yet sometimes this is done. And rarely does a parent feel humiliated for having a dyslexic child, believing the condition is something shameful, that it must mean "tainted" blood in the family, or something to that effect. Yet this too sometimes happens.

Such attitudes change when dyslexia is carefully explained to the parents and they understand just what it means for their child to have dyslexia, what can be done for the child—and how important their love and support is at this time.

I have seen tears in the eyes of mothers—and of fathers—at the relief of finding out at last what was wrong with their child and knowing that something could be done about the problem. So often, their instinct had told them that there really was something wrong, that their child was not just being lazy or rebellious in school. Often one hears statements such as, "I *knew* there was something really wrong. I *knew* it in my heart, but the teacher kept telling me that he was smart and could do the work if he just *tried*, but that he's lazy and doesn't want to work."

I shall always remember the time when a father asked me to step into my office with him. He shut the door and turned to me with tears streaming down his face. He began with, "I know you think that men shouldn't cry [which I don't think], but I have to tell you that I am so *relieved* now. We have been so worried, so up-tight, so frustrated for so long. We reached the point where everyone in the family was snapping at everybody else. I don't know how to thank you enough for what you've done for our son, whom we love so much."

The dyslexic child has been through so much in his young life that it is crucial that he have the support, encouragement, and understanding of his parents. He must know that they are behind him in all his efforts to improve, that he has their love no matter what has happened in the past or may yet happen, and that they will love him in spite of his poor schoolwork, low grades, and occasional outbursts of frustration.

The cooperation and support of parents is also needed by the classroom teacher and by the reading specialist or other special person who is alleviating the dyslexia. Understanding the child's behavior at home, reducing the pressure for high grades, showing an interest in the progress of the child, however small this might be at first, expressing positive feelings about the teachers and what the school is doing for the student—all will help those who are working with your child.

The Cooperation and Understanding of the Classroom Teacher

It is not easy for a teacher to have a dyslexic student in the classroom who needs special work prepared at a level which he can do successfully. Books must be gathered about the specific topics in the curriculum at his lower reading level. Textbook chapters will have to be rewritten at an easier reading level. Directions may have to be repeated. Help must be given with any note-taking, and other adjustments will have to be made in instruction and achievement expectations.

Teachers already work hard for all their students. Planning effective lessons can take hours each week outside of the regular classroom day. While it is customary for secondary school teachers to have at least one period free during the day, which can be used for planning lessons, making materials, grading papers, and keeping records, there is never sufficient time, and the teacher often finds that afternoons, evenings, and weekends must also be used for these purposes. If the teacher is also a coach of some sport, or adviser of a school club, or if there are grade-group or other faculty meetings, the afternoons may not be available either.

Most elementary school teachers have no daily break at all—no reserved time for such planning and teaching preparation. Their afternoons, too, are often filled with school responsibilities other than teaching.

The point is: Teachers are BUSY people. They *have* to care about children and enjoy teaching to work so hard! And when there are special students in the classroom who need additional attention, teachers must work even harder. They do this because they are conscientious, professional persons dedicated to teaching and helping young people. They know the results of their labor can be well worth the effort and time. But they also know that their responsibilities extend to all the students in their class, not just to the dyslexic student.

The classroom teacher needs to work cooperatively with the parents and with the reading specialist, who can offer suggestions on how to work with the dyslexic in the regular classroom, and who can help to gather special materials that may be needed. The teacher should not hesitate to ask any questions of the reading specialist, who also serves as a resource person.

Understanding that the dyslexic student is working hard to help himself, that he cannot change the fact that he has dyslexia, that he needs special attention, and that his condition is extremely frustrating to *him* (as well as to the teacher), will help the child, the parents, and the specialist working with the dyslexic.

The Duration and Frequency of Periods and Length of Remediation

The amount of time allowed for each period of remediation, the number of times each week that the specialist works with the dyslexic student, and the continuation of the remediation until his condition has been alleviated, all will affect the progress of the dyslexic. Much more can be accomplished in hour-long periods than those lasting only thirty minutes. Remediation five times a week will result in faster progress than two or three times a week.[2,3] It may take a year or two, or longer, to show significant results.[4]

Working with dyslexics intensively for two to three hours a day over a six-week period in our summer clinic has accomplished notable improvement, but we always explain that this is only a beginning. Parents and students must undertake any program of remediation with patience.

Remediation: One-to-One or Small Group?

The fastest remediation can be achieved on a one-to-one basis; that is, one person working with one child on that particular child's special needs.

All the efforts of the specialist are centered upon the child and his needs. The child has no other children to distract him from what he is learning.

This is usually the situation when parents hire trained reading specialists to remediate their dyslexic child on a private basis. There is a financial cost, but parents tend to consider the faster remediation well worth it.

The higher the grade in which a child is placed, the more important reading, spelling, writing, listening, and speaking become. This is due to the heavy vocabulary load in textbooks, the preparation of science and social studies reports, the lecture method of teaching, the need for note-taking, and the additional homework assignments involving reading and writing exercises.

At our clinic we have found that a one-to-two ratio can work well if students are carefully matched according to age, grade, needs, and sex. Two boys or two girls together, not one boy and one girl. We learned the hard way that at any age both girls and boys are very conscious of each other, and can be easily embarrassed or become flirtatious, thus detracting from the task at hand. To provide opportunities for social growth and mingling of the sexes, there are times when a teacher will work with small groups or when all the students will form one group for a particular purpose.

Most public (and private) schools do not have the resources for remediation on a one-to-one or one-to-two basis. Remediation of those students with problems is usually done in groups of from six to ten or more. In those cases, remediation will occur at a slower rate (due to less individual attention), which is unfortunate for the dyslexic student.

Notes

1. Anita N. Griffiths, *Teaching the Dyslexic Child* (Novato, Calif.: Academic Therapy, 1978), p. 35.

2. My own work over the years, as well as that of those teachers who work with dyslexics throughout the year after the diagnosis has been made in our clinic, has shown that those students who attend remedial sessions a greater number of times per week make more rapid improvement. Private remedial sessions always last at least an hour. Clinic remedial lessons are never less than two hours per day.

3. In a study of a group of dyslexics at the Northwestern University clinic, the late Doris J. Johnson, professor of learning disabilities, found that these students made significantly more progress in remediation when they received the intensive help of six hours of remediation per week, instead of only two hours a week. Doris J. Johnson, "Persistent Auditory Disorders in Young Dyslexic Adults," *Bulletin of the Orton Society* 30 (1980), pp. 268–69.

4. Carl L. Kline, clinical professor of medicine at the University of British Columbia in Vancouver, and Carolyn Lacey Kline, a psycho-educational consultant in

Vancouver, confirmed that length of treatment is an important factor in successful remedial therapy. Their experience indicated that most cases of dyslexia require up to two years of remedial therapy and that those with an especially severe dyslexic condition require three or more years of regular remediation. Carl L. Kline and Carolyn Lacey Kline, "Follow-Up Study of 216 Dyslexic Children," *Bulletin of the Orton Society* 25 (1975), p. 144.

CHAPTER 14

BEWARE OF "QUICK FIXES"
(or SHORT CUTS TO NOWHERE)

So quick bright things come to confusion.
—*William Shakespeare*

Anxious to help their son or daughter in any way that they can, parents of dyslexic children often fall prey to unsubstantiated new "cures" for dyslexia. Days of frustration and nights of sleepless worry leave parents vulnerable to ill-founded promises for alleviation of their child's problems in school.

A succession of reports of purported remedies for dyslexia appear in daily newspapers, in Sunday supplements, and on television talk shows. Seldom do these "cures" have the support of well-designed, carefully controlled research with full documentation to show unbiased results.

For a while the sorcerer's apprentice shines in the limelight—until partially eclipsed by someone with even more spectacular claims. These claims are likely to fade into some disrepute after pointed questions and additional research have raised serious doubts about their validity.

The alleged cures are numerous, varied, and controversial. They range from medication with different drugs, massive doses of vitamins (megavitamins) and trace elements, and special nutritional diets (such as the Feingold diet), to neurophysiological retraining (patterning), various visual exercises (vision training), tinted lenses in glasses, applied kinesiology (chiropractic treatment), and more.

Parents should be wary of magic-pill approaches. Knowledge of some of these approaches should be helpful in appraising others as they appear. Knowledge should make parents less vulnerable to the immoderate claims of the "quick fixers" of dyslexia. Parents should realize that however much they may wish for a faster process they should expect to find none. Professional reading specialists and trained special education teachers are able to apply effective techniques, based on empirical evidence to help dyslexics. Research continues with long-range, follow-up studies. Additional help should soon be on the way, based upon a recognition of the subtypes of dyslexia (see Chapters 3, 4, and 5) and an understanding that remedial techniques may vary depending upon the subtype. No longer will all dyslexics be lumped together for the same treatment.

It should be noted that in none of the "new cures" described below is any differentiation made with respect to the subtypes of dyslexia. All children are referred to as just "dyslexic."

Medication

Levinson's Approach

The possible causes of dyslexia, discussed in Chapter 9, concluded with a brief discussion of the validity of Levinson's[1] theory of cerebellar-vestibular (C-V) dysfunction. He claims that this dysfunction can be successfully treated with combinations of medication, drugs such as ritalin, dramamine, marezine, antivert, and benedryl, as well as with vitamin B complex, B_6, B_{12}, niacin, ginger root, and other chemicals and nutrients. He professes to have cured over ten thousand dyslexics in the past ten years with these drugs and nutrients. (He also says that his medication has cured deafness and stuttering as well as dyslexia.)

Levinson has not provided sufficient scientific evidence to support his theory that dyslexia is even caused by a cerebellar-vestibular dysfunction, much less that dyslexia can be cured by the combinations listed above.[2,3] This same conclusion applies to other vestibular stimulation proponents.[4]

Piracetam

Piracetam is a psychostimulant suggested by some to improve a disabled child's attention span and memory skills (cognitive and memory functioning), especially short-term memory. Various researchers have been using this medication with dyslexics to determine its effect upon the dyslexic condition. Piracetam is not considered a *cure* but rather a means of helping the dyslexic child cope with his environment. Findings of research on the medication are inconclusive. Perhaps this is because children used in some of the studies are not truly dyslexic. For example, two researchers define the dyslexic as one who has "(1) a WISC-R performance or verbal IQ which was greater than or equal to 90, with the other score being at least 80, and (2) a reading quotient equal to or less than 0.85 as determined by the formula developed by Harris and Sipay."[5]

The researchers go on to explain that a younger child with an IQ of 100 had to be at least one year behind in reading, and an older child of similar intelligence had to be at least two years behind in reading to be included in the study. (The reading quotient merely reflects the child's reading achievement in relation to his IQ.) In Chapter 1, several valid reasons are given as to why a student may be performing below grade level (or ability), other than being dyslexic. There is much more to diagnosing dyslexia than determining a child's intelligence quotient and reading level. Other researchers investigating the effects of piracetam on dyslexic children have made the same error in selecting subjects for their studies.[6]

In addition to the faulty criteria used for diagnosing a dyslexic condition, these researchers failed to take into consideration the subtypes of dyslexia. As in so many studies, the "dyslexic" students were lumped together in one ill-defined group. Furthermore, they continued receiving instruction at the time. As explained in Chapter 15, some dyslexic children are hyperactive (have an attention deficit disorder [ADD]), some are not.

One researcher (and her associates) found that during a twelve-week treatment period, children taking piracetam had a six-month improvement in their scores on a reading test requiring recognition of single words in isolation. In contrast, both the treatment group and the *non-treatment* group had almost the *same* amount of improvement on an oral reading accuracy test.[7]

Results are confusing, controversial, and inconclusive. We need much more positive information in this area before parents can consider the use of such medication as treatment for their dyslexic children. At this point, it cannot even be considered a temporary "quick fix."

Megavitamin and Trace Element Therapy

Massive doses of vitamins were first used to treat schizophrenia in 1960.[8] In 1973, a Task Force Report on Vitamin Therapy of the American Psychiatric Association carefully reviewed the claims in the literature of the orthomolecular[9] psychiatrists. ("Orthomolecular" refers to the treatment of a disease by changing body concentrations of certain normally occurring substances.) The task force members concluded that the use of megavitamins was without value in the treatment of schizophrenia.[10]

In 1971, Dr. Allan Cott, a practicing physician in New York, wrote a paper, "Orthomolecular Approach to the Treatment of Learning Disabilities,"[11] which launched the concept of using megavitamins as a treatment for children with learning disabilities. He claimed that massive doses of vitamins administered to five hundred children in clinical trials proved to be a valuable adjunct to the treatment of learning disabilities. (Many of the children used in his study were either autistic or schizophrenic.)[12] He offered no data to support his statements. His conclusions have not been confirmed by other researchers.

In 1976, the Committee on Nutrition of the American Academy of Pediatrics reviewed the data and published a paper, "Megavitamin Therapy for Childhood Psychoses and Learning Disabilities," which concluded that "megavitamin therapy as a treatment for learning disabilities and psychoses in children, including autism, is not justified on the basis of documented clinical results."[13]

Trace elements include such substances as copper, zinc, chromium, magnesium, iron, sodium, and calcium. Sometimes in "treatments" these are included along with the doses of vitamins. There is no research data that provides supporting evidence that this therapy leads to a cure or, indeed, to any improvement in the dyslexic condition. In fact there is evidence that the hair analysis technique used to measure the level of trace elements in the body may not be reliable.[14]

Parents should resist any attempt by anyone to administer massive doses of vitamins or trace elements to their child as a remedy for dyslexia. Indeed, high doses of certain vitamins and trace elements over a period of time may lead to a variety of physical ailments, such as severe neurologic impairment, liver damage, persistent redness of the skin associated with some local inflammation, itching of the skin, an excessively fast heartbeat, an increase in blood sugar, an abnormal amount of uric acid or calcium in the blood or urine, and other serious problems.[15]

Food Additives and Preservatives

The idea that the elimination of artificial coloring and flavoring of foods and beverages may help children with various forms of minimal brain dysfunction (including reading disorders and other learning and memory difficulties) started with Dr. Benjamin Feingold in 1974. He claimed, at a meeting of the American Medical Association in New York City, that he had achieved "dramatic results" by removing synthetic colors and flavors from his subjects' diets.[16] His book, *Why Your Child is Hyperactive*,[17] which was published in 1975, and described his clinical experiences, presented no research data to support his conclusions. The book received a great deal of publicity in the news media and popular magazines. Various researchers began work in this area.[18] Feingold's claims needed either to be verified or discounted.

In 1982, the National Institute of Child Health and Development sponsored a conference on "Defined Diets and Childhood Hyperactivity." A panel of authorities concluded that while for a very small group of children there does seem to be a limited positive association between the elimination diet and hyperactivity, there is no adequate evidence that would identify the small number of children for whom the diet might be of some help.[19]

Dr. Larry B. Silver, clinical professor of psychiatry at Georgetown University and director of Tri-Services' National Institute of Dyslexia in Chevy Chase, Maryland, states:

> The Feingold diet is not effective in treating hyperactivity in most children. There may be a small percentage (1% to 2%) who appear to respond positively to the diet for reasons that are not yet clear. There is no way for the physician to identify in advance which patients might be part of this "small percentage."[20]

In 1983, Dr. Jeffrey A. Mattes of the Carrier Foundation (formerly medical director of the Child Development Clinic at the Long Island Jewish-Hillside Medical Center) reviewed all of the published, completed controlled studies concerning the Feingold diet. In a summary of his findings, he noted that

> this review illustrates the need for controlled objective investigations of any treatment intervention, no matter how enthusiastically endorsed. This area may well be a good example of how long research can continue on the basis of a popular "fad" and chance positive results. The popularity of the Feingold diet might be seen as an outgrowth of sociological factors (e.g., the desire for "naturalness," and suspicion of an "establishment" which includes large food manufacturers) rather than true beneficial results.
>
> Clearly there is no rationale for being an advocate *for* artificial food colorings; these additives serve no function except cosmetic. But concerns regarding their effects on the behavior and learning of children seem to be unwarranted.[21]

As stated, some dyslexics are hyperactive; some are not. Certainly nothing has proved to be helpful to the dyslexic *condition* itself. Parents should not consider any such diet as Dr. Feingold's.

Neurological Patterning Exercises

Claims by Carl H. Delacato (an educational psychologist) and Glen Doman (a physical therapist) that exercises such as crawling, creeping, moving the limbs in a specific manner, and sleeping in a certain position, would result in improvement of reading and spelling achievement triggered a major controversy.[22] Delacato and Doman theorized that some children failed to move through their developmental stages in the appropriate sequence, thereby disrupting neurological integration at the subcortical level of the brain. For those children who *had* achieved neurological integration, Delacato and Doman attributed reading and spelling problems to lack of cerebral dominance (usually indicated by mixed eye-hand dominance). In this case, treatment consisted of occluding the eye not on the side of the dominant hand. Once consistent dominance and neurological integration had been achieved, learning could continue by normal developmental patterns.

This theory rests on rather oversimplified concepts of hemispheric dominance and the relationship of the sequential phylogenic development of an individual. Eight prestigious medical and health organizations,[23] concerned about the questionable underlying theory and claims made for this treatment, issued a joint statement in 1968 describing the theory on which the treatment is based as "without merit," and charged that the Philadelphia group (Delacato, Doman, and their Institute for the Achievement of Human Potential) was making undocumented claims of cures.[24]

In the meantime, independent researchers continued to investigate this treatment. They uncovered no evidence to support the Doman-Delacato treatment.[25]

In 1982, the American Academy of Pediatrics, concerned about the media coverage and numerous inquiries from parents and public officials, reviewed the current status of the Doman-Delacato treatment. The Academy issued a policy statement that concluded:

> The Institutes for the Achievement of Human Potential differ substantially from other groups treating developmental problems in (1) the excessive nature of their poorly documented claims for cure and (2) the major demands placed on parents in unswervingly carrying out an unproven technique to the smallest detail.
>
> In most instances, improvement observed in patients undergoing this method of treatment can be accounted for on the basis of growth and development, the intensive practice of certain isolated skills, or the nonspecific effects of intensive stimulation.
>
> Physicians and therapists should acquaint themselves with the issues

in the controversy and the available evidence. Based on past and current analyses, studies, and reports, we must conclude that patterning treatment offers no special merit, that claims of its advocates are unproven, and that the demands on families are so great that in some cases there may be harm in its use.[26]

Albert J. Harris and Edward R. Sipay, in a discussion of this particular approach in their book, *How to Increase Reading Ability*, write, "Reading specialists can safely ignore the Delacato-Doman approach."[27] To this I would add that parents, classroom teachers, special education teachers, and other school personnel should not even consider this "treatment" for dyslexic children.

Visual Training and Exercises

Visual training is a term used to describe various remedial programs that claim reading can be improved by "training" a person's vision through a variety of exercises designed to improve ocular and perceptual skills. The assumption is that dyslexia and other reading disabilities are caused by a malfunction in the primary visual system. To varying degrees, depending upon the particular program, children are required to do eye exercises, binocular control tasks, balance beam drills, eye-hand motor coordination tasks, and to practice on tachistoscopes (machines that flash letters, numbers, and so on). They are even given tasks dealing with color and form discrimination.

As in the case of the other "quick fixes" discussed in this chapter, research findings are inconsistent. Many of these studies do not meet rigorous research standards. Many are not reported in professional and scientific publications. Reviews of the literature show no proof that these visual training programs are effective. In spite of this lack of evidence, visual training therapists continue to offer their quick solutions—even though as long ago as March 1972, they should have been alerted by a joint statement of the American Academy of Pediatrics, the American Academy of Ophthalmology and Otolaryngology, and the American Association of Ophthalmology concerning visual training in the treatment of dyslexia and associated learning disabilities:

> The problem of learning disability has become a matter of increasing public concern, which has led to exploitation by some practitioners of the normal concern of parents for the welfare of their children. . . .
> The eye and visual training in the treatment of dyslexia and associated

learning disabilities have recently been reviewed with the following conclusions. . . .

(1) Learning disability and dyslexia . . . require a multi-disciplinary approach from medicine, education, and psychology in diagnosis and treatment. *Eye care should never be instituted in isolation when a patient has a reading problem.*

(2) Since clues in word recognition are transmitted through the eyes to the brain, it has become common practice to attribute reading difficulties to subtle ocular abnormalities presumed to cause faulty visual perception. Studies have shown that *there is no peripheral eye defect which produces dyslexia and associated learning disabilities.*

(3) No known scientific evidence supports claims for improving the academic abilities of learning-disabled or dyslexic children with treatment based solely on: (a) visual training (muscle exercises, ocular pursuit, glasses); (b) neurologic organizational training (laterality training, balance board, perceptual training).

(4) Excluding correctable ocular defects, glasses have no value in the specific treatment of dyslexia or other learning problems. In fact, unnecessarily prescribed glasses may create a false sense of security that may delay needed treatment.

(5) The teaching of learning-disabled and dyslexic children is a problem of educational science.[28]

In 1984, Dr. Richard L. Metzger and Dr. David B. Werner of the Department of Psychology, Pennsylvania State University, reviewed the ophthalmologic, optometric, and psychological literature to determine the validity of vision training for reading disabilities. They too found no evidence to support the assumption that there is a relationship between reading failure and perceptual ability.[29]

Another policy statement, "Learning Disabilities, Dyslexia, and Vision," issued jointly in 1984 by the American Academy of Pediatrics, the American Association for Pediatric Ophthalmology and Strabismus, and the American Academy of Ophthalmology, supported the use of traditional, accepted eye care and appropriate educational methods for the diagnosis and treatment of reading disorders.[30]

In 1985, Dr. Barbara Keogh, professor of special education at the University of California at Los Angeles, presented a critical review of research on visual training programs. She (and her co-researcher, Michele Pelland) state, "Our goal in this review was to determine if optometric vision therapy is an effective treatment for learning disabled children."[31] The answer was no. Dr. Keogh found little agreement on the content of optometric training and limited consensus concerning the suitable targets of the training. She found little clear evidence of the effectiveness of visual training. Despite this lack of "a firm research base," they note that developmental vision training continues to be used.

In 1987, concern over the persistent use of visual training for dyslexia prompted the development of a Clinical Module for Ophthalmologists by the editorial board of "Focal Points" in the *Journal of Learning Disabilities*. They invited Dr. Eugene M. Helveston, professor of ophthalmology and director of the Section of Pediatric Ophthalmology, Indiana University School of Medicine in Indianapolis, to review the management of dyslexia and related learning disabilities. Respondents to certain questions raised by the Advisory Committee of the American Academy of Ophthalmology were Dr. Creig S. Hoyt, professor and director of Pediatric Ophthalmology, University of California in San Francisco, and Dr. Andrea Cibis Tongue, associate clinical professor of ophthalmology, Oregon Health Sciences University in Portland, Oregon.

Dr. Helveston concluded, "At present, there is no valid scientific confirmation of most of the benefits claimed for eye exercises in improving reading or learning ability. . . . At this time, an educationally based approach appears to hold the most promise for the management of dyslexia and related learning disorders."[32]

In the question-and-answer section of this article, Dr. Tongue noted, "At this time, there is no scientific evidence to support the claims of visual training programs or their underlying hypotheses."[33]

Dr. Hoyt pointed out that since 1978 it has been known that "tracking" eye movements have no relationship to reading skills. Dr. Tongue responded that the "tracking" of eye movements performed by a number of educators and optometrists are not used in actual reading. She emphasized that "one of the more definitive" studies suggests that there is no difference in the saccadic eye movements of dyslexic children and those of nondyslexic children.[34]

Vision training programs are not likely to help your dyslexic child in any way. Indeed, the false expectations of success, as well as the time and effort expended in this direction, may cause your child to fall farther behind in other ways.

Glasses with Tinted Lenses

As is often the case, the media raised false hopes for dyslexics when an article, "Glasses Hope for Dyslexia," appeared in London's *The Sunday Times* on December 22, 1985.[35] The lead paragraph read, "Thousands of schoolchildren with reading and learning difficulties because they suffer from dyslexia may benefit if claims made for specially designed spectacles prove true." An

American psychologist, Norman Murphy, brought to London glasses with lenses tinted in a variety of colors. Through tests that lasted from one to two hours, Murphy claimed he could determine which color tint, or combination of colors, would best reduce overstimulation of the light-sensitive cells in each dyslexic's eyes. His theory was that visual dyslexia is a result of overstimulation of light receptors on the retina.

Murphy admitted that the tinted lenses were not a cure for dyslexia and that remediation was still required, but claimed that the lenses increased the dyslexic's concentration. He reported that this treatment was developed by Helen Irlen, another American psychologist. Murphy had investigated her claims of success and as a result, he, too, was convinced of the value of tinted lenses.

But British experts on dyslexia urged parents to be "extremely cautious" before paying Murphy the £110 to £120 charge for an examination and a pair of glasses. The British Dyslexia Association refused to endorse the glasses until Murphy's claims of success could be thoroughly investigated and substantiated.

On March 31, 1987, the BBC Television News raised hopes again with a report that wearing glasses with tinted lenses could relieve the dyslexic condition.[36] On May 8, 1988, in the United States, CBS's "Sixty Minutes" featured these glasses, as developed by Helen Irlen. They explained that the idea behind her theory is that glare is reduced by the tinted lenses when a dyslexic tries to read print on white paper, thus increasing the sharpness of the image seen.

Irlen believes that many dyslexics are sensitive to light, thereby creating focusing problems. (She calls this problem "scotopic sensitivity.") Irlen reports that dyslexics treated at the Irlen Institute with glasses containing tinted lenses progressed in reading. The evidence for this improvement is slim. It consists of observations of thirty-seven learning disabled students, eighteen to forty-nine years of age, who were pretested and then tested again after wearing the tinted lenses for one month. Evidence of improvement was based on how long a person read before becoming frustrated and how much his rate of reading increased, not on progress in reading level. Apparently no consideration was given to the possibility that the special attention these persons were getting, their motivation, or the Hawthorne effects could well have accounted for the results obtained. No control group was used in this study[36]—a critical element in any well-designed experimental study.

Sensitivity to light is not dyslexia. The dyslexic condition lies with faulty information processing by the brain. Since the problem does not lie with the dyslexic's vision, special glasses (or vision training as previously discussed) will not correct or help the dyslexic condition. It is through appropriate educational intervention that the dyslexic can best be helped with his processing of information, sequencing, reversals, organization, short-term memory, comprehension, and revisualization and/or reauditorization problems. Indeed, Dr. Harry Chasty of the British Dyslexia Institute says the effects of the lenses can be duplicated simply by placing the book one wants to read in a pale blue plastic bag.[37]

Applied Kinesiology

Applied kinesiology refers to chiropractic treatment. Some chiropractors are advertising that they can now cure dyslexia, based on the writings and work of Carl A. Ferreri whose claims are truly amazing. He has written a short article and, with Richard B. Wainwright, a book on his technique. In his article he states:

> By using the principles of Applied Kinesiology and Cranial techniques (with special eye muscle techniques) the condition known as Dyslexia and its lesser cousin known as Learning Disabilities are curable.
>
> The most amazing part of this new approach is that although this condition has been recognized for over 100 years and has resisted even definite diagnosis, let alone any viable treatment; the cure is simple, inexpensive, uses no drugs and is almost instant.
>
> The techniques are designed to organize the central nervous system, establish right-brain, left-brain coordination, establish an intact cloacal reflex system, stabilize the gait mechanisms, establish normal cranial function and reset the proper eye muscle function with body and hand coordination; then the condition known as Dyslexia is no more.[38]

Ferreri and Wainwright claim that most of the learning disabled patients responded positively with one to three treatments, though they were kept on a schedule of bimonthly reinforcement visits. Full-fledged dyslexics needed five to eight treatments of a more far-reaching nature. These dyslexics are placed on a biweekly schedule of investigation and correction, if needed.[39] All they have to do now is to learn to read and write, to "catch up." Their dyslexia is cured, but remedial tutoring is necessary to learn all that was not learned prior to the cure. If tutoring does not result in progress, Ferreri and Wainwright imply that the cranial bones may have slipped out of position.

Ferreri's article (slightly over one page) did not appear in a respected scientific journal that reports standard research practices. The article provides no research data. Instead there is just a description of his theory.

While a few brief case histories are described in Ferreri and Wainwright's book, no solid research data to support this theory is included. No independent research studies are noted. No objective, valid evidence is provided that his treatment actually works with dyslexics. Indeed, this treatment is not based on any known research, and some of the anatomical concepts upon which this theory is based are not supported by the majority of anatomists (for example, that the cranial bones move, thus affecting certain brain functions in a negative way and causing learning disabilities).

Parents should beware of the claims of such charlatans. There is no evidence to substantiate the notion of applied kinesiology as a "quick fix."

Summary

It is not easy for parents of children with dyslexia to accept the fact that there is no instant fix, no magic cure that can suddenly make the dyslexic condition disappear. Thus the stream of alleged cures can be expected to continue in the future. It is no simple matter to have to accept the fact that the alleviation of their child's difficulty is going to take a great deal of time. But patient they must be—for their child's sake and for the whole family's sake.

Notes

1. Harold N. Levinson, *A Solution to the Riddle Dyslexia* (New York: Springer-Verlag, 1980); *Smart But Feeling Dumb* (New York: Warner Books, 1984); see also Jan Frank and Harold N. Levinson, "Seasickness Mechanisms and Medications in Dysmetric Dyslexia and Dyspraxia," *Academic Therapy* 12 (Winter 1976–1977), pp. 133–49.

2. Richard Masland and Celia Usprich, "Review of *A Solution to the Riddle Dyslexia* by Harold N. Levinson . . . ," *Bulletin of the Orton Society* 31 (1981), pp. 256–61.

3. Larry B. Silver, "The 'Magic Cure'; A Review of the Current Controversial Approaches for Treating Learning Disabilities," *Journal of Learning Disabilities* 20 (October 1987), pp. 500–501.

4. (a) Ayres is cautious in drawing conclusions based upon the vestibular, postural, and tactile stimulation treatment models. Final conclusions are not offered. A. Jean Ayres, "Improving Academic Scores Through Sensory Integration," *Journal of Learning Disabilities* 5 (1972), p. 339; see also A. Jean Ayres, *Sensory Integration and Learning Disorders* (Los Angeles: Western Psychological Services, 1973) and A. Jean Ayres, "Learning Disabilities and the Vestibular System," *Journal of Learning Disabilities* 11 (1978), pp. 30–41.

(b) Two studies concerning dyslexic children and vestibular responses will interest the reader: Brian Brown, Gunilla Haegerstrom-Portnoy, Charles D. Yingling, Jeannine Herron, David Galin, and Marilyn Marcus, "Dyslexic Children Have Normal Vestibular Responses to Rotation," *Archives of Neurology* 40 (June 1983), pp. 370–73, and, by the same authors, more research on another population of dyslexics and controls: "Static Postural Stability is Normal in Dyslexic Children," *Journal of Learning Disabilities* 18 (January 1985), pp. 31–34.

5. C. Keith Conners and Mark Jay Reader, "The Effect of Piracetam on Reading Achievement and Visual Event-Related Potentials in Dyslexic Children," *Developmental Dyslexia and Learning Disorders,* D. Bakker, C. Wilsher, H. Debruyne, and N. Bertin, eds. (New York: Karger, 1987), pp. 75–90.

6. Various criteria used in determining dyslexia:

(a) "On the WISC-R a performance and verbal scale IQ greater than 80, with at least one of the two scores greater than 90. . . . A reading quotient (RQ) at least one standard deviation below expected level, i.e., less than or equal to 0.85 [Harris and Sipay formula]" (p. 111). The statement *was* made that teacher confirmation was required as to the fact that the student was having reading difficulties in the classroom. [Much more information is needed here for the accurate diagnosis of dyslexia.] Elayne Helfgott, Rita G. Rudel, Harold Koplewicz, and Jonathan Krieger, "Effect of Piracetam on Reading Test Performance of Dyslexic Children," in Dirk J. Bakker (et al.), op. cit., pp. 110–22.

(b) "(1) Were at least 2 years behind expectancy, in one of the reading and writing studied parameters, i.e., reading comprehension, reading accuracy, reading speed, writing accuracy. (2) Had a WISC performance and verbal IQ greater than or equal to 85 with the other score being at least 90 at the beginning of the experiment or during the 6 previous months" (pp. 130–31). G. Levi and E. Sechi, "A Study of Piracetam in the Pharmacological Treatment of Learning Disabilities," in Dirk J. Bakker et al. op. cit., pp. 128–39.

(c) "Both boys and girls participated who were between the ages of 7.5 and 12.9, had normal intelligence (Wechsler Intelligence Scale for Children—Revised WISC-R) and a significant reading impairment as measured by the Gray Oral Reading Test using a Reading Quotient [Harris and Sipay]." C. Chase and P. Tallal, "Piracetam and Dyslexia," in Dirk J. Bakker et al., op. cit., pp. 140–47.

7. The test of recognition of isolated words was the Wide Range Achievement Test (WRAT). The one requiring reading accuracy, which consisted of prose reading, a task similar to the natural act of reading, was the Gilmore Oral Reading Test. E. Helfgott, R.G. Rudel, and J. Kreiger, "Effect of Piracetam on the Single Word and Prose Reading of Dyslexic Children," *Psychopharmacology Bulletin* 20 (Fall 1984), pp. 688–90.

8. A. Hoffer and H. Osmond, *The Chemical Basis of Clinical Psychiatry.* (Springfield, Ill.: Charles C. Thomas, 1960).

9. The noted Nobel Laureate in biochemistry, Linus Pauling, originally coined the term "orthomolecular medicine." (His term now encompasses the use of other additional substances, such as riboflavin, ascorbic acid, calcium panthotenate, folic acid, vitamin B_{12}, riboflavin, NAD, and trace minerals—all in doses much in excess of the RDA—for a wide range of problems, such as arthritis, geriatric problems, etc.) Linus Pauling, "Orthomolecular Psychiatry," *Science* 160 (April 1968), p. 265.

10. "Megavitamin and Orthomolecular Therapy in Psychiatry," Task Force Report No. 7 (Washington, D.C.: American Psychiatry Association, 1973). See also: "Megavi-

tamin and Orthomolecular Therapy in Psychiatry: Excerpts from the Report of the Task Force on Vitamin Therapy in Psychiatry," *Nutrition Review* 32 (1974), p. 44.

11. Allan Cott, "Orthomolecular Approach to the Treatment of Learning Disabilities," *Schizophrenia* 3 (1971), pp. 95–107. See also his "Megavitamins: The Orthomolecular Approach to Behavioral Disorders and Learning Disabilities," *Academic Therapy* 7 (1972), pp. 245–58.

12. Silver, op. cit., p. 502.

13. "Megavitamin Therapy for Childhood Psychoses and Learning Disabilities," Committee on Nutrition, American Academy of Pediatrics (1976) *Pediatrics* 58 (December 1976), p. 911.

14. Silver, op. cit., p. 502.

15. Cautions regarding the administration of megadoses of vitamins and minerals:

(a) "Surplus retinol [vitamin A] is stored in the liver until needed, and an excess can produce liver toxicity and other harmful side effects." Charles H. Hennekens, Robert J. Lipnick, Sherry L. Mayrent, and Walter Willett, "Vitamin A and Risk of Cancer," *Journal of Nutrition Education* 14 (December 1982), p. 135.

(b) An article in the *Canadian Medical Association Journal* described a four-year-old boy who, for two and a half years, had asthma accompanied by lethargy; pain in his feet and legs; headaches; cracked and swollen lips; a red, blotchy rash; and a sore on the tip of his penis. A year before the above symptoms appeared, his parents took him to a chiropractor (because of his asthma) for food allergy testing. The chiropractor recommended the avoidance of certain foods and supplements to build up his strength, including 30,000 IU per day of vitamin A. This was more than eighteen times the recommended daily intake of 1,665 IU for children four to six years of age. When his condition became worse, he was hospitalized. Laboratory tests confirmed vitamin A intoxication. The vitamin A dosage was discontinued, and his condition improved rapidly. (Subsequent allergy testing reflected a negative reaction to the foods that had been previously identified as being allergenic.) Piyush Patel, Rhona M. Hanning, et al. "Intoxication From Vitamin A in an Asthmatic Child," *Canadian Medical Association Journal* 139 (October 15, 1988), pp. 755–56.

(c) "Moreover, there is some evidence that long-term administration of high doses of nicotinic acid [vitamin B complex] in man may lead to persistent skin erythema, pruritis, tachycardia, liver damage, hyperglycemia, and hyperuricemia." Committee on Nutrition, American Academy of Pediatrics, "Megavitamin Therapy for Childhood Psychoses and Learning Disabilities," *Pediatrics* 58 (December 1976), p. 911.

(d) "Vitamin B, and its amide derivative appear to injure the liver in certain susceptible patients if taken in large doses over extended periods. . . . " Stephen L. Winter and James L. Boyer, "Hepatic Toxicity from Large Doses of Vitamin B_3 (Nicotinamide)," *New England Journal of Medicine* 289 (November 29, 1973), p. 1182.

(e) "Megadosage [of vitamin D] is not recommended . . . [it] is associated with a substantial incidence of hypercalcemia and hypercalciuria." Quoted from "Vitamin D Dosage Alert," in Sally Wicklund, Marilyn Devroye, Shirley Morrison, and Sam Uretsky, eds., "Nurses Drug Alert," *American Journal of Nursing* 10 (January 1986), p. 70.

(f) Large dosages of niacin can cause nausea, diarrhea, gout, liver function abnormalities, aggravation of peptic ulcer disease, an abnormal amount of uric acid in the blood, low blood pressure, irregular action or tremors of a heart muscle, and dermatologic side effects such as reddening, pruritus, rash, and thickening of the skin with black, brown, or gray pigmentation. Mark R. Goldstein, "Potential Problems With the Widespread Use of Niacin," *American Journal of Medicine* 85 (December 1988), p. 881.

(g) In an article on vitamin and mineral overdosage, *American Family Physician* lists the following adverse effects of excessive vitamin and mineral intake:

Element	Adverse Effects
Vitamin A	Can cause deformed fetus, dysfunction of the brain, pseudotumors of the brain, abnormal growth of bonelike tissue, bone pain, overgrowth of skin tissue
Vitamin B$_1$	Abnormal rapidity of heart action, fatty liver
Riboflavin	Itching, hives or nettle rash, numbness or prickling sensation
Niacin	Flushing, liver malfunction, increased uric acid, cardiac arhythmia
Vitamin B$_6$	Diseases of the nervous system, partial paralysis
Folate	Masks vitamin B$_{12}$ deficiency
Vitamin C	Modifies drug and vitamin metabolism diarrhea, kidney stones
Vitamin D	Can cause deformed fetus, excessive amount of calcium in blood, kidney failure, change calcification in the brain, retardation
Vitamin E	Fatigue, headache, delayed wound healing, increased bleeding, muscle weakness
Chromium	Respiratory disease (rare)
Cobalt	Bone marrow toxicity, rapid growth, abnormal increase of cells (without formation of tumor, but with increase in size of an organ or part)
Copper	Gastrointestinal and central nervous system toxicity
Fluoride	Chronic fluorine poisoning, sometimes marked by mottling of tooth enamel, and other tooth and bone abnormalities
Iodine	Hyperthyroidism, thyroid abnormalities
Iron	Acute: gastrointestinal bleeding, central nervous system toxicity; chronic: dark pigment deposits in tissue or organs
Manganese	Central nervous system toxicity
Molybdenum	Gout (acute arthritis and inflammation of the great toe and of the joints)
Selenium	Central nervous system and kidney toxicity, hair loss
Zinc	Cholesterol abnormalities, can cause deformed fetus
Lithium	Interactions with other minerals, can also cause deformed fetus

"Vitamin and Mineral Overdosage," *American Family Physician* 35 (March 1987), p. 282.

16. Larry B. Silver, "Acceptable and Controversial Approaches to Treating the Child with Learning Disabilities," *Pediatrics* 55 (March 1975), p. 413.

17. Benjamin F. Feingold, *Why Your Child is Hyperactive* (New York: Random House, 1975). See also his article, "Hyperkinesis and Learning Disabilities Linked to the Ingestion of Artificial Food Colors and Flavors," *Journal of Learning Disabilities* 9 (November 1976), pp. 551–59.

18. (a) Conners et al. found results of studies unclear. The researchers noted that the children's *teachers* noticed improvement in behavior in a few students, but this occurred only when the control diet was given first, followed by the elimination diet. When the diet order was reversed, this result was not observed. (This type of investigation is called a "dietary crossover study.") C. Keith Conners, Charles H. Goyette, et al., "Food Additives and Hyperkinesis. A Controlled Double-Blind Experiment," *Pediatrics* 58 (1976), pp. 154–66. See also C. Keith Conners, *Food Additives and Hyperactive Children* (New York: Plenum Press, 1980).

(b) Other researchers found that the Feingold diet has no significant effect on hyperactivity and achievement in the reading of thirty-six boys, ages six to twelve. They stated that there *may* be a subset of hyperactive younger children who may be helped by some aspect of the diet, but this group is either exceptionally small or the diet's effectiveness is not what Feingold claims it to be. See J. Preston Harlet, Roberta S. Ray, et al., "Hyperkinesis and Food Additives: Testing the Feingold Hypothesis," *Pediatrics* 61 (1978), p. 826.

(c) Since no significant findings to prove Feingold's diet theory were found in the crossover studies, researchers used a different approach, which considered the specific role of the synthetic coloring and flavoring in foods and beverages. Children were periodically placed on a diet containing the additives. The researchers then observed them to see if the hyperkinethesis occurred (or was aggravated by the additive). (This type of study is called a "specific challenge study," because the child is "challenged" with a particular additive.) The researchers concluded that elimination of food coloring from a child's diet is not likely to be a major factor in bringing about or reducing hyperkinesis. However, as suggested in the above studies, a small subset of children *may* respond to certain facets of Feingold's diet. Charles H. Goyette, C. Keith Conners, et al., "Effects of Artificial Colors on Hyperkinetic Children. A Double-Blind Challenge Study," *Psychopharmacology Bulletin* 13 (1984), pp. 39–40.

19. National Institute of Health, Conference on "Defined Diets and Childhood Hyperactivity," *Journal of The American Medical Association* 245 (1982), pp. 290–92.

20. Silver, op. cit., p. 503.

21. Jeffrey A. Mattes, "The Feingold Diet: A Current Reappraisal," *Journal of Learning Disabilities* 16 (June/July 1983), p. 322.

22. Carl H. Delacato, *Treatment and Prevention of Reading Problems* (Springfield, Ill.: Charles C. Thomas, 1959); Carl H. Delacato, *The Diagnosis and Treatment of Speech and Reading Problems* (Springfield, Ill.: Charles C. Thomas, 1963); Carl H. Delacato, *Neurological Organization and Reading* (Springfield, Ill.: Charles C. Thomas, 1966); Glenn Doman and Carl H. Delacato, "Doman-Delacato Philosophy," *Human Potential* 1 (1968), p. 113–16.

23. The professional organizations issuing the joint statement about the Doman-Delacato treatment were the American Academy for Cerebral Palsy, American Academy of Physical Medicine and Rehabilitation, American Congress of Rehabilitation Medicine, Canadian Association for Children with Learning Disabilities, Canadian Association for Retarded Children, National Association for Retarded Children, American Association on Mental Deficiency, and the American Academy of Pediatrics. Robert Reinhold, "A Therapy System for Young Scored," *The New York Times*, May 7, 1968, p. 42.

24. Ibid.

25. Melvyn P. Robbins, "A Study of the Validity of Delacato's Theory of Neurological Organization," *Exceptional Children* 32 (April 1966), pp. 517–23; Gene V. Glass and Melvyn P. Robbins, "A Critique of Experiments on the Role of Neurological Organization in Reading Performance," *Reading Research Quarterly* 3 (Fall 1967), pp. 5–52; P.A. O'Donnell and J. Eisenson, "Delacato Training for Reading Achievement and Visual-Motor Integration," *Journal of Learning Disabilities* 2 (1969), pp. 441–46; William H. Kohlmorgen, "A Study of the Effects of Delacato's Program of Neurological Organization on Reading Achievement," Doctoral Dissertation, New York University, 1971.

26. American Academy of Pediatrics, Policy Statement, "The Doman-Delacato Treatment of Neurologically Handicapped Children," *Pediatrics* 70 (November 1982), p. 811.

27. Albert J. Harris and Edward R. Sipay, *How to Increase Reading Ability*, 7th ed., (New York: Longman, 1985), p. 289.

28. Ad hoc committee of the American Academy of Pediatrics, the American Academy of Ophthalmology and Otolaryngology, and the American Association of Ophthalmology, Joint Organizational Statement, "The Eye and Learning Disabilities," *Pediatrics* 49 (March 1972), p. 454.

29. Richard L. Metzger and David B. Werner, "Use of Visual Training for Reading Disabilities: A Review," *Pediatrics* 73 1(June 1984), pp. 824, 828.

30. "Learning Disabilities, Dyslexia, and Vision," Policy Statement, American Academy of Ophthalmology, San Francisco, 1984.

31. Barbara K. Keogh and Michele Pelland, "Vision Training Revisited," *Journal of Learning Disabilities* 18 (August/September 1987), p. 234.

32. Eugene M. Helveston, "Vol. III Module I: Management of Dyslexia and Related Learning Disabilities," *Journal of Learning Disabilities* 20 (August/September 1987), p. 418.

33. Ibid., p. 420.

34. Ibid.

35. David Connett, "Glasses Hope for Dyslexia," *The Sunday Times*, December 22, 1985, p. 3.

36. Helen Irlen, "Successful Treatment of Learning Disabilities." Paper presented to the American Psychological Association, August 1983, as cited in Colin R. Wilsher, "Treatment of Specific Reading Difficulties (Dyslexia)," *Child Health Development* 5 (1987), pp. 95–109; see also Colin R. Wilsher and J.A. Taylor, "Commentary: Tinted Glasses and Dyslexia," *Journal of Research in Reading* 11 (1988), pp. 50–52.

37. "Therapies," *UPDATE*, (Chevy Chase, Maryland: National Institute of Dyslexia, Spring 1988), p. 7.

38. Carl A. Ferreri, "Dyslexia and Learning Disabilities Cured," *The Digest of Chiropractic Economics* (May/June 1983), p. 74.

39. Carl A. Ferreri and Richard B. Wainwright, *Breakthrough for Dyslexia and Learning Disabilities* (Pompano Beach, Fla.: Exposition Press of Florida, 1984), p. 114.

CHAPTER 15

WHAT CAN PARENTS DO?

Not everything that is faced can be changed; but
nothing can be changed until it is faced.
—*Anon*.

The very first thing that you, as parents, must do after an accurate diagnosis is to face the reality of the situation and accept the fact that your child has dyslexia. Admit it to yourselves. Admit it to others. It is not something to hide. Be thankful, in fact, that the dyslexia has been discovered, because now your child can get help for his problems. Now positive steps can be taken. Dyslexia is nothing to be ashamed of—any more than is a broken leg or tuberculosis or diabetes. It is not an indictment against your performance as parents or your family genes or your own intelligence. Dyslexia is a disorder that can be treated. Your feeling should be one of relief, for you have known that your child has had a problem, and now you know what that problem is.

The second thing that you must realize is that remediation will take time. There is no instant cure for dyslexia. At the same time, dyslexia should not be used as a "cop-out" or as a "status symbol." One sometimes overhears parents and teachers saying, "Johnny can't learn to read or spell; he has dyslexia."

Well, no and yes. Johnny can learn, and Johnny will.

Your perception of dyslexia and how you handle the situation is critical to your child's success in overcoming his difficulties, for he will sense your feelings and react accordingly—with hope or despair, with faith or doubt, with confidence or uncertainty, with courage or fear. He must know that you love him, that you accept him regardless of his problem, that you do not resent the restrictions that may have been placed upon the family, such as tighter finances if private help must be obtained. Always keep in mind that he loves *you*, that he really is sorry for any problems he has caused you at home and at school, and that because of these problems, he has been carrying guilt feelings around for some time.

Again, there should be a sense of *relief* to find out exactly what has been causing your child to have so many problems in school, to know that he really is not lazy or being deliberately disobedient. There should be a lessening of worry and tension in the whole family as a result of the diagnosis.

The Home Environment

Show your child that you care about him. Make it evident by your actions that you miss him during the day while he is at school. Give him a big hug when he gets home or when you get home from work. Hold him close for a minute or two—Dad as well as Mom. Ask him about his day—and *listen* to what he tells you. Share some of your day's experiences with him. Draw him into your family discussions. Try to arrange dinner time so that all family members can eat together and share the events of their days, and never let this time degenerate into arguments. Leave the television off at mealtime so that you can give each other your undivided attention.

Show an interest in the papers your child brings home from school. Ask him to tell you about them. Look for the correct things on the papers and comment on them. In other words, commend him for the parts that are well done and let him know that you are aware he is trying very hard at school to do his best. Remain calm about low grades and papers covered with red ink. Never lose your temper or ridicule your child about his schoolwork. Remember, dyslexics are very sensitive, and the situation will change in time. As he progresses and his work improves, be sure to let him know that you are pleased with the improvement and his hard work. He needs your support and approval very much. Make sure he gets them.

A Quiet Work Place

Parents can help by providing a quiet place where the child can do his work—away from the distractions of the television and the movement of the rest of the family. If the apartment or house is small, set aside each school day a certain time for schoolwork to be done by all the children and use the old-fashioned tradition of the kitchen table. At this time, the television and radio should be turned off. Why not pick up a magazine or book to read while the children are working? Sit at the table with the others and read quietly. Your presence will be appreciated and will provide a certain measure of security, for they know you are there if help is needed. Your presence will also help keep the children to their task.

Helping with Homework Assignments

I hope any assignment that your child brings home will be at a level that he can read with ease and understanding, whether it involves books or dittoed work sheets. Sometimes, though, a child with dyslexia will have a teacher who finds it difficult to individualize instruction and prepare work at varying levels. Unfortunately, it's "READ OR FAIL" with some teachers. Parents and older children in the family can help the child with dyslexia by using a tape recorder and taping chapters of his textbook on cassettes. The dyslexic can then listen to this taped material as often as he needs to and can stop the cassette at passages that he needs to have repeated. He can also listen to the tape as he "reads" along in the book, following the words on the page. This will help him learn new words. Whoever does the taping can later discuss the chapter with the dyslexic. This will help his understanding of the new concepts and will aid in clearing up any misunderstandings that he may have about the material in the book.

If you are thinking, "What! Tape a *whole* book!"—hold it. This is not such an awesome task when you realize that the book may be taped in chapter sections. You only need to stay one or two chapters ahead. The book can be done piecemeal.

Your child will know that all of you are truly interested in helping him when you or his brothers or sisters take the time to help him in this way.

It may be, of course, that your child will be fortunate enough to have a teacher who has already taped the various chapters and you need only to check these out. Still, it would be helpful if you could take the time to listen to or read the material and discuss it with your child.

A Regular Routine

Children with dyslexia need the security of a routine within which they can function. Try to stick to a regular time for meals and going to bed. Avoid late television for your child, because this interferes with his getting enough sleep, not just because of the late time but because he will be stimulated and for a while will be unable to relax and fall asleep. Your child needs to be rested and alert during the day in order to learn. If he is tired and sleepy he will be more likely to give in to his frustrations—and the tolerance level is always low for a child with dyslexia.

A mother once said to me, "How do you get a child to stop watching TV?" My answer to her was simple: "All TVs come equipped with a button. Just turn it off. After all, *you* are the parent." I did not intend to be either curt or facetious. I suppose I just wanted her to use her common sense in such matters.

Giving Directions

Your dyslexic child has trouble following oral directions, especially if there are several given at one time. No doubt you have found yourself becoming exasperated when he has not done what you told him to do. Keep in mind that he is not being deliberately disobedient. He did hear you, but he cannot remember all that you say and he tends to get what he hears all mixed up. He cannot help this. But there are ways you can help him with directions:

1. Keep your directions clear and short; avoid wordiness.

2. Give only one or two directions at a time.

3. If you need to give more than one or two directions at a given time, write them on paper in list form, as done here.

4. Go over the list with your child.

5. If there are words that give him trouble, draw a picture of what is to be done—for example,

"Make your bed."

"Hang up your clothes."

6. Have your dyslexic draw a line through each direction when the task has been completed.

7. Post the list in the kitchen, in his bedroom, in the garage, in the tool shed—wherever it is to be used—for easy reference and to prevent the list from being misplaced or lost.

Reading Together

In years past it was a common practice for families to read together. Often this consisted of reading the Bible around the kitchen table. Some families often read other books together—classics, fairy tales, histories. Read to your child from books of his selection as often as you have time. Share portions from your book or magazine that are especially interesting. Encourage him to read silently while you read a book or article of your choice and give him help as needed with unrecognized words.

Your child will need books that are at a reading level that he can read easily and with enjoyment. There should be no struggling and no frustration. This is sometimes called his "free reading level" or "independent reading level." Your child's teacher will know the level appropriate for him. Do not hesitate to ask the teacher to send home books for this extra reading at home. If you find that he is missing too many words (more than one or two out of a one-hundred-word passage) and he seems to be struggling and not enjoying the material, or if he refuses to read, return the book to the school and tell the teacher. I should not have to add that these leisure reading books should be about things that are of interest to your child.

Appendix C includes lists of publishers (and their addresses) of books written at lower reading levels for older students who have had problems in learning to read. These books are not babyish and will not embarrass your dyslexic child. Most of the stories and topics should interest your child. When you find out your child's independent reading level from the teacher, you may want to write to some of the publishers and request a catalog from which to order. These books will make good presents for birthdays, Christmas, or just "I think you are great!" gifts.

You may wish to purchase Nancy Larrick's *A Parent's Guide to Children's Reading,*[1] which can help you in selecting books to read to your child or for him to read.

What about those monthly children's book clubs? I urge caution here. Often these books are not at the appropriate reading level for your child really to enjoy them. Even children who are "normal" readers will have trouble with some of the books. I have heard parents say, "I don't understand it. That book he's reading came two years ago. He refused to read it then, but now he says it's a good book." Of course, you could read these books *to* your child if they are too hard for him.

It is important that your child see you reading and enjoying books and magazines. Parents serve as models for their children to emulate. Children whose parents sit glued to the "tube" night after night are not going to place a high priority on learning to read.

Shopping Together

Take your child shopping with you. Talk about the prices of foods. Discuss the bargains and how much you may be saving. Take along a small hand calculator. Let him total the prices as you select the items for the week. (But check his entries so you can call his attention to reversed and transposed numerals). Show your child how to compare prices by weight. Talk about good nutrition and why you buy certain foods even though they may not be the favorites of all in the family. Ask him to take on the job of recording the food needs at home and making up the grocery list for the week—with your help as needed, of course. Writing words will help him with his spelling and reading. This will also help to focus his attention on some of his particular difficulties and thus alert him to the occurrence of these errors.

Planning Trips

Trips are usually planned by the parents. Include your dyslexic child (and other children) in the planning. Sit down with the road map and talk about the trip together. Ask everyone to make a list of what should be taken to the beach, to the mountains, or the camping trip, to grandmother's, or wherever you plan to go. Then discuss the contents of all the lists and make one master list together. If possible, get extra maps or make copies of your marked map so that each member of the family has one showing the roads to take. If traveling by airplane, try to get the airline's map and use it to discuss the states or countries over which you will be flying, the direction of the route, how fast you will be flying, and how long it will take to reach your destination.

When in the car, call attention to the different signs and billboards. See how many your child can read—always gently giving him help whenever he needs it. Point out special features of letters and shapes of signs and words.

These activities should be looked upon as fun for all, not as a chore. Make games of them. And when your child begins to show that he is losing interest in some such activity, discontinue it.

Journal of Important Events

Suggest to your dyslexic child that he keep a record of the family's important events. This does not have to be kept every day, but it should be kept at least weekly. The small books with blank pages available in most bookstores are ideal for this purpose. Tell him that you will help him to spell words when necessary, but that he should try to spell them first. Suggest ideas for entries in the journal. Try to find a daily occurrence that could be recorded. Once a week let him read to the family his record for the week. Parents who have followed this suggestion have told me that the journal is an enjoyable experience for the whole family, and they look forward to the reading each week!

Keeping a Diary of Feelings

Give your child a diary, preferably with a small lock and key. Tell him it is for his eyes only, and that his privacy will be respected. The diary should include special things or incidents that made him happy, or excited him, or made him angry or sad. His dreams and aspirations, his fears and worries can all be written in the diary. He can write what happened from his viewpoint and tell how it made him feel.

"Get it out and get it down!" should be his motto. Help him to view keeping his diary as a kind of talking to himself. It is amazing how such a diary will help the child with dyslexia to come to terms with himself, to understand why he reacts the way he does sometimes, and in time you will find that he will begin to share some of the things that he has written in this special diary. This sharing should always be voluntary, of course. He must know that you will not invade the privacy of his diary unless he chooses to reveal what he has written.

Helping at Home

A family plays together. A family works together. Chores around the home are the responsibility of all. Encourage your child to help in the kitchen as you cook, with setting the table, or to work in the yard, or on the car. Foods are cooked in a certain order. Setting the table is done according to a certain form. Chores in the yard and repairs to the car are also done in an order. All these activities will help your child with his sequencing problems.

When cooking, call attention to the words and pictures on the cans and boxes of food. Let him open them. Ask if he can tell you what sound the word "bean" (or "asparagus" or "rice" or "lettuce") begins with. (Answer: the *b* sound—not *buh*). He will be associating the concrete items with the abstract phonemes (sounds). Do this when you set the table, or put clothes in the washer, or work in the yard or on the car.

Make all this fun and entertaining. Enjoy these activities yourself! It really *can* be fun. When your child gives you an incorrect answer, just smile and say, for example, "No, fork begins with the *f* sound."

Passing Notes

It does not take long to write a short note to your child telling him that you love him or like something in particular that he has done, or asking him to help you with something. In the note ask him to write you an answer. Set up a "family mailbox" in the kitchen or on the porch. Do *not* criticize the spelling errors! Be patient. Just keep writing him notes and reading and answering the notes from him. You will find that the spelling errors will become less frequent in time.

Slip short, cheery notes in his lunch box, his math book or reader, or the pocket of his jacket, sweater, or pants. Notes like:

—Have a nice day! See you this afternoon.
—This weekend we'll have a picnic in the back yard. What would you like to eat?
—We're having your favorite dish for supper tonight. Yes, it's fried chicken.
—Those were good papers you brought home for us to see. We're proud of your hard work.
—Keep trying! You're doing fine.

And always at the end be sure to write, "Love, Mom (or Dad)" or "Mom and Dad."

Helpful Games to Play

"My Father Owns a . . ."

Games such as, "My father owns a grocery store [which may be purely imaginary], and in it he has something that begins with an 'A' " or, "My father owns a toy store and in it he has something that begins with an 'A' "—with the correct answer beginning with the required letter, such as "apple" or "asparagus" or "almonds" (or "air gun" or "airplane" or "anagrams game" if it's a toy store)—can be most worthwhile for the dyslexic child and fun for all. On trips it helps the time pass quickly and keeps everyone in good spirits.

You can vary the categories to keep the games interesting. For example, you might try, "My father owns a . . . ":

drugstore	pet shop	cafeteria
bookstore	zoo	aquarium
circus	farm	ice cream shop
carnival	meat store	used-car-lot
beach shop	fruit store	furniture store

Games such as these can be played at home, in the back yard, at the pool, on the way to the grocery store or, as mentioned, on trips. How can they help? In several ways: by developing a sense of sequencing and reinforcing knowledge of the alphabet, by using recall, by naming objects and associating these names with the beginning letters, by developing vocabulary, and by using auditory memory.

Let's Pretend

Act out a story commonly known to all family members, or an old familiar fairy tale, or a television show that all have watched together. Here again, memory is being brought to the fore, attention must be paid to the sequencing of events, vocabulary is being developed and used, associations are being made, and feelings and attitudes of characters are being brought out into the open. If your child gets the events out of order, talk about what came first, then next, then next. If he makes other mistakes, discuss these together. For example, point out why a character may have behaved or responded the way he or she did.

Alphabet Meals

Let one night in each week be a special alphabet letter evening. This is a lot of fun and can present a real challenge at times. Choose the first letter of the alphabet. Together, as a family, try to plan a nutritional meal of foods that begin with that letter. Next week, choose another letter. I recommend that you begin with the letter "A" and proceed in sequence through the alphabet. Each week ask the question, "What meals have we already had?" Answer: "Meals that begin with *A, B, C, D, E,* and next we should think of foods that begin with *F.*" Your dyslexic child needs practice with sequencing and reviewing the alphabet whenever he can get it.

Here are some examples of foods that begin with the letters *A* and *B*:

A Foods	*B Foods*
apple cider	banana milkshake
anchovies	beefburgers with brown
asparagus, acorn squash, artichokes	gravy
	biscuits and butter
almond rice	beans, beets, broccoli, Brussels sprouts
avocado or aspic salad	baked potatoes
angel food cake, apricot pie	butterscotch pie, Boston cream pie

This appears to be simple, but you'll discover that remembering a variety of foods beginning with a particular letter is not always easy, especially for some letters. Try to recall the foods at first without anyone referring to a cookbook, though you may have to as a last resort. You may have to use your imagination and improvise a little, which can generate whoops of laughter. For example, for Y you may have to resort to "yesterday's left-overs perked up with yeast bread, and yellow cake for dessert." Of course you could come up with "yolk omelettes or yams with ham, and yellow squash." The letter Z is a real challenge! You may have to reach as low as "zoo stew with zesty seasoned onions and a zippy dip made of zucchini." Your ingenuity will really be needed for the letter X, and you may have to devise such foods as "X-tra long hot dogs or X-citing fruit salad." This is fudging a bit, but what can you do with X? After all, it's just a game, and the nonsense makes it even more fun.

One last suggestion for this family game: Be sure to write out the menu on a card or poster so that it can be read by all. You want your dyslexic child to *see* these food words as well as *hear* them. He will be getting experience in associating items of food with the beginning letter and sound. He will also be getting experience in trying out new foods and discovering new tastes as well as learning about balanced diets for good health. All this will aid him in developing a store of associations which are being made in a concrete, sensory way and which will probably stay with him permanently.

Let's See!

At any free moment during the day, or on car trips, whether to the grocery store, school, or the next state, play the game "Let's See!" It is a good deal of fun and does help the dyslexic child. Take turns listing words for things seen along the way. "I see a road and road begins with an *r*" or, "I see a church and church begins with *ch*." The catch is, each time someone "sees" something and says the name and the beginning letter(s) he has to repeat all the words seen before. For example, "I see a horse and horse begins with an *h* . . . road, church, horse." Since this is just a game that is to be enjoyed by all (while helping the dyslexic child with his recall of words, association of letters with words, auditory memory, and sequencing), it is permissible to give a little help when needed. The game stops when everyone bogs down. Then it starts all over again with one word.

Helping Your Child: Things to Avoid Doing

Avoid Comparisons

I cannot emphasize too strongly the need for you to accept your dyslexic child as he is and not compare him with any of his brothers and sisters. It does not help the dyslexic child at all to be told "Your sister is two years younger than you and yet she is reading better than you are" or "Your brother was reading a book a year ahead of his grade when he was your age."

A child with dyslexia knows quite well that he has not been living up to expectations or achieving at the levels of his brother or sister, whether younger or older. Please do not take the heart out of him by making such comparisons. Just believe in him and have faith that he will progress. Give him the support and encouragement that he needs so very much. Let him know that you understand that he is doing the best he can at the present time.

Watch Those "Put-Downs"

There is a natural amount of kidding and bantering that goes on within a family, and this is usually healthy for family relations. But there is one kind that usually takes place between older and younger children that can be harmful. The child with dyslexia is thin-skinned to begin with, and he does not have a strong, positive self-concept. He harbors certain feelings of inadequacy and insecurity, although he may put on an air of not caring that can fool some people.

Often these put-downs by an older brother or sister are only meant to be funny. The problem is that they don't come across that way; they are taken seriously by the dyslexic child. A younger child tends to look up to the older one. The younger boy admires his older brother and emulates him. He may even put him on a pedestal—he can do no wrong in the eyes of the younger child; what he says is Truth.

So when the older brother comes out with cracks such as "Hey, stupid, watch where you're walking!" or "What a dumbbell!" or "Hey, birdbrain, what's the matter with you? *Anyone* knows that word!" the young dyslexic wonders if his older brother really thinks he's dumb and stupid and a birdbrain. After all, look at all the problems he's having with reading and spelling and writing and math and everything. Deep inside, the dyslexic has long wondered if he has inferior intelligence. Put-downs only make him hurt inside and cause him to feel different from others and inadequate.

If this particular kind of put-down bantering is going on in your family, have a talk with the older brothers and sisters and explain how words such as those used in the examples above are perceived by the child with dyslexia. Tell them that they must not call him by these words. After all, he has a name, call him by it. Also help them to understand the problems he's having and how very important it is for them to let him know that they really care for him and believe in him. He needs help and encouragement from his brothers and sisters as well as from his parents.

Drug Therapy?

The administration of drugs to dyslexics as a "quick fix" was discussed in the previous chapter. Here, with specific reference to what parents can do, a few additional comments are needed.

I am not referring here to the use of drugs to "cure" dyslexia, but rather to the possible use of drugs with dyslexic children to help parents and teachers in managing them. This is a highly debatable topic. I am not a physician, and therefore I must be careful not to overstep the boundaries of my professional training; however, I can speak from experience with children who have been prescribed drugs for various reasons, and from my observations of their behavior, reactions, and achievement in the classroom and clinic.

The usefulness of stimulant therapy has been well validated for the hyperactive group. It has not been for dyslexics. Most reviews of studies indicate that drugs have little or no effect on reading performance.[2] So it is questionable that the use of such drugs provides any help at all for the dyslexic child.

But what about children who are both dyslexic and hyperactive? The drug may help the child in social situations but will leave untouched the dyslexic elements that still have to be taken care of through remediation. What about students who have both hyperkinesis and dyslexia? In this case there may be some justification for the proper use of stimulant therapy.[3] Only a medical doctor can, of course, make such a decision. I would hope there would be follow-through conferences not only with the parents but also with the child's teachers about the effect of the drug on the child's behavior and performance at home and at school.

Based upon my experience with children with all kinds of problems, I have grave reservations about the use of drug therapy. Certainly drugs should be prescribed *only* if they actually help the child—not to appease parents or teachers who want the child to "sit still and be quiet." Parents should never seek drug therapy lightly. The side effects can be serious and may actually detract from the child's attempts to do his work as expected. Sometimes children become snappy and irritable, or they may develop nausea and cramps or headaches. They may get the "jitters" and find it difficult to sleep at night and so come to school tired and sleepy and thus unable to learn in class. Some children lose their appetite and become underweight and malnourished, deprived of the necessary vitamins and other nutrients to develop normally.

There is another concern with children who are regularly taking drugs, over and above any dependency that may possibly occur. The "pill-popping" habit may continue with them and could lead to more serious drug taking. Dyslexics have so many frustrations, ego-cutting experiences, and failures that avenues of escape are sometimes sought—escape from a world of unhappiness to a world of chemical fantasies.

When children who have been taking prescribed drugs for behavior attend our clinic for diagnosis of their academic difficulties, the parents are requested to ask the doctor if the medication can be stopped during the testing and the following remedial lessons. In every case, this request has been granted by the psychiatrist or other medical doctor—who, I might add, is always interested in the consequences.

Without exception, no child has had to return to the medication during his stay with us. True, one or two children have had one or two rough incidents of temper and balkiness, but these passed. An environment of acceptance, faith, caring, and encouragement, with varied, brief, structured lessons built on what the child can do, yet structured upon his needs so that he can achieve and can see his progress, and with opportunities to stretch, move around, and get the kinks out before settling down again—all seem to be what the dyslexic needs to find a new direction for his life.

Sometimes teachers confuse learning style with hyperactivity and suggest to parents that drug therapy should be considered. One year when I was teaching third grade, there was a girl, Heidi, in my class. She was rather large for her age, exceptionally intelligent, and very energetic. She had apparently driven her second-grade teacher to distraction, if one can judge by certain comments in the cumulative record. "Hyperactive, won't sit still and stay at her desk, wiggles constantly" were typical observations. This particular second-grade teacher kept her students in their seats copying volumes of work from the chalkboard most of the time. She had suggested to the parents several times that they should consider "giving Heidi a drug to calm her down and make her stay in her seat." Her parents were not convinced that this was the answer to Heidi's problems in school.

I found that Heidi would conscientiously do whatever work was given her if she could quietly get up every now and then and walk over to the window, or get a drink of water from the fountain, or just stand up and stretch. She did not disturb the other children. She would return to her seat, slip into it quietly, and return to her work. This need for activity was part of her learning style. When allowed the freedom to do these things, she was a very cooperative and successful student in every way.

Heidi's story is related here as an example to parents that they need to ask why a child is behaving in a particular manner in school. They should ask the teacher for specific examples of negative behavior, and then they and the child's teacher should explore possible reasons for this behavior. Children like Heidi need no drug therapy.

It is questionable whether the majority of dyslexics need any drug therapy at all. Perhaps what is more important is for dyslexic students to have understanding, flexible teachers who provide an environment suitable to their learning styles and special needs—including opportunities to move about.

The Parents' Relations with the School

What I suggest here will not be easy for some parents because of unfortunate experiences with school personnel. In some cases the schools have been most conscientious in discovering which students have dyslexia and then providing the remedial care for these children. Others have been negligent in this respect. This negligence is not always the fault of either the teachers or the principal of a particular school, and the parents should realize this. The teachers and principal may wish very much to have a qualified reading specialist in their school who can detect those students who have dyslexia and then work with them to alleviate their condition. The decision may well rest with the "central office" and "higher-ups," who may not see the need for the funding or who may place a greater priority on other expenditures, such as enlarging the football stadium or the parking lot.

If your child has been diagnosed elsewhere as having dyslexia and you have been frustrated in your attempts to get remedial help, do not be too hasty in blaming your child's teacher or his principal. Even though you may ask them why this service is not provided, they may not be in a position to help or to give you satisfactory reasons. It will not help either your child or you if you criticize the school principal for not having the qualified person to work with your child.

The matter should be pursued with the superintendent of instruction, or the superintendent of special services, if there is one, and then if you receive no satisfaction, do not hesitate to carry the matter to the superintendent of schools. This is the person who can take the necessary steps to provide the funds for specialists in the schools to work with dyslexic children. The lonely principal can only ask for such help and dream. Discuss your feelings with the principal but seek help from those who determine the priorities for the whole school system.

Teacher Conferences

Never, *never* hesitate to request a conference with your child's teacher if you have any questions or are concerned about the progress of your child.

This also applies to the specialist who may be working with your child in support of the classroom teacher. Most teachers are delighted to have parents who are truly concerned about their children, who care about their progress, and who want to help the teacher in any way they can.

If your child's teacher has an unlisted telephone number, as some now have, by all means send a note with your child, or a letter by mail, requesting that the teacher call you, and giving a choice of times when you will be home. At this time, set up an appointment and go to the school to talk with the teacher of your dyslexic child rather than discuss the matter on the telephone, because you will want to see samples of your child's work and the results of tests he has taken.

Be prepared for the conference. Make a written list of your questions. During the conference, if you do not understand the teacher's "educational jargon," which we all tend to slip into at times, by all means ask her to explain and give examples. If you have not been trained in education you cannot be expected to be familiar with some of the terms used, no matter how intelligent or educated you may be.

If, for example, your child's teacher says to you during a conference, "He has a lot of trouble with his suffixes. He just can't seem to get his prefixes and suffixes straight," and you are not sure what she is talking about—stop her. Ask the teacher to explain each unknown term so you can understand fully what she is telling you about your child. There is no need to be embarrassed about this. It is no reflection upon your intelligence.

If the teacher does not already have available for your inspection examples of your child's work and test results in support of what she is telling you about his difficulties, be sure to ask for them. They will add to your understanding and perception of the situation.

Keeping Your Cool

In most cases, the parents and school are able to cooperate amiably in helping the dyslexic child. Each understands the other's position and all want to do whatever they can to alleviate the dyslexic's problems—the number one priority.

Unfortunately, this is not always the case. At times parents and school personnel seem to lock horns. This may have happened to you when you sought help for your dyslexic child. You may be disappointed and frustrated because the school cannot, or will not, provide the help your child needs in spite of the federal law for disabled children, PL 94–142. This may be the result of insufficient funding, the priorities placed on funds, the lack of qualified personnel, or a lack of interest for one reason or another.

The school may want to place your child in a self-contained special education class with children who have all kinds of handicaps, rather than placing him in a regular classroom with a competent teacher who will work cooperatively with the specialist to whom he should go regularly for special remediation classes. Some parents have found that their child has been placed in a class with mentally retarded students, emotionally disturbed students, or students with certain physical and other handicaps. The school may want to place the dyslexic child in a crowded special class where individual attention would be difficult. Or it may want to place him with someone who has not had special training in alleviating dyslexia—which could be disastrous.

Whatever the circumstances, you may find yourself becoming anxious about what is happening to your child, frightened that he may not get the remediation necessary to alleviate his dyslexia, angry that the school personnel do not appear to realize the seriousness of the situation, and frustrated about the whole state of affairs. It would be natural to lose your temper, to want to yell and shout and punch someone in the nose. But you can't. Nothing would be accomplished except a worsening of an already difficult relationship.

So, for the sake of your dyslexic child you must remain cool, calm, and collected. His welfare must always be your first priority. Nor do you want to give the school an excuse for writing you off as an "overanxious, unpredictable, emotionally disturbed terror," or just another "irate parent." You can accomplish more by a courteous, attentive manner—even though you may be boiling inside. It may be that at a later date you will need to ask that your child be excused from school for remedial lessons with a private specialist. This trained person should be able to visit the school and work cooperatively with your child's classroom teacher, helping her to understand the nature of a dyslexic's problems, perhaps suggesting special techniques that will help him, and sharing testing results—in other words, good relations must be maintained. You may even have other children who attend or will be attending the school, unless you move to another area (which some parents have done to get the necessary help for their dyslexic child).

Following is a letter written by the mother of a visual dyslexic boy to a person in the central office of her school system. She sent a copy to me, knowing that I would be interested in her son's situation at school. He had attended our clinic where the diagnosis of his condition was made. We always send to a child's school the results of testing along with the implications of such findings for the child's achievement in school, and with suggestions to teachers that will help them work with the student. We have found that most schools are delighted to have children tested and to have suggestions on helping them. Teachers appreciate the helpful ideas and often call to report on the progress of the child. Of course, no teacher is "told how to teach."

The mother has given me permission to share her letter with you. The letter was seven pages long and written in small handwriting, so some parts have had to be omitted. Nevertheless, the thread of frustration, anguish, and despair with her son's experiences in this particular school system pour through her words. Names have been changed.

Dear Mr. Johnson,

I have two children in advanced classes and one in the gifted [class] at Main School and I know your contribution to this system has made this possible for them to achieve to the best of their ability.

My concern is not for my other three children but for my ten-year-old in an L.D. [Learning Disabled] classroom in Grace School. . . . My child, Tommy, was placed in the L.D. class when he seemed to be out in space, as told by his first-grade teacher. . . . When they placed him in the L.D. system, naturally I became curious when I couldn't find out what his problem was with reading. I felt that surely they would have professionals that would immediately diagnose his problem, but I was in for a rude awakening. . . . I was told by the school psychologist that my child walked funny, that something was wrong with him, as he breathed with his mouth open which was a sign of a mental problem. . . . I explained . . . that all of my children walked funny as they had crooked legs, that they all breathed through their mouths as they had asthma, allergies, and bronchial problems . . .

[A year later] still not knowing why he was an L.D. student, I got in touch with Dr. Anne Marshall Huston at Lynchburg College. . . . She did numerous tests and found that he had visual dyslexia. She recommended a private reading teacher and she also was kind enough to send a letter to his teachers telling them the best methods to teach him. Mrs. Albert, his teacher at Grace School, said she didn't appreciate Dr. Huston telling her how to teach and if he had a private reading teacher, she [that teacher] would teach as she [Mrs. Albert] told her to. . . . She [Mrs. Albert] had never heard of dyslexia. . . . Mrs. Albert's animosity toward me for seeking outside help for my child was met to her satisfaction by taking out her spite on my child. He could do no right. When he finally realized this he did everything he could to stay out of her class. This last year was spent in the office helping the janitor. He became so disturbed and disoriented that now he has a real social problem.

Mrs. Smith agreed to place him in her regular science class, against Mrs. Albert's wishes, after I finally convinced the system that he could function in a classroom setting. There, he has no problems, as Mrs. Smith calls out his tests orally, however I asked that he be placed in other classes, and I am informed that he is now a behavior problem so these other teachers don't have to take him. I've asked for help from resource teachers that seem to have extra time when I'm in the school, but they don't have to take L.D. children, they only work with slow children. They prefer I don't get any outside help in reading as this may confuse my child. . . .

John David [school psychologist] insists that I put my child on drugs to shut him up. . . . I went to my Dr. W. [who] called Dr. Jackson [superintendent of schools] and expressed his concern that John was using this way out to correct these problems. Dr. W. became very concerned when John suggested I change doctors. We [parents and Tommy] decided to go to Dr. Lasser [private clinical psychologist] at $65 an hr. and she also felt that Tommy didn't need drugs. She and Dr. W. were also nice enough to take their time and attend our last [school] meeting . . . to prove their point. We are trying to keep kids off of drugs, not to put them on [them].

I wrote a similar letter to Dr. Jackson during the summer and he was very nice to inform me that he would pay closer attention to the L.D. system and also that Mrs. Albert would be leaving. . . . This year the children . . . have a concerned teacher, Bob Wilson, but without any help other than an aide, he can't accomplish miracles. He has a combination of hearing problems, reading problems, wheelchairs, abused kids, gifted kids and any kind of kids that regular teachers are not required to take. . . . Please get in touch with someone that cares and get additional help for these teachers so that they can accomplish more than their checklists and provide adequate education for each child in these centers. It's spend the money now or destroy them and their parents and let society pay later.

I apologize for this monologue but hope you will understand my . . . sincerity in hoping that all of these children will have an equal opportunity to function.

Sincerely,
Gladys W. Fisher

Private Help for Your Child

If your school has no one trained in working with dyslexics, and if there is someone in your area who is trained in the diagnosis and remediation of dyslexia and will work privately with your child on a one-to-one basis, by all means secure this help. This will add to your financial burden and may represent a sacrifice for the whole family, but in the long run the expense will be worth it. A professional person who knows exactly what to do, who has the materials necessary for effective remediation, and who will work with your child alone will be able to alleviate the dyslexia much more quickly than could be done in school, where he is likely to be in a group of eight to twelve other students. Even more effective would be for your child to receive the help not only of this specialist but also of a trained school person who will work with him several times a week—the two working cooperatively with the classroom teacher to alleviate his dyslexia. This, of course, is the ideal situation for the dyslexic child, but it is not always possible to obtain.

The time factor is of the utmost importance. As your dyslexic child moves up the grades, his work in textbooks will increase, whether in math, social studies, science, or English. The sooner he is helped with his reading, writing, and spelling, the better the student and the happier the child will be, and the more contented you, his parents, will be.

Due Process and What This Means to Parents

Public Law 94–142 (and Section 504 of the 1973 Vocational Rehabilitation Act) has provided certain legal safeguards for parents of disabled children.[4] Due process is an example of such legal safeguards.

You have the right to know what the school is planning with regard to the identification, evaluation, and placement of your child. School personnel must consult with you, and involve you, in all of it. At the conferences, if you do not understand some of the professional terms used, ask for an explanation. If you wonder about the purpose of certain tests—that is, what information they are seeking—do not hesitate to ask why they are being given to your child. If you do not agree with what is suggested by the school, you may present evidence to contradict the school's recommendations and planned course of action. You also have the right to suggest your own proposals for the education of your child.

Your consent, as parents, is required for the placement of your child in any special education class. In other words, you do not have to agree to this arrangement if you do not believe it is appropriate for your child. Actually, your dyslexic child is likely to do better in a regular classroom—*provided* the teacher understands his special needs and is willing to take him as he is, adapting the instruction, teaching him at his current level of achievement, and modifying performance expectations until his difficulties have been alleviated. Your dyslexic belongs in the regular classroom with a caring and understanding teacher, sensitive to the dyslexic child's anxieties, and one who can be flexible in instruction and the use of materials.

Your dyslexic child also needs, on a regular basis, the help of the school reading specialist if the specialist is trained in the remediation of dyslexia. This was discussed in the previous section. *Be sure to inquire about this person's specific training in dyslexia*. There are both reading specialists and learning disability teachers in the schools who have not had this training. If the school does not have such a qualified person, then you must seek additional help on a private basis. If your child is excused from school to get this outside help, as is done in some school systems, you will probably be responsible for the transportation. This may be inconvenient for you, but the important thing is to get the necessary help for your child.

In your conferences with the school, try to keep in mind that school personnel are usually sincere people who are earnestly trying to help your child. Their views may differ from yours, and you may strongly disagree with what they recommend. Keep calm and listen to what they have to say. Then present your case in the same manner, courteously and firmly. Parents of dyslexic children have often gone through so much and have had so many frustrations that this is not always easy to do.

The following is a list of rights that some parents may not know they have:

1. You must receive written notice as to the time and date of any hearing.

2. You may have access to any and all records about your child.

3. You have the right to get a separate, independent evaluation of your child (other than that provided by the school).

4. You may decide whether the hearing will be open or closed.

5. Your child may be kept at his present grade placement until all due process hearing appeals have been completed.

6. You may have your attorney with you at any hearing.

7. Your child may be present at the hearing if you wish.

8. You may present any evidence or testimony that you have obtained.

9. You may prevent any information or other evidence from being presented if it was not disclosed at least five days before the hearing.

10. You have the right to challenge any testimony of any persons or any evidence presented at the hearing.

11. You may request a verbatim transcript (which is usually an audiotape), and there will be a reasonable charge for this, but I strongly urge that you do this as you may need it for future reference.

12. You may appeal the decision of the members of the hearing panel or the hearing officer—you do not have to buckle under if you disagree strongly.

Public Law 99–372, the Handicapped Children's Protection Act, became effective in August 1986. This provides a partnership of Public Law 94–142 and Section 504, so that Section 504 may be used to enforce the accommodation of dyslexic students in a regular classroom, rather than placing them in a separate special education class. Failure on the part of a public school system to provide such arrangements for dyslexics can result in the loss of federal funds.

This law can reduce the number of due process hearings and help school systems conform with Public Law 94–142. While the new law provides for legal fees and costs to parents who succeed in due process or court proceedings, payment is limited to those awarded in comparable types of proceedings. If parents reject a timely written offer of settlement by the school system and do not obtain better relief through the hearing or court decision, then the fees may not be recoverable by the parents. Consequently, parents might give serious thought to a negotiated settlement rather than proceed with a due process hearing.[5,6]

Family Education Rights and Privacy Act (The Buckley Amendment)

In 1974 Congress passed the Family Education Rights and Privacy Act (FERPA). Parents and their disabled children now have the right to know what information is in the school cumulative folder and other confidential school records of the child. Do not hesitate to ask to see the "confidential" files, as schools often have two sets of files. Parents may also challenge the comments in the files and correct any errors in the school records. The act also provides one other protection that parents should use: the right of the parents to control the accessibility of the child's school records.

Parents are urged to request to examine these records. This is your child! Ask questions, challenge certain negative comments. Request specific examples of your child's behavior and written observational records to support the negative comments. Do your dyslexic child's records contain comments by teachers such as "lazy, defiant, has to be pushed, is smart but won't do the work, is capable but won't work," and the like? Was he diagnosed as being a dyslexic after these remarks? During? Of course such comments should be stricken from the records of a dyslexic student. Are you aware that your child's academic folder and other school records may follow him throughout his life?

Under the new confidentiality law you have the right to see any psychological assessment of your child. It may be helpful if a psychologist is present to explain the test results and answer any questions you may have.

The Importance of Keeping Records

Parents of dyslexic children need to be very conscientious about keeping a file of all kinds of records. These records can provide the necessary documentation you may need at some time to justify your requests for special services and to hold your child's school system accountable for its obligations. Your file should include school report cards, progress reports, evaluation reports and copies of Individual Educational Programs (IEPs), samples of schoolwork, copies of questions asked of school personnel and other professionals (with their answers), notes of visits to the school, conferences with teachers and others, problems at school that occurred (and results of suggested solutions), and records of your child's medical and developmental history.

Go over your child's cumulative file at school and ask for copies of any information you think should be included in your home file. As time passes, jot down comments and reactions made by your child as well as your own observations and reactions.

Keeping such a file up-to-date will take discipline. Notes of conferences, and telephone conversations, should be written as soon after their occurrence as possible. Be sure that all records are dated. You will probably want to keep the records filed in chronological order.

Boarding Schools for Dyslexic Students

Sometimes I am asked about special boarding schools for dyslexics. The question usually comes about as a result of the parents' dissatisfaction with what the child's school has to offer in the way of remediation of the dyslexia or the locked-horns situation previously discussed in this chapter—the parents just want to get their child "out of that school."

Brochures and catalogs are available from these special schools, but the information must be read with caution. The materials cannot always be taken at face value. Remember: this is advertising material to get you interested and to sell the school. The actual program may not be any different from that which the child is getting at his present school, although it is possible that the curriculum may be somewhat more individualized. Naturally, any school considered should be visited by the parents and the dyslexic student. In addition to the usual visit with the headmaster and admissions person, you should visit the classrooms while instruction is going on. Listen to the teachers and note how they relate to the students. Observe the students and their reactions in class. Are they interested and motivated? Do they appear prepared for the class and do they participate in the discussion? Are they considerate of their classmates? Stop the students on the grounds and outside of classes and ask them how they are doing in the school, if they are progressing, and so on. Note their attitude toward their teachers and the school as a whole. What individual attention will your child be getting?

These special boarding schools tend to be very expensive. Parents must give careful thought to whether what their child is going to get from the school is really worth the high tuition and probable family financial sacrifice it will entail. You also need to find out if your dyslexic child truly wants to leave home and go off to school. Remember, he has had many unhappy and frustrating experiences, his self-concept is poor, and he tends to feel insecure and inadequate as it is. He must not think that you want "to get rid of him" because he is such a burden and not the kind of son he thinks you would like to have.

I personally believe that the best situation is for the dyslexic child to remain at home and receive private remedial help on an individual basis, as discussed earlier. You may have to fight hard (but always diplomatically, of course) to get special help at school. Regardless of these problems, your child has you to stand behind him, to give him the needed support and encouragement, and the security of your love and acceptance. He would miss you terribly if you sent him away and you would miss him as much.

Notes

1. Nancy Larrick, *A Parent's Guide to Children's Reading*, 4th ed. (New York: Bantam Books, 1975).

2. Michael E. Thomson, *Developmental Dyslexia: Its Nature, Assessment and Remediation* (London: Edward Arnold, 1984), p. 226.

3. Marcel Kinsbourne et al., "Questions People Ask About Dyslexia," *The Dyslexic Child*, Drake D. Duane and Paula Dozier Rome, eds. (New York: Insight Publishing, 1979), pp. 23–24.

4. Public Law 94–142, Education of the Handicapped Act of 1975. The implementation of Part B dealing with specific learning disabilities was published in the *Federal Register* on December 29, 1977, and went into effect in September 1978. On October 30, 1990, the name of Public Law 94–142 was changed to *Individuals with Disabilities Education Act (IDEA)*.

5. Justine Maloney, "Public Law 99–372, The Handicapped Children's Protection Act, Deemed Significant," *ACLD Newsbriefs* 176 (September/October 1988), p. 21.

6. Ibid.

CHAPTER 16

WHAT CAN THE CLASSROOM TEACHER DO?

> We are all sufferers from our continued failure to
> fulfill the educational obligations of a democracy.
> We are all the victims of a school system
> that has only gone halfway along the road
> to realize the promise of democracy.
> —*Mortimer J. Adler*

As I have stated, the best situation for the dyslexic student is to be in a regular classroom (the traditional self-contained type) while receiving regular help from a specialist who is trained in the remediation of dyslexia and who cooperates with the classroom teacher to provide the best possible environment and instruction for the student to alleviate his dyslexia. This is a form of "mainstreaming," which some think is a fairly new concept. It is not. For years regular classroom teachers have had children with all kinds of handicaps who have achieved at different levels in their classrooms—beginning with the teachers in one-room schoolhouses, who not only had students of varying handicaps but also of different ages and in different grades. Teachers have been dealing with these problems for years and have been successfully educating the young people in their charge.

Fads come and go in education. People are prone to jump on bandwagons before research and experience indicate they are good for our children. The American "open" classroom concept (so different from that in Great Britain), which abolished the traditional self-contained classroom in some schools and actually tore down walls between rooms so that as many as ninety or so young children were in a large area with several teachers, did not achieve the results predicted. Some students who had learned successfully before found that the distraction of so many people in one area, often talking and moving around, interfered with their learning. Teachers could not get to know the individual students as well as in the traditional classroom, where they were with the same group of children all day each day for the entire school year. Teachers and administrators found that tearing down walls did not necessarily create the "open" classroom—the new concept could be as structured and inhibiting as the old. At last educators have come to realize that an "openness" of learning can exist within the self-contained classroom, which can provide a flexibility of planning and instruction and individualization not available in a situation where there are large numbers of students in one big room.

Today, there is growing acceptance in American schools of the so-called "Whole Language Program." This program is more of a set of beliefs and philosophy than a distinctive method. It carries a danger that the variability of quality, overall structure, and consistency of programs may doom it to the same fate as the "Individualized Reading" programs of a few years ago—a program with many of the same tenets. Some schools are jumping on the bandwagon without the necessary planning, in-service training of teachers, and materials. In some instances the pendulum has swung from the excessive drills and skills in isolation approach to the opposite end of the continuum with no attention to certain specific needs.

In the authentic whole-language classroom, the emphasis on building on the language knowledge and strategies that the student already has, the integration of language use into learning activities, working with whole, authentic texts, and having real purposes for reading, writing, speaking, and listening, together with the development of a positive self-esteem, should enhance the dyslexic's motivation and progress. So, too, will the practice of using hands-on activities, books containing interesting stories and natural language usage, integrated assignments and projects, and numerous opportunities for active learning.

At the same time, however, the student with dyslexia has specific gaps in knowledge and strategies that limit his progress in and understanding of material read or heard. These deficiencies must be attended to. If placed in a classroom where instruction and materials are at either extreme of the continuum, the dyslexic student will flounder. His best chance for progress will be in a well-balanced program where his particular needs will receive special attention.

I have also stated that the "departmentalized" class procedure is difficult for the dyslexic student. Here he has to move from room to room for each subject he is taking, usually with a different teacher. The pressure is on him to complete his work within the class period. The "tyrant" (the clock) is always on the wall watching him, hurrying him, reminding him that time is slipping away.

The departmentalized class procedure has been customary for older students for a long time, and the dyslexic student will have to accept that situation. Ideally, the teachers will understand the dyslexic's problems and will be flexible enough to make certain adaptations in both instruction and expectations of work. Unfortunately, the practice has moved to some primary and elementary schools where young children are expected to be miniature adolescents, able to move efficiently to each class and to adjust to a variety of teacher personalities and methods of instruction from hour to hour. Fortunately, teachers' voices are being heard—as are those of parents—and there is already a move to modify the departmentalized class procedure in some primary and elementary schools.

Whatever the arrangement within your school at the present time, you and the specialist working with the dyslexic student will be the two most important people in the school for him. As a matter of fact, if you are in a self-contained or "block" departmentalized situation (several subjects taught by one teacher), you will probably spend many more hours with him than will the specialist. You will be his source of security within the school. You will, in a sense, be his guardian. If in the past you have not knowingly had the responsibility of a dyslexic in your class the thought may at first appear to be a little frightening, but you can deal with it successfully—and you will find the rewards worth the effort. The experience can be challenging and even exciting. I have known teachers who have become so interested in working with a dyslexic student that they have, on their own, requested his parents to let him stay a little while after school so that they could give him more help with his classroom work. I call such dedicated teachers "angels of mercy." Would there were more!

The Classroom Environment

The environment of the classroom must be one in which the dyslexic student feels secure and safe, accepted and *liked* by his teacher and his classmates. You, the teacher, create the environment within your classroom. The other students will observe your relationship with the dyslexic student. They will be aware of the dignity and respect with which you treat him, your friendly attitude and acceptance of him, your willingness to give him special help, your tolerance of certain dyslexic symptoms that he cannot help—such as the spoonerisms or slow responses to questions—and they will pick up your attitude and will respond to him accordingly.

In Chapter 13 certain instructional materials needed to alleviate dyslexia are described. These materials will be exceptionally helpful to anyone working with dyslexic students. You will find that the materials will also help you with the other children in your class who are having academic problems.

As you will discover, your dyslexic student can participate in class discussions. If he does, give yourself a pat on the back, for it means that he feels a part of the class, wants to make a contribution, and is not afraid to go out on a limb and take a chance. It means that he feels his response will be accepted. He does not have to be afraid of ridicule.

You should know that sometimes a dyslexic student will be "behind" in answering a certain question. You may have already gotten one response from another student and moved on to the next question when the dyslexic student finally raises his hand and gives a response to the former question. This happens because of the "language disconnection" that occurs at times. His mind is still working on and processing the information in answer to the former question. Your reaction to this is very important. Some teachers, not understanding the nature of the dyslexic student, react with impatience or ridicule. If this happens, he is not likely to volunteer to answer a question again. He is more likely to withdraw mentally and emotionally from a situation that is painful for him.

Remember that *he cannot help this behavior*, any more than we can help a sneeze. Accept his answer to the earlier question. You might say, "That's a good answer. It's the right answer to the question [repeat the question asked earlier]. Both you and [the other student's name] have given good answers and know the information. Now, back to the question I just asked. . . . " By replying in this manner you have preserved his self-respect and yet have courteously and kindly indicated that another question has been asked.

You will also find that not all work for the dyslexic student will have to be individualized and specially prepared for him. Besides, there are likely to be others in the class who have similar problems with reading and writing and learning the subject matter, and need the same concepts and skills. These students can form a group according to their particular needs. If you use the unit method of teaching, then the dyslexic student will be able to read books about the subject (written at his reading level), participate in various groups, and contribute as he is able. If you use one textbook for all students in the class, expecting every student to be at the same place on the same page at the same time, then it will be more difficult for you to work with the dyslexic student. If you have one textbook but are willing to be flexible in your instruction, there are several ways to adapt to the needs of the dyslexic student.

Taping Textbook Chapters and Other Assignments

One way of dealing with the dyslexic's inability to read the textbooks for his various subjects is for the classroom teacher (or a volunteer helper who enunciates clearly) to record the different chapters. This, of course, need not be done all at once. The chapters can be recorded one at a time as long as they are ready when needed. The dyslexic student can then either listen to the tape at school or take the cassette home overnight, in which case he will need a cassette recorder. I have found that in the few cases where students did not have their own cassette recorder, the parents have been quite willing to get one for their dyslexic child.

The dyslexic student can listen to the voice on the tape and look at the words in the book at the same time. Another advantage is that he can stop the tape and replay it any time he gets overwhelmed with information and needs to pick up the thread of thought. He can replay the tape as often as he needs to in order to learn the material.

Textbooks are usually adopted for use for a certain number of years. This means that once you have taped the chapters, you need not tape again until a new textbook is chosen by your school system.

You will probably have other students who are unable to read the textbook required for your class. There are media setups containing earphones whereby as many as six or more students can listen to one tape. You will find that other work and special assignments can also be taped and used in this way by the dyslexic student.

Rewriting Material

Another way of dealing with material in books that are too difficult for the dyslexic student to read is for the classroom teacher to rewrite the material so that it can be read comfortably and with understanding by the student. By doing this, the teacher can make sure that the student is acquiring the major concepts in the curriculum for that particular subject. Some teachers rewrite textbook chapters during the summer in order to have them ready before school starts. They do this not only for their dyslexic students but for their other students who cannot read the textbook with ease. Once a chapter is rewritten, as many copies as needed can be reproduced on a copy machine.

Special Subject Matter Books

For whatever subject you may be teaching, books dealing with the content and major concepts of the subject are written at lower reading levels. Some teachers request these books for the use of their dyslexic students and other students unable to read the required textbook adequately. The reading specialist in your school will be able to help you in selecting and ordering these books. You will have to make a list, along with the publisher, address, and prices, and submit it to your principal who must approve the funds. When I was a public school teacher and did this, I found my principals always supportive. I sincerely hope that you will be as fortunate.

Listed in Appendix C are some names of publishers and their addresses, which may be of help in ordering your books. Your reading specialist will be able to provide additional ones. Appendix D lists some books and materials for different subjects. These are examples that can be used in adapting your instruction. They will be especially helpful in unit teaching.

Films

There is a saying that "one picture is worth a thousand words." This may or may not be so, depending upon the particular picture. There are films that can be obtained free or at a nominal cost (usually from your State Department of Education), rented, or purchased, which can be used in your classroom to present or reinforce certain subject matter. Films can be helpful to the dyslexic student in learning material that he cannot get from his textbook. They can enhance your lessons and provide some variety in your instruction. It helps to use the visual and auditory modalities at the same time, and the classroom discussion following the film will help to organize the information for the students as well as provide you with insights as to which concepts need to be reviewed.

You will want *always* to preview the film before showing it to your students. You may decide that it is not appropriate after all, in spite of what the film's write-up says. If you find it appropriate, then you will know how best to introduce the film to your students and what advance information they will need before they view the film. A preview will also enable you to prepare the questions you will want to use in guiding the discussion after the viewing.

While it is true that ordinarily films should be used sparingly with a generation of students already addicted to watching television, and that films do not have the novelty they once did, for the student with dyslexia educational films are one way to learn new material contained in textbooks that he cannot read on his own.

Giving Directions

Remember that dyslexic students have trouble with both oral and written directions. Give prior thought to the directions that you plan to give so that they will be organized, clear, concise, and to the point, with no ambiguity. Give only one or two oral directions at one time, and always reinforce these visually for the student by writing them on the chalkboard or a chart. Do this when giving directions for homework assignments—and make sure the student copies the assignments correctly.

Think about any written directions you plan to include in a lesson or on a test. Are you certain that your dyslexic student can read all the words in the directions so that he understands what is being asked? If not, read the directions to him. Never let yourself fall into the practice of telling students to "read the directions and then do the work" without being sure they can.

Give Tests and Examinations Orally

You will want to consider giving tests and examinations to your dyslexic student orally. This will remove the threat of his having to read the questions. Read the question to him. Let him tell you the answer. Dyslexics often know the answers to questions that they cannot read, for they pick up a great deal of information by "osmosis" in class and often bring much from their previous background to the class. If they have heard taped textbook chapters, read rewritten material, and seen films about a particular subject, they will probably have learned the information asked for in a test.

Dyslexic students have problems with tests and examinations because (1) they often cannot read all the words in the test questions and are not sure what is being asked; (2) they have trouble writing out the answers; and (3) their writing is slow and laborious, and they are caught in the limits of time.

You may wish to tape the test or examination. You will find that evaluating the answers will probably be more valid, and you can keep the cassette on file if you desire.

Some teachers are critical of this method of giving a test. Perhaps what needs to be considered is this: Is the test being given to determine what information a student knows and how much he has learned about a particular topic, or as a measure of his reading and speed in writing?

Wait-Time

Keep in mind that the dyslexic has trouble with processing information. He needs more time to think, to make sense of what he has seen and heard, and if asked a question in class, to produce the information in a sensible answer. When you ask the dyslexic student a question in class, wait. Do not expect an immediate answer from him. Give him time to think. Wait at least six (or more) seconds for his answer.

Even regular students respond better when there is a wait-time of three to five seconds on the part of the teacher. The length of the answer increases. There are more unsolicited (but correct) answers from students. And there are fewer incorrect answers.[1]

Give your dyslexic student a chance to give you the answer you expect. Give him time to think. Wait, be patient.

Use Multisensory Techniques

The best way to help dyslexics to make associations and relate ideas and to retain information is to take advantage of all the senses and to use concrete materials in instruction as often as possible. This applies to learning new reading and spelling words, studying the geography of a country, doing arithmetic computations—actually, everything in every subject. The dyslexic student needs to hold and feel, to see and hear and touch, to do and act out, to sing and draw—whenever possible. *Both hemispheres of his brain need to be involved in learning.*

One of the most effective sixth-grade teachers whom I have known was a young man who taught in this multisensory, multiexperience manner. He had a typical heterogeneous class—students of varying abilities and differing achievement, with a couple falling in the handicapped classification. What he did with these students in a school year was nearly miraculous. The children turned from "so-so" pupils into excited, eager, curious, knowledgeable students tuned in to learning.

How did he accomplish this? One example will illustrate his technique. The social studies curriculum required a study of the continent of Africa. Of course, the students also had reading, writing, spelling, arithmetic, science, music, and other information to learn. This young man had insisted on having a self-contained classroom, even at this grade. Otherwise, teaching the way he did and accomplishing so much with his students might not have been possible.

The students pushed back the desks and chairs in the classroom, and on the floor they drew to scale a large map of the continent of Africa. They drew in the countries with the respective capitals and other important cities, and the deserts, mountains, rivers, seas, and oceans. They brought in sand for the deserts, molded the mountains out of papier-mâché, and used blue paper for the rivers and neighboring seas and oceans. They calculated the size of the pyramids and made models to scale. (They didn't realize they were learning math when they were doing all this.) They wrote stories about the

Africans and shared these by reading some aloud in class and making booklets of them to be read at free times. They acted out excerpts from Shakespeare's *Antony and Cleopatra* and excerpts from the biblical Book of Exodus. They made their own costumes and prop materials. They learned to sing "Lady of the Nile" and other relevant songs.

Was he teaching his students the necessary subjects in the "curriculum"? More thoroughly than in any other class, and the students enjoyed it so much that they were not aware of the effort they were putting into the process of learning. Their scores on the required standardized achievement tests at the end of the year? Amazing.

A dyslexic student could fit in well in such a class with the flexibility, individualizing, group work, sharing, reinforcement, multisensory approach to learning, and the opportunities for not only mental growth but also social and emotional growth.

Reading Aloud

The Teacher

Read to your students each day. This will not only help the dyslexic student in your class but all your students. It will help them to make the "language connection." Whether you are a fourth-grade, seventh-grade, or eleventh-grade teacher, each day read aloud from a story or a selection dealing with your subject. Your students will listen to you reading and learn new vocabulary and concepts as you read, internalize the flow and melody of our language, and develop an understanding of the relationship between a writer and his reader—who in this case is also the speaker—and the listeners, who are the students. This reading aloud need only take ten minutes, with an additional few to talk about what has been read, but a great deal is being accomplished in this short time.

The Student

Do not require your dyslexic student to read aloud in front of the class, whether from the textbook or his reader. Dyslexics are very self-conscious about their reading mistakes and feel humiliated and ashamed when this occurs in front of others. Most regular textbooks are too difficult for the dyslexic to read anyhow.

Even the elementary teacher, during a formal reading lesson, should avoid having the dyslexic student read aloud in front of the others. I have already mentioned the ineffectiveness of the round-robin method used by some to teach reading.

If your dyslexic *volunteers* to read a story that he has written, or tell how a certain character said something in a story, or repeat a funny joke he has read and enjoyed, this is different. *This* is coming from *him*. He is not being "made" to read aloud from a particular book—and he knows that he can read what he has volunteered to read.

Reading aloud should be required of the dyslexic only for diagnostic purposes, in a one-to-one situation.

Reading Instruction

Even though your dyslexic student is spending time regularly with the specialist who is working specifically on alleviating his dyslexia, you have the responsibility to complement his reading instruction in the classroom. The specialist will help you here. As a regular classroom teacher you already know how to find the instructional reading level of your students, the level used to teach reading when using basal readers. Some classroom teachers are more comfortable if the reading specialist reaffirms this level.

It is of the utmost importance that your dyslexic student not be expected to read a book too difficult for him. As in the case of your other students, he should be learning from a reading book that is at his instructional level—lightly lower if he is more self-confident at this level. It is possible that you will have other nondyslexic students at this same level. If so, you can form a group of those who have the same instructional reading level.

Somehow, in the past, the myth arose that the ideal classroom arrangement for teaching the art of reading is to have three groups, even though in a typical classroom there are likely to be more than three levels of reading. In spite of what some appear to believe, there is no Eleventh Commandment that says, "Thou shalt have only three reading groups." To teach reading effectively (and to learn effectively), there should be as many groups as needed by the students in your class. This will assure that you are providing more effective reading instruction, and that you truly will be complementing the work that the specialist is doing with your dyslexic student.

As a classroom teacher, you are familiar with the overall lesson plan of the basal readers. Keep in mind that the dyslexic student will need to be prepared for any new story in the reader by your introducing the new concepts and the new vocabulary in a manner relevant to him through the use of concrete materials and multisensory techniques. In no way can the dyslexic learn new words if you simply write them on the chalkboard or chart, read them aloud, and have him repeat them to you. He has to tackle new words and become involved with them!

After reading a story, let him act it out. This will help him with any sequencing problems. Correct him gently if he makes mistakes in the sequence. Let him draw pictures of events in sequence and put these up on the chalk tray and talk about them. Let him make dioramas to illustrate scenes—again with your help in rectifying any omissions. Let him (and others in his group) make charts, maps, illustrations of the characters, and the like.

Always stress meaning—the meaning of new words, the meaning of words as they appear in sentences, the meaning of passages, or the main idea of the story as a whole. Remember that meaning is critical to the dyslexic's success in learning.

Computers

The latest bandwagon that educators are hurrying to jump on is the use of computers in the classroom. Here, again, one must be cautious in giving either blanket approval or disapproval, especially concerning dyslexic students. I have already mentioned the problems dyslexics have when using computers by reason of their reversing letters and numerals, transposing symbols, and confusing similar letters in words or words similar in appearance, and also confusing similar numerals.

I fear that some teachers will want "to plug" the dyslexic child into these machines and let the computer do the work—which it cannot do. If this happens, it is a neglect of responsibility on the part of the teacher. Students have been "plugged" into workbooks, mechanical tachistoscopes, and automatic "readers" in the past, none of which has resulted in much progress on the part of the child, and none of which can take the place of a warm, caring, competent human being.

At the present time it appears that advances in the production of the actual computers (called hardware) have shot ahead of the special programs designed for their use (called software). I do not mean to imply that there are not a number of educational programs available that may be compatible with the different brands of computers that schools have purchased. What concerns me is the content of such programs. There is a saying in the computer world, "garbage in, garbage out," sometimes referred to as GIGO. Reading is a *process*—not an accumulation of bits and pieces of skills that together make a whole. The dyslexic student has already had his share of drill and more drill in isolated skills, so much so that he has enough meaningless debris (garbage) floating around in his brain to clog his learning. Computer programs of drill and practice and more drill and practice fall under the category of "garbage in, garbage out," with the possible reinforcement of errors.

Tutorial types of programs should be evaluated carefully by the teacher. Here the student moves from one step to another by answering questions. One must ask if what is being stressed is really what the student needs to learn. Is the information in each step needed? Or is it more "garbage in, garbage out?" Are there other ways of teaching this information that would be more meaningful and effective?

There are still other programs that contain questionable material. Could anyone trained in education and the nurture of children possibly have designed the program that responds to a mistake by a student with "Wrong answer, dummy!"? Or the one that gives an ugly, mocking, "raspberry" sound when the student makes an error? Students with dyslexia already have a low enough self-concept, and they secretly worry about really being "dumb." They are very sensitive to criticism, especially the put-down type. Such responses, even if made by a machine, only serve to reinforce the dyslexic's negative ideas about himself and to increase his anxiety in learning.

The ability to transfer any new skills and concepts to reading and writing is *essential*. Some teachers have trouble getting their students to transfer and apply new learning in reading and writing language because they have taught these in isolation to their students. In the same way, I am concerned about the transfer of skills learned from the computer to the actual tasks of reading and writing.

As for the word processor, it may be beneficial in writing papers and its spelling program may catch some misspelled words, but the dyslexic student will still have certain problems, already mentioned.

Careful thought should be given to whether and how computers can help the dyslexic student, and whether the expense is justifiable. Perhaps other means would be more effective given the expense involved—for instance, the employment of a full-time reading specialist.

The Reading Specialist in Your School

The reading specialist is able to suggest special activities in the classroom to reinforce what is being done with the dyslexic student in the reading clinic. The specialist can also help in acquiring various materials that you may need and in selecting and ordering other special materials and books suited to your dyslexic student.

The Teacher's Aide/The Volunteer

If you have a teacher's aide or a volunteer mother or other helper, be sure always to give careful instructions as to what they should do—and how they should do it. Keep in mind that their job is not to "teach" but to help you with your dyslexic student while you are working with the other students in your classroom. They can read a story or chapter of a textbook to him, *review* certain skills and new words previously taught by you, help with his spelling, and use the kinesthetic technique for teaching new reading and spelling words. (See Appendix E for an effective kinesthetic approach.)

Do *not* have these helpers simply sit and flash isolated words on cards to the dyslexic student. This is a meaningless drill and can be a frustrating and useless experience for a child with dyslexia. Instead, have them use sentence strips in which the sentence contains the word, which is underlined. (The student should be able to read the sentence, of course.) The word could also be written on another strip, and the child could match that word with the same word in the sentence, and then make up his own sentence using the word. The sentence strip could be placed at the top of the pocket chart and the helper could then proceed with another sentence strip. Each time, though, the dyslexic student should read the preceding sentences before moving to another one.

Public Law 94–142, Individuals with Disabilities Education Act (IDEA)

In 1975, Congress passed Public Law 94–142 (Federal Register, 1977), which requires the states to provide educational programs for all handicapped children between the ages of three and twenty-one. The right to "free, appropriate public education" for handicapped children, geared to their particular needs, has been mandated for, but not necessarily received by, all disabled children.

The term *disabled children* is broad and includes those who are deaf, hard of hearing, mentally retarded, orthopedically impaired, severely emotionally disturbed, speech impaired, visually handicapped, and learning disabled. Learning disability is defined in the regulations for Public Law 94–142 as follows:

A disorder in one or more of the basic psychological processes involved in understanding or in using language, spoken or written, which may manifest itself in imperfect ability to listen, think, speak, read, write, spell, or to do mathematical calculations. The term includes such conditions as perceptual handicaps, brain injury, minimal brain dysfunction, dyslexia, and developmental aphasia. The term does not include children who have learning problems which are primarily the result of visual, hearing, or motor handicaps, or mental retardation, or of environmental, cultural or economic disadvantage.[2]

When this law went into effect in September 1978, funds were provided for the states and localities to help in the education of handicapped children. Unfortunately, many superintendents of school systems and directors of instruction and special services were and still are confused as to what services are reimbursable under the law.[3] Consequently, some students who have serious reading and spelling problems are not getting the help they need.

Dyslexia was specifically named in the definition of learning disability in the mandate by the federal government. Nevertheless, in a number of schools, the dyslexic student is not getting the kind of help that he needs. There are several possible explanations for this. Some teacher-training institutions have not adequately prepared their reading specialists and learning disability teachers in the diagnosis and remediation of dyslexia. In some institutions there are those who deny that dyslexia exists and therefore their graduates leave the college or university ignorant and insensitive to the problems of the dyslexic student. In some public school systems there are insufficient reading specialists and learning disability teachers to take care of the number of students in need. There are few in-service programs dealing with dyslexia to help the public school classroom teacher deal with students who have this disability.

The Age Limits of PL 94–142

The range of ages, from three to twenty-one, has implications for the schools. More and more pressure for early identification of problems is being brought to bear upon school personnel. Certainly we want to identify children with vision or hearing defects, the orthopedically impaired, the emotionally disturbed, and those children with severe speech impediments and brain damage.

But where determining "mentally retarded" can be tricky at the early age of three, and identifying certain speech problems can be precarious, detecting dyslexia at the age of three is ludicrous! The reasons have been explained in Chapter 6 dealing with the early identification of dyslexia— before the age of eight—and there is no need for repetition here.

The upper limit of twenty-one years of age means that our high school dyslexic student can remain in school longer to continue receiving special services of remediation. If the young person is able and wants to remain in school—does not have to work—then this is to be desired, as he needs all the help he can get for as long as he can get it. But most young persons, especially those who have had difficulties and frustrations along the way, are anxious to get out of school and on with their lives. I doubt that many dyslexics will continue to stay in school—too many, as it is, drop out of school as soon as they reach the legal age.

The Classroom Teacher's Rights Under PL 94–142

Classroom teachers may have the notion that Public Law 94–142 provides rights only for handicapped students and their parents, and perhaps for the special education professional.[4] This is not the case. You, too, have the following rights:

1. To have a student adequately diagnosed
2. To participate in the program planning process, especially if a student is "mainstreamed" into your classroom
3. To work with the education specialist who is alleviating the student's dyslexia
4. To have adequate resources for your instruction of the dyslexic student
5. To receive the assistance of parents in complementing the school program at home.

Sometimes regular classroom teachers believe they are considered less important, even less intelligent, than the reading or special education specialist, the school psychologist, or other special personnel in the school. This may be so even though they too have a master's degree from an eminent school of education. The feeling may be due to the fact that often the classroom teachers are not included in some conferences concerning a child, or perhaps their specific recommendations are ignored. They become hesitant about taking the initiative with a child, and reticent about making suggestions that they believe appropriate—standing up for what they know is right. Like the dyslexic student, these teachers begin to lose their self-confidence, and they become sensitive and somewhat defensive. *Do not let this happen to you!* Recall that I began this chapter by saying that you are important to the dyslexic child: "You will be his source of security within the school. You will, in a sense, be his guardian." Remember these words and draw courage from them. The dyslexic child in your classroom needs you. Do not let him down.

Individual Educational Program

Public Law 94–142 requires that an individual educational program (IEP) be prepared in detail for each child. Annual overall goals must be set with a list of short-term objectives to serve as steps in achieving each annual goal. Special instructional materials used for each task must be listed along with the criteria for success, and tests and other evaluation procedures to determine if the objectives are being met—if the student is learning what he is supposed to be learning as planned.

The regular classroom teacher may or may not participate in the IEP, depending upon the policy of the particular school.

The advantages often cited for an IEP are:

1. The teacher and other personnel must focus upon the child himself.

2. Individual strengths and weaknesses of the child become known.

3. Progress of the child is noted.

4. The IEP says, "This is where we're going, how we're to get there, and how we will know when we've arrived."[5]

5. Since the parents' approval is required, they are more likely to feel as though they have been involved in the process.

IEP's are criticized for these reasons:

1. IEP's require the spelling out of detailed, specific behavioral objectives which permit only a very narrow definition of both curriculum and competence.[6]

2. In this behavioral approach, various skills are broken down into fragmented pieces, and our dyslexic students already have too many bits and pieces of garbage floating around in their heads.

3. The isolated approach to reading prevents students from understanding what reading is all about. Learning skills becomes the end rather than the means to successful reading. Many of our dyslexics have already begun to internalize this erroneous concept of the reading process.

4. Success criteria of 80 percent accuracy on task (or 85 percent or 90 percent or 75 percent) still leave gaps in knowledge and can contribute to additional problems with skills at a higher level. (For example, not knowing the consonant "*l*" can affect the learning of the "*l*" blends [*bl, cl, fl* . . .].)

5. Preparing the IEP and short-term daily (or weekly) objectives in a professional manner is extremely time consuming and reduces the time that could be spent in planning motivating lessons and making creative materials to achieve more effectively the objectives.

6. While the IEP is supposed to stress individualization, in the section on procedures, instructional methods, media/materials, and evaluation procedures, lists such as this are found:

"Hayes ditto worksheet"
"Workbook, page 20"
"Workbook, page 21"
"Workbook, page 22"
"Commercial and teacher worksheets"
"Blend ditto worksheet"

"Digraph ditto worksheet"
"Commercial and teacher worksheets"
"Completed worksheet"
. . . and so on . . . and on . . .

7. IEPs too often fail to emphasize the sustained silent reading needed for the transfer and application of skills and new words learned, the creating of experience charts and word banks, and creative writing by students. These activities are all aimed at "meaning" and could certainly be used with IEPs.

To return for a moment to the listed advantages of the IEP, it should be noted that conscientious teachers have always focused upon the child as an individual with individual strengths and needs. For years teachers have kept progress charts of various kinds to indicate how well a student is achieving. In order to be effective, all teachers must plan and set objectives—and work hard to meet the overall goals set for students. The only thing new about the IEP is, perhaps, that a separate program must be written for each child.

Programs to Avoid

There are certain commercial programs and kits that have been reputedly good for working with dyslexic students. As we have learned more about the diagnosis and alleviation of dyslexia, we have found that certain programs and approaches are suitable—but others are not. Some to avoid are those that

1. Do not stress meaning and understanding on the part of students. (This is critical to a dyslexic's success in acquiring new concepts, vocabulary, and skills.)

2. Emphasize the teaching of the phonic elements in isolation. (The rationale for this has already been presented in detail.)

3. Use an orthography other than our traditional alphabet, including color coding of words or sounds or a restructured alphabet to represent the forty-four sounds in our language, or special pictures to represent the sounds of the alphabet or words. (The dyslexic has enough difficulty mastering his own alphabet: the visual dyslexic, with difficulty in revisualization that causes unstable letter formations and incomplete recall of details in pictures; and the auditory dyslexic, with processing the sounds represented by the letters of our alphabet. Moreover, our books are written in traditional orthography and these must be used to transfer the skills learned.)

4. Stress any kind of speed reading, tachistoscope flashing, controlled reading, or require fast-paced verbal responses. (The dyslexic needs *time* to

process information. Any pressure for speed and quantity can cause him undue stress.)

5. Require a dyslexic to proceed through workbook pages on his own in a programmed manner and without supervision. (The dyslexic has special needs requiring attention. Any program where students go through a workbook working all the pages one after the other is not meeting the individual needs of a student. This "canned" approach will not help the dyslexic who needs guidance and attention to specific difficulties.)

6. Are highly structured regarding what the teacher is to say and do as well as what the child is to say in response. (The dyslexic student needs flexibility of instruction, creativity on the part of the teacher, and individualization based on specific needs.)

7. Permit an undue amount of noise, such as the students' shouting out the answers all at once. (The dyslexic student tends to be sensitive to noise and movement, and these will distract him and cause confusion.)

8. Attempt to remediate dyslexia by having the student creep, crawl, balance on beams, jump on trampolines, and the like. (These may be fun for the dyslexic student and perhaps help his coordination, but they will not help alleviate his dyslexia.)

9. Require spelling lists where the words must be memorized in rote fashion. (The dyslexic needs to use the words, associate them with things and experiences in his background, and write the words.)

10. Rely heavily on drills of words and skills in isolation. (The dyslexic needs to use words and skills in context where they will have meaning and be better retained.)

11. Do not use multisensory techniques for learning new concepts, vocabulary, and skills. (The dyslexic student needs to say and hear and see and touch, drawing on his senses.)

12. Ignore the use of concrete manipulative materials. (Again, the dyslexic needs to see and feel; he also needs to smell and hold and manipulate materials representing new concepts. This enables him to make associations, gives him mnemonic cues that he can draw on when needed, and makes learning come alive for him.)

13. Emphasize one particular word recognition strategy. (The dyslexic student needs to learn a variety of strategies to help him, for some work better than others, depending on the situation.)

14. Use optical devices and exercises to remediate dyslexia.[7]

15. Use chemicals and vitamins reputed to "cure" dyslexia.

16. Use ridicule or put-downs when the student makes an error or is confused.

Communicating with Parents

I suggest that you have a conference with the parents of your dyslexic student fairly soon after the beginning of school and that it include the reading specialist or other specialist working with the student. By doing this the parents will see that the two of you are working cooperatively to create the best learning environment and instruction for their child. Later, you may wish to meet with them in your classroom to discuss special things that you may be doing with him and the class as a whole.

Sometimes parents come in with what may appear to be a chip on their shoulder. Try to understand that this is the result of what may be years of frustration and anxiety in trying to get help for their child, to get him placed with a classroom teacher who understands his particular problems. Some parents feel truly battered. Some have been shunted and pushed aside or ignored or ridiculed in their search for help.

Accept the parents as you accept the student with dyslexia: with interest and caring and understanding and faith. Let the parents talk out their problems, explain what has happened in the past, what they hope will happen—and then it will be done. *Listen attentively* to what they have to say. You may be astounded at what information they reveal. Let them know that you are pleased to have their child and will work very hard to help him. This is what parents need to hear.

For conferences with parents, be sure to have samples of the student's work and the results of tests and other papers to show the parents and substantiate the information you are giving them. Keep samples for yourself so that later in the year you and the parents can compare the student's work at various times and see the progress he is making.

Telephone the parents occasionally or send home a short note telling them about something that the dyslexic student has done especially well. This will make the student and his parents happy, and it will show them that you do care and are interested in his progress.

There will be times when you are discouraged. When this happens try to remember that in any child's progress, especially a dyslexic's, there are plateaus and peaks, troughs and crests, crawls and leaps in learning. Have faith in the dyslexic. Trust him. And trust yourself as his teacher.

When report card time comes around you may wish to invite the dyslexic's parents in to discuss his marks. Or you may wish to write a special note to accompany the report card. In either case you should begin with the student's strengths and taper off with what he still needs to work on.

When I taught in elementary school I used to write such notes with the report card of every child in my class. I found that this contributed a great deal to good parent-teacher relations, and years later when I happened to run into the parents, they would make a point of expressing their appreciation. This takes time—and a thorough knowledge of the student's strengths and weaknesses—but it is well worth the effort.

Most of all, you will find that parents want to know that their child is happy in school, happy with you, and happy with his classmates. They want to know that he is learning and making progress. They realize that because of his special problems you must work harder and longer. While they may not say so, they are grateful to you. Remember that always and resolve that you will never let them down—nor your student with dyslexia—nor yourself as a professional, dedicated teacher. Remember to keep your feet on the ground and use your common sense when working with the dyslexic student—and both of you will learn together.

Notes

1. Mary Budd Rowe, "Wait-Time and Rewards as Instructional Variables, Their Influence on Language, Logic, and Fate Control: Part One—Wait-Time," *Journal of Research in Science Teaching* Vol. 2 (1974), pp. 81, 89–93.

2. Public Law 94–142, Education of the Handicapped Act of 1975. The implementation of Part B dealing with specific learning disabilities was published in the *Federal Register* on December 29, 1977, and went into effect in September 1978, 121a.5[9].

3. Leslie Burg and Maurice Kaufman, "Laws about special education: Their impact on the use of reading specialists," *The Reading Teacher* Vol. 34, No. 2 (November 1980), p. 189.

4. "The Teacher's Rights in PL 94–142," editor's interview with Attorney Reed Martin in *Journal of Reading Disabilities* Vol. 11 (June/July 1978), p. 332.

5. George Kaluger and Clifford J. Kolson, *Reading and Learning Disabilities*, 2nd ed. (Columbus, Ohio: Charles E. Merrill, 1978), p. 215.

6. Lenore H. Ringler and Carol K. Weber, *A Language-Thinking Approach to Reading, Diagnosis and Teaching* (New York: Harcourt, Brace, Jovanovich, 1984), p. 358.

7. *The Role of the Ophthalmologist in Dyslexia*, Report of International Seminar (Melbourne, Fla.: Institute for Development of Educational Activities, 1969), p. 10.

CHAPTER 17

FUTURE DIRECTIONS: WHERE DO WE GO FROM HERE?

There are two ways of spreading light: to be the
candle or the mirror that reflects it.
—*Edith Wharton*

Unfortunately, Voltaire was right in his statement, "Common sense is not so common." Surely in the area of dyslexia the lack of common sense is evident. Individuals in various fields seem to delight in going off on all kinds of tangents, making questionable statements about what dyslexia is, the subtypes of dyslexia, what causes the condition, who can have it, how many people are dyslexic, and how to remediate it.

To find out what we need to know about dyslexia, and then to provide real help for those who have this condition, we must overcome the roadblocks to progress and make the necessary changes in direction. As more valid data emerge, researchers, schools, teacher-training institutions, and the state and federal governments all must assume responsibility for moving in the right direction.

The Research

Too many universities have failed to provide the needed direction. Indeed, some of them have contributed further to the confusion. Policies of "publish or perish" have created pressures that have led researchers to a plethora of ill-founded assumptions in defiance of common sense. These conclusions often do more harm than good. Slipshod research hampers real progress in answering our many questions about dyslexia.

As Dr. Carl L. Kline of the Faculty of Medicine, University of British Columbia, Vancouver, notes:

> Unfortunately many findings are of little value because of inadequate diagnostic data and poorly researched progress reports. Some comprise such small numbers of cases that they are statistically invalid. Other studies do not specify the kind of remedial therapy, often failing even to indicate the frequency or the length of sessions.[1]

In some studies of the prevalence of dyslexia, the researchers simply asked families or teachers if a child had had any serious difficulty in reading or learning to read. What may seem serious to one may not appear so to another. A child may have difficulty in reading for many reasons other than dyslexia (school absences, quality of reading instruction, parental influence, motivation, overall health, vision or hearing problems, intellectual ability, and so on).

Some researchers "diagnose" a child as being dyslexic if he is reading at a certain level below his grade (six months to one or more years, depending on the researcher). In their "diagnoses," some investigators administer only a word-recognition test of either real or nonsense words listed in isolation, a task not representative of an actual reading situation involving narrative paragraphs with checks on comprehension.

Some researchers "determine" dyslexia on the basis of a spelling test. Others use a test that purports to test spelling by having a child look at four words and select the one correctly spelled. No writing of words is involved in this test, so the task really becomes one of word recognition rather than spelling.

The practice in many studies of lumping all dyslexics into one group, without regard to subtypes, can neutralize the findings in many ways. Indeed, if there is a difference in the numbers of dyslexics in the subtypes and if all are grouped together in one study, the results may be skewed in a way that makes the findings invalid. Combining partially remediated dyslexics with dyslexics just diagnosed as such will also confound the findings.

Some studies appear to reflect the bias of researchers who seem bent on proving that a particular method of remediation is the "right" one for all dyslexics, regardless of subtype or the degree of dyslexia. Often a kit or special program or certain materials can be purchased—for a substantial price.

In many studies, researchers give very little information as to just exactly what was involved in a particular remedial program, or the training of the tutors, the number of students in a training session, the length of a remedial period, the frequency of the remediation sessions, and how long in months or years remediation was given. They give scanty information, if any, about the pretesting and post-testing situations, the number of students completing the remedial program, and so on. And too often, they have used no control groups.

Such questionable research broadens the credibility gap that already exists in the dyslexia area and contributes to the confusion and misinterpretations that are still all too common.

Suggestions for Researchers

In order to uncover the needed information about dyslexia, we must tighten up our research, resist the pressure for "hurry-up research" that is done in as short a time as possible to stay within the limits of available funds or prior to the due date of a dissertation, or to "prove" that a particular program works. We must approach our research in a measured, controlled, professional, and ethical manner, knowing that valid research takes careful planning, careful procedures, and often much time. We must keep in mind the following:

1. The *manner*[2] in which sample units are selected is critical. This requires accurate diagnoses and consideration of the subtypes of dyslexia. The larger the sample, the better.[3] Finding a sizable sample can present a problem in research, simply because of the limited number of dyslexics in our society.

2. The diagnosis of dyslexia must be based on the administration of a *battery of tests*—not on a single test, nor on a child's merely reading below grade level,[4] nor on a certain discrepancy between a student's IQ and his reading level.

At a symposium sponsored by the Division of Learning Disabilities of the Council for Exceptional Children, the Utah State Office of Education, and others, Dr. Carol Weller concluded:

> If researchers and decision-makers continue to focus on definition of discrepancy rather than definition of [learning disability], the implications for the field are staggering. . . . Lack of precision in selection of research samples will persist, and adequate validation of instructional strategies and assessment tools will remain impossible.[5]

By definition, dyslexia is a language communication disability involving reading, writing, spelling, speaking, and listening. Thus the determination of dyslexia must be based on tests and documented observations dealing with all of these areas. Since other problems may show symptoms similar to those of dyslexia, tests to eliminate such possibilities must be administered. These would include tests for vision, hearing, finger agnosia, intelligence, and others. The child's chronological age must be taken into account because of maturation factors. The subtypes of the dyslexic condition must be determined on the basis of the results of this series of tests.

For verification purposes, researchers should conduct their own testing rather than merely taking those students "diagnosed by the schools" as having dyslexia.

3. Bias is an ever-present danger. We must consider the possibility of bias in the research design—and the implications of such bias. Data obtained in the descriptive survey or observational type of research are especially susceptible to distortion through the introduction of bias into a research design. Every effort must be made to safeguard the data from any influence of bias.[6] Yet many studies on dyslexia ask teachers to select students having problems in reading, or ask teachers or parents to complete questionnaires. And then there is the type of bias that enters when a researcher wants to "prove" a hypothesis. Researchers must have an intellectual acuity that looks honestly and objectively at procedures used and results obtained.

4. Control is basic to experimental research. Dyslexic groups and control groups must be matched as closely as possible. Chronological ages, grade levels, achievement, IQ, size of groups, sex, race, and opportunity to learn are all important factors to be considered. (Some studies on dyslexics match younger students with older students, and small groups are compared to large groups!)

5. In historical research, reliable sources must be used to ensure the integrity of these studies. This also tends to strengthen the reliability. Failure to compare sources and to study primary data is a major reason for the development of the fallacy that Einstein, Edison, Wilson, Churchill, Patton, Leonardo da Vinci, and others mentioned in Chapter 12 were all dyslexic. Indeed, an examination of primary sources gives considerable assurance that these notable people were not dyslexic. True, academic problems of one kind or another existed, but these problems were not the result of dyslexia.

6. In pretesting and post-testing, the same tests (or a different form of the same test) should be given, and regression factors cannot be ignored. Two different tests of reading achievement, or spelling, or even intelligence may not be measuring the same information or tasks.

7. Long-range studies are needed. Dyslexic students need to be followed into adulthood. Follow-up data is needed on educational and occupational attainment and on the social and marital adjustment of dyslexics.

8. Research on remediation of dyslexia should spell out in detail the

type of remedial treatment, and the materials and instruction used, the training of the persons doing the remediating, the length and frequency of the remediation session, and how long in months or years the remediation continued. Was remediation on a one-to-one or group basis? If done on a group basis, how many students were included in each remedial session? Was one remedial teacher with the student throughout the remediation or was there a change in teachers at one time or another? If so, when did the change occur?

The Schools

The schools have a major responsibility for their dyslexic students. True, they have a responsibility to educate all those who come under their jurisdiction but in the future the schools must place more emphasis on helping dyslexics. All too often, such students are not diagnosed properly. Some are placed in special education classes with students who have a multitude of problems—slow learners, emotionally disturbed students, and those with other types of learning disabilities. Their needs are not adequately met in a number of ways. Such children do not receive the professional remediation required for alleviation of the dyslexic condition.

Some schools may have a special education teacher but no specialist trained in the diagnosis and remediation of reading, writing, and spelling disabilities. True, there are schools that do have reading specialists as well as special reading clinics where children may be helped, but, unfortunately, many schools have no full-time reading specialist trained in diagnosis and remedial procedures. Some schools try to sweep such problems under the rug and deny that they have any students with such disabilities.

In the future, schools will feel more and more pressure to provide the remedial teachers, resource persons and space, materials, and instruction needed by dyslexic students at all levels: elementary school, middle school, and high school. Classroom teachers will receive in-service training to help them work with dyslexics within their classrooms. They will learn to adapt instruction, materials, and performance expectations as needed. The number of students in each classroom will need to be small so that the teacher may be able to provide more individual help to all students, not just the dyslexic.

Schools will need to adjust priorities when it comes to expenditures. Helping *all* at-risk students may receive a higher priority in the future, and more attention than perhaps a sports team of a few students, or stadium lights, or even the purchase of computers costing thousands of dollars that in many schools few students use for any length of time or on any regular basis. It is truly striking how one can determine the real priorities of a school system by looking at the services offered—especially those to help students with problems. How many special efforts to help dyslexic students are written up in the newspapers?

In the future, schools will consider untimed tests for the dyslexic student, since he tends to work more slowly than the nondyslexic. Test questions may be taped or presented orally by teachers. Dyslexics may respond orally, or on tape, or perhaps be permitted to type answers to test questions either on a typewriter or a word processor. Since filling in the computer-scored answer sheets is difficult for the visual dyslexic, teachers may permit the student to circle or underline the correct answer on achievement tests.

Since dyslexics need more than just dictionary definitions, more concrete, direct experiences will need to be provided by the schools. Dyslexic students will receive instruction on the use of computers and will be permitted to use a word-processing program along with a speller software program for taking notes and writing papers. Both visual and auditory dyslexics will need to be exempt from foreign language requirements.

Teacher-Training Institutions

Teacher training institutions must assume responsibility for preparing teachers to work with dyslexic students in the classrooms as well as in reading clinics and resource rooms. Improved programs for teacher preparation are essential. Too often this special training has been minimal. In some higher education institutions teacher candidates may hear no more than a half-hour lecture or report on dyslexia (usually at the graduate level). That is the extent of their "training" for working with our dyslexic students. No wonder these teachers report that they are insecure, lack confidence, and do not really know how to work with dyslexic students. I speak not only of the regular classroom teachers, but of those supposedly trained at the graduate level as reading specialists and special education teachers majoring in learning disabilities. Due to ignorance of the problem, they sometimes compound it.

In the future we can expect teacher-training institutions to work with school systems to provide special in-service training for regular classroom teachers to help them become adept at working with the dyslexic student. Teachers will learn what to do for those students who cannot read the textbooks or do the work at a particular level.

In addition, higher education institutions will work with school systems to provide special in-service training for those reading specialists and learning disability specialists who are not trained in the diagnosis and remediation of dyslexia. Where nearby colleges offer on-campus programs in remediation and diagnosis, school systems will provide tuition assistance to enable untrained specialists to take the necessary courses and participate in clinical experiences with dyslexic students.

Eventually, the corps of expertise in the accurate diagnosis of dyslexia and the alleviation of the condition will reach the point where all dyslexic students are able to get the help they need. This specialized training will develop more quickly in some places than in others. Indeed, this is already beginning in some parts of the country.

The State and Federal Governments

Many of us have fallen into the habit of looking for federal funds to solve almost any problem. First, however, we should look to local resources. Still, the federal government does have a responsibility to help our dyslexic students. The Department of Education must take the initiative in this direction, by providing aid for research and teacher education, grants for special programs, and help in establishing school clinics and purchasing needed materials.

Our society must have leaders who speak out and work to help dyslexics. No doubt partly because of her dyslexic son and her understanding of the problems that dyslexics must face, Barbara Bush is very active in the promotion of literacy. In June of 1987, the officers and Literacy Award Committee members of the Greater Washington Reading Council awarded its first annual Literacy Award to Mrs. Bush in recognition of her significant contributions. Hereafter the award will be named the Barbara Bush Literacy Award to honor Mrs. Bush's long-term commitment to the elimination of illiteracy, and for making it her special area of emphasis as the wife of the president (then vice president) of the United States.[7]

We must guard against too much reliance on the government to serve as watchdog, but someone must assess school systems on the qualifications of their teachers, their programs, their in-service training, and the diagnostic and remedial facilities that they make available to help dyslexic students. The responsibility for providing services and maintaining professional standards should lie first with the school districts, second with the state, and lastly with the federal government.

In the final analysis, the responsibility lies with each of us to initiate steps to improve the disheartening situation in which many dyslexics now find themselves. We need to visit the schools and ask questions about what is being done. City councils, school boards, and county boards of supervisors must set up fact-finding committees and arrange meetings with school administrators. Directors and superintendents of personnel in the schools need to question prospective teachers on their knowledge of and attitude toward dyslexia. This information should be passed on to teacher-training institutions (who want all their graduates to get jobs). Interested members of the community might set up study sessions and support groups for dyslexic families.

Medical Research

As we search for a deeper understanding of the causes and the nature of the dyslexic condition (including the genetic factors), medical research must concentrate on *accurately* diagnosed dyslexics.

Research such as that being done on the brains of deceased dyslexics by Dr. Galaburda at the Laboratory for the Biological Foundations of Dyslexia at Harvard Medical School's Department of Neurology, Beth Israel Hospital in Boston, must continue. While this anatomical analysis of the brain, involving architectonics, the study of cellular architecture and the connections among cells, is exceptionally time consuming (requiring hundreds of hours for the preparation of each brain to undergo examination), such work is critical to our understanding of dyslexia.[8]

In a special article concerning his work, Dr. Galaburda points out that:

> More epidemiological work is needed to uncover the immunological illnesses that increase this risk [for dyslexia], and the developmental stages at which they do. Moreover, specific autoantibodies must be identified, which may serve, in part, as early markers for the risk for dyslexia. One of the possible general implications of the findings and hypotheses . . . include the presence of a heretofore poorly understood group of disorders caused by abnormal immune interactions during fetal life, which may lead to a variety of intellectual deficits depending on the exact types and times of the interactions, as well as on the availability of compensatory mechanisms. Thus it is possible that developmental disorders of language, emotional behavior, and attention will eventually be explained by these mechanisms affecting different parts of the brain during different developmental epochs.[9]

Research must continue on the possibility that a gene localized on chromosome 15 may play an important role in the occurrence of dyslexia— and on whether this disorder is inherited as an autosomal dominant trait.

Additional studies should be made on the possible linkage between dyslexia and chromosomal anomalies such as the 47,XXY, 47,XYY, and 47,XXX karyotypes as well as those missing all or part of an X chromosome (called X monosomy). We are still a long way from understanding the full implications of such chromosome irregularities.

Further work is needed on the possibility that the presence of anti-Ro antibody in mothers may be associated with dyslexia.

While I have been somewhat critical of the use of computerized tomography, often called CT scans (see Chapter 9), it is possible that additional advances in technology may result in better resolution (and if clinical clusters are used to predict the locus of abnormality), it may be that sometime in the future CT scans will reveal more specific findings in regard to dyslexia.[10]

The Dyslexic's Future

The future is promising for the dyslexic, although progress toward fulfillment of the promise is slow. It will not be realized soon enough to help some already out there in the Dyslexia World of Frustration. But we *are* finding out more about the condition. We know that there is a genetic factor in the cause of dyslexia, and therefore we can be alert to the occurrence in some families and provide the immediate help as needed. We now know how to diagnose dyslexia accurately; the problem lies in disseminating and using this knowledge. Unfortunately, some people seem to be unwilling to give up pet theories or special tests that they have devised (which also bring a certain profit). We know that, because of maturational factors, an accurate diagnosis of dyslexia at the present time ordinarily cannot be made before a child has reached about the age of eight.

We know that dyslexia can be alleviated, and that the most appropriate time to begin remediation for a child is at about the age of eight. It is far easier to remediate the condition at this early age than at an older age, when certain behaviors and attitudes have been internalized. Of course the severity of the dyslexic condition will affect the success and length of remediation, (as will other factors, which were discussed in Chapter 13, "Alleviating Dyslexia").

More information is being distributed about dyslexia; and thus more people are aware of the condition and are becoming concerned about helping dyslexics. Society recognizes the need to provide the dyslexic with opportunities for remediation, opportunities to learn and to develop normally, and opportunities to become what he is capable of becoming.

The challenge of dyslexia must be met by all: parents, schools, researchers, teacher-training institutions, the federal government, society as a whole—and the dyslexic himself. For it will take all of us working together to accomplish what must be accomplished—what can be done. We must make this challenge the focus of our efforts.

Notes

1. Carl L. Kline and Carolyn L. Kline, "Follow-Up Study of 216 Dyslexic Children," *Bulletin of the Orton Society* 25 (1975), p. 127.
2. Paul D. Leedy, *Practical Research, Planning and Design*, 2nd ed. (New York: Macmillan, 1980), p. 112.
3. Ibid., p. 116.
4. Typical of many studies are statements by the researchers such as, "A reading level at least 2 years below expected grade level was used as the guideline for diagnosis." The same researchers also reported that "the primary criteria for the diagnosis of specific dyslexia in adults were pronounced difficulty in reading and spelling along with a positive family history." Shelley D. Smith, Bruce F. Pennington, William J. Kimberling, and Herbert A. Lubs, "A Genetic Analysis of Specific Reading Disability," *Genetic Aspects of Speech and Language Disorders,* Christy L. Ludlow and Judith A. Cooper, eds. (New York: Academic Press, 1983), p. 171.

The following statement is another example of using this type of criteria in diagnosis: "Dyslexia in this study was operationally defined as reading retardation on the Wide-Range Achievement Test two or more grades below the level appropriate for age. Eighty-two children were classified as dyslexic." Steven Mattis, Joseph H. French, and Isabelle Rapin, "Dyslexia in Children and Young Adults: Three Independent Neuropsychological Syndromes," *Developmental Medicine and Child Neurology* 17 (1975), p. 151.

Even more dubious is the claim "all subjects defined as dyslexic read more than six months below grade leve'," as stated in Karen R. Sobotka and James G. May, "Visual Evoked Potentials and Reaction Time in Normal and Dyslexic Children," *Psychophysiology* 14 (1977), p. 19.

Some researchers varied the arbitrary criteria of reading retardation as: "To qualify for the dyslexic group, . . . 1.0 or more years of reading retardation in Grades 2 and 3, 1.5 or more years in Grades 4, 5, and 6, and 2.5 or more years in Grades 7 and 8." Patricia A. Szeszulski and Franklin R. Manis, "A Comparison of Word Recognition Processes in Dyslexic and Normal Readers at Two Reading-Age Levels," *Journal of Experimental Child Psychology* 44 (1987), p. 367.
5. Carol Weller, "Response" (to James D. McKinney's "Research on the Identification of Learning-Disabled Children: Perspectives on Changes in Educational Policy), *Research in Learning Disabilities, Issues and Future Directions,* Sharon Vaughn and Candace S. Bos, eds. (Boston: College-Hill, 1987), p. 234.
6. Paul D. Leedy, op. cit., p. 124.
7. "Literacy Award Presented to Barbara Bush," *Virginia State Reading Association Newsletter* (Fall 1987), p. 1.
8. "History of the Research Division of the Orton Dyslexia Society: Medical Research," *Perspectives on Dyslexia, Medical Research Update* (May 1987), p. 1.
9. Albert M. Galaburda, "The Pathogenesis of Childhood Dyslexia," *Language, Communication, and the Brain*, F. Plum, ed. (New York: Raven Press, 1988), pp. 134–35.
10. Martha B. Denckla, Marjorie LeMay, and Catherine A. Chapman, "Few CT Scan Abnormalities Found Even in Neurologically Impaired Learning Disabled Children," *Journal of Learning Disabilities* 18 (March 1985), p. 135.

APPENDIXES

APPENDIX A

ERRORS CAUSED BY FAULTY
PHONICS INSTRUCTION

The following are examples of errors made by nondyslexic students on a diagnostic test given to determine how the phonic elements had been taught to them. The key word confusions are quite logical when one considers how the sounds were taught. Here we have a glimpse of how their minds have used incorrect information to arrive at incorrect key words—words *not* beginning with the blends. Such errors are similar to those of the dyslexic and could result in a misdiagnosis if the examiner is not aware of how the child was taught phonics. If a dyslexic student is taught in this nonsensical manner, his problems will be compounded.

The students said:	*And gave one of these words as a key word:*
sound of *br* is "bur"	burn, Bert, Burrhead Jones
sound of *cr* is "cur"	curve, curt, curtsy
sound of *dr* is "dur"	derby, dirt, dirty
sound of *pr* is "pur"	purr, purple, person, purgatory
sound of *tr* is "tur"	turtle, turn, termite, term,
sound of *fl* is "ful"	full, Fulton, full-grown
sound of *sk* is "suhkuh"	sucker, suckle
sound of *sp* is "suhpuh"	supper, superb, support
sound of *cl* is "kul"	color, culprit, cool, couple
sound of *sn* is "ssss," a hiss sound followed by "nnnnn"	sun, sin, soon

APPENDIX B

TWIN STUDIES

Knud Hermann. *Reading Disability, A Medical Study of Word-Blindness and Related Handicaps* (Springfield, Ill.: Charles Thomas, 1959).

Hermann pooled the findings of three studies concerning twins: In one study, Hallgren (1950) used six sets of twins of which three were identical twins and three nonidentical pairs. Norrie (1954) used twenty-eight sets, of which seven were identical and twenty-one were nonidentical. Norrie had also completed another study, unpublished at that time, where she studied eleven sets of twins, of which two pairs were identical and nine were nonidentical.

Of the total forty-five pairs of twins studied, all of the identical twins were concordant. Twenty-seven pairs of the nonidentical twins were concordant (33 percent). Hermann concluded that "since all the uniovular twins showed concordance, it is evident that heredity is the only decisive factor." (p. 87)

Edith Zerbin-Rubin. "Congenital Word-Blindness," *Bulletin of the Orton Society* 17 (1967), p. 50.

Zerbin-Rubin summarized nine studies on twins: Hallgren (1950), Norrie (1954), Brander (1935), Ley and Tordeur (1936), Jenkins, Brown, and Elmendorf (1937), Schiller (1937), vonHarnack (1948), Weinschenck (1962), and Spiel (1953). Of Norrie's thirty-nine sets of twins, all nine identical sets were concordant, with only ten of the thirty nonidentical sets concordant. Of Hallgren's six sets, all three identical twins were concordant, with only one of the three nonidentical pairs being concordant. Single case studies of concordant identical sets of twins were reported by Brander; Ley and Tordeur; Jenkins, Brown, and Elmendorf; Schiller, and vonHarnack. One concordant nonidentical (boy-girl) pair was reported by Weinschenck. Two concordant sets of unknown zygocity were reported by Spiel and Weinschenck.

In summary, all seventeen identical twins were concordant, twelve of the thirty-four nonidentical twins were concordant, and two concordant sets of unknown zygocity were reported.

*   *   *

Note: While these two summaries of twin studies are often referred to in articles and books on dyslexia, no mention has been made that there may be some overlapping of the results. It would appear that Hallgren's sets of twins are the same for both studies. And are Hermann's seven identical and twenty-one nonidentical sets from Norrie a part of the larger number of twin pairs used in Zerbin-Rubin's summary?

APPENDIX C

PUBLISHERS AND THEIR ADDRESSES

In this Appendix are the names and addresses of some publishers who distribute books and other materials that are suitable for working with the dyslexic. Since some publishing companies may change names, others go out of business, and addresses change from time to time, you will want to check any in which you may be interested. This can usually be done at your local library. Ask for *Books in Print,* which is published each year.

Addison-Wesley Publishing Company, 2725 Sand Hill Road, Menlo Park, CA 94025–9915.

Ann Arbor Publishers, Inc., P.O. Box 7249, Naples, FL 33941.

American Guidance Service, P.O. Box 31552, Richmond, VA 23294.

Barnell Loft, 111 S. Centre Avenue, New York, NY 11571.

Benefic Press, 1250 Sixth Avenue, San Diego, CA 92101.

Bowmar/Noble Publishers, Inc., 4563 Colorado Boulevard, Los Angeles, CA 90039.

Curriculum Associates, 5 Esquire Road, N. Billerica, MA 01862–2589.

D.C. Heath & Company, Center Square, Hanover, PA 17331.

Developmental Learning Materials, One DLM Park, P.O. Box 4000, Allen, TX 75002.

Doubleday Publishing, 666 Fifth Avenue, New York, NY 10103.

Educational Activities, P.O. Box 392, Freeport, NY 11520.

Educators Publishing Service, Inc., 75 Moulton Street, Cambridge, MA 02238–9101.

Fearon Publishers, Inc., 500 Harbor Boulevard, Belmont, CA 94002.

Follett Publishing Company, 4506 Northwest Highway, Crystal Lake, IL 60014–3397.

Ginn & Company, 4343 Equity Drive, P.O. Box 2649, Columbus, OH 43216.

Globe Book Company, 50 W. 23rd Street, New York, NY 10010.

Harcourt Brace Jovanovich, Inc., 1250 Sixth Avenue, San Diego, CA 92101.

High Noon Books, 20 Commercial Boulevard, Suite 303, Novado, CA 94947–6191.

Holt, Rinehart, and Winston, 16237 Woodland Avenue, Austin, TX 78741.

Houghton Mifflin Company, One Beacon Street, Boston, MA 02108.

Jamestown Publishers, P.O. Box 9168, Providence, RI 02940.

Janus Book Publishers, 2501 Industrial Parkway, West, Dept. JANC, Hayward, CA 94545.

Macmillan Company, Front & Brown Streets, Riverside, NJ 08075–1197.

McGraw-Hill Book Company, 1221 Avenue of the Americas, New York, NY 10020.

Merrill Publishing Company, 1300 Alum Creek Drive, Columbus, OH 43216.

Milton Bradley Company, 74 Park Street, Springfield, MA 01101.

Modern Curriculum Press, 13900 Prospect Road, Cleveland, OH 44136.

Pendulum Press, Inc., Department C., Box 509, West Haven, CT 06516.

Prentice-Hall, Inc., 1230 Avenue of the Americas, New York, NY 10020.

PRO-ED, 5341 Industrial Oak Boulevard, Austin, TX 78735.

Psychological Corporation, 555 Academic Court, San Antonio, TX 78204–0952.

Quercus Corporation, 4343 Equity Drive, P.O. Box 2649, Columbus, OH 43216.

Random House, Inc., 201 East 50th Street, New York, NY 10022.

Reader's Digest Services, Educational Division, Pleasantville, NY 10570. (Random House handles some of their materials.)

Scholastic, Inc., 2931 E. McCarty Street, P.O. Box 7501, Jefferson City, MO 65102.

Scott, Foresman & Company, 1900 East Lake Avenue, Glenview, IL 60625.

Slosson Educational Publications, Inc., P.O. Box 280, East Aurora, NY 14052.

Steck-Vaughn Company, P.O. Box 26015, Austin, TX 78755.

APPENDIX D

MATERIALS TO HELP WITH SPECIAL SUBJECTS

Reading Level
(Grade Equivalent)

SCIENCE

1	*Science for You:* *You Can See*
2	*You Can Do*
3	*You Can Learn*
4	*You Can Explore*
5	*You Can Discover*
6	*You Can Experience*
2.3	*Wonders of Science: The Human Body, Water Life, The Earth and Beyond, Land Animals, Matter, Motion, and Machines, Plant Life*
	(Steck-Vaughn)

1	*Science Work:* *Science is Looking*
2	*Science is Measuring*
3	*Science is Comparing*
4	*Science is Inquiring*
5	*Science is Experimenting*
6	*Science is Predicting*
3–4	*Insights Into Science* (Interest Level: Students in grades 4–6)

Reading Level
(Grade Equivalent)

3–4   *Experience in Science* (Pathways Text) (Interest Level:
                 Students in grades 4–6)
             (Modern Curriculum Press)

2.2   *Earth Science*
2.3   *Physical Science*
2.4   *Environmental Science*
2.4   *Human Biology* (also has accompanying lab book)
2.5   *Biology of Plants and Animals* (also has accompanying
                 lab book)
             (Quercus Corporation)

5–6   *Pathways in Science,* Revised Edition (geared for junior-
                 high level students and above)
                 Life Science
                 Earth Science
                 Chemistry
                 Physics
             (Globe Book)

7–9   *Ideas and Investigations in Science* (geared for junior-
                 high level students and above)
                 Life Science
                 Earth Science
                 Physical Science
             (Prentice-Hall Educational Book Division)

3–6   *Science Readers* (Interest Level: Students in grades 3–9)
             (Reader's Digest Services)

Reading Level
(Grade Equivalent)

2.5	*Life Science in Action:*
	Human Systems
	Animals
	Green Plants
	The Five Senses
2.5	*Earth Science in Action:*
	Earth Resources
	Changing Earth
	Weather
	The Solar System
2.5	*Physical Science in Action:*
	Energy
	Electricity
	Machines
	Sound
	(Janus Book Publishers)

---

700 Science Experiments for Everyone (Doubleday)

	SOCIAL STUDIES
	(HISTORY/GEOGRAPHY/GOVERNMENT)
3	*Geography Skills Series:* *Lands at Homes*
4	*Regions of the World*
5	*The American Continents*
6	*Continents Overseas*
	(Interest Level: Students in grades 7-8-9-10)
7	*World Geography*
8	*American Adventures* (Interest Level: Students in grades 7–9)
4	*Our Country Today*
5	*Our Country's History*
6	*Our World Today*
5–6	*Our U.S.A., Part 1*
5–6	*Our U.S.A., Part 2*
7–8	*Our Nation's Story, Part 1*

Reading Level
(Grade Equivalent)

7–8	*Our Nation's Story, Part 2*
JHS	*Our Democracy,* 2nd edition
	(In addition to the above, some state histories may be obtained from Steck-Vaughn. These include Alabama, Arkansas, California, Florida, Georgia, Kentucky, Louisiana, Mississippi, Missouri, New York, Tennessee, Texas, and Virginia. Since the reading levels vary, you will need to send for Steck-Vaughn's catalog.)
2.5	*It's Our Government, Congress, the President, and the Courts*
2.5	*Government at Work, from City Hall to State Capitol*
2.5	*Electing the President*
2.8	*Stamp and Story Histories: Highlights of American History*
2.8	*Famous Americans*
	(Janus Book Publishers)

(Comic book format)   *The Basic Illustrated History of America Series*

The New World 1500–1700
The Fight for Freedom 1750–1783
The United States Emerges 1783–1800
Problems of the New Nation 1800–1830
Americans Move Westward 1800–1850
Before the Civil War 1830–1860
The Civil War 1850–1876
The Industrial Era 1865–1915
America Becomes a World Power 1890–1920
The Roaring Twenties and the Great Depression 1920–1940
World War II 1940–1945
America Today 1945–1981

(Pendulum Press. Note: Cassettes and filmstrips are available for the above.)

Reading Level
(Grade Equivalent)

K–3	*Map Skills 1* (RC 01343): Includes basic map concepts, map symbols and legends, map directions, map distance and scale; also includes four sound film–strips with cassettes.
4–6	*Map Skills 2* (RC 01344): Includes What Is a Map?, Travel Maps, Social Purpose Maps, Political Maps; also includes four sound filmstrips with cassettes.
K–3	*Globe Skills 1* (RC 01345): Includes What Is a Globe?, What Does a Globe Do?, Where Do We Live?, How Do We Get Night and Day?; also includes four sound filmstrips with cassettes.
4–6	*Globe Skills 2* (RC 01346): Includes Hemispheres and Parallels; Latitude and Longitude; Yesterday, Today, Tomorrow; The Four Seasons; also includes four sound filmstrips with cassettes.
1–6	*Success With Maps* (Books A–F)
1–6	*Map Skills* (Books 1–6)
	(Scholastic)
4	*American Democracy Series:*
	America the Beautiful
	Electing Our Presidents
	The FBI
	The Making of the United States
	The Office of the President
	The Statue of Liberty Comes to America
	The Story of the Boy Scouts
	The Story of the United States Flag
	The Supreme Court in America's Story
4	*Living in Today's World Series:*
	Canada, Giant Nation of the North
	Ethiopia, Mountain Kingdom
	Iran, Crossroads of Caravans
	The People's Republic of China, Red Star of the East
	The Soviet Union, Land of Many Peoples
	(Addison-Wesley)

Reading Level
(Grade Equivalent)

2.5–4.0   MATH
           Math in Action Series:
               Math Language
               Understanding Word Problems
               Solving Word Problems
               Estimation
               Using a Calculator
           (Janus Book Publishers)

4–6   *Tables, Charts, and Graphs* (Books A–C)
3–8   Problem Solving in Math (Books 3–8)
       (Scholastic)

2–4   *Math-A-Riddle I*
3–5   *Math-A-Riddle II*
1–5   *Math-A-Dot* (Books 1–5)
       (Fearon Publishers)

3–8   *Practicing Problem Solving* (Books 3–8)
       (Random House)

       HEALTH
1–8   *Choosing Good Health Series* (Books 1–8)
2.3   *Health and You* (two books: Book 1 and Book 2, with
           interest levels for grades 5–10)
2   *Steck-Vaughn Health Series:*
           Your Growth
3   *Growing and Changing*
4   *Your Healthy Body*
5   *Your Growing Body*
6   *Your Health*

Reading Level
(Grade Equivalent)

7	*Better Health*
8–9	*Keeping Your Health*
	(Interest levels are for students in grades 5–10.)
	(Steck-Vaughn)

2.4	*First Aid Plus Biology*
2.3	*Take Care of Yourself*
	(Quercus Corporation)

4–5   *Pathways to Health Series:*
        Drugs
        Alcohol and Tobacco
        Facing the Facts
        The Pollution Problem
        Protecting our Environment
        Protecting Your Health
        Battling Disease
        Safety and First Aid
        Avoiding Accidents
        Mental Health
        Improving Your Human Relations
        Inquiry Into Consumer Education
        Getting It Together
(Globe Book)

LANGUAGE ARTS
2–8   See the Random House catalog for various books on
        capitalizing, punctuation, grammar, writing,
        vocabulary, poetry.

2.3	*Story Starters, Part 1*
4–6	*Story Starters, Part 2*
	(Steck-Vaughn)

Reading Level
(Grade Equivalent)

1–6   *Text Extenders* (Collection of paperback books of
                          children's literature)
                      Sprint Libraries: for students in grades 4–6
2.0–2.4   *Sprint Library 1-A*
2.1–2.4   *Sprint Library 1-B*
2.0–2.4   *Sprint Library 1*
2.5–2.9   *Sprint Library 2-A, 2-B, and 2*
                      Scholastic Listening Skills, Unit 1
                      Scholastic Listening Skills, Unit 2
                      (Scholastic, Inc.)

Comic book   *Shakespeare:*
format, but
well done.

                          As You Like It
                          Hamlet
                          Julius Caesar
                          King Lear
                          Macbeth
                          The Merchant of Venice
                          A Midsummer Night's Dream
                          Othello
                          Romeo and Juliet
                          The Taming of the Shrew
                          The Tempest
                          Twelfth Night
                      (Pendulum Press. Note: Each of the above is available
                      with filmstrip and cassette.)

APPENDIX E

HUSTON MULTISENSORY APPROACH TO LEARNING NEW READING AND SPELLING WORDS

Word cards should be prepared in advance. Words should be written in manuscript if the child writes in manuscript. If the child uses cursive writing, the words should be written in cursive.

Using a black magic marker, write the word on a card. Take a small bottle of Elmer's glue and go over the word with a thin line of glue. Sprinkle fine sand on the card and shake the card, making sure that all the glue is covered. Set the word card aside to dry. This usually takes about five minutes.

Teaching Technique:

1. Pronounce the word.
2. Ask the child to say the word.
3. Use the word in a sentence.
4. Ask the child to make up a sentence using the word.
5. Have the child act out the word. For example, if the word is "on," the child can climb on a book, on a chair, on a box; if "under," the child can crawl under a table, under a desk; if "dog," the child can imitate a dog, bark like a dog; if "house," the child can draw a house in the air with his hands or pretend he is a house with his hands over his head and fingers touching at a point to illustrate the roof.
6. Demonstrate how the child is to trace the word on the prepared word card, pronouncing the word as he traces it. (Note: The *word* is pronounced as it is spoken. Do NOT sound the phonemes in isolation.) The tip of the forefinger ("pointer") should be used for tracing the word.
7. Have the child trace the word *five* times, each time pronouncing the word as he traces it.
8. Turn the word card over and ask the child to write the word on a sheet of paper.

9. If the child writes the word correctly, proceed to Step 10; if not, repeat Step 7. (Note: The child must write the entire word correctly at one time. If he bogs down, he may not look back at the word card and complete the word. He must repeat the tracing five times.)

10. Ask the child to draw a picture of his new word. If the new word has no concrete referral such as the word "on," ask the child to draw a picture of something lying or sitting on an object.

11. Have the child write a sentence about the picture.

12. Ask the child to underline the new word in his sentence, say the word, and read the entire sentence.

NOTE: This teaching technique may be used with a small group of children as well as with an individual child.

GLOSSARY

alexia: refers to one who has previously been literate but has lost the ability to read as a result of disease or acquired injury to the central nervous system.

ambidextrous: able to use both hands with ease for certain tasks; can do this even if one hand is considered to be the dominant or preferred hand.

ambivalent use of hands: simultaneous conflicting use of the hands; no dominant (preferred) hand has been established; one hand is used just about as much as the other, sometimes referred to as *unestablished dominance.*

anecdotal records: brief descriptions of specific instances of a child's behavior.

aniseikonia: a condition in which the lenses of the eyes are not in focus; may cause readers to mix letters in words, make reversals, lose their place, and read slowly.

anti-Ro antibody: a substance that assaults the Ro antigen, which exists in the brains (and hearts) of developing fetuses, causing irritation and inflammation.

antonyms: words that are opposite in meaning, such as open/shut, up/down, big/little, in/out.

aphasia: loss of speech.

application: the ability to use a skill, a rule, a method, or some new concept in a new situation.

astigmatism: an impairment of the eye that results in inability to bring the light rays to a single focal point; vision tends to be blurred and distorted, similar letters and words may be confused, sustained reading is fatiguing.

attention deficit disorder: difficulty with paying attention or staying on task, hyperactivity.

audiometer: machine used to test hearing.

auditory acuity: overall hearing; the sharpness or clearness of sounds transmitted to the brain.

auditory discrimination: ability to discern similarities and differences among sounds.

auditory dyslexia: a type of language communication disability characterized by problems in integrating and processing what is heard and recalling those sounds and applying them to the printed symbols representing them; at times referred to as auditory-linguistic dyslexia.

auditory image: a mental representation (remembrance) of what has been heard.

auditory-linguistic dyslexia: see auditory dyslexia.

auditory memory: retention of sounds in the sequence heard.

basal reader: the "textbook" (basic book) used in the teaching of reading, at successive reading levels of increasing difficulty beginning with the preprimer.

Broca's area: the area of brain relating to speech function.

cerebral trauma: an injury to an area of the brain.

chunking: organizing discrete units into larger meaningful units or chunks; a chunk of letters make up a word; a chunk of words form a sentence.

cognitive development: the intellectual development of a child as he matures.

concepts: higher and more abstract level of cognitive functioning; idea; thought; general notion.

configuration: the general form or shape of a letter, word, or object.

congenital: existing at or dating from birth; acquired during development in the uterus and not through heredity.

context clues: method of determining the meaning of a word from other words in a passage.

corrective reader: a student who has minor problems in reading that can be corrected by the classroom teacher; the services of the reading specialist are not needed.

decentration: the ability to take account of several features of an object or event at the same time (Piaget).

decoding: changing the written message into a spoken message; figuring out the relationship between the writing system and the sound system.

departmentalized classes: an organization of classes whereby the student moves from class to class throughout the day, changing periods and teachers according to subjects.

diacritical markings: symbols used in the dictionary to designate the pronunciation of words.

diagnosis: the process of identifying a disorder, such as visual or auditory dyslexia, on the basis of particular symptoms, characteristics, and test patterns.

diagnostic battery: a variety of standard and informal tests administered to determine specific strengths and deficiencies in different areas.

dialect: a regional variety of language distinguished by features of vocabulary, grammar, and pronunciation from other regional varieties; differs from the standard form of the language.

digraph: two letters that represent a single speech sound, such as the consonant digraphs *ch* in *chip, th* in *this, sh* in *shed;* or the vowel digraphs *ea* in eat, oa in *boat,* or *ai* in *paid.*

diorama: three-dimensional picture usually constructed in a box with objects or animals placed in front of a painted background; similar to a stage with props and actors or to a museum display.

directionality: refers to the knowledge of left and right.

disorientation: losing one's bearings; confusion as to time and space.

dizygotic twins: nonidentical twins.

dyslexia: a language communication disability including three general categories. The first, visual dyslexia (sometimes referred to as visuospatial dyslexia), is characterized by reversals of letters and numerals; faulty sequencing of letters in words, numbers in series, and events in narratives; disorientation in time and space relationships and problems in processing, interpreting, and recalling visual images. The second, auditory dyslexia (sometimes referred to as auditory-linguistic dyslexia), is characterized by problems of integrating and processing what is heard and recalling those sounds and applying them to the printed symbols representing them. The third is a combination of the two in varying degrees. Dyslexia is not attributable to any vision or hearing defect; it persists beyond that time when most childhood developmental conditions normally mature.

electroencephalogram (EEG): graphic record of brain waves.

empathy: capacity to sense and participate in another person's feelings or ideas.

etymology: the study of the origins and development of words.

experience charts: charts dictated by a student or students to the teacher who acts as a scribe, recording what they have to relate about a particular happening (experience).

expressive language: writing and speaking; information emerges from a person in the form of written or spoken words to be read or heard by others.

eye-hand coordination: ability of eyes and hands to work together; required for such tasks as copying or writing; sometimes referred to as visual-motor coordination.

farsightedness: hyperopia (the eye is too short and the image falls behind the retina); refers to near-point vision; can affect reading and other close work.

feature analysis: a process by which children recognize letters and words according to their distinctive features.

finger agnosia: relative or absolute inability to show or name the fingers that have been touched, or how many fingers have been touched, in a particular test; sometimes referred to as a "short circuit" in the neural pathways from the brain to the fingers or vice versa.

fixations: stops that the eyes make as they progress along a line of print. It is during the fixations that reading occurs.

functional literacy: the skills needed for a person to perform productively in our society.

grade equivalent: the grade level representing a given score—a 5.7 is the seventh month of the fifth grade.

grade level: comparable to the equivalent grade in school.

hyperactivity: excessively active behavior that deviates frequently from that considered to be within a normal range.

hyperopia: See farsightedness.

illiterate: as defined by the Census Bureau—someone at least fourteen years old who has not completed the fifth grade.

independent reading level: the level at which a student can read material with ease, understanding, and enjoyment, and without teacher assistance; sometimes called *free-* or *easy-reading level.*

individualization: adapting instruction and materials to meet each student's individual needs, while building upon each student's individual strengths.

individualized educational program (IEP): a curriculum plan that includes objectives, methodology, specific curriculum changes, and any classroom adjustments; IEPs are required by PL 94–142 for handicapped children.

instructional reading level: the level used for the formal teaching of reading with basal readers; the student misses no more than five words out of a running one hundred and has a good understanding of what he reads.

integration: combining of separate elements into a structured or unified whole.

intelligence quotient (IQ): a ratio of mental ability of an individual based on performance on an intelligence test and chronological age; refers to rate of mental development.

$$(IQ = \frac{MA}{CA} \times 100$$

irregular words: words that are not spelled according to the way they are sounded or do not adhere to the phonics rules; sometimes called *unpredictable words.*

language: a system of communication by means of spoken or written symbols (or gestures).

lateral awareness: ability to discriminate right from left.

linguistic development: the development of language structure, function, and changes as a child matures.

linguistics: the study of the nature and structure of language.

lip movements: moving lips while silently pronouncing words to self as one reads.

long-term memory: that aspect of memory that has a great capacity, lasts over a long period of time, and has organized or chunked information into patterns.

mainstreaming: placing dyslexic or other handicapped children in regular classes and integrating them into the regular school program while providing support from special teachers.

maturation: those aspects of development that are a part of the biological make up of a child, and which inevitably will occur if the child's environment is reasonably appropriate.

maturational lag: a late development of areas of the brain controlling certain perceptual and motor functions.

mnemonic device: something used to help in remembering.

monozygotic twins: identical twins (single ovum).

motivation: interest, drive, incentive to do something; intrinsic motivation comes from within, extrinsic from outside as a result of rewards or punishments.

mutant: produced by mutation, a change in hereditary material.

myelin sheath: the fatty substance that covers the axon, along which nerve impulses travel.

myopia: See nearsightedness.

nearsightedness: myopia (the eye is too long and the image falls in front of the retina); refers to far-point vision; can affect reading correctly from the chalkboard, charts, or an overhead projector.

negative transfer: a term used to indicate when a child has been taught something a certain way, then has to "unlearn" it, and learn it again.

occipital lobe: area of brain concerned with vision.

open classroom: an organization of classes whereby large groups of students work in large central areas with several teachers; a decentralized classroom arrangement.

oral reinforcement: saying the words softly to one's self as one reads.

orthography: way of writing; the letters of our alphabet (Aa, Bb, Cc) are a form of orthography.

parietal lobe: area of brain concerned with visual association.

phonological shifts: developmental shifts in speech sounds and changes of sounds as children mature.

polygenic: a group of nonallelic genes that collectively control the inheritance of a quantitative character or modify the expression of a qualitative character.

positive reinforcement: the strengthening of a response by an encouraging comment, action, or reward.

practical charts: charts prepared especially for teaching the new vocabulary in basal reader stories.

preprimer: first "formal" book used in the teaching of reading.

prerequisite knowledge: the readiness necessary to acquire new learning; the basic understanding, skills, and knowledge that serve as the foundation and springboard for information to be learned.

problem solving: using thinking to combine principles and obtain new solutions.

process: continuous actions or operations toward an end, as in the *reading process.*

processing: the handling of information by a series of active steps.

readability: the difficulty of reading material.

reading level: the level at which a child is reading, usually expressed in terms of grade level. A student in the fourth grade may have a reading level of fourth grade, third grade, or fifth grade; that is, lower or higher than the school grade in which he is placed.

reading readiness: the basic understanding, skills, and maturational development that serve as the foundation and bridge into formal reading instruction; can also apply to the reading of textbooks as one moves up through the grades.

reading retardation: reading performance significantly below one's ability to read.

reauditorize: to remember and "hear" in one's mind the sound of something one has heard.

recall: the remembrance of what has been seen or heard (or experienced in another way).

receptive language: reading and listening; that which is read and heard, and filters into the brain for processing.

regressive eye movements: a shift of the eye to the left along a line of print to return to a word or words to get another look.

reliability: the degree to which a test gives consistent results.

remedial reader: a student who is not reading according to his ability and whose achievement and difficulties are such that he needs special help by the reading specialist in addition to what he receives in his regular classroom.

retention: learning that permits later recall or recognition.

return sweep: the diagonal sweep of the eyes from the end of a line of print to begin reading on the next line of print.

reversals: changing the position or orientation of numbers, letters, parts of a word, or words, such as 6 for *9, d* for *b*, w for *m, iorn* for *iron*, or *was* for *saw.*

revisualize: to remember and "picture" in one's mind something one has seen.

round-robin teaching: refers to the practice of having children take turns reading orally from the basal reader (or textbook); sometimes called the "next, next" procedure.

saccades: jerky movements of the eyes along a line of print.

schwa: a softened, unaccented vowel sound; represented by the symbol ə; the vowel sound *a* in *about*, the *o* in but*o*n; any of the vowels may represent the schwa sound in certain words.

self-concept: how a child views himself and how he perceives that others see him.

semantical shifts: developmental shifts in the relations between referents and names, and concepts and names, as children mature.

sequencing: placing ideas, events, letters, and words in logical or chronological order, and numbers in a certain numerical order.

short-term memory: that aspect of memory that is limited in capacity, lasts only briefly, and has rapid input and output; sometimes called our working memory.

sight vocabulary: stock of words that a child can recognize instantly without having to resort to the application of word recognition strategies.

space: the three-dimensional extension in which objects and events exist, occur, and have relative position and direction.

specialized vocabulary: words indigenous to particular subject matter, such as those used in science, social studies or math.

spoonerism: a transposition of initial sounds of two or more words, such as *sons* of *toil* for *tons* of *soil*; a characteristic of auditory dyslexia.

standardized test: a test with specific procedures and certain tasks, and for which norms have been established so that comparable measurements may be obtained in different geographical regions.

strabismus: muscular imbalance resulting from an incoordination of the muscles that move the eyeball; can cause omission of letters, losing place on line, displacement of words.

strephosymbolia: "twisted symbols" as in reversing *no* and *on* or *saw* and *was* (coined by Dr. Samuel Orton).

syndrome: a cluster of symptoms or characteristics which together indicate a disorder.

syntactical shifts: developmental shifts in grammatical relations as children mature.

tachistoscope: a mechanical device that rapidly exposes reading material at differing rates of speed.

telebinocular: machine used to test vision.

traditional self-contained classroom: a classroom where students are with the same teacher for the entire day and where the teacher teaches the different subjects to the class.

transfer of learning: learning a concept or skill in one situation and being able to apply it in another; learning one thing helps in learning something else.

transposition: a change in sequence of letters (or sounds) within a word, such as *iorn* for *iron* or *emeny* for *enemy*; or words in a phrase or sentence, such as *gray, little fox* for *little, gray fox*; a type of reversal.

unpredictable words: words that are not spelled according to the way they are sounded, or do not adhere to the phonics rules; sometimes called irregular words.

validity: the extent to which a test represents a balanced and adequate sampling of the instructional outcomes it is intended to cover.

visual acuity: refers to overall vision; the sharpness or clearness of a visual image transmitted to the brain.

visual discrimination: the ability to discern similarities and differences in letters and words when looking at them.

visual dyslexia: a type of language communication disability characterized by reversals of letters and numerals; faulty sequencing of letters in words, numbers in series, and events in narrative; disorientation in time and space relationships; and problems in processing, interpreting, and recalling visual images; sometimes referred to as visuospatial dyslexia.

visual image: a mental representation (remembrance) of what has been seen.

visual memory: the retention of objects, events, or words seen.

visual-motor coordination: the ability of the hands and eyes to work together, sometimes called eye-hand coordination; required for such tasks as copying or writing.

visuospatial dyslexia: see visual dyslexia.

word banks: a file of known words that a student selects from his own stories or language experience charts.

word-blindness: a term formerly used to indicate the inability to read words as a result of congenital or acquired causes.

BIBLIOGRAPHY

Aaron, Ira E., "Translating research into practice: Reading readiness, visual perception, and auditory perception," in Helen K. Smith, ed., *Perception and Reading* (Newark, Del.: International Reading Association, 1968), pp. 130–35.

Aaron, P. G., "Developmental dyslexia: Is it different from other forms of reading disability?" *Annals of Dyslexia* Vol. 37 (1987), pp. 109–25.

―――, "The neuropsychology of developmental dyslexia," in R. N. Malatesha and P. G. Aaron, eds., *Reading Disorders, Varieties and Treatments* (New York: Academic Press, 1982), pp. 5–67.

Aaron, P. G., and Bakes, Catherine, "Empirical and heuristic bases for diagnosis and remediation of specific reading disabilities," *Topics in Learning and Learning Disabilities: Issues in Reading Diagnosis* Vol. 2, No. 4. (Gaithersburg, Md.: Aspen Systems, January 1983).

Aaron, P. G., and Kuchta, Steven, "Is there such a thing called dyslexia?" *Bulletin of the Orton Society* Vol. 38 (1988), pp. 33–49.

Adams, Richard B., "Dyslexia: A discussion of its definition," *Journal of Learning Disabilities* Vol. 2 (December 1969), pp. 616–26.

Adler, Mortimer, *How to Speak, How to Listen* (New York: Macmillan, 1983).

Adler, Mortimer J., and Van Doren, Charles, *How to Read A Book* (New York: Simon and Schuster, 1972).

Alexander, J. Estill, ed., *Teaching Reading*, 3rd ed., (Glenview, Ill.: Scott, Foresman/ Little, Brown, 1988).

Algozzine, Bob, and Yeseldyke, James E., "The future of the LD field: Screening and diagnosis," *Journal of Learning Disabilities* Vol. 19, No. 7 (August/September 1986), pp. 394–98.

American Academy of Ophthalmology, Policy Statement, "Learning disabilities, dyslexia, and vision" (San Francisco: American Academy of Ophthalmology, 1984).

American Academy of Pediatrics, Policy Statement, "The Doman-Delacato treatment of neurologically handicapped children," *Pediatrics* Vol. 70, No. 5 (1982), pp. 810–12.

American Academy of Pediatrics, Committee on Nutrition, "Megavitamin therapy for childhood psychoses and learning disabilities," *Pediatrics* Vol. 58, No. 6 (1976), pp. 910–12.

American Academy of Pediatrics, American Academy of Ophthalmology and Otolaryngology, and the American Association of Ophthalmology, Joint Organizational Statement, "The eye and learning disabilities," *Pediatrics* Vol. 49, No. 3 (1972), pp. 454–55.

American Psychiatric Association, Task Force Report No. 7 on Vitamin Therapy in Psychiatry, "Megavitamin and orthomolecular therapy in psychiatry," (Washington, D.C., 1973).

Anderson, Paul S., ed., *Linguistics in the Elementary School Classroom* (New York: Macmillan, 1971).

Ansara, Alice, Geschwind, Norman, Galaburda, Albert, Albert, Marilyn, and Gartrell, Nanette, *Sex Differences in Dyslexia* (Towson, Md.: The Orton Dyslexia Society, 1981).

Atteberry, Mary Wade, "Dyslexia, do its 'victims' have unusual ability?" *The Indianapolis Star* (Nov. 4, 1984), Section F, pp. 1–2.

Auten, Anne, "The ultimate connection: Reading, listening, writing, speaking, thinking," *The Reading Teacher* Vol. 36, No. 6 (February 1983), pp. 584–87.

Ayers, Floyd W., and Torres, Fernando, "The incidence of EEG abnormalities in a dyslexic and a control group," *Journal of Clinical Psychology* Vol. 23 (1967), pp. 334–36.

Ayres, A. Jean, "Improving academic scores through sensory integration," *Journal of Learning Disabilities* Vol. 5 (1972), pp. 338–43.

———, "Learning disabilities and the vestibular system," *Journal of Learning Disabilities* Vol. 11, No. 1 (January 1978), pp. 30–41.

———, *Sensory Integration and Learning Disorders* (Los Angeles: Western Psychological Services, 1972).

Backman, Joan, Bruck, Margaret, Hebert, Martine, and Seidenberg, Mark S., "Acquisition and use of spelling-sound correspondences in reading," *Journal of Experimental Child Psychology* Vol. 38 (1984), pp. 114–33.

Baddeley, A. D., Ellis, N. C., Miles, T. R., and Lewis, V. J., "Developmental and acquired dyslexia: A comparison," *Cognition* Vol. 11 (1982), pp. 185–199.

Bader, Lois A., *Reading Diagnosis and Remediation in Classroom and Clinic* (New York: Macmillan, 1980).

Baker, Ray Stannard, *Woodrow Wilson, Life and Letters; Youth 1856–1890* (Garden City, N.Y.: Doubleday, 1927).

Bakker, Dirk J., "Hemispheric differences and reading strategies: Two dyslexias?" *Bulletin of the Orton Society* Vol. 29 (1979), pp. 84–100.

Bakker, Dirk J., and Satz, Paul, eds., *Specific Reading Disability: Advances in Theory and Method* (The Netherlands: Rotterdam University Press, 1970).

Bakker, Dirk J., van Leeuwen, H. M. P., and Spyer, G., "Neuropsychological aspects of dyslexia," in Dirk J. Bakker, Colin R. Wilsher, H. Debruyne, and N. Bertin, eds., *Developmental Dyslexia and Learning Disorders* (New York: Karger, 1987), pp. 30–39.

Bakker, Dirk J., and Vinke, Jan, "Effects of hemisphere-specific stimulation on brain activity and reading in dyslexics," *Journal of Clinical and Experimental Neuropsychology* Vol. 7, No. 5 (1985), pp. 505–25.

Bakker, Dirk J., Wilsher, Colin R., Debruyne, H., and Bertin, N., eds., *Developmental Dyslexia and Learning Disorders* (New York: Karger, 1987).

Balajthy, Ernest, "Computers and instruction: Implications of the rising tide of criticism for reading education," *Reading Research and Instruction* Vol. 28, No. 1 (1988), pp. 49–59.

———,"Reinforcement and drill by microcomputer," *The Reading Teacher* Vol. 37, No. 6 (February 1984), pp. 490–94.

Bannatyne, Alexander, *Language, Reading and Learning Disabilities* (Springfield, Ill.: Charles C. Thomas, 1971).

Barnett, Lincoln, "The English language," in Hal D. Funk and DeWayne Triplett, eds., *Language Arts in the Elementary School: Readings* (Philadelphia: Lippincott, 1972), pp. 95–103.

Bateman, Barbara, *Learning Disorders, Reading* Vol. 4 (Seattle, Wash.: Special Child Publications, 1971).

Battle, James, and Labercane, George, "Comparing achievement, ability, with visual memory and visual association," *Read-Horizons* Vol. 25, No. 2 (1985), pp. 87–94.

Baumann, James F., and Stevenson, Jennifer A., "Understanding standardized reading achievement test scores," *The Reading Teacher* Vol. 35, No. 6 (March 1982), pp. 648–54.

Bayliss, Janet, and Livesey, P. J., "Cognitive strategies of children with reading disability and normal readers in visual sequential memory," *Journal of Learning Disabilities* Vol. 18, No. 6 (June/July 1985), pp. 326–32.

Beers, Carol S., "The relationship of cognitive development to spelling and reading abilities," in Edmund H. Henderson and James W. Beers, eds., *Developmental and Cognitive Aspects of Learning to Spell: A Reflection of Word Knowledge* (Newark, Del.: International Reading Association, 1980), pp. 74–84.

Beers, James W., "Developmental strategies of spelling competence in primary school children," in Edmund H. Henderson and James W. Beers, eds., *Developmental and Cognitive Aspects of Learning to Spell: A Reflection of Word Knowledge* (Newark, Del.: International Reading Association, 1980), pp. 36–45.

Beers, James W., and Henderson, Edmund H.,"A study of developing orthographic concepts among first graders," *Research in the Teaching of English* Vol. 11 (Fall 1977), pp. 133–48.

Beery, Keith E., *Monograph: Visual-Motor Integration* (Chicago: Follett, 1967).

Behan, Wilhelmina M. H., Behan, P. O., and Geschwind, Norman, "Anti-Ro antibody in mothers of dyslexic children," *Developmental Medicine and Child Neurology* Vol. 27 (1985), pp. 538–39.

Bender, Bruce G., Puck, Mary H., Salbenblatt, James A., and Robinson, Arthur, "Cognitive Development of Children with Sex Chromosome Abnormalities," in Shelley D. Smith, ed., *Genetics and Learning Disabilities* (San Diego, Calif.: College-Hill Press, 1986).

Benirschke, Kurt, "Accurate recording of twin placentation, a plea to the obstetrician," *Obstetrics and Gynecology* Vol. 18 (September 1961), pp. 334–47.

Benton, Arthur L., "Developmental dyslexia: Neurological aspects," in Walter J. Friedlander, ed., *Current Reviews of Higher Nervous System Dysfunction* (New York: Raven Press, 1975), pp. 1–45.

————, "Dyslexia in relation to form perception and directional sense," in John Money, ed., *Reading Disability, Progress and Research Needs in Dyslexia*, (Baltimore: Johns Hopkins Press, 1968), pp. 81–102.

————, "Right-left discrimination," *Pediatric Clinics of North America* Vol. 15 (1968), pp. 747–58.

————, *Right-Left Discrimination and Finger Localization* (New York: Harper and Brothers, 1959).

————, "Significance of systematic reversal in right-left discrimination," *Acta Psychological et Neurological* Vol. 33 (1957), pp. 129–37.

Benton, Arthur L., and Pearl, David, eds., *Dyslexia: An Appraisal of Current Knowledge* (New York: Oxford University Press, 1978).

Bettman, Jerome W., Jr., Stern, Earl L., Whitsell, Leon J., and Gofman, Helen F., "Cerebral dominance in developmental dyslexia," *Archives of Ophthalmology* Vol. 78 (December 1967), pp. 722–29.

Bireley, Marlene, and Manley, Eleyse, "The learning disabled student in a college environment: A report of Wright State University's Program," *Journal of Learning Disabilities* Vol. 13, No. 1 (January 1980), pp. 7–10.

Blank, Marion, "A word is a word—or is it?" in David B. Gray and James F. Kavanagh, eds., *Biobehavioral Measures of Dyslexia* (Parkton, Md.: York Press, 1987), pp. 261–77.

Blue, Rose, *Me and Einstein* (New York: Human Sciences, 1979).

Blumenson, Martin, *The Patton Papers* Vols I and II (Boston: Houghton Mifflin, 1974).

Boder, Elena, "Developmental dyslexia: A diagnostic approach based on three atypical reading-spelling patterns," *Developmental Medicine and Child Neurology* 15 (1973) pp. 663–87.

————, "Developmental dyslexia: A diagnostic screening procedure based on three characteristic patterns of reading and spelling," in Barbara Bateman, ed., *Learn-*

ing Disorders, Reading Vol. 4 (1971) (Seattle, Wash.: Special Child Publications), pp. 297–342.

———, "Developmental dyslexia, a new diagnostic approach based on the identification of three subtypes," *The Journal of School Health* Vol. 40, No. 6 (June 1970), pp. 289–90.

———, "Developmental dyslexia: Prevailing diagnostic concepts and a new diagnostic approach," in Helmer R. Myklebust, ed., *Progress in Learning Disabilities* Vol. II (New York: Grune and Stratton, 1971), pp. 293–321.

Bond, Guy L., Tinker, Miles A., Wasson, Barbara B., and Wasson, John B., *Reading Difficulties, Their Diagnosis and Correction*, 5th ed., (Englewood Cliffs, N.J.: Prentice-Hall, 1984).

Boyd, Gertrude A., *Teaching Communication Skills in the Elementary School* (New York: Van Nostrand Reinhold, 1970).

Brander, T., cited by Edith Zerbin-Rubin in "Congenital word-blindness," *Bulletin of the Orton Society* Vol. 17 (1967), pp. 47–54.

Broadbent, Sir William Henry, "Note on Dr. Hinshelwood's communication on word-blindness and visual memory," *The Lancet* (January 4, 1896), p. 18.

———, "On the cerebral mechanism of thought," *Medico-Chirurgical Transactions* Vol. 37 (London: The Royal Medical and Chirurgical Society of London, Longmans, Green, Reader, and Dyer, 1872), pp. 145–94.

Brown, Brian, Haegerstrom-Portnoy, Gunilla, Yingling, Charles, Herron, Jeannine, Galin, David, and Marcus, Marilyn, "Dyslexic children have normal vestibular responses to rotation," *Archives of Neurology* Vol. 40 (June 1983), pp. 370–73.

———, Haegerstrom-Portnoy, Gunilla, Yingling, Charles D., Herron, Jeannine, Galin, David, and Marcus, Marilyn, "Tracking eye movements are normal in dyslexic children," *American Journal of Optometry and Physiological Optics* Vol. 60, No. 5 (1983), pp. 376–83.

———, Haegerstrom-Portnoy, Gunilla, Adams, Anthony J., Yingling, Charles D., Galin, David, Herron, Jeannine, and Marcus, Marilyn, "Predictive eye movements do not discriminate between dyslexic and control children," *Neuropsychologia* Vol. 21, No. 2 (1983), pp. 121–28.

———, Haegerstrom-Portnoy, Gunilla, Herron, Jeannine, Galin, David, Yingling, Charles D., and Marcus, Marilyn, "Static postural stability is normal in dyslexic children," *Journal of Learning Disabilities* Vol. 18, No. 1 (January 1985), pp. 31–34.

Brown, Don A., *Reading Diagnosis and Remediation* (Englewood Cliffs, N.J.: Prentice-Hall, 1982).

Bruck, Maggie, "The word recognition and spelling of dyslexic children," *Reading Research Quarterly* Vol. 23, No. 1 (1988), pp. 51–69.

Bryant, Peter, and Impey, Lawrence, "The similarities between normal readers and developmental and acquired dyslexics," *Cognition* Vol. 24 (1986), pp. 121–37.

Burg, Leslie, and Kaufman, Maurice, "Laws about special education: Their impact on the use of reading specialists," *The Reading Teacher* Vol. 34, No. 2 (November 1980), pp. 187–91.

Burns, Paul C., Roe, Betty D., and Ross, Elinor P., *Teaching Reading in Today's Elementary Schools* (Boston: Houghton Mifflin, 1984).

Burns, Paul G., and Broman, Betty L., *The Language Arts in Childhood Education*, 4th ed. (Chicago: Rand McNally, 1979).

Calder, Richie, *Leonardo and the Age of the Eye* (New York: Simon and Schuster, 1970).

Caldarelli, David D., and Campanella, Ruth S., "Ear," *The World Book Encyclopedia* Vol. 6 (1985), pp. 5–8.

Calfee, Robert, "Literacy and illiteracy: Teaching the nonreader to survive in the modern world," *Annals of Dyslexia* Vol. 32 (1982), pp. 71–91.

Calvin, William H., and Ojemann, George A., *Inside the Brain* (New York: New American Library, 1980).

Carlson, Thorsten, ed., *Administrators and Reading* (New York: Harcourt Brace Jovanovich, 1972).

Carlton, Lessie, and Moore, Robert H., *Reading, Self-Directive Dramatization and Self-Concept* (Columbus, Ohio: Charles E. Merrill, 1968).

Carter, John L., and Russell, Harold L., "Use of EMG biofeedback procedures with learning disabled children in a clinical and an educational setting," *Journal of Learning Disabilities* Vol. 18, No. 4 (April 1985), pp. 213–16.

Chalfant, James C., and Flathouse, Virgil E., "Auditory and visual learning," in Helmer R. Myklebust, ed., *Progress in Learning Disabilities* Vol. II (New York: Grune and Stratton, 1971), pp. 252–92.

Chall, Jeanne S., "Learning to Read: The great debate 20 years later—," *Phi Delta Kappan* Vol. 70 (March 1989), pp. 521–38.

Chase, C., and Tallal, P., "Piracetam and dyslexia," in D. J. Bakker, Colin R. Wilsher, H. Debruyne, and N. Bertin, eds., *Developmental Dyslexia and Learning Disorders* (New York: Karger, 1987), pp. 140–47.

Chomsky, Carol, "Reading, writing and phonology," *Harvard Educational Review* Vol. 40 (May 1970), pp. 287–309.

———, "Write first, read later," *Childhood Education* Vol. 47 (March 1971), pp. 296–99.

Chomsky, Noam, and Halle, Morris, *The Sound Patterns of English* (New York: Harper and Row, 1968).

Clark, Diana B., *Dyslexia: Theory and Practice of Remedial Instruction* (Parkton, Md.: York Press, 1988).

Cohen, Elizabeth G., Intilli, Jo-Ann K., and Robbins, Susan Hurevitz, "Teachers and reading specialists: Cooperation or isolation?" *The Reading Teacher* Vol. 32, No. 3 (December 1978), pp. 281–87.

Collins-Cheek, Martha, and Cheek, Earl H., Jr., *Diagnostic-Prescriptive Reading Instruction, A Guide for Classroom Teachers* (Dubuque, Iowa: William C. Brown, 1984).

Conners, C. Keith, "A critical review of electroencephalographic and neurophysiological studies in dyslexia," in Arthur L. Benton and David Pearl, eds., *Dyslexia, an Appraisal of Current Knowledge* (New York: Oxford University Press, 1978).

_____, "The effect of piracetam on reading achievement and visual event-related potentials in dyslexic children," in D. J. Bakker, Colin R. Wilsher, H. Debruyne, and N. Bertin, eds., *Developmental Dyslexia and Learning Disorders* (New York: Karger, 1987), pp. 75–90.

_____, "Event-related potentials and quantitative EEG brain-mapping in dyslexia," in D. Bakker, Colin R. Wilsher, H. Debruyne, and N. Bertin, eds., *Developmental Dyslexia and Learning Disorders* (New York: Karger, 1987), pp. 9–21.

_____, *Food Additives and Hyperactive Children* (New York: Plenum Press, 1980).

Conners, C. Keith, Goyette, Charles H., et al., "Food additives and hyperkinesis. A controlled double-blind experiment," *Pediatrics* Vol. 58 (1976), pp. 154–56.

Connett, David, "Glasses hope for dyslexia," *The Sunday Times* (London) (December 22, 1985) p. 3.

Cook, Louisa, "Misspelling analysis in dyslexia: Observation of developmental strategy shifts," *Bulletin of the Orton Society* Vol. 31 (1981), pp. 123–34.

Cott, Allan, "Megavitamins: The orthomolecular approach to behavioral disorders and learning disabilities," *Academic Therapy* Vol. 7 (Spring 1972), pp. 245–58.

_____, "Orthomolecular approach to the treatment of learning disabilities," *Schizophrenia* Vol. 33 (1971), pp. 95–107.

Cox, Aylett R., "Syllable division: Prerequisite to dyslexics' literacy," *Annals of Dyslexia* Vol. 38 (1988), pp. 226–42.

Cranston, Ruth, *The Story of Woodrow Wilson* (New York: Simon and Schuster, 1945).

Criqui, Orvel A., "An administrator's view of reading programs," *The Reading Teacher* Vol. 30, No. 4 (January 1977), pp. 356–58.

Crisculolo, Nicholas P., "Effective ways to communicate with parents about reading," *The Reading Teacher* Vol. 34, No. 2 (November 1980), pp. 164–66.

Critchley, Macdonald, *The Dyslexic Child* (Springfield, Ill.: Charles C. Thomas, 1970).

_____, "Some problems of the ex-dyslexic," *Bulletin of the Orton Society* Vol. 23 (1973), pp. 7–14.

Critchley, Macdonald, and Critchley, Eileen A., *Dyslexia Defined* (Springfield, Ill.: Charles C. Thomas, 1978).

Cronnel, Bruce, "Phonics for reading vs. phonics for spelling," *The Reading Teacher* Vol. 32, No. 3 (December 1978), pp. 337–40.

Crosby, Robert M. N., "Reading: The dyslexic child," *Today's Education* Vol. 60, No. 7 (October 1971), pp. 46–48.

Cunningham, Pat, "Horizontal reading," *The Reading Teacher* Vol. 34, No. 2 (November 1980), pp. 222–24.

Dallman, Martha, Rouch, Roger L., Char, Lynette Y. C., and DeBoer, John J., *The Teaching of Reading*, 6th ed. (New York: Holt, Rinehart and Winston, 1982).

Daniels, Josephus, *The Life of Woodrow Wilson* (Chicago: John C. Winston, 1924).

Dauzat, Jo Ann, and Dauzat, Sam V., *Reading: The Teacher and the Learner* (New York: John Wiley, 1981).

Debray-Ritzen, P., "Diagnosis and natural history of dyslexia in children," in D. J. Bakker, Colin R. Wilsher, H. Debruyne, and N. Bertin, eds., *Developmental Dyslexia and Learning Disorders* (New York: Karger, 1987), pp. 22–29.

Dechant, Emerald, *Diagnosis and Remediation of Reading Disabilities* (Englewood Cliffs, N.J.: Prentice-Hall, 1981).

———, *Improving the Teaching of Reading* (Englewood Cliffs, N.J.: Prentice-Hall, 1970).

Decker, Sadie N., and Bender, Bruce G., "Converging evidence for multiple genetic forms of reading disability," *Brain and Language* Vol. 33 (1988), pp. 197–215.

Decker, Sadie N., and Corley, Robin P., "Bannatyne's 'Genetic Dyslexic' subtype: A validation study," *Psychology in the Schools* Vol. 21 (July 1984), pp. 300–304.

Decker, Sadie N., and DeFries, J. C., "Cognitive abilities in families with reading disabled children," *Journal of Learning Disabilities* Vol. 13, No. 9 (1980), pp. 53–57.

Decker, Sadie N., and Vandenberg, Steven G., "Colorado twin study of reading disability," in David B. Gray and James F. Kavanagh, eds., *Biobehavioral Measures of Dyslexia* (Parkton, Md.: York Press, 1987), pp. 123–35.

DeFries, J. C., and Decker, S. N., "Genetic aspects of reading disability: A family study," in R. N. Malatesha and P. G. Aaron, eds., *Reading Disorders, Varieties and Treatments* (New York: Academic Press, 1982), pp. 255–79.

Delacato, Carl H., *Neurological Organization and Reading* (Springfield, Ill.: Charles C. Thomas, 1966).

———, *Treatment and Prevention of Reading Problems* (Springfield, Ill.: Charles C. Thomas, 1959).

Denckla, Martha B., "Issues of overlap and heterogeneity in dyslexia," in David B. Gray and James F. Kavanagh, eds., *Biobehavioral Measures of Dyslexia* (Parkton, Md.: York Press, 1985), pp. 41–46.

Denckla, Martha B., LeMay, Marjorie, and Chapman, Catherine A., "Few CT Scan abnormalities found even in neurologically impaired learning disabled children," *Journal of Learning Disabilities* Vol. 18, No. 3 (March 1985), pp. 132–35.

De Quiros, Julio B., "Diagnosis of vestibular disorders in the learning disabled," *Journal of Learning Disabilities* Vol. 9, No. 1 (January 1976), pp. 50–55.

DeStefano, Johanna S., and Fox, Sharon E., *Language and the Language Arts* (Boston: Little, Brown, 1974).

Dinklage, Kenneth T., "Inability to learn a foreign language," in Graham B. Blaine, Jr., and Charles C. McArthur, eds., *Emotional Problems of the Student* (New York: Appleton-Century-Crofts, 1971), pp. 185–206.

DiStefano, Philip P., and Hagerty, Patricia J., "Teaching spelling at the elementary level: A realistic perspective," *The Reading Teacher* Vol. 38 (January 1985), pp. 373–77.

Divoky, Diane, "Ritalin: Education's fix-it drug?" *Phi Delta Kappan* (April 1989), pp. 599–605.

Doehring, Donald G., *Patterns of Impairment in Specific Reading Disability* (Bloomington, Ind.: Indiana University Press, 1968).

Doehring, Donald G., Trites, Ronald L., Patel, P. G., and Fiedorowicz, A. M., *Reading Disabilities, The Interaction of Reading, Language, and Neuropsychological Deficits* (New York: Academic Press, 1981).

Doman, Glenn, and Delacato, Carl H., "Doman-Delacato philosophy," *Human Potential* Vol. 1 (1968), p. 113–16.

Done, D. J. and Miles, T. R., "Learning, memory, and dyslexia," in M. M. Gruneberg, P. E. Morris, and R. M. Sykes, eds., *Practical Aspects of Memory* (London: Academic Press, 1978), pp. 553–60.

Downing, John, *Comparative Reading, Cross-National Studies of Behavior and Processes in Reading and Writing* (New York: Macmillan, 1973).

Drake, William E., Jr., "Clinical and pathological findings in a child with a developmental learning disability," *Journal of Learning Disabilities* Vol. 1, No. 9 (September 1968), pp. 486–502.

Duane, Drake D., "Commentary on dyslexia and neurodevelopmental pathology," *Journal of Learning Disabilities* Vol. 22, No. 4 (April 1989), pp. 219–20.

———, "Neurodiagnostic tools in dyslexic syndromes in children: Pitfalls and proposed comparative study of computed tomography, nuclear magnetic resonance, and brain electrical activity mapping," in George Th. Pavlidis and Dennis F. Fisher, eds., *Dyslexia: Its Neuropsychology and Treatment* (New York: John Wiley, 1986), pp. 65–84.

———, "A neurologic overview of specific language disability for the non-neurologist," *Bulletin of the Orton Society* Vol. 24 (1974), pp. 5–36.

Duane, Drake D., and Rawson, Margaret B., eds., *Reading, Perception and Language*, papers from the World Congress on Dyslexia (Baltimore: York Press, 1974).

Duane, Drake D., and Rome, Paula Dozier, eds., *The Dyslexic Child* (New York: Insight Publishing, 1979).

Duffy, Frank H., Denckla, Martha B., Bartels, Peter H., and Sandini, Giulio, "Dyslexia: Regional differences in brain electrical activity by topographic mapping," *Annals of Neurology* Vol. 7, No. 5 (May 1980), pp. 412–20.

Duffy, Frank H., Denckla, Martha B., Bartels, Peter H., Sandini, Giulio, and Kiessling, Louise S., "Dyslexia: Automated diagnosis by computerized classification of brain electrical activity," *Annals of Neurology* Vol. 7, No. 5 (1980), pp. 421–28.

Duffy, Frank H., McAnulty, Gloria B., and Schachter, Steven C., "Brain electrical activity mapping," in Norman Geschwind and Albert M. Galaburda, eds., *Cerebral Dominance, The Biological Foundations* (Cambridge, Massachusetts: Harvard University Press, 1984), pp. 53–74.

Dunn, Rita, "Learning style and its relation to exceptionality at both ends of the spectrum," *Exceptional Children* Vol. 49, No. 6 (April 1983), pp. 496–506.

"Dyslexia, The Hidden Handicap," special educational needs report of the Committee of Enquiry into the education of handicapped children and young people (Peppard, Oxfordshire: British Dyslexia Association, n.d.).

Echenne, B., and Cheminal, R., "The Physiopathological bases of dyslexia," in D. J. Bakker, Colin R. Wilsher, H. Debruyne, and N. Bertin, eds., *Developmental Dyslexia and Learning Disorders* (New York: Karger, 1987), pp. 40–47.

Edwards, R. Phillip, Alley, Gordon R., and Snider, William, "Academic achievement and minimal brain dysfunction," *Journal of Learning Disabilities* Vol. 4, No. 3 (March 1971), pp. 17–21.

Eiterman, R. D., Abel, L. A., Daroff, R. B., Dell'Osso, L. F., and Bornstein, J. L., "Eye movement patterns in dyslexic children," *Journal of Learning Disabilities* Vol. 13, No. 1 (January 1980), pp. 11–16.

Ekwall, Eldon E., *Diagnosis and Remediation of the Disabled Reader* (Boston: Allyn and Bacon, 1976).

———, *Locating and Correcting Reading Difficulties*, 4th and 5th eds. (Columbus, Ohio: Charles E. Merrill, 1985, 1989).

———, ed., *Psychological Factors in the Teaching of Reading* (Columbus, Ohio: Charles E. Merrill, 1973).

Ekwall, Eldon E., and Shanker, James L., *Teaching Reading in the Elementary School* (Columbus, Ohio: Charles E. Merrill, 1985).

Elkind, David, *Children and Adolescents Interpretive Essays on Jean Piaget,* 2nd ed. (New York: Oxford University Press, 1974).

Elkind, David, Horn, John, and Schneider, Gerrie, "Modified word recognition, reading achievement and perceptual decentration," *The Journal of Genetic Psychology* Vol. 107 (December 1965), pp. 235–51.

Ellis, Andrew W., "The cognitive neuropsychology of developmental (and acquired) dyslexia: A critical survey," *Cognitive Neuropsychology* Vol. 2, No. 2 (1985), pp. 169–205.

———, *Reading, Writing and Dyslexia: A Cognitive Analysis* (Hillsdale, N.J.: Lawrence Erlbaum, 1984).

Ellis, N. C., and Miles, T. R., "Visual information processing in dyslexic children," in M. M. Gruneberg, P. E. Morris, and R. N. Sykes, eds., *Practical Aspects of Memory* (London: Academic Press, 1978), pp. 561–69.

Erion, R. Joel, "Chronological age, immaturity and the identification of learning disabilities," *Educational Research Quarterly* Vol. 11, No. 1 (1986–1987), pp. 2–7.

Evans, James R., "Neuropsychologically based remedial reading procedures: Some possibilities," in R. N. Malatesha and P. G. Aaron, eds., *Reading Disorders, Varieties and Treatments* (New York: Academic Press, 1982), pp. 371–88.

Evans, James S., *An Uncommon Gift* (Philadelphia: Westminister Press, 1983).

Evans, Martha M., *Dyslexia, An Annotated Bibliography* (Westport, Conn.: Greenwood Press, 1982).

Farago, Ladislas, *Patton: Ordeal and Triumph* (New York: Dell, 1963).

Farr, Roger, and Roser, Nancy, *Teaching a Child to Read* (New York: Harcourt Brace Jovanovich, 1979).

Feingold, Benjamin F., "Hyperkinesis and learning disabilities linked to the ingestion of artificial food colors and flavors," *Journal of Learning Disabilities* Vol. 9 (November 1976), pp. 551–59.

————, *Why Your Child is Hyperactive* (New York: Random House, 1975).

Fernald, Grace, *Remedial Techniques in Basic School Subjects* (New York: McGraw-Hill, 1971/1943).

Ferreri, Carl A., "Dyslexia and learning disabilities cured," *The Digest of Chiropractic Economics* (May/June, 1983), pp. 74, 148.

Ferreri, Carl A., and Wainwright, Richard B., *Breakthrough for Dyslexia and Learning Disabilities* (Pompano Beach, Fla.: Exposition Press of Florida, 1984).

Finucci, Joan M., "Approaches to subtype validation using family data," in David B. Gray and James F. Kavanagh, eds., *Biobehavioral Measures of Dyslexia* (Parkton, Md.: York Press, 1987), pp. 137–53.

————, "Follow-up studies of developmental dyslexia and other learning disabilities," in Shelley D. Smith, ed., *Genetics and Learning Disabilities* (San Diego, Calif.: College-Hill, 1986), pp. 97–121.

————, "Genetic considerations in dyslexia," in Helmer R. Myklebust, ed., *Progress in Learning Disabilities* Vol. IV (New York: Grune and Stratton, 1978), pp. 41–63.

Finucci, Joan M., and Childs, Barton, "Dyslexia: Family studies," in Christy L. Ludlow and Judith A. Cooper, eds., *Genetic Aspects of Speech and Language Disorders* (New York: Academic Press, 1983), pp. 157–67.

Finucci, Joan M., Guthrie, John T., Childs, Anne L., Abbey, Helen, and Childs, Barton, "The genetics of specific reading disability," *Annals of Human Genetics* Vol. 40 (London: 1976), pp. 1–23.

Fleming, Elizabeth, *Believe the Heart* (San Francisco, Calif.: Strawberry Hill, 1984).

Flood, James, and Lapp, Diane, "Reporting reading progress: A comparison portfolio for parents," *The Reading Teacher* Vol. 42 (March 1989), pp. 508–15.

Frank, Jan, and Levinson, Harold N., "Seasickness mechanisms and medications in dysmetric dyslexia and dyspraxia," *Academic Therapy* Vol. 12, No. 2 (Winter 1976–1977), pp. 133–49.

Frauenheim, John G., "Academic achievement characteristics of adult males who were diagnosed as dyslexic in childhood," *Journal of Learning Disabilities* Vol. 11, No. 8 (October 1978), pp. 21–28.

Frith, Uta, and Frith, Christopher, "Relationships between reading and spelling," in James F. Kavanagh and Richard L. Venezky, eds., *Orthography, Reading, and Dyslexia* (Baltimore: University Park Press, 1980), pp. 287–95.

Funk, Hal D., and Triplett, DeWayne, *Language Arts in the Elementary School: Readings* (Philadelphia: Lippincott, 1972).

Furth, Hans G., *Piaget for Teachers* (Englewood Cliffs, N.J.: Prentice-Hall, 1970).

Gaddes, William H., *Learning Disabilities and Brain Function, A Neuropsychological Approach* (New York: Springer-Verlag, 1980).

Galaburda, Albert M., "Anatomical asymmetries," in Norman Geschwind and Albert M. Galaburda, eds., *Cerebral Dominance, The Biological Foundations* (Cambridge, Mass.: Harvard University Press, 1984), pp. 11–25.

———, "Developmental dyslexia: Current anatomical research," *Annals of Dyslexia* Vol. 33 (1983), pp. 41–53.

———, "Developmental dyslexia: A review of biological interactions," *Annals of Dyslexia* Vol. 35 (1985), pp. 21–33.

———, "Symmetry and asymmetry in the human posterior thalamus, II. Thalamic lesions in a case of developmental dyslexia," *Archives of Neurology* Vol. 39 (June 1982), pp. 333–36.

———, "The pathogenesis of childhood dyslexia," in F. Plum, ed., *Language, Communication, and the Brain* (New York: Raven Press, 1988), pp. 127–37.

Galaburda, Albert M., and Kemper, Thomas L., "Cytoarchitectonic abnormalities in developmental dyslexia: A case study," *Annals of Neurology* Vol. 6 (August 1979), pp. 94–100.

Galaburda, Albert M., Sherman, Gordon F., and Geschwind, Norman, "Developmental dyslexia: Third consecutive case with cortical anomalies," *Society for Neuroscience, Abstracts* Vol. 9 (1983), p. 940.

Galaburda, Albert M., Sherman, Gordon F., Rosen, Glenn D., Aboitiz, Francisco, and Geschwind, Norman, "Developmental dyslexia: Four consecutive patients with cortical anomalies," *Annals of Neurology* Vol. 18 (1985), pp. 222–33.

Gambrell, Linda B., "Dialogue journals: Reading-writing interaction," *The Reading Teacher* Vol. 38 (February 1985), pp. 512–15.

———, "Think-time: Implications for reading instruction," *The Reading Teacher* Vol. 34, No. 2 (November 1980), pp. 143–46.

Gamby, Gert, "Talking books and taped books: Materials for instruction," *The Reading Teacher* Vol. 36, No. 4 (January 1983), pp. 366–69.

Ganschow, Leonore, "Analysis of written language of a language learning disabled (dyslexic) college student and instructional implications," *Annals of Dyslexia* Vol. 34 (1984), pp. 271–84.

———, "Analyze error patterns to remediate severe spelling difficulties," *The Reading Teacher* Vol. 38 (December 1984), pp. 288–93.

Gentry, J. Richard, "An analysis of developmental spelling in GNYS AT WRK," *The Reading Teacher* Vol. 36, No. 2 (November 1982), pp. 191–92.

———, "Learning to spell developmentally," *The Reading Teacher* Vol. 34, No. 4 (January 1981), pp. 378–81.

Geschwind, Norman, "The biology of dyslexia: The after-dinner speech," in David B. Gray and James F. Kavanagh, eds., *Biobehavioral Measures of Dyslexia* (Parkton, Md.: York Press, 1985), pp. 1–19.

———, "The brain of a learning-disabled individual," *Annals of Dyslexia* Vol. 34 (1984), pp. 319–27.

———, "Dyslexia, cerebral dominance, autoimmunity, and sex hormones," in George Th. Pavlidis and Dennis F. Fisher, eds., *Dyslexia: Its Neuropsychology and Treatment* (New York: John Wiley, 1986), pp. 51–63.

———, "Why Orton was right," *Annals of Dyslexia* Vol. 32 (1982), pp. 13–30.

Geschwind, Norman, Galaburda, Albert, and LeMay, Marjorie, "Morphological and physiological substrates of language and cognitive development," in Robert Katzman, ed., *Congenital and Acquired Cognitive Disorders* (New York: Raven Press, 1979), pp. 31–41.

Gibson, Eleanor J., Gibson, James J., Pick, Anne D., and Osser, Harry, "A developmental study of the discrimination of letter-like forms," *Journal of Comparative and Physiological Psychology* Vol. 55 (1962), pp. 897–906.

Gillespi-Silver, Patricia, *Teaching Reading to Children with Special Needs* (Columbus, Ohio: Charles E. Merrill, 1979).

Gillet, Jean Wallace, and Temple, Charles, *Understanding Reading Problems, Assessment and Instruction* (Boston: Little, Brown, 1982).

Gittelman, Rachel, "Indications for the use of stimulant treatment in learning disorders," *Journal of the American Academy of Child Psychiatry* Vol. 19 (1980), pp. 623–36.

Glass, Gene V., and Robbins, Melvyn P., "A critique of experiments on the role of neurological organization in reading performance," *Reading Research Quarterly* Vol. 3 (Fall 1967), pp. 5–52.

Goldberg, Herman K. and Schiffman, Gilbert B., *Dyslexia Problems of Reading Disabilities* (New York: Grune and Stratton, 1972).

Goldberg, Herman K., Schiffman, Gilbert B., and Bender, Michael, *Dyslexia, Interdisciplinary Approaches to Reading Disabilities* (New York: Grune and Stratton, 1983).

Goldberg, Morton F., "Eye," *The World Book Encyclopedia*, Vol. 6 (1985), pp. 358–67.

Goldstein, Mark, "Potential problems with the widespread use of niacin," *The American Journal of Medicine* Vol. 85 (December 1988), p. 881.

Goodman, Kenneth S., *What's Whole in Whole Language?* (Portsmouth, N.H.: Heinemann, 1986).

Goodman, Kenneth S., and Fleming, James T., eds., *Psycholinguistics and the Teaching of Reading*, selected papers from the IRA Pre-Convention Institute held in Boston, April 1968. (Newark, Del.: International Reading Association, 1972).

Gordon, Harold W., "Cognitive asymmetry in dyslexic families," *Neuropsychologia* Vol. 18 (1980), pp. 645–55.

Gosse, Edmund, "Andersen, Hans Christian," *The Encyclopedia Britannica*, 11th ed., Vol. 1 (1911), pp. 958–59.

Gottfredson, Linda S., Finucci, Joan M., and Childs, Barton, "The adult occupational success of dyslexic boys: A large scale, long-term follow up," Report No. 334 (March 1983) (Baltimore: The Center for Social Organization of Schools at The Johns Hopkins University).

Gow, David W., "Dyslexic adolescent boys: Classroom remediation is not enough," *Bulletin of the Orton Society* Vol. 24 (1974), pp. 154–63.

Goyette, Charles H., Conners, C. Keith, et al., "Effects of artificial colors in hyperkinetic children. A double-blind challenge study," *Psychopharmacology Bulletin* 13 (1984), pp. 39–40.

Grabe, Mark, and Grabe, Cindy, "The microcomputer and the language experience approach," *The Reading Teacher* Vol. 38 (February 1985), pp. 508–11.

Granschow, Leonore, "Analyze error patterns to remediate severe spelling difficulties," *The Reading Teacher* Vol. 38 (December 1984), pp. 288–93.

Graves, Donald H., *Writing: Teachers and Children at Work* (Exeter, N.H.: Heinemann, 1983).

Gray, David B., and Kavanagh, James F., *Biobehavioral Measures of Dyslexia* (Parkton, Md.: York Press, 1985).

Griffiths, Anita N., *Teaching the Dyslexic Child* (Novato, Calif.: Academic Therapy, 1978).

Gross-Glenn, Karen, Lewis, D. C., Smith, Shelley D., and Lubs, H. A., "Phenotype of adult familial dyslexia: Reading of visually transformed texts and nonsense passages," *International Journal of Neuroscience* Vol. 28 (1985), pp. 49–59.

Grossman, Ronald P., "XY and LD," *Journal of Learning Disabilities* Vol. 16 (January 1983), p. 65.

Gunning, Thomas G., "Wrong level test: Wrong information," *The Reading Teacher* Vol. 35, No. 8 (May 1982), pp. 902–5.

Guthrie, John T., "Research views: Classroom management," *The Reading Teacher* Vol. 36, No. 6 (February 1983), pp. 606–8.

Hall, Mary Anne, *Teaching Reading as a Language Experience* (Columbus, Ohio: Charles E. Merrill, 1981).

Hallahan, Daniel P., and Cruickshank, William M., *Psychoeducational Foundations of Learning Disabilities* (Englewood Cliffs, N.J.: Prentice-Hall, 1973).

Hallgren, Bertil, *Specific Dyslexia ("Congenital Word-Blindness"); A Clinical and Genetic Study* (Copenhagen: Ejnar Munksgaard, 1950). Translated from the Swedish by Erica Odelberg. (Stockholm: Esselte aktiebolag, 1950).

Hanley, John, and Sklar, Bernard, "Electroencephalographic correlates of developmental reading dyslexia: Computer analysis of recordings from normal and dyslexic children," in Gerald Leisman, ed., *Basic Visual Processes and Learning Disability* (Springfield, Ill.: Charles C. Thomas, 1976), pp. 217–43.

Harley, J. Preston, Ray, Roberta S., Tomasi, Lawrence, et al., "Hyperkinesis and food additives: Testing the Feingold hypothesis," *Pediatrics* 61 (1978), pp. 818–28.

Harris, Albert J., and Sipay, Edward R., *How to Increase Reading Ability*, 7th and 8th eds. (New York: Longman Press, 1980, 1985).

_____, *How to Teach Reading* (New York: Longman Press, 1979).

_____, *Readings on Reading Instruction*, 3rd ed. (New York: Longman Press, 1984).

Harris, Larry A., and Smith, Carl B., *Reading Instruction, Diagnostic Teaching in the Classroom*, 3rd ed. (New York: Holt, Rinehart and Winston, 1980).

Harris, Larry A., and Smith, Carl B., *Reading Instruction, Diagnostic Teaching in the Classroom,* 4th ed. (New York: Macmillan, 1986).

Hartman, Rhona C., and Krulwich, Maxine T., "Learning disabled adults in postsecondary education," *Health Resource Center* (Washington, D.C.: Higher Education and the Handicapped Resource Center, 1983), pp. 1–11.

Hartwig, Elinor L., ed., "History of the research division," *Medical Research Update: Perspectives on Dyslexia* (Baltimore, Md.: The Orton Dyslexia Society, 1984).

Haslam, Robert H. A., Dalby, J. Thomas, Johns, Robert D., and Rademaker, Alfred W., "Cerebral asymmetry in developmental dyslexia," *Archives of Neurology* Vol. 38 (November 1981), pp. 679–82.

Heilman, Arthur W., *Phonics in Proper Perspective*, 5th ed. (Columbus, Ohio: Charles E. Merrill, 1985).

Heilman, Arthur W., Blair, Timothy R., and Rupley, William H., *Principles and Practices of Teaching Reading*, 7th, 6th, and 5th eds. (Columbus, Ohio: Charles E. Merrill, 1990, 1986, 1981).

Helfgott, Elayne, Rudel, Rita G., and Dreiger, Jonathan, "Effect of piracetam on reading test performance of dyslexic children," in Dirk J. Bakker, C. R. Wilsher, H. Debruyne, and N. Bertin, eds., *Developmental Dyslexia and Learning Disorders* (New York: Karger, 1987), pp. 110–22.

_____, "Effect of piracetam on the single word and prose reading of dyslexic children," *Psychopharmacology Bulletin* Vol. 20 (Fall 1984), pp. 688–90.

Helveston, Eugene M., "Management of dyslexia and related learning disabilities," *Journal of Learning Disabilities* Vol. 20, No. 7 (August/September 1987), pp. 415–21.

Henderson, Edmund H., and Beers, James W., eds. *Developmental and Cognitive Aspects of Learning to Spell, A Reflection of Word Knowledge* (Newark, Del.: International Reading Association, 1980).

Hennekens, Charles H., Lipnick, Robert J., Mayrent, Sherry L., and Willett, Walter, "Vitamin A and Risk of Cancer," *Journal of Nutrition Education* Vol. 14, No. 4 (December 1982), pp. 135–36.

Hermann, Knud, *Reading Disability, A Medical Study of Word-Blindness and Related Handicaps* (Springfield, Ill.: Charles C. Thomas, 1959).

Herrick, Virgil E., "Children's experiences in writing," in Virgil E. Herrick and Leland B. Jacobs, eds., *Children and the Language Arts* (Englewood Cliffs, N.J.: Prentice-Hall, 1955), pp. 271–72.

Hier, Daniel B., LeMay, Marjorie, Rosenberger, Peter B., and Perlo, Vincent P., "Developmental dyslexia, evidence for a subgroup with a reversal of cerebral asymmetry," *Archives of Neurology* Vol. 35 (February 1978), pp. 90–92.

Hillerich, Robert, "Let's teach spelling—not phonetic misspelling," *Language Arts* Vol. 54 (March 1977), pp. 301–307.

Hinshelwood, James, "A case of dyslexia: A peculiar form of word-blindness," *The Lancet* (November 21, 1896), pp. 1451–54.

———, "A case of 'word' without 'letter' blindness," *The Lancet* (Feb. 12, 1898), pp. 422–25.

———, "Congenital word-blindness," *The Lancet* (May 26, 1900), pp. 1506–8.

———, *Congenital Word-Blindness* (London: H. K. Lewis, 1917).

———, *Letter-, word-, and mind-blindness* (London: H. K. Lewis, 1900).

———, "Word-blindness and visual memory," *The Lancet* (Dec. 21, 1895), pp. 1564–70.

"History of the research division of the Orton dyslexia society," *Perspectives on Dyslexia: Medical Research Update* (May 1987), pp. 1–4.

Hochberg, Julian, "Attention in perception and reading," in Francis A. Young and Donald B. Lindsley, eds., *Early Experience and Visual Information Processing in Perceptual and Reading Disorders* (Washington, D.C.: National Academy of Sciences, 1970), pp. 319–624.

Hoffer, A., and Osmond, H., *The Chemical Basis of Clinical Psychiatry* (Springfield, Ill.: Charles C. Thomas, 1960).

Horn, Ernest, "Spelling," *Encyclopedia of Educational Research*, 3rd ed. (New York: Macmillan, 1960), p. 1337.

Hornsby, Bevé, *Overcoming Dyslexia* (New York: Arco, 1984).

Housman, David, Smith, Shelley D., and Pauls, David, "Applications of recombinant DNA techniques to neurogenetic disorders," in David B. Gray and James F. Kavanagh, eds., *Biobehavioral Measures of Dyslexia* (Parkton, Md.: York Press, 1987), pp. 155–62.

Hsu, Chen-chin, "Correlates of reading success and failure in logographic writing system," *Thalamus* Vol. 6 (Spring 1988), pp. 33–59.

Huey, Edmund Burke, *The Psychology and Pedagogy of Reading* (Cambridge, Mass.: MIT Press, 1908/1968).

Hughs, John R., "The electroencephalogram and reading disorders," in R. N. Malatesha and P. G. Aaron, eds., *Reading Disorders, Varieties and Treatments* (New York: Academic Press, 1982), pp. 234–53.

———, "Evaluation of electrophysiological studies on dyslexia," in David B. Gray and James F. Kavanagh, eds., *Biobehavioral Measures of Dyslexia* (Parkton, Md.: York Press, 1987), pp. 71–86.

Huston, Anne Marshall, "Dyslexia, who can have it?", *Journal of Instructional Psychology* Vol. 14, No. 4 (December 1987), pp. 201–5.

———, "Helping students with auditory memory problems," *The Guidance Clinic* (January 1988), pp. 7–12.

———, "Reading and writing problems: The difficulties of early identification," *The Journal of the Virginia College Reading Educators* Vol. 8, No. 1 (Spring 1988), pp. 53–70.

———, "In one ear and out the other; How to stop it inbetween—Or, the effects of poor auditory memory on reading and writing," paper read at The Reading Association of Ireland, 13th Annual Conference, Dublin, Ireland (September 17, 1988).

Huttenlocher, Janellen, and Burke, Deborah, "Why does memory span increase with age?" *Cognitive Psychology* Vol. 8 (1976), pp. 1–31.

Hynd, George W., and Cohen, Morris, *Dyslexia, Neuropsychological Theory, Research, and Clinical Differentiation* (New York: Grune & Stratton, 1983).

Hynd, George W., and Hynd, Cynthia R., "Dyslexia: Neuroanatomical/neurolinguistic perspectives," *Reading Research Quarterly* Vol. 19, No. 4 (Summer 1984), pp. 482–98.

Hynd, George W., and Semrud-Clikeman, Margaret, "Dyslexia and neurodevelopmental pathology: Relationships to cognition, intelligence, and reading skill acquisition," *Journal of Learning Disabilities* Vol. 22, No. 4 (April 1989), pp. 204–16, 220.

Ingram, T. T. S., Mason, A. W., and Blackburn, J., "A retrospective study of 82 children with reading disability," *Developmental Medicine and Child Neurology* 12 (1970), pp. 271–81.

Ingram, Thomas T. S., "The nature of dyslexia," in Francis A. Young and Donald B. Lindsley, eds., *Early Experience and Visual Information Processing in Perceptual and Reading Disorders* (Washington, D.C.: National Academy of Sciences, 1970), pp. 405–44.

Inouye, Dillon K., and Sorenson, Matthew R., "Profiles of dyslexia: The computer as an instrument of vision," in David B. Gray and James F. Kavanagh, eds., *Biobehavioral Measures of Dyslexia* 3 (Parkton, Md.: York Press, 1987), pp. 297–321.

Irlen, Helen, "Successful treatment of learning disabilities,"paper presented to American Psychological Association, August 1983.

Jacob, Stanley W., Francone, Clarice A., and Lossow, Walter J., *Structure and Function in Man*, 4th ed. (Philadelphia: W. B. Saunders, 1978).

Jansky, Jeannette, and De Hirsch, Katrina, *Preventing Reading Failure: Prediction, Diagnosis, Intervention* (New York: Harper and Row, 1972).

Jenkins, R. L., Brown, A. W., and Elmerdorf, L., "Mixed dominance and reading disability," as cited in Edith Zerbin-Rubin, "Congenital word-blindness," *Bulletin of the Orton Society* Vol. 17 (1967), pp. 47–54.

Johnson, Doris J., "Persistent auditory disorders in young dyslexics," *Bulletin of the Orton Society* Vol. 30 (1980), pp. 268–76.

——, "Remediation for dyslexic adults," in George Th. Pavlidis, ed., *Dyslexia: Its Neuropsychology and Treatment* (New York: John Wiley, 1986), pp. 249–62.

Johnson, Doris J., and Myklebust, Helmer R., *Learning Disabilities, Educational Principles and Practices* (New York: Grune and Stratton, 1967).

Jordan, Dale R., *Dyslexia in the Classroom*, 2nd ed. (Columbus, Ohio: Charles E. Merrill, 1977).

Kail, Robert V., Jr., and Hagen, John W., eds., *Perspectives on the Development of Memory and Cognition* (Hillsdale, N.J.: Lawrence Erlbaum, 1977).

Kaluger, George, and Kolson, Clifford J., *Reading and Learning Disabilities* (Columbus, Ohio: Charles E. Merrill, 1978).

Karlin, Robert, *Teaching Elementary Reading, Principles and Strategies*, 3rd ed. (New York: Harcourt Brace Jovanovich, 1980).

Karnowski, Lee, "Using LEA with process writing," *The Reading Teacher* Vol. 42, No. 7 (March 1989), pp. 462–65.

Katzman, Robert, ed., *Congenital and Acquired Cognitive Disorders* (New York: Raven Press, 1979).

Kavanagh, James F., and Mattingly, Ignatius G., eds., *Language by Ear and by Eye* (Cambridge, Mass.: MIT Press, 1972).

Kavanagh, James F., and Venezky, Richard L., *Orthography, Reading and Dyslexia* (Baltimore: University Park Press, 1980).

Kemper, Thomas L., "Asymmetrical lesions in dyslexia," in Norman Geschwind and Albert M. Galaburda, eds., *Cerebral Dominance, The Biological Foundations* (Cambridge, Mass.: Harvard University Press, 1984), pp. 75–86.

Kennedy, Helen, "Reversals, reversals, reversals!" *Journal of Experimental Education* Vol. 23 (December 1954), pp. 161–70.

Keogh, Barbara K., and Pelland, Michele, "Vision training revisited," *Journal of Learning Disabilities* Vol. 18, No. 4 (April 1985), pp. 228–36.

Kerr, James, "School hygiene, in its mental, moral, and physical aspects," *Journal of the Royal Statistical Society* Vol. 60 (1897), pp. 613–80.

Kinsbourne, Marcel, "The analysis of learning deficit with special reference to selective attention," in Dirk J. Bakker and Paul Satz, eds., *Specific Reading Disability: Advances in Theory and Method* (The Netherlands: Rotterdam University Press, 1970), pp. 115–22.

———, "Developmental gerstmann syndrome," *Pediatric Clinics of North America* Vol. 15, No. 3 (August 1968), pp. 771–77.

———, "Minimal brain dysfunction as a neurodevelopmental lag," *Annals of the New York Academy of Sciences* Vol. 205 (1973), pp. 268–73.

———, "Models of dyslexia and its subtypes," in George Th. Pavlidis, ed., *Dyslexia: Its Neuropsychology and Treatment* (New York: John Wiley, 1986), pp. 165–80.

———, "Prospects for the study of developmental reading backwardness," *The British Journal of Disorders of Communication* Vol. 2, No. 2 (1967), pp. 152–54.

———, "The role of selective attention in reading disability," in P. G. Aaron and R. N. Malatesha, eds., *Reading Disorders, Varieties and Treatments* (New York: Academic Press, 1982), pp. 199–214.

Kirby, Edward A., and Grimley, Liam K., *Understanding and Treating Attention Deficit Disorder,* 4 (New York: Pergamon Press, 1986).

Klasen, Edith, "Helping dyslexics—A task for sharing," *Annals of Dyslexia* Vol. 38 (1988), pp. 22–30.

———, *The Syndrome of Specific Dyslexia* (Baltimore: University Park Press, 1972).

Kline, Carl L., and Kline, Carolyn L., "Follow-up study of 216 dyslexic children," *Bulletin of The Orton Society* Vol. 25 (1975), pp. 127–44.

Kohlmorgen, William H., "A Study of the effects of Delacato's program of neurological organization on reading achievement," Doctoral dissertation, New York University, 1971.

Kolers, Paul A., "Three stages of reading," in Harry Levin and Joanna Williams, eds., *Basic Studies in Reading* (New York: Basic Books, 1970), pp. 90–118. Also in Frank Smith ed., *Psycholinguistics and Reading* (New York: Holt, Rinehart and Winston, 1973).

Koppitz, Elizabeth M., *The Bender Gestalt Test for Young Children* (New York: Grune and Stratton, 1971).

LaBuda, Michele C., and DeFries, J. C., "Genetic and environmental etiologies of reading disability: A twin study," *Annals of Dyslexia* Vol. 38 (1988), pp. 131–38.

Lapp, Diane, and Flood, James, *Teaching Reading to Every Child* (New York: Macmillan, 1978).

Larrick, Nancy, *A Parent's Guide to Children's Reading*, 4th ed. (New York: Bantam Books, 1975).

Lebrun, Y., "Dyslexia in left-handers," in D. J. Bakker, Colin R. Wilsher, H. Debruyne, and N. Bertin, eds., *Developmental Dyslexia and Learning Disorders* (New York: Karger, 1987), pp. 148–56.

Lee, Y. C., ed., *Annual Report of the Tung-mun Elementary School*, (Taipei: Taipei City Bureau of Education, 1986).

Leedy, Paul D., *Practical Research, Planning and Design*, 2nd ed. (New York: Macmillan, 1980).

Lehr, Fran, "Grade repetition vs. social promotion," *The Reading Teacher* Vol. 36, No. 2 (November 1982), pp. 234–237.

LeMay, Marjorie, "Are there radiological changes in the brains of individuals with dyslexia?" *Bulletin of the Orton Society* Vol. 31 (1981), pp. 135–41.

Lenkowsky, Linda Klein, and Saposnek, Donald T., "Family consequences of parental dyslexia," *Journal of Learning Disabilities* Vol. ll, No. 1 (January 1978), pp. 59–65.

Lerner, Janet W., *Children with Learning Disabilities* (Boston: Houghton Mifflin, 1971).

———, "Learning disabilities and cultural diversity," *Educators' FORUM* (Boston: Houghton Mifflin, Fall 1989), p. 3.

———, "Learning disabilities in jeopardy," *ACLD Newsbriefs* 176 (September/October, 1988), pp. 9, 24.

———, "Remedial reading and learning disabilities: Are they the same or different?" *Journal of Special Education* Vol. 9 (Feb. 19, 1975), pp. 119–31.

Levi, G., and Sechi, E., "A study of piracetam in the pharmacological treatment of learning disabilities," in Dirk J. Bakker et al., eds. *Developmental Dyslexia and Learning Disorders* (New York: Karger, 1987), pp. 128–39.

Levin, Harry, and Williams, Joanna P., eds., *Basic Studies on Reading* (New York: Basic Books, 1970).

Levinson, Harold N., *Smart But Feeling Dumb* (New York: Warner Books, 1984).

———, *A Solution to the Riddle Dyslexia* (New York: Springer-Verlag, 1980).

Ley, J., and Tordeur, G. W., "Alexie et agraphie d'évolution chez des jumeaux monozygotiques," *Journal Belgium Neurological Psychiatry* Vol. 36 (1936), p. 102, as cited in Edith Zerbin-Rubin, "Congenital word-blindness," *Bulletin of the Orton Society* Vol. 17 (1967), pp. 47–54.

Liberman, Alvin M., "General discussion of Templin's study of articulation and language development during the early school years," in Frank Smith and George A. Miller, eds., *The Genesis of Language, A Psycholinguistic Approach* (Cambridge, Mass.: MIT Press, 1966).

Link, Arthur S., *Wilson, The Road to the White House* (Princeton, N.J.: Princeton University Press, 1947).

Linksz, Arthur, *On Writing, Reading, and Dyslexia* (New York: Grune and Stratton, 1973).

"Literacy award presented to Barbara Bush," *Newsletter* (Virginia State Reading Association, Fall 1987).

Loban, Walter, "What language reveals," in James B. MacDonald and Robert R. Leeper, eds., *Language and Meaning* (Washington, D.C.: Association for Supervision and Curriculum Development, 1966), p. 73.

Loomer, Bradley M., *Educator's Guide to Spelling Research and Practice* (Des Moines, Iowa: Iowa State Department of Public Instruction; Iowa City, Iowa: University of Iowa, 1978), pp. 1–33.

Losen, Stuart M., and Losen, Joyce Garskof, *The Special Education Team* (Boston: Allyn and Bacon, 1985).

Lovett, Maureen W., "A developmental perspective on reading dysfunction: Accuracy and rate criteria in the subtyping of dyslexic children," *Brain and Language* Vol. 22 (1984), pp. 67–91.

———, "The search for subtypes of specific reading disability: Reflections from a cognitive perspective," *Annals of Dyslexia* Vol. 34 (1984), pp. 155–78.

Ludlow, Christy L., and Cooper, Judith A., eds., *Genetic Aspects of Speech and Language Disorders* (New York: Academic Press, 1983).

Mackworth, Norman H., "Visual noise causes tunnel vision," *Psychonomic Science* Vol. 3 (1965), pp. 67–68.

Makita, Kiyoshi, "The rarity of reading disability in Japanese children," *American Journal of Orthopsychiatry* Vol. 38 (1968), pp. 599–614.

Malatesha, R. N., and Dougan, Deborah R., "Clinical subtypes of developmental dyslexia," in R. N. Malatesha and P. G. Aaron, eds., *Reading Disorders, Varieties and Treatments* (New York: Academic Press, 1982), pp. 69–92.

Malatesha, R. N., and Whitaker, H. A., *Dyslexia: A Global Issue* (Boston: Martinus Nijhoff, 1984).

Malmstrom, Jean, *Understanding Language, A Primer for the Language Arts Teacher* (New York: St. Martin's Press, 1977).

Maloney, Justine, "Public Law 99–372, the handicapped children's protection act, deemed significant," *ACLD Newsbriefs* Vol. 176 (September/October 1988), p. 21.

Manis, Franklin R., Szeszulski, Patricia A., Holt, Liana K., and Graves, Kathryn, "A developmental perspective on dyslexic subtypes," *Annals of Dyslexia* Vol. 38 (1988), pp. 139–53.

Marain, S. Donald, ed., *Human Development and Reading Instruction* (Cambridge, Mass.: Educators Publishing, 1977).

Martin, Reed, "The teacher's rights in PL. 94–142," editor's interview, "A Conversation with Attorney Reed Martin," *Journal of Learning Disabilities* Vol. 2 (June/July 1978), pp. 4–14.

Marzano, Robert J., Hagerty, Patricia J., Valencia, Sheila W., and DiStefano, Philip P., *Reading Diagnosis and Instruction, Theory Into Practice* (Englewood Cliffs, N.J.: Prentice-Hall, 1987).

Masland, Richard L., "The advantages of being dyslexic," *Bulletin of the Orton Society* Vol. 26 (1976), pp. 10–18.

Masland, Richard, and Usprich, Celia, review of Levinson's book in *Bulletin of the Orton Society* Vol. 31 (1981), pp. 256–61.

Mason, George E., "The computer in the reading clinic," *The Reading Teacher* Vol. 36, No. 6 (February 1983), pp. 504–6.

———, "The word processor and teaching reading," *The Reading Teacher* Vol. 37, No. 6 (February 1984), pp. 552–53.

Massaro, Dominic V., ed., *Understanding Language, An Information-Processing Analysis of Speech Perception, Reading, and Psycholinguistics* (New York: Academic Press, 1975).

Matejek, Zdenek with Rawson, Margaret B., "Dyslexia, an international problem: A report from Czechoslovakia," *Bulletin of the Orton Society* Vol. 15 (1965), pp. 24–30.

Mattes, Jeffrey A., "The Feingold Diet: a current reappraisal," *Journal of Learning Disabilities* Vol. 16, No. 6 (June/July 1983), pp. 319–23.

Mattis, Steven, French, Joseph H., and Rapin, Isabelle, "Dyslexia in children and young adults: Three independent neuropsychological syndromes," *Developmental Medicine and Child Neurology* Vol. 17 (1975), pp. 150–63.

McCarthy, James J., and McCarthy, Joan F., *Learning Disabilities* (Boston: Allyn and Bacon, 1969).

McClelland, Jane, "Adolescents: It's never too late to learn," *Bulletin of the Orton Society* Vol. 24 (1974), pp. 141–53.

McCorduck, Pamela, and Russell, Avery, "Computers in the schools," *The Key Reporter* (Washington, D.C.: Phi Beta Kappa, Winter 1986–1987), pp. 2–4.

McGrady, Harold J., "Eligibility: Back to basics," in Sharon Vaughn and Candace S. Bos, eds., *Research on Learning Disabilities* (New York: College-Hill, 1987), pp. 105–15.

McKeever, Walter F., and VanDeventer, Allan D., "Dyslexic adolescents: Evidence of impaired visual and auditory language processing associated with normal lateralization and visual responsivity," *Cortex* Vol. 11 (1975), pp. 361–78.

McKinney, James D., "Research on the identification of learning-disabled children: Perspectives on changes in educational policy," in Sharon Vaughn and Candace S. Bos, eds., *Research in Learning Disabilities, Issues and Future Directions* (Boston: College-Hill, 1987), pp. 215–37.

———, "The search for subtypes of specific learning disability," *Journal of Learning Disabilities* Vol. 17, No. 1 (January 1984), pp. 43–50.

McNeil, John D., *Reading Comprehension, New Directions for Classroom Practice* (Glenview, Ill.: Scott, Foresman, Inc., 1984).

McWilliams, John R., "Eye," *The World Book Encyclopedia* Vol. 6 (Chicago: Ill.: Field Enterprises Educational Corp., 1969, 1985), pp. 357–63.

"Megavitamin and orthomolecular therapy in psychiatry: Excerpts from the Report of the Task Force on Vitamin Therapy in Psychiatry," *Nutrition Review* Vol. 32 (1974), p. 44.

Mencken, H. L., *The American Language, An Inquiry Into the Development of English in the United States* (New York: Alfred A. Knopf, 1980).

Menyuk, Paula, *The Acquisition and Development of Language* (Englewood Cliffs, N.J.: Prentice-Hall, 1971).

_____, *Language and Maturation* (Cambridge, Mass.: MIT Press, 1977).

Mercer, Cecil D., *Students With Learning Disabilities* (Columbus, Ohio: Charles E. Merrill, 1983).

_____, *Students With Learning Disabilities,* 3rd. ed. (Columbus, Ohio: Merrill, 1987).

Metzger, Richard L., and Werner, David B., "Use of visual training for reading disabilities: A review," *Pediatrics* Vol. 73, No. 6 (June 1984), pp. 824–29.

Miccinati, Jeannette, "The Fernald technique: Modifications increase the probability of success," *Journal of Learning Disabilities* Vol. 12, No. 3 (March 1979), pp. 6–9.

Micklos, John, "Reading levels of newspapers," *Reading Today '84* Vol. 1, No. 4 (International Reading Association, February 1984).

Miles, T. R., "Dyslexia: Anomaly or normal variation?" *Annals of Dyslexia* Vol. 36 (1986), pp. 103–17.

_____, *Dyslexia, the Pattern of Difficulties* (Springfield, Ill.: Charles C. Thomas, 1983).

_____, "On the persistence of dyslexic difficulties into adulthood," in George Th. Pavlidis, ed., *Dyslexia: Its Neuropsychology and Treatment* (New York: John Wiley, 1986), pp. 149–63.

Miles, T. R., and Miles, Elaine, *Help for Dyslexic Children* (London: Methuen, 1983).

Miller, George A., *The Psychology of Communication* (New York: Basic Books, 1967).

Moats, Louisa Cook, "A Comparison of the spelling errors of older dyslexic and second-grade normal children," *Annals of Dyslexia* Vol. 33 (1983), pp. 121–40.

Money, John, ed., *Reading Disability, Progress and Research Needs in Dyslexia* (Baltimore: Johns Hopkins Press, 1962).

Morency, Anne, "Auditory modality, research and practice," in Helen K. Smith, ed., *Perception and Reading* (Newark, Del.: International Reading Association, 1968), Vol. 12, Part 4, pp. 17–21.

Morgan, W. Pringle, "A case of congenital word blindness," *British Medical Journal* (Nov. 7, 1896), p. 1378.

Moyer, Sandra B., and Newcomer, Phyllis L., "Reversals in reading: Diagnosis and remediation," *Exceptional Children* Vol. 43, No. 7 (April 1977), pp. 424–29.

Murray, Joseph N., "Understanding and use of chemotherapy by learning disabilities and behavior disorders teachers," *Journal of Learning Disabilities* Vol. 13, No. 7 (August/September 1980), pp. 356–60.

Mussen, Paul H., Conger, John J., and Kagan, Jerome, *Readings in Child Development and Personality,* 2nd ed. (New York: Harper and Row, 1970).

Myklebust, Helmer J., *Development and Disorders of Written Language, Picture Story Language Test* Vol. 1 (New York: Grune and Stratton, 1965).

———, *Development and Disorders of Written Language, Studies of Normal and Exceptional Children* Vol. 2 (New York: Grune and Stratton, 1973).

———, ed., *Progress in Learning Disabilities* Vol. II (New York: Grune and Stratton, 1971).

———, ed., *Progress in Learning Disabilities* Vol. IV (New York: Grune and Stratton, 1978).

Naidoo, Sandhya, *Specific Dyslexia, The Research Report of the ICAA Word Blind Centre for Dyslexic Children* (New York: John Wiley, 1972).

———, "Symposium on reading disability: Specific developmental dyslexia," *British Journal of Educational Psychology* Vol. 41 (February 1971), pp. 19–21.

National Institute of Health, Conference on "Defined diets and childhood hyperactivity," *Journal of the American Medical Association* Vol. 245 (1982), pp. 290–92.

NATO Advanced Study Institute on Dyslexia: A Global Issue, Dyslexia, The Hague, published in cooperation with NATO Scientific Affairs Division (Hingham, Mass.: M. Nishoff, 1984).

Newby, Robert F., Caldwell, JoAnne, and Recht, Donna R., "Improving the reading comprehension of children with dysphonetic and dyseidetic dyslexia using story grammar," *Journal of Learning Disabilities* Vol. 22, No. 6 (June/July 1989), pp. 373–80.

Newton, Margaret, and Thomson, Michael, *Dyslexia, A Guide for Teachers and Parents* (London: University of London Press, 1975).

Noblitt, Gerald L., "Rejoinder on using scores from standardized reading tests," *The Reading Teacher* Vol. 36, No. 4 (January 1983), pp. 452–53.

Nolan, William, and Siegel, Paul, "Remediating letter reversals: Cost Considerations," *Journal of Learning Disabilities* Vol. 13, No. 9 (November 1980), pp. 483–86.

Norrie, E., "Ordblindhedens (dyslexiens) arvegang. Laesepaedagogen" 2 (1954), p. 61, as cited in Knud Hermann, *Reading Disability, A Medical Study of Word-Blindness and Related Handicaps* (Springfield, Ill.: Charles C. Thomas, 1959), and by Edith Zerbin-Rubin, "Congenital word-blindness," *Bulletin of the Orton Society* Vol. 17 (1967), pp. 45–55.

Obrzut, John E., "Dyslexia and neurodevelopmental pathology: Is the neurodiagnostic technology ahead of the psychoeducational technology?" *Journal of Learning Disabilities* Vol. 22, No. 4 (April 1989), pp. 217–18.

O'Donnell, P. A., and Eisenson, J., "Delacato training for reading achievement and visual-motor integration," *Journal of Learning Disabilities* Vol. 2 (1969), pp. 441–46.

Olson, David R., "Language and thought: Aspects of a cognitive theory of semantics," *Psychological Review* Vol. 77 (July 1970), pp. 257–73.

Olson, Richard, Wise, Barbara, Conners, Frances, Rack, John, and Fulker, David,

"Specific deficits in component reading and language skills: Genetic and environmental influences," *Journal of Learning Disabilities* Vol. 22, No. 6 (June/July 1989), pp. 339–48.

Omenn, Gilbert S., and Weber, Bruce A., "Dyslexia: Search for phenotypic and genetic heterogeneity," *American Journal of Medical Genetics* Vol. 1 (1978), pp. 333–42.

Orton, Samuel T., "'Word-blindness' in school children," *Archives of Neurology and Psychiatry* Vol. 14, No. 5 (November 1925), pp. 581–615.

_____, *Reading, Writing and Speech Problems in Children* (New York: W. W. Norton, 1937).

Otto, Wayne, and Smith, Richard J., *Corrective and Remedial Teaching* (Boston: Houghton Mifflin, 1980).

Outhred, Lynne, "Word processing: Its impact on children's writing," *Journal of Learning Disabilities* Vol. 22, No. 4 (April 1989), pp. 262–63.

Owen, Freda W., Adams, P. A., Forrest, T., Stolz, L. M., and Fisher, S., "Learning disorders in children: Sibling studies," *Monographs of the Society for Research in Child Development* Vol. 36 (Chicago: University of Chicago Press, 1971).

Palermo, David S., and Molfese, Dennis L., "Language acquisition from age five onward," *Psychological Bulletin* Vol. 78, No. 6 (December 1972), pp. 409–28.

Patel, P., et al., "Intoxication from vitamin A in an asthmatic child," *Canadian Medical Association Journal* Vol. 139 (October 15, 1988), pp. 755–56.

Pauling, Linus, "Orthomolecular psychiatry," *Science* Vol. 160 (April 1968), pp. 265–71.

Pavlidis, George Th., "Eye movements in dyslexia: Their diagnostic significance," *Journal of Learning Disabilities* Vol. 18, No. 1 (January 1985), pp. 42–50.

_____, "The role of eye movements in the diagnosis of dyslexia," in George Th. Pavlidis, ed., *Dyslexia: Its Neuropsychology and Treatment* (New York: John Wiley, 1986), pp. 97–110.

Pavlidis, George, and Mills, T. R., eds., *Dyslexia Research and Its Applications to Education* (New York: John Wiley, 1981).

Pearson, P. David, ed., *Reading Theory, Research and Practice* (Clemson, S.C.: The National Reading Conference, 1977).

Pennington, Bruce F., "Issues in the diagnosis and phenotype analysis of dyslexia: Implications for family studies," in Shelley D. Smith, ed., *Genetics and Learning Disabilities* (San Diego, Calif.: College-Hill, 1986), pp. 69–96.

Perlo, Vincent P., and Rak, Elsie T., "Developmental dyslexia in adults," *Neurology* Vol. 21 (December 1971), pp. 1231–35.

Perry, Anthony R., Dember, William N., Warm, Joel S., and Sacks, Joel G., "Letter identification in normal and dyslexic readers: A verification," *Bulletin of the Psychonomic Society* Vol 27, No. 5 (1989), pp. 445–48.

Petty, Walter T., and Jensen, Julie M., *Developing Children's Language* (Boston: Allyn and Bacon, 1980).

Petty, Walter T., Petty, Dorothy C., and Becking, Marjorie F., *Experiences in Language, Tools and Techniques for Language Arts Methods* (Boston: Allyn and Bacon, 1973).

Piaget, Jean, "The stages of the intellectual development of the child," in Paul Henry Mussen, John Janeway Conger, and Jerome Kagan, eds., *Readings in Child Development and Personality*, 2nd ed. (New York: Harper and Row, 1970), pp. 291–98.

Picturesque Word Origins (Springfield, Mass.: Merriam, 1933).

Pirozzolo, Francis J., "Language and brain: Neuropsychological aspects of developmental reading disability," *School Psychology Review* Vol. 10, No. 8 (1981), pp. 350–55.

————, *The Neuropsychology of Developmental Reading Disorders* (New York: Praeger, 1979).

Public Law 94–142, Education of the Handicapped Act of 1975. The implementation of Part B dealing with specific learning disabilities, *Federal Register* (Dec. 29, 1977), effective September 1978.

Public Law 99–372, The Handicapped Children's Protection Act, restoring the partnership of PL 94–142 and Section 504, *Federal Register* (August 1986).

Purtell, Thelma C., *Can't Read, Can't Write, Can't Talk Too Good Either* (New York: Walker, 1973).

Rawson, Margaret B., *Developmental Language Disability: Adult Accomplishments of Dyslexic Boys* (Baltimore: Johns Hopkins Press, 1968).

————, "The many faces of dyslexia," *Annals of Dyslexia* Vol. 36 (1986), pp. 179–91.

Rayner, Keith, "Eye movements and the perceptual span: Evidence for dyslexic typology," in George Th. Pavlidis, ed., *Dyslexia: Its Neuropsychology and Treatment* (New York: John Wiley, 1986), pp. 111–30.

"Reading disorders in children," *The Journal of the American Medical Association* Vol. 206, No. 3 (Oct. 14, 1968).

"Readings . . . Finding New York's Finest," *Harper's* (February 1986), pp. 16–18.

Reese, Hayne W., ed., *Advances in Child Development and Behavior* (New York: Academic Press, 1975).

Reid, D. Kim, and Hresko, Wayne P., eds., *Topics in Learning and Learning Disabilities: Issues in Reading Diagnosis* Vol. 2, No. 4 (January 1983) (Gaithersburg, Md.: Aspen Systems).

Reinhold, Robert, "A therapy system for young scored," *The New York Times* (May 7, 1968), p. 42.

Restak, Richard M., *The Brain* (New York: Bantam Books, 1984).

Richardson, Ellis, "The reliability, validity, and flexibility of the Decoding Skills Test for reading research," in David B. Gray and James F. Kavanagh, eds., *Biobehavioral Measures of Dyslexia* (Parkton, Md.: York Press, 1987), pp. 279–96.

Ringler, Lenore H. and Weber, Carol K., *A Language-Thinking Approach to Reading Diagnosis and Teaching* (New York: Harcourt Brace Jovanovich, 1984).

Robeck, Mildred C., and Wilson, John A. R., *Psychology of Reading: Foundations of Instruction* (New York: John Wiley, 1974).

Robbins, Melvyn P., "A Study of the validity of Delacato's theory of neurological organization," *Exceptional Children* Vol. 32 (1966), pp. 517–23.

Rockefeller, Nelson A., "Don't accept anyone's verdict that you are lazy, stupid or retarded," *TV Guide* (Oct. 16, 1978), pp. 12–14.

"The Role of the Ophthalmologist in Dyslexia," report of an international seminar held in Indianapolis, Indiana; Institute for Development of Educational Activities, an affiliate of the Charles F. Kettering Foundation, IDEA, Melbourne, Florida, 1969.

Rourke, Byron P., Bakker, Dirk J., Fisk, John L., and Strang, John D., *Child Neuropsychology, an Introduction to Theory, Research, and Clinical Practice* (New York: Guilford Press, 1983).

Rowe, Mary Budd, "Wait-time and rewards as instructional variables, their influence on language, logic, and fate control: Part one—wait-time," *Journal of Research in Science Teaching* Vol. 2 (1974), pp. 81–94.

Rowse, A. L., "Why a contemporary Shakespeare?" in *King Lear* (Lanham, Md.: University Press of America, 1984), pp. 3–19.

Rubin, Dorothy, *Diagnosis and Correction in Reading Instruction* (New York: Holt, Rinehart and Winston, 1982).

Rumsey, Judith M., Berman, Karen F., Denckla, Martha B., Hamburger, Susan D., Kruesi, Markus J., and Weinberger, Daniel R., "Regional cerebral blood flow in severe developmental dyslexia," *Archives of Neurology* Vol. 44 (November 1987), pp. 1144–50.

Rumsey, Judith M., Dorwart, Robert, Vermess, Michael, Denckla, Martha B., Kruesi, Markus J., and Rapoport, Judith L., "Magnetic resonance imaging of brain anatomy in severe developmental dyslexia," *Archives of Neurology* Vol. 43 (October 1986), pp. 1045–46.

Rupley, William H., and Blair, Timothy R., *Reading Diagnosis and Remediation* (Chicago, Ill.: Rand McNally, 1983).

Rutherford, William L., "What is your D.Q. (Dyslexia Quotient)?" *The Reading Teacher* Vol. 25 (December 1971), pp. 262–66.

Samuels, S. Jay, "Diagnosing reading problems," *Topics in Learning and Learning Disabilities: Issues in Reading Diagnosis* Vol. 2, No. 4 (January 1983) (Gaithersburg, Md.: Aspen Systems), pp. 1–11.

Satz, Paul, Morris, Robin, and Fletcher, Jack M., "Hypotheses, subtypes, and individual differences in dyslexia: Some reflections," in David B. Gray and James F. Kavanagh, eds., *Biobehavioral Measures of Dyslexia* (Parkton, Md.: York Press, 1987), pp. 25–40.

Satz, Paul, and Sparrow, Sara S., "Specific developmental dyslexia: A theoretical formulation," in Dirk J. Bakker and Paul Satz, eds., *Specific Reading Disability: Advances in Theory and Method* (The Netherlands: Rotterdam University Press, 1970), p. 17 ff.

Scarborough, Hollis S., "Continuity between childhood dyslexia and adult reading," *British Journal of Psychology* Vol. 75 (1984), pp. 329–48.

Schiller, M., "Zwillingsprobleme, dargestellt auf Grund von Untersuchungen an Stuttgarter Zwillingen," *Z. Menschl. Vererb.—U. Konstit.—Lehre* 20 (1937), p. 284, as cited in Edith Zerbin-Rubin, "Congenital word-blindness," *Bulletin of the Orton Society* Vol. 17 (1967), pp. 47–54.

Schmitt, Clara, "Developmental alexia: Congenital word-blindness or inability to learn to read," *The Elementary School Journal* Vol. 18 (1918), pp. 680–88.

School, Beverly A., and Cooper, Arlene, *The IEP Primer* (Novato, Calif.: Academic Therapy, 1979).

Schwalb, Eugene, Blau, Harold, and Blau, Harriet, "Developmental and symptomatic dyslexia: Differential diagnosis and remediation," in Barbara Bateman, ed., *Learning Disorders, Reading* Vol. 4 (1971) (Seattle, Wash.: Special Child Publications), 343–83.

Seidenberg, Mark S., Bruck, Margaret, Fornarolo, Gail, and Backman, Joan, "Who is dyslexic? Reply to Wolf," *Applied Psycholinguistics* Vol. 7 (1986), pp. 77–83.

Share, David L., McGee, Rob, McKenzie, Dean, Williams, Sheila, and Silva, Phil A., "Further evidence relating to the distinction between specific reading retardation and general reading backwardness," *British Journal of Developmental Psychology* Vol. 5 (1987), pp. 35–44.

Shucard, David W., Cummins, Katharine R., Gay, Elizabeth, Lair-Smith, Judy, and Welanko, Phillip, "Electrophysiological studies of reading-disabled children: In search of subtypes," in David B. Gray and James F. Kavanagh, eds. *Biobehavioral Measures of Dyslexia* (Parkton, Md.: York Press, 1987), pp. 87–106.

Shuck, Annette, Ulsh, Florence, and Platt, John S., "Parents encourage pupils (PEP): An inner-city parent involvement reading project," *The Reading Teacher* Vol. 36, No. 6 (February 1983), pp. 524–28.

Silver, Archie A., and Hagin, Rosa A., "Specific reading disability: Follow-up studies," *American Journal of Orthopsychiatry* Vol. 34, No. 1 (1964), pp. 95–102.

————, "Specific reading disability: A twelve-year follow-up study," *American Journal of Orthopsychiatry* Vol. 33 (March 1963), pp. 338–39.

Silver, Larry B., "Acceptable and controversial approaches to treating the child with learning disabilities," *Pediatrics* Vol. 55, No. 3 (March 1975), pp. 406–15.

————, "The 'magic cure': A review of the current controversial approaches for treating learning disabilities," *Journal of Learning Disabilities* Vol. 20, No. 8 (October 1987), pp. 498–504, 513.

Sittig, Linda Harris, "Involving parents and children in reading for fun," *The Reading Teacher* Vol. 36, No. 2 (November 1982), pp. 166–68.

Slobin, Dan I., *Psycholinguistics* (Glenview, Ill.: Scott, Foresman, 1971).

Smith, Frank, ed., *Psycholinguistics and Reading* (New York: Holt, Rinehart and Winston, 1973).

_____, *Reading Without Nonsense* (New York: Teachers College, Columbia University, 1985).

_____, *Understanding Reading* (New York: Holt, Rinehart and Winston, 1971).

_____, *Understanding Reading* (Hillsdale, N.J.: Lawrence Erlbaum, 1988).

Smith, Frank, and Miller, George A., eds., *The Genesis of Language, A Psycholinguistic Approach* (Cambridge, Mass.: MIT Press, 1966).

Smith, Lawrence L., Johns, Jerry L., Ganschow, Leonore, and Masztal, Nancy Browning, "Using grade level vs. out-of-level reading tests with remedial students," *The Reading Teacher* Vol. 36, No. 6 (February 1983), pp. 550–53.

Smith, Nancy J., "The word processing approach to language experience," *The Reading Teacher* Vol. 38 (February 1985), pp. 556–59.

Smith, R. J. and Johnson, D. D., *Teaching Children to Read*, 2nd ed. (Reading, Mass.: Addison-Wesley, 1980).

Smith, Shelley D., and Goldgar, David E., "Single gene analyses and their application to learning disabilities," in Shelley D. Smith, ed., *Genetics and Learning Disabilities* (San Diego, Calif.: College-Hill, 1986).

Smith, Shelley D., Goldgar, David E., Pennington, Bruce F., Kimberling, William J., and Lubs, Herbert A, "Analysis of subtypes of specific reading disability: Genetic and cluster analytic approaches," in George Th. Pavlidis, ed., *Dyslexia: Its Neuropsychology and Treatment* (New York: John Wiley, 1986), pp. 181–202.

Smith, Shelley D., Kimberling, William J., Pennington, Bruce F., and Lubs, Herbert A., "Specific reading disability: Identification of an inherited form through linkage analysis," *Science* Vol. 219 (March 18, 1983), pp. 1345–47.

Smith, Shelley D., Pennington, Bruce F., Kimberling, William J., and Lub, Herbert A., "A genetic analysis of specific reading disability," in Christy L. Ludlow and Judith A. Cooper, eds., *Genetic Aspects of Speech and Language Disorders* (New York: Academic Press, 1983), pp. 169–78.

Snow, Katherine, "A comparative study of sound substitutions used by 'normal' first grade children," *Speech Monographs* Vol. 31 (1964), pp. 135–42.

Snowling, Maggie, Stackhouse, Joy, and Rack, John, "Phonological dyslexia and dysgraphia—a developmental analysis," *Cognitive Neuropsychology* Vol. 3, No. 3 (1986), pp. 309–39.

Snowling, Margaret J., "The development of grapheme-phoneme correspondence in normal and dyslexic readers," *Journal of Experimental Psychology* Vol. 29 (1980), pp. 294–305.

_____, *Dyslexia, A Cognitive Developmental Perspective* (Oxford: Basil Blackwell, 1987).

————, "Phonemic deficits in developmental dyslexia," *Psychological Research* Vol. 43 (1981), pp. 219–234.

Sobotka, Karen R., and May, James G., "Visual evoked potentials and reaction time in normal and dyslexic children," *Psychophysiology* 14 (1977), pp. 12–24.

Spache, George D., *Diagnosing and Correcting Reading Disabilities*, 2nd ed. (Boston: Allyn and Bacon, 1981).

Spache, George D., and Spache, Evelyn B., *Reading in the Elementary School,* 5th ed. (Boston: Allyn and Bacon, 1986).

Sperling, George, "Short-term memory, long-term memory, and scanning in the processing of visual information," in Francis A. Young and Donald B. Lindsley, eds., *Early Experience and Visual Information Processing in Perceptual and Reading Disorders* (Washington, D.C.: National Academy of Sciences, 1970), pp. 198–215.

Spiel, W., "Beitrag zur kongenitalen Lese—und Schreibstorung," *Wien Z. Nervenheilk* 7 (1953), p. 20, as cited in Edith Zerbin-Rubin, "Congenital word-blindness," *Bulletin of the Orton Society* Vol. 17 (1967), pp. 47–54.

Springer, Sally P., and Deutsch, Georg, *Left Brain, Right Brain,* (New York: Freeman, 1985).

Stanovich, Keith E., "Explaining the difference between the dyslexic and the garden-variety poor reader: The phonological-core variable-difference model," *Journal of Learning Disabilities* Vol. 21, No. 10 (December 1988), pp. 590–604, 612.

————, "Matthew effects in reading: some consequences of individual differences in the acquisition of literacy," *Reading Research Quarterly* Vol. 21, No. 4 (Fall 1986), pp. 360–407.

Stanovich, Keith E., Nathan, Ruth G., and Vala-Rossi, Marilyn, "Developmental changes in the cognitive correlates of reading ability and the developmental lag hypothesis," *Reading Research Quarterly* Vol. 21, No. 3 (Summer 1986), pp. 267–83.

Stanovich, Keith E., Nathan, Ruth G., and Zolman, Judith E., "The developmental lag hypothesis in reading: longitudinal and matched reading-level comparisons," *Child Development* Vol. 59 (1988), pp. 71–86.

Stauffer, Russell, Abrams, Jules C., and Pikulski, John J., *Diagnosis, Correction and Prevention of Reading Disabilities* (New York: Harper and Row, 1978).

Stein, J. F., and Fowler, S., "Diagnosis of dyslexia by means of a new indicator of eye dominance," *British Journal of Ophthalomology* Vol. 66 (1982), pp. 332–36.

Stevenson, Harold W., "Orthography and reading disabilities," *Journal of Learning Disabilities* Vol. 17, No. 5 (May 1984), pp. 296–301.

Stevenson, Lillian P., "WISC-R analysis: Implications for diagnosis and intervention," *Journal of Learning Disabilities* Vol. 13, No. 6 (June/July 1980), pp. 60–63.

Strauss, Alfred A., and Lehtinen, Laura E., *Psychopathology and Education of the Brain-Injured Child* (New York: Grune and Stratton, 1947).

Szeszulski, Patricia A., and Manis, Franklin R., "A comparison of word recognition processes in dyslexic and normal readers at two reading-age levels," *Journal of Experimental Child Psychology* Vol. 44 (1987), pp. 364–76.

Tanner, Nancy B., "Phonics," in J. Estill Alexander, ed., *Teaching Reading,* 3rd ed. (Glenview, Ill.: Scott, Foresman/Little, Brown, 1988), p. 78.

Taylor, Pamela, *The Notebooks of Leonardo da Vinci* (New York: New American Library, 1960).

Taylor, Robert Lewis, *Winston Churchill, An Informal Study of Greatness* (Garden City: Doubleday, 1952).

Taylor, Stanford E., "Listening," *What Research Says to the Teacher* No. 29 (1964) (Washington, D.C.: National Education Association).

Temple, Charles, and Gillet, Jean Wallace, *Language Arts, Learning Processes and Teaching Practices* (Boston: Little, Brown, 1984).

Temple, Christine M., and Marshall, John C., "A case study of developmental phonological dyslexia," *British Journal of Psychology* Vol. 74 (1983), pp. 517–33.

Templeton, Shane, "Spelling, phonology and the older student," in Edmund H. Henderson and James W. Beers, eds., *Developmental and Cognitive Aspects of Learning to Spell: A Reflection of Word Knowledge* (Newark, Del.: International Reading Association, 1980), pp. 85–96.

Templin, Mildred C., "The study of articulation and language development during the early school years," *A Genesis of Language, A Psycholinguistic Approach* (Cambridge, Mass.: MIT Press, 1966), pp. 173–80.

"Therapies," *UPDATE* (Chevy Chase, Md.: National Institute of Dyslexia, Spring 1988), p. 7.

Thomas, James Blake, *Introduction to Human Embryology* (Philadelphia: Lea and Febiger, 1968).

Thompson, Lloyd J., "Language disabilities in men of eminence," *Journal of Learning Disabilities* Vol. 4 (January 1971), pp. 34–45.

Thomson, Michael, *Developmental Dyslexia* (London: Edward Arnold Publishers Ltd., 1984).

Tomkins, Calvin, "The last skill acquired," *New Yorker* Vol. 39 (Sept. 14, 1963), pp. 127–57.

Torgesen, Joseph K., and Dice, Carl, "Characteristics of research on learning disabilities," *Journal of Learning Disabilities* Vol. 13, No. 9 (December 1980), pp. 531–35.

Torgeson, Joseph K., and Wolf, Nancy, "Computers and reading instruction: Lessons from the past, promise for the future," in George Th. Pavlidis, ed., *Dyslexia: Its Neuropsychology and Treatment* (New York: John Wiley & Sons, 1986), pp. 279–96.

Treiman, Rebecca, and Hirsh-Pasek, Kathy, "Are there qualitative differences in reading behavior between dyslexics and normal readers?" *Memory and Cognition* Vol. 13, No. 4 (1985), pp. 357–64.

Turaids, Dainis, Wepman, Joseph M., and Morency, Anne, "A perceptual test battery: Development and standardization," *Elementary School Journal* Vol. 72, No. 7 (April 1972), pp. 351–61.

Vail, Priscilla L., *Smart Kids With School Problems* (New York: Dutton, 1987).

Valett, Robert E., *Dyslexia, a Neuropsychological Approach to Educating Children With Severe Reading Disorders* (Belmont, Calif.: Fearon Pittman, 1980).

Van Hout, A., "Dyslexia, neurolinguistic diagnostical and remediation methods," in D. J. Bakker, Colin R. Wilsher, H. Debruyne, and N. Bertin, eds., *Developmental Dyslexia and Learning Disorders* (New York: Karger, 1987), pp. 157–63.

Varney, Nils R., and Damasio, Antonio R., "Acquired dyslexia," in R. N. Malatesha and P. G. Aaron, eds., *Reading Disorders, Varieties and Treatments* (New York: Academic Press, 1982), pp. 305–14.

Vaughn, Sharon, and Bos, Candace S., eds., *Research in Learning Disabilities, Issues and Future Directions* (Boston: College-Hill, 1987).

Vawter, Jacquelyn M., and Vancil, Marybelle, "Helping children discover reading through self-directed dramatization," *The Reading Teacher* Vol. 34, No. 3 (December 1980), pp. 320–23.

Veatch, Florence Sawick; Elliott, Geraldine; Barnette, Eleanor; and Blakey, Janis, *Key Words to Reading: The Language Approach Begins* (Columbus, Ohio: Charles E. Merrill, 1973).

Vellutino, Frank, "Dyslexia," *Scientific American* Vol. 256, No. 3 (March 1987), pp. 34–41.

———, "Dyslexia: Perceptual deficiency or perceptual inefficiency," in James F. Kavanagh and Richard L. Venezky, eds., *Orthography, Reading, and Dyslexia* (Baltimore: University Park Press, 1980), pp. 251–70.

———, *Dyslexia: Theory and Research* (Cambridge, Mass.: MIT Press, 1979).

Venezky, Richard L., "Regularity in reading and spelling," in Harry Levin and Joanna P. Williams, eds., *Basic Studies on Reading* (New York: Basic Books, 1970), pp. 30–42.

Vernon, M. C., *Backwardness in Reading, A Study of its Nature and Origin* (Cambridge: Cambridge University Press, 1958).

"Vitamin and mineral overdosage," in "Tips from Other Journals," *American Family Physician* Vol. 35, No. 3 (March 1987), p. 282.

Vogler, George P., DeFries, J. C., and Decker, Sadie N., "Family history as an indicator of risk for reading disability," *Journal of Learning Disabilities* Vol. 18, No. 7 (August/ September 1985), pp. 419–21.

Vogel, Susan Ann, *Syntactic Abilities in Normal and Dyslexic Children* (Baltimore: University Park Press, 1975).

vonHarnack (1948), as cited in Edith Zerbin-Rubin, "Congenital word-blindness," *Bulletin of the Orton Society* Vol. 17 (1967), pp. 47–54.

Vukelich, Carol, "Parents' role in the reading process: A review of practical suggestions and ways to communicate with parents," *The Reading Teacher* Vol. 37, No. 6 (February 1984), pp. 472–77.

Wagner, Rudolph F., *Dyslexia and Your Child* (New York: Harper and Row, 1971).

―――, "Rudolf Berlin: Originator of the term dyslexia," *Bulletin of the Orton Society* Vol. 23 (1973), pp. 57–63.

Walberg, Herbert J., and Tsai, Shiow-Ling, "Matthew effects in education," *American Educational Research Journal* Vol. 20, No. 3 (1983), pp. 359–73.

Wallace, Gerald, and McLoughlin, James A., *Learning Disabilities, Concepts and Characteristics* (Columbus, Ohio: Charles E. Merrill, 1975).

Waller, T. Gary, and MacKinnon, G. E., eds., *Reading Research, Advances in Theory and Practice* (New York: Academic Press, 1979).

Wardhaugh, Ronald, *Reading: A Linguistic Perspective* (New York: Harcourt, Brace and World, 1969).

Watson, Alan J., "Developmental spelling: A word categorizing instructional experiment," *Journal of Educational Research* Vol. 82, No. 2 (September/December 1988), pp. 82–88.

Weinschenk, C., "Die erbliche Lese-Rechtschreibeschwache and ihre sozialpsychiatrischen Auswirkungen," Schweiz. Z. Psychol. Beih (1962), p. 44, as cited in Edith Zerbin-Rubin, "Congenital word-blindness," *Bulletin of the Orton Society* Vol. 17 (1967), pp. 47–54.

Welchman, Marion, "The current status of dyslexia in Great Britain," *Bulletin of the Orton Society* Vol. 31 (1981), pp. 245–50.

Welchman, Marion, and Will, Stewart Obe, "Dyslexia 1972–1983," *British Dyslexia Association* (Peppard, Oxfordshire: British Dyslexia Association, 1982).

Wheeler, T. J., and Watkins, E. J., "Dyslexia: A review of symptomatology," *Dyslexia Review* Vol. 2, No. 1 (1979), pp. 12–16.

Whiting, Sally A., and Jarrico, Sylvia, "Spelling patterns of normal readers," *Journal of Learning Disabilities* Vol. 13, No. 1 (January 1980), pp. 45–47.

Wicklund, Sally, "Permanent nerve damage from vitamin B_6 overdose," in "Nurses' Drug Alert," *American Journal of Nursing* 88 (May 1988), p. 687.

Wicklund, Sally, Morrison, Shirley, and Uretsky, Sam, eds., "Vitamin D dosage alert," in "Nurses' Drug Alert," *American Journal of Nursing* 86 (January 1986), pp. 69–70.

Wiegel-Crump, Carole Ann, "Rehabilitation of acquired dyslexia of adolescence," in T. Gary Waller and G. E. Mackinnon, eds., *Reading Research, Advances in Theory and Practice* Vol. 1 (New York: Academic Press, 1979), pp. 171–86.

Wildman, Terry M., "Cognitive theory and the design of instruction," *Educational Technology* (July 1981), pp. 14–19.

Wilsher, Colin R., "Treatment of specific reading difficulties (dyslexia)," in D. J. Bakker, Colin R. Wilsher, H. Debruyne, and N. Bertin, eds., *Developmental Dyslexia and Learning Disorders* (New York: Karger, 1987), pp. 95–109.

Wilsher, Colin R., Atkins, George, and Manfield, Pauline, "Effect of Piracetam on dyslexic's reading ability," *Journal of Learning Disabilities* Vol. 18, No. 1 (January 1985), pp. 19–25.

Wilsher, Colin R., and Taylor, J. A., "Commentary: Tinted glasses and dyslexia," *Journal of Research in Reading* Vol. 11 (1988), pp. 50–52.

Wilson, Edith Bolling, *My Memoir* (New York: Bobbs-Merrill, 1938).

Wilson, Louis Ada, "A study of some influencing factors upon and the nature of young children's written language," *The Journal of Experimental Education* Vol. 31, No. 4 (Summer 1963), pp. 371–80.

Wilson, Robert M., *Diagnostic and Remedial Reading for Classroom and Clinic*, 4th ed. (Columbus, Ohio: Charles E. Merrill, 1981).

Winter, Stephen L., and Boyer, James L., "Hepatic toxicity from large doses of vitamin B₃ (nicotinamide)," *New England Journal of Medicine* Vol. 289 (November 1973), pp. 1180–82.

Witelson, Sandra F., "Developmental dyslexia: Two right hemispheres and none left," *Science* Vol. 195 (January 1977), pp. 309–11.

Wolf, Maryanne, "Rapid alternating stimulus naming in the developmental dyslexias," *Brain and Language* Vol. 27 (1986), pp. 360–79.

Yo, Guo, et al., "A survey on prevalence of reading disabled children in Tainan City," Collected Papers, Taiwan Provincial Health Administration, 1984, pp. 253–59.

Young, Francis A., and Lindsley, Donald B., eds., *Early Experience and Visual Information Processing in Perceptual and Reading Disorders* (Washington, D.C.: National Academy of Sciences, 1970).

Zahalkova, M., Vrzal, V., and Kloboukova, E., "Genetical investigations in dyslexia," *Journal of Medical Genetics* Vol. 9 (1972), pp. 48–52.

Zerbin-Rubin, Edith, "Congenital word-blindness," *Bulletin of the Orton Society* Vol. 17 (1967), pp. 47–55.

Zintz, Miles V., *Corrective Reading* (Dubuque, Iowa: Wm. C. Brown, 1981).

Zintz, Miles V., and Maggart, Zelda R., *The Reading Process, the Teacher and the Learner*, 4th ed. (Dubuque, Iowa: Wm. C. Brown, 1984).

INDEX

ABOUT THE AUTHOR

Anne Marshall Huston is professor of education and human development and director of the reading programs and the reading clinic at Lynchburg College in Virginia.

In addition to teaching, study and research, and being involved in reading clinics for the diagnosis and remediation of reading, spelling, and writing disabilities, including dyslexia, Dr. Huston has been a reading consultant to various public school systems. She has conducted numerous professional workshops for school systems and conferences, and has read papers throughout the United States, and in Ireland and England.

Her publications include *Common Sense About Dyslexia, Under the Double Cross* (co-authored with husband, James Huston), *Symposium Readings: Classical Selections on Great Issues,* 10 vols. (co-edited with Faculty Group, Lynchburg College), and numerous articles on reading and writing problems, dyslexia, early identification, and related educational topics. The recipient of the 1988 Distinguished Faculty Scholar Award at Lynchburg College, she is also a member of Phi Delta Kappa, Phi Eta Sigma, Kappa Delta Pi, Gold Key, and is listed in *World Who's Who of Women in Education* and *Outstanding Educators in Exceptional Education.*

Currently completing a book on the alleviation of reading, writing, and spelling difficulties, including dyslexia, she resides in Lynchburg, Virginia.